Investigating Internet Crimes

Investigating Internet Crimes
An Introduction to Solving Crimes in Cyberspace

Todd G. Shipley

Art Bowker

Technical Editor

Nick Selby

AMSTERDAM • BOSTON • HEIDELBERG • LONDON
NEW YORK • OXFORD • PARIS • SAN DIEGO
SAN FRANCISCO • SINGAPORE • SYDNEY • TOKYO
Syngress is an imprint of Elsevier

Publisher: *Steven Elliot*
Editorial Project Manager: *Benjamin Rearick*
Project Manager: *Malathi Samayan*
Designer: *Greg Harris*

Syngress is an imprint of Elsevier
225 Wyman Street, Waltham, MA 02451, USA

Library of Congress Cataloging-in-Publication Data
Shipley, Todd G.
Investigating internet crimes:an introduction to solving crimes in cyberspace/Todd Shipley, Art Bowker. -- 1 Edition.
pages cm
Includes bibliographical references and index.
ISBN 978-0-12-407817-8 (alk. paper)
1. Computer crimes–Investigation. I. Bowker, Art. II. Title.
HV8079.C65S55 2014
363.25'968--dc23

2013036146

British Library Cataloguing-in-Publication Data
A catalogue record for this book is available from the British Library

For information on all Syngress publications,
visit our website at store.elsevier.com/Syngress

I dedicate my work on this book to my friend, confidant and former business partner, Bill Siebert. Every day you have been gone has been a loss to our field. I still can't remove you from my Skype contact list. I miss you Bill, thanks for believing in the mission.

Todd G. Shipley

I would like to dedicate my efforts on this book to my family. May they all be safer online and in the real world as the result of our work to educate law enforcement and the private sector on investigating cyber malfeasance. Additionally, it would be remiss for me not to also second Todd's dedication to his close friend, Bill Siebert, a true leader and pioneer in Internet and computer investigations.

Art Bowker

Contents

Foreword

Cybercrime, security and digital intelligence are important work of great relevance in today's interconnected world and one that nobody with an interest in enforcement, risk or technology should be without. In the mid 1990's the Secret Service was at the forefront of cybercrime because of its financial crimes and identity theft legal responsibilities to protect the country's financial systems. Almost all cybercriminals at that time were focused on penetrating private sector institutions for financial and personal information. As stated by a Secret Service "target hacker" at the time, "why financial institutions? Because that is where the money is".

Today's digital economy is even more dependent on the Internet, yet few users or decision makers have more than a rudimentary understanding of the online risks that threaten all of us.

Advances in computer technology and greater access to personal information via the Internet have created a virtual marketplace for transnational cyber criminals to share stolen information and criminal methodologies. As a result, the Secret Service has observed a marked increase in the quality, quantity and complexity of cybercrimes targeting private industry and critical infrastructure. These crimes include network intrusions, hacking attacks, development and use of malicious software, and account takeovers leading to significant data breaches affecting every sector of the world economy. As large companies have adopted more sophisticated protections against cyber-crime, criminals have adapted as well by increasing their attacks against small and medium-sized businesses, banks, and data processors. Unfortunately, many smaller businesses do not have the resources to adopt and continuously upgrade the sophisticated protections needed to safeguard data from being compromised.

From a different perspective, cybercrime is no longer just in a sophisticated hacker's purview. Internet crime can literally be committed by anyone and no one is immune to becoming a victim of an internet crime. The media is full of stories of sex offenders, cyber stalkers, cyber bullies and all manner of Internet malfeasance. Social media is also increasing being used to perpetrate all kinds of criminal activity. There are even cases of serial killers going online to stalk and trap their victims. In this day and age who has not received a notice from their financial institution that their personal information may have been compromised and is being offered identity theft insurance and monitoring as a precaution? All investigative departments and agencies now need this expertise available in their investigative toolbox. Internet investigations are therefore necessary law enforcement ability and yet they are fully understood by only a small minority of state and local law-enforcement agencies.

According to federal and state law enforcement officials, the pool of qualified of cyber-crime investigator candidates is limited because those investigating or examining cyber-crime cases must be highly trained specialists, requiring both investigative and technical skills, including knowledge of various IT hardware and software, electronic chain of custody rules and advanced forensic tools.

As more and more sensitive information is stored in cyberspace, target-rich environments are created for both the sophisticated and un-sophisticated cyber criminals. With proper computer and network security, personal users and businesses can provide a first line of defense by knowing who they are communicating with and safeguarding the information they collect. Such efforts can significantly limit the opportunities for cyber criminals.

In order to investigate and prosecute cyber-crime, law enforcement agencies need skilled investigators, up-to-date computer forensic examiners, calculated evidence collection and state and local prosecutors with cyber-crime familiarity and know-how. Todd Shipley and Art Bowker's book is a roadmap for not only new criminal investigators tasked to investigate Internet crime but also seasoned investigators who are in need of a quick and easy to follow reference guide to help them assemble complex online cybercrime cases.

Todd Shipley understands and is unequally qualified to help criminal investigators navigate through a cyber-crime investigation from beginning to end. Todd's work with the U.S. Secret Service in the early days of financial crime, digital forensics and cyber investigations helped the agency collect cyber intelligence, combat financial fraud and internet crime. Todd is one of the true cyber-crime experts today that has worked with numerous law enforcement agencies and can translate his knowledge and experience into the many uses of scenario-based digital investigations. Art Bowker's experience is drawn not only from conducting financial criminal investigations but also from being responsible for investigating and supervising convicted federal cyber offenders.

Their combined experiences and knowledge provide the reader with a more engaged, interactive instructional environment. This book offers the most comprehensive, and understandable account of cybercrime currently available to all different skill levels of investigators. It is suitable for novices and instructors, across the full spectrum of digital investigations and will appeal to both advanced and new criminal investigators. It will no doubt become a must have text for any law enforcement or corporate investigator's investigative library.

Larry D. Johnson
Current CEO at Castleworth Global LLC
Former Chief Security Officer at Genworth Financial and
Special Agent in Charge, Criminal Investigative Division USSS Retired

Preface

We conceived this book during a weekend telephone call when Art said we need to write a book on Internet investigations. Todd thought it was a great idea and just so happened to have a draft outline he had written in the hopes of someday writing this book. From the start we wanted to provide to the investigative community a reference book that would help them deal with the growing issues of Internet-related crime. Over the years as we both have taught these topics elicited herein, we heard the frustration with the lack of published material specific to Internet investigations, as opposed to the numerous computer forensic texts. This book was intended to fill the void and provide a focused approach to investigating, documenting, and locating Internet criminals.

In Chapter 1, we define Internet crime and follow with a discussion in Chapter 2 regarding the offenders that were making the Internet their criminal playground. In Chapter 3, we provide an understanding how Internet crimes can be investigated. We then discuss in Chapter 4 the legal issues associated with collecting online electronically stored information (ESI). Chapter 5 commences the process of properly documenting online ESI. Together Chapters 4 and 5 stress the importance of collecting, preserving, and documenting online ESI so it can be admitted as evidence in any legal proceeding.

In Chapter 6, we present various tools for investigating Internet crime. Chapter 7 discusses how investigators need to prepare their equipment and protect themself online. In Chapter 8, we lay out the investigative process of following online data to identify an investigative target. We cover in Chapter 9 how the investigator can work unseen on the Internet and in Chapter 10, we furthered that discussion with detailing how to conduct covert investigations. In Chapter 11, we outline the processes an investigator uses to respond to Internet crime in their community. Chapter 12 focuses on resources the investigator can use to locate online evidence. In Chapter 13, we outline how to investigate websites. We devoted Chapter 14 to looking at social media and how it has impacted investigations. In Chapter 15, we discuss a variety of Internet communication methods and how to investigate them. Chapter 16 provides approaches to detecting and preventing Internet crimes. In Chapter 17, we bring it all together with scenarios that lay out a set of investigative circumstances and how to go about solving online crime.

Most of the scenarios found throughout this book may be similar to real investigations in the field. None of the information mentioned is from a real investigation and should not be inferred as such or associated with any wrongdoing. The cases mentioned as real are referenced to their sources and quoted based on known published facts.

Readers should find that this book takes a practical, hands-on approach to dealing with the techniques and tools defined in each chapter. Our intent is not to provide you with enormous amounts of technical data on the topic, but balance the explanation of Internet processes with techniques to aid in your investigation. You should find that you can immediately employ the techniques in your investigations. We hope that you find *Internet Crime Investigations* a useful resource in making the Internet a part of your regular beat.

The target audience

The material and techniques described in this book are basic information that the new Internet investigator should know and understand. Individuals familiar with the material will also find the book useful as a reference in their ongoing investigations. The examples and material provided come not only from the United States but also from the entire world. We have made a conscience effort to include examples and laws from numerous regions, such as Australia, Canada, China, the European Union, and the United Kingdom. The book obviously provides resources for criminal investigators. However, we also strive to provide information that would be helpful for civil or corporate investigators, recognizing that civil disputes and injustices are oftentimes an online reality.

About the Authors

Todd G. Shipley is a retired City of Reno Police Detective Sergeant, where he served for 25 years. There he started and managed Nevada's first cybercrime unit. Upon retirement he was selected as the Director of Systems Security and High Tech Crime Prevention Training for SEARCH, The National Consortium for Justice Information and Statistics. He oversaw a national program that provided expert technical assistance and training to local, state, and federal justice agencies on successfully conducting high-technology computer crimes investigations. In 2007 he formed Vere Software, a company dedicated to developing tools to aid in the investigation of online crime. He was the primary designer of the patented software "WebCase" that aids investigators(in) document(ing) their online investigation. He has also developed free to the investigative community the Internet Investigators Toolkit (IITK) and the Internet Investigators Toolbar. He also developed and teaches Vere Software's Cybercrime Survival courses nationally.

Mr. Shipley has also authored works regarding cybercrime and speaks nationally and internationally on cybercrime investigations. He is a Certified Fraud Examiner through the Association of Certified Fraud Examiner (ACFE) and a Certified Forensics Computer Examiner through the International Association of Computer Investigative Specialists (IACIS). He has also served on the International Executive Committee of the High Technology Crime Investigation Association (HTCIA) and was the 2010 International President. He is a founding member of the board of directors of the Consortium of Digital Forensic Specialists (CDFS) and the National Forensic Data Recovery Training Center (NFDRTC). He holds the US patent, US 8417776 B2, for online evidence collection. You can follow him on Twitter at @webcase or on the Vere Software blog at www.veresoftware.com/blog.

Art Bowker has over 28 years experience in law enforcement/corrections and is recognized as an expert in managing cyber risk in offender populations. He is the author of *The Cybercrime Handbook for Community Corrections: Managing Offender Risk in the 21st Century* (Charles C. Thomas Publisher, Ltd., March 20, 2012). He has also had numerous articles published in professional publications, such as the *FBI Law Enforcement Bulletin*.

In 2013, Mr. Bowker received the American Probation and Parole Association (APPA) Sam Houston State University Award for his writing contributions to promote awareness of cybercrime and tools for helping the community corrections field combat computer crime. He is an APPA member and serves on its Technology Committee. Additionally, Mr. Bowker was recognized as the 2013 Great Lakes Region, Thomas E. Gahl Line Officer of the Year by the Federal Probation and Pretrial Officer Association for his work in the cybercrime area. Mr. Bowker is also a lifetime High Technology Crime Investigation Association (HTCIA) member and served in various positions on its Executive Committee, including International President in 2008. Additionally, he writes a blog, the Three C's: Computers, Crime, and Corrections (http://corrections.com/cybercrime) and has his own website, Computer PO (http://computerpo.com). He can be followed on Twitter, @Computerpo.

About the Technical Editor

Nick Selby is co-founder and CEO of StreetCred Software. He was sworn as a Texas police officer in 2010, and he regularly leads and assists on investigations into Internet-based crime. Previously Nick co-founded N4Struct, Inc, a consultancy that provided cyber incident response to the Fortune 500.

Nick is co-author of *Blackhatonomics: the Economics of Cybercrime* (Syngress, 2012), and of the Police-Led Intelligence blog, on which he writes about law enforcement and government technology, intelligence, and cybercrime. He is a regular guest on FOX Business, where he discusses government and law enforcement technology, and he regularly speaks at conferences including The RSA Conference. In 2005, Nick founded the enterprise security practice at industry analyst firm, The 451 Group, where he conducted in-depth interviews with and consulted more than 1,000 technology vendors, and a range of Fortune 1.000 and government clients.

Acknowledgments

We have numerous people to thank for this book's production. First of all the Syngress staff was exceptionally helpful in putting to the page and editing our ramblings to make this an actual book. We need to especially thank Steve Elliot for believing in the project and Ben Rearick for guiding us through the process. Our thanks also go out to our families without whom we would never have gotten through this process, Nick Selby for reviewing the material and providing comments throughout the process, and Larry Johnson for spending the time to write this book's foreword.

Todd would like to thank Linda, my beautiful wife and Eva, my ever brilliant daughter.

Art would like to thank Kathy, my beautiful wife, my children, Stephanie and Mark, my grandchildren, Scarlett and Raylan, and my parents, Harry and Martha. Additionally, thank you Todd for allowing me to work on this book with you. It has been a pleasure.

Introduction to Internet Crime

The Internet is like a giant jellyfish. You can't step on it. You can't go around it. You've got to get through it.

(John B. Evans, former senior News Corporation executive and pioneer in electronic publishing, 1938–2004)

In less then 20 years, the Internet has affected every element of modern society. Worldwide Internet usage increased from almost nothing in 1994 to nearly 2 billion users worldwide at the start of 2012 (Figure 1.1). Seventy-eight percent of North Americans were online in 2011. The current social networking leader, Facebook®, had over 800,000,000 worldwide users on March 31, 2012 (At the time of publishing Facebook according to their website has over one billion users). The Americas alone had over 300 million Facebook® users (Internet World Stats, Usage and Population Statistics, 2012).

Internet connectivity is, however, not limited to just humans. In 2008, the number of things connected to the Internet, exceeded the Earth's human population. Evans (2011) noted "these things are not just smartphones and tablets. They're everything." He cites as an example a Dutch start-up company using wireless cattle sensors to report on each cow's health. Similar medical sensors are being developed for humans. For years many automobiles have been connected to the Internet. By 2020, he notes there will be an estimated 50 billion devices connected to the Internet (Evans, 2011).

Expanding Internet connectivity has been extremely beneficial to many human endeavors, such as communication, education, commerce, transportation, and recreation to name a few. Unfortunately, criminals have also found ways to take advantage of the Internet's benefits, such as increased opportunities to find and target victims. This translates into a higher likelihood that an Internet crime victim will be walking in the doors of the world's "brick and mortar" police departments.

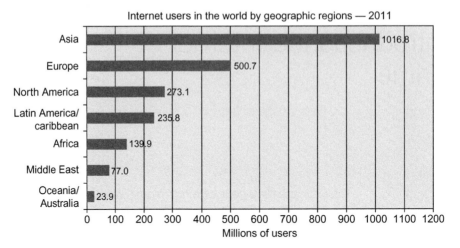

FIGURE 1.1

Internet users in the world by geographical regions—2011.

Source: Internet World Stats—www.internetwordstats.com/stat.htm

Defining Internet crime

Criminal acts on the Internet are as varied as there are crimes to commit. In the Internet's early years, the notorious criminals were the Kevin Mitnicks[1] of the hacker world. Common then was the breaking into phone service and social engineering their way into computer networks. Today hacking has been brought to the masses with the introduction of various "crimeware," malicious code designed to help the average criminal automate his attacks. But what does the term cybercrime mean? A broad definition would be a criminal offense that has been created or made possible by the advent of technology, or a traditional crime which has been transformed by technology's use. Internet crimes by definition are crimes committed on or facilitated through the Internet's use. There is often an over use of the term cybercrime to be all inclusive of many Internet crime categories, including computer intrusion and hacking. Texts have been devoted to the investigation and prevention of computer intrusions and hacking. This book's primary focus is to provide law enforcement with the basic skills to understand how to investigate traditional crimes committed on the Internet.

Internet crime's prevalence

Internet crime estimates vary widely depending on the data collection method. Most studies are done through surveying victims and businesses in an attempt to

---

[1]Kevin Mitnick, a.k.a. Condor, was an infamous hacker of the 1990s. He gained notoriety after being wanted by federal authorities.

quantify the actual scope of the problem. The Computer Security Institute (CSI) Computer Crime and Security Survey[2] solicits information from security experts. Symantec/Norton™ Cybercrime Index interviews individuals on their victimization. The High Technology Crime Investigation Association (HTCIA) solicits input from its members, who are made up of law enforcement, corporate, and private investigators, on cybercrime. Other studies look at investigative data, such as Verizon Data Breach Reports. Others collect data concerning specific incidents, such as McAfee Threats Reports, which cover malware[3] incidents. Some are concerned with the data collection methods used by many of these studies. After all why would a company selling security products report anything but a high incidence of cybercrime? Normally crime data is collected by law enforcement or criminal justice agencies who presumably do not have a profit motivation.

US crime statistics are reported on a national level by individual law enforcement agencies to the Federal Bureau of Investigation (FBI) under the uniform crime reports (UCR) process. Data is collected on crimes committed by law enforcement agencies under specific guidelines and forwarded to the FBI. The FBI compiles the data and publicly discloses the information in its annual crime reports. Current UCR data collection efforts *do not* focus on "high-tech" offenses, such as hacking and computer intrusions. There is a hesitancy by some to report cybercrime to the authorities. Publicly traded companies are reluctant to supply information on cyber-incidents fearing such disclosures will damage their image, negatively affect stock prices and/or spark lawsuits (Lardner, 2012).

The reporting requirements also do not mandate the reporting of any information about crimes committed on the Internet or whether a computer was used in the offense. Goodman (2001) points out that those traditional offenses may be classified under something that does not reflect the presence of a computer or Internet use. For instance, an Internet fraud scheme might be classified as a simple fraud. Additionally, cyberstalking might be classified as a criminal threat offense or stalking case.

One ironic data twist concerns sexual enticement cases. These cases are frequently undercover sting operations, in which the suspect believes he[4] is communicating via the Internet with a minor. In reality there is no minor. The suspect makes online sexual comments, including his desire to have sex with the fictitious

---

[2]From 1999 to 2006, the survey was known as the CSI/FBI survey. In 2007, the survey was renamed with the "FBI nomenclature" being discontinued and the survey being entirely administered by CSI. Source: *CSI Survey 2007: The 12th Annual Computer Crime and Security Survey.* Retrieved from http://gocsi.com/sites/default/files/uploads/2007_CSI_Survey_full-color_no%20marks.indd_pdf.

[3]Malware is short for "malicious software," a term used to collectively refer to software programs designed to damage or do other unwanted actions on a computer system. Examples include viruses, worms, Trojan horses, and spyware (http://www.techterms.com).

[4]Internet crime is by no means solely a male activity. The vast majority of enticement cases involve male suspects. However, females have also been involved in this criminal conduct. Throughout this book we will use the male gender, unless we are discussing a real case in which a female was involved.

minor. The suspect is arrested when he goes to meet the "minor." This crime is likely to be classified as sex crime even though there is no real minor or even victim. This is not to minimize the offense's seriousness or to argue that it should not be counted as sex offense. The computer element and Internet use in this type of offense is clearly apparent and is largely being ignored in the data collection. It is an Internet-based crime but classified as a sex crime where no victim ever existed. This lack of clarity can have important implications for officers attempting to secure resources and training to properly investigate Internet crime.

It is also possible to look to media reports on cybercrime. The important caveat is that such reports tend to focus on the sensational and may not be representative of the vast majority of cybercrime cases. A case may make the headlines because it was novel or was particularly heinous, harmful, or otherwise "newsworthy." Such crimes may have been isolated incidents and not the norm.

The above realities make it difficult but not impossible to determine the scope of the Internet crime. We obviously can't definitively state the exact number of Internet crime victims, their actual loss, or even how many possible online criminals are preying on our citizens. We can, however, get a broad outline of Internet crime's prevalence in our society by examining numerous data sources.

CSI 2010/2011 Computer Crime and Security Survey

The CSI has been a leading educational membership organization for information security professionals for over 30 years. Their study involves sending surveys by post and email to security practitioners. In the 2011, CSI sent out 5,412 such surveys to its members with a total of 351 returns or a 6.3% response rate. The survey looked at the period June 2009 to June 2010. Some of the major findings were as follows:

- Approximately 67% noted malware infections continued to be the most commonly seen attack;
- Almost half the respondents experienced at least one security incident. Slightly more than 45% of these respondents indicated they had been the subject of at least one targeted attack;
- Slightly more than 8% reported financial fraud incidents, which was down compared to previous years;
- At the same time fewer respondents than ever were willing to share specific information about dollar losses suffered (CSI, 2011).

Norton™ Cybercrime Report 2011[5]

Symantec provides information security solutions including software, commonly referred to as Norton™ anti-virus and anti-spyware. Symantec under the trade

---

[5]Commencing on February 16, 2011, Norton started a "real-time" cybercrime index, purporting to reflect the newest attack. See http://us.norton.com/theme.jsp?themeid=protect_yourself.

name Norton™, surveyed a total of 19,636 individuals in 24 countries[6] from February 6, 2011 to March 14, 2011. The survey participants included 12,704 adults (including 2,956 parents), 4,553 children (aged 8–17), and 2,379 teachers (of students aged 8–17). Participants were asked if they ever experienced one or more of the following: a computer virus or malware appearing on their computer; responding to a phishing[7] message thinking it was a legitimate request; online harassment; someone hacking into their social networking profile and impersonating them; an online approach by sexual predators; responding to online scams; experiencing online credit card fraud or identity theft; responding to a smishing[8] message or any other type of cybercrime on their cell/mobile phone or computer. The survey found that more than a million individuals become a cybercrime victim every day. Fourteen adults become a cybercrime victim every second. The top three cybercrimes were computer viruses/malware (58%), online scams (11%), and phishing (10%). Ten percent of the online adults indicated that they experienced cybercrime on their mobile phone (Symantec, 2011).

The Norton™ study also did some data extrapolation and determined the financial losses due to cybercrime to be $114 billion annually. Additionally, they estimated the dollar figure for time individuals lost due to their victimization to be $274 billion. They combined these two amounts for an annual global cybercrime cost of $388 billion. They further noted that this cost was more than the combined global black market in marijuana, cocaine, and heroin ($288 billion) (Symantec, 2011).

HTCIA 2011 Report on Cybercrime Investigation

HTCIA is the largest worldwide organization dedicated to the advancement of training, education, and information sharing between law enforcement and corporate cybercrime investigators. Its over 3,000 members are located in 41 chapters worldwide. Eight-five percent of the membership is located in the United States, with 14% located in other countries, including Canada, Europe, the Asia-Pacific Rim, and Brazil. Since 2010, HTCIA has annually solicited input on cybercrime from their membership. In 2011, 445 members responded to the survey. The 2011 Report found:

---

[6]The 24 countries were Australia, Belgium, Brazil, Canada, China, Denmark, France, Germany, Holland, Hong Kong, India, Italy, Japan, Mexico, New Zealand, Poland, Singapore, South Africa, Spain, Sweden, Switzerland, United Arab Emirates, United Kingdom, and United States.

[7]Think of fishing in the lake, but instead of capturing fish, individuals are trying to steal personal information. They accomplish this by sending out emails, which appear to be from legitimate sources, such as your bank. The email purports that your information needs updated or your account needs validated and requests you to enter your user name and password, after clicking a link. In reality you are providing your identifiers to the phisher (http://www.techterms.com).

[8]Smishing is similar to phishing. However, instead of email the offender sends fraudulent messages over SMS (text messages). The term is therefore a combination of "SMS" and "phishing" (http://www.techterms.com).

- An increase in criminal use of digital technology: Members reported increases for the second year in a row in all four ways computers and/or the Internet are used to commit crime, specifically: for research or planning to commit the offense, as a direct instrument in the offense, as a communication device between offenders and/or victims, and as a record keeping or storage device.
- Improvement needed in information sharing: Members noted that a lack of resources has made it harder for investigators to collaborate and share information.
- Better training at multiple levels needed: Members reported that civilians, judges, prosecutors, and even middle and upper level management have a hard time understanding cybercrimes' complexities.
- Better reporting, strategy and policy needed: Members recognized the continuing problem of no uniform mechanism for cybercrime reporting.
- Perhaps more importantly members noted that law enforcement agencies and corporations may have widely divergent policies and strategies based on the extent to which they understand the cybercrime problem.

McAfee® Threats Reports

McAfee® is a wholly owned subsidiary of Intel® Corporation and is leader in anti-virus software. It has a lab which studies the detection of new and evolving online threats and provides threat assessments on a quarterly basis. In 2012, they reportedly had 100 million pieces of malware in their "zoo." These threats are important for the investigator to be aware of, not only for understanding Internet crime but to remain virulent during online investigations. As the *2012 First Quarter Threats Report* notes "The web is a dangerous place for the uninformed and unprotected." Some of the 2012 trends noted were as follows:

- Data breaches by the third quarter of 2012, reached an all time high, exceeding all of 2011 figures.
- Increases in active malicious uniform resource locators (URLs)[9] were noted with almost 64% of newly discovered suspicious URLs located in North America. By September 2012, McAfee® had identified 43 million suspicious URLs.
- The United States is frequently the location of both the attacker and target of attacks. Additionally, the United States was most often noted as location of newly discovered botnet[10] command servers.

---

[9]A malicious URL is frequently a fraudulent version of a legitimate website, which contains malware that will infect the unsuspecting user.

[10]A botnet is a group of computers controlled by an offender or group of offenders. A botnet can be a few hundred or several thousand computers. An offender's control of these computers is often unknown by the legitimate user. Frequently a botnet will be used to launch a denial of service attack (DNS) against a website. By directing all computers in a botnet to make requests of a website they can either overload it or make it impossible for legitimate users to get access. Botnets are also referred to as zoobie armies (http://www.techterms.com).

- Malware trends included increasing targeting of mobile devices, notably Androids and Macintosh®[11] computers. Additionally, Ransonware[12] attacks were seen as growing.
- McAfee® detected a growth of established rootkits[13] as well as the emergence of new ones. Of particular concern were the rebounding of password stealing Trojans.[14]
- They also observed global spam[15] volume decrease but noted there were significant differences of volume by country. Some countries, such as South Korea, Russia, and Japan, saw decreases while others saw increasing volumes. For instance, Saudi Arabia saw a spike in August 2012 of more than 700%. The most common spam subject line involved drugs.
- McAfee® noted that botnet software was actively being marketed for as low as $450.00. One particularly rootkit program that McAfee® observed as a growing threat was Blackhole. Gallagher (2012) describes it as a "...web-based software package which includes a collection of tools to take advantage of security holes in web browsers to download viruses, botnet Trojans, and other forms of nastiness to the computers of unsuspecting victims. The exploit kit is offered both as a 'licensed' software product for the intrepid malware server operator and as malware-as-a-service by the author off his own server."
Cost ranges from a 1-day rental of $50 up to a month-long lease of $500. Those interested in purchasing a 3-month license for their own sever (which includes software support) were looking at $700 up to $1,500 for a full year, plus $200 for the multidomain version. Special "site cleanup" package is priced at $300.

In 2012, McAfee® also observed not only malware's use for profit but also cyberattacks in retaliation of such events, such as the release of YouTube anti-Islam video (Poeter, 2012). They concluded that estimating and understanding the growth of malware is a continuing challenge, in part due to the differences in

---

[11]Malware have been developed for Windows-based personal computers as they had the lion share of the market. This increasing targeting of Macintosh® computers by offenders is a recognition that their usage is becoming more common place.

[12]Ransonware infects a user's computer and extorts money from its victim. It often purports to be from a law enforcement agency, accusing the user of illegal activity, locking the computer, and demanding payment of a "fine" to unlock the device.

[13]A rootkit is probably the most serious of malware. It is designed to give the offender administrator level access to a computer without being detected. Once such access is gained the offender can perform all manner of criminal activity, from stealing or destroying data to using the computer to launch an attack against another system (http://www.techterms.com).

[14]Everyone is probably familiar with the story about the Trojan Horse and how some Greek soldiers hid inside the "gift" presented to the Trojans. In this manner, the Greeks were able to get inside the Trojan's fortifications and open the gates. A Trojan is malware hidden inside another program, such as a game or screen saver, that once executed does something the user did not wish to happen (http://www.techterms.com).

[15]Spam is electronic junk mail, named after Hormel's canned meat (http://www.techterms.com).

enemy motivations. We will go into more detail about this idea in the next chapter, suffice to say the *2012 Third Quarter Report* notes:

> *Where our industry lacks insight is into the conditions and motivations of the enemy; today's cybercriminals and other classes of attackers. Cyber-criminal's motivations are pretty straightforward, making money from malware and related attacks. This goal yields malware of certain types and functionalities. However, with hacktivist or state-sponsored attacks, their motivations and goals are completely different. Thus the code and attacks will be of a very different order. These underlying dynamics lead to the wide swings in sophistication we see in many classes of malware and attacks. Cybercrime malware exhibits far different behaviors than Stuxnet, Dugu, or Shamoon because the goals of the attackers are different: Cybercrime malware seeks a profit and (form the most part) stealth: Stuxnet and Dugu are concerned with sabotage and espionage; and Shomoon sows chaos and destruction (McAfee®, 2012, p. 9).[16]*

2012 Data Breach Investigations Report

This study was conducted by the Verizon RISK Team[17] with cooperation from the numerous law enforcement agencies.[18] This study was based upon "...first-hand evidence collected during paid external forensic investigations conducted by Verizon" and data submitted by the law enforcement based upon their investigations. Unlike the other studies, this one focuses solely on data breaches. In 2011, the study looked at 855 incidents, involving 174 million compromised records, which was the second-highest data loss since they started keeping records in 2004. The study found that 98% of the breaches were from outside agents. Eighty-one percent involved some form of hacking and 69% incorporated the use of malware. Most profound was the report's Executive Summary which noted:

> *The online world was rife with the clashing of ideals, taking the form of activism, protests, retaliation, and pranks. While these activities encompassed more than data breaches (e.g., DDoS attacks), the theft of corporate and personal information was certainly a core tactic. This reimagined and reinvigorated*

---

[16]Stuxnet and Dugu were reportedly malware developed to thwart and gather information about the Iranian nuclear program (Nakashima & Warrick, 2012; Sulemanzp, 2011). Shamoon was the malware that attacked Saudi Arabia's state oil company, ARAMCO, replacing crucial system files with an image of a burning US Flag (Reuters, 2012).

[17]Verizon is a company that designs, builds, and operates networks, information systems, and mobile technologies. Their risk team provides security products and services and gathers intelligence as part of that function. Source: http://www.verizonbusiness.com/Products/security/risk/.

[18]The law enforcement agencies were Australian Federal Police, Dutch National High Tech Crime Unit, Irish Reporting and Information Security Service, Police Central e-Crime Unit, and United States Secret Service.

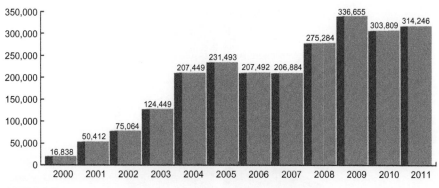

FIGURE 1.2

IC3 yearly complaint comparisons.

Source: IC3 2011 Internet Crime Report

specter of 'hacktivism' rose to haunt organizations around the world. Many, troubled by the shadowy nature of its origins and proclivity to embarrass victims, found this trend more frightening than other threats, whether real or imagined. Doubly concerning for many organizations and executives was that target selection by these groups didn't follow the logical lines of who has money and/or valuable information. Enemies are even scarier when you can't predict their behavior.

Internet Crime Compliant Center

In June 2000, a partnership between the FBI and the National White Collar Crime Center (NW3C) was created "...to serve as a means to receive Internet-related criminal complaints and to further research, develop, and refer the criminal complaints to federal, state, local, or international law enforcement and/or regulatory agencies for any investigation they deem to be appropriate." From this partnership, the Internet Crime Complaint Center (IC3)[19] was eventually formed (IC3, 2011).

One function of the IC3 is to analyze and report on the online victimization complaints received. During 2000, its first year of existence, 16,383 complaints were received. Unfortunately, there has been an almost steady increase in the complaints received since then (Figure 1.2). In 2011, 314,246 complaints were received. These complaints involved an adjusted total dollar loss of $485.3 million. Additionally, 2011 marked the third year in a row that IC3 received over 300,000 complaints, which was a 3.4% increase over 2010 (IC3, 2011).

---

[19]Initially the IC3 was called the Internet Fraud Complaint Center. It was renamed in October 2003 to better reflect the broad character of Internet crimes.

Top five reported crime types

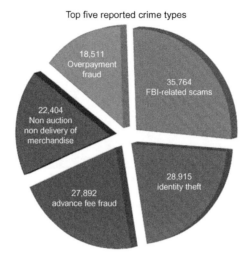

FIGURE 1.3

Top five reported crime types.

Source: IC3 2011 Internet Crime Report

The vast majority of complaints were fraud related with FBI-related scams being the most prevalent. The IC3 reported the following top five crime categories in 2011 (Figure 1.3):

- FBI-related scams: Offenses in which the suspect posed as the FBI to defraud victims.
- Identity theft: Unauthorized use of a victim's personal identifying information to commit fraud or other crimes.
- Advance fee fraud: Suspects convince victims to pay a fee to receive something of value, but do not deliver anything of value to the victim.
- Non-auction/non-delivery of merchandise: Purchaser does not receive items purchased.
- Overpayment fraud: An incident in which the complainant receives an invalid monetary instrument with instructions to deposit it in a bank account and send excess funds or a percentage of the deposited money back to the sender.

Internet harassment

Noticeably absence from the *2011 Internet Crime Report* are incidents concerning cyberharassment, cyberbullying, and cyberstalking, which Smith (2008) collectively refers to as Internet harassment offenses. Cyberbullying and stalking have become regular events that require significant investigative attention. Cyberbullying has become publicly significant due to the number of teenagers who have committed suicide over Internet harassment and comments posted online about them. Baum, Catalano, Rand, and Rose (2009) note that approximately 3.4 million people are stalked annually and one in four victims report that the offense includes a cyberstalking act. Law enforcement estimates that electronic communications are a factor in 20–40% of all stalking cases (National Conference of State Legislatures, 2009). Cyberstalking victims report that 83% of the perpetrated acts are via email and 35% are via instant messaging (Baum et al., 2009).

Traditional crimes and the Internet

Kaspersky (2012) recently noted that "social media is the latest tool in the arsenal of cybercrimes, with groups using social networking websites, such as Twitter, to 'manipulate the masses' into thinking a certain way" (Barwick, 2012). Cellular telephones, particularly through their easy access to social media, have added another dimension to the investigation of Internet crime. In 2011, we saw the coordination of mass mayhem via "flash mobs" or "flash robs,"[20] through the use of cell phones and social media by individuals in the United Kingdom and the United States (Pinkston, 2011). One parole officer found through a mobile phone examination and checking a social networking site that a violent offender was participating in a gang called M.O.B. (Money Over Bitches), which involved individual pimps trading prostitutes on the west coast (Korn, 2011). The connection of the Internet through cell phones is also becoming a prevalent communication method for gangs. The *2009 National Gang Threat Assessment* reflects:

> *Gang members often use cell phones and the Internet to communicate and promote their illicit activities. Street gangs typically use the voice and text messaging capabilities of cell phones to conduct drug transactions and prearrange meetings with customers. Members of street gangs use multiple cell phones that they frequently discard while conducting their drug trafficking operations. For example, the leader of an African American street gang operating on the northside of Milwaukee used more than 20 cell phones to coordinate drug-related activities of the gang; most were prepaid phones that the leader routinely discarded and replaced. Internet-based methods such as social networking sites, encrypted email, Internet telephony, and instant messaging are commonly used by gang members to communicate with one another and with drug customers. Gang members use social networking Internet sites such as MySpace®, YouTube®, and Facebook® as well as personal web pages to communicate and boast about their gang membership and related activities (p. 10).*

---

[20]Flash mobs were coordinated in the United Kingdom through posts on Twitter, usually via cell phones to meet at a specific location and to commence rioting and looting. Flash robs occurred in the United States, where a specific location, such as a store, was targeted for mass shoplifting, with the attack being coordinated through social media and cell phones.

Sex offenders have been using the Internet, almost since its inception to view, store, produce, receive, and/or distribute child and other forms of pornography; to communicate, groom, and entice children and others for victimization; and to validate and communicate with other sex offenders. Since 2007, MySpace® has reportedly removed 90,000 sex offenders from its social networking site (Wortham, 2009). Facebook® prohibits sex offenders from accessing their site. Major dating sites are moving to screen sex offenders from their membership (NYDailyNews.com, 2012). Legislatures in many states are working to make it illegal for a sex offender to access social networking sites that may be used by minors (Bowker, 2012a,b).

Countless criminals have also been caught after boasting about their illegal activities online. In December 2011, three "geniuses" were caught after two of them were bragging about their bank robbery on their Facebook® profile wall (Hernandez, 2011). Another robber skipped out on supervision conditions and fled the jurisdiction, only to be later apprehended after his taunting Facebook® posts lead officers to his location (DesMarais, 2012). Others have logged into their social networking profiles from houses they are burglarizing or from stolen cell phones, which have lead authorities to their identity and arrest (DesMarais, 2012).

There have been numerous media reports of criminals using the Internet to attempt to intimidate or harass victims and/or witnesses. A Sarasota Florida woman was arrested after making threats on Facebook® against witnesses in her brother's murder trial (Eckhart, 2012). One of the most brazen offenders was a Cook County burglar who would cyberstalk witnesses and victims, posting malicious allegations that they had committed criminal acts (Gorner & Meizner, 2012). In one incident, he ran online ads claiming a witness was running prostitution out of her home, resulting in several men erroneously knocking on her door thinking they had appointments. In one recent United Kingdom case, a convicted killer was accused of threatening a female trial witness by sending her Facebook® messages while he was incarcerated (Traynor, 2012).

Unfortunately, it is not unusual for inmates to have social networking profiles, which are oftentimes accessed through smuggled cell phones (Bowker, 2012a).

Investigators are also seeing the use of premade kits to commit crime on the Internet. Criminals can buy "crimeware" software that can enable them to commit crimes, hide themselves, and setup networks of computers to support their efforts. All of the efforts can then be funneled through online money exchange sites like Bitcoin to hide their profits from the authorities. This can make investigating these crimes difficult.

Investigative responses to Internet crime

Compounding the problem is how law enforcement and corporate investigators response to Internet-related crimes. There are over 18,000 law enforcement agencies in the United States. Most are small departments with little ability to respond to Internet-based crime. Some in fact still believe that crimes committed on the Internet are not their problems. "The Internet is not my Jurisdiction" was stated by a senior law enforcement administrator not so long ago. Many times the Internet is thought to be solely federal law enforcement's purview and not local law enforcement's responsibility.

Yet there are certainly many within state and local law enforcement agencies that understand the problem and are aggressively working on addressing segments of online crime. Particularly of note are the efforts of the Internet Crimes Against Children (ICAC) Task Forces nationwide. The ICAC is a federally funded program that is run by the state and local members of each task force. The program focuses on protecting children and finding and arresting those that would abuse and exploit them through the Internet. What is significant is that the program is run by the state and local investigators, and over the years they have developed a common national policy and procedures for their investigations of these crimes.

In the United States, there is no national cybercrime/cyber-terrorism reporting procedure or clearing house. This lack of a concise reporting process for victims, state and local law enforcement agencies, and the federal government leads to an under reporting of cybercrime and a true lack of understanding of the exact magnitude of the crime. To truly understand the significance of the cybercrime problem, a national plan to address law enforcements response and a method to measure the effects of the crime need to be implemented. The contributing factors that lead to continuing problems related to law enforcements' response to cybercrime include:

- our ongoing national dependence on technology and the Internet;
- a lack of understanding of computer and Internet security risks by both users and law enforcement;
- a lack of funding for adequate network security and investigations tools;
- the ease of committing acts of terrorism or crimes through technology and the Internet;
- the continued difficulty in tracking the cyber-terrorist and cyber-criminal through the Internet;
- an inadequate national strategy to address cybercrime investigation;
- difficulty of collecting evidence from the Internet.

All of this does not mean that law enforcement and corporate investigators have sat back and done nothing since the Internet went public. In fact pre-1994 law enforcement was well on its way to building responses to technology crime. In 1989, HTCIA was formed to bring law enforcement and corporate investigators together to fight technology crime. In 1990, the International Association of Computer Investigative Specialists (IACIS) was formed to train law enforcement investigators to examine computers and analyze digital evidence. Both of these organizations are leaders in the field of technology investigations and have greatly influenced the law enforcement response to cybercrime on an International level.

The individual members have impacted cybercrime and have driven individual agencies response to cybercrime. This local law enforcement response has varied through depending on the agency and its leaderships' understanding of the problem. Although things have improved over the past decade, there are still some law enforcement administrators that think the Internet is not their jurisdiction. Funding is a major problem associated with investigating cybercrime. Much of the local and state law enforcements response is dependent on the local funding for the problem. Nationally there has never been any consistent federal funding to local and state agencies to address the overall cybercrime problem. The US government as many governments around the world, have increasingly made cybercrime and cyber-terror investigations a priority. Federal agencies are recruiting engineers and computer scientists for their critical skills and they are dedicating more agents to cybercrime investigations. Throughout the last decade they have also created regional task forces across the nation to deal with the cybercrime issue.

Why investigate Internet crime?

Law enforcement for 30 years has understood the need to address crime in neighborhoods even at the lowest level. In 1982, a theory was introduced by George L. Kelling and James Q. Wilson, which has been referred to as the "Broken Windows Theory." They suggested:

> ... that "untended" behavior also leads to the breakdown of community controls. A stable neighborhood of families who care for their homes, mind each other's children, and confidently frown on unwanted intruders can change, in a few years or even a few months, to an inhospitable and frightening jungle. A piece of property is abandoned, weeds grow up, a window is smashed. Adults stop scolding rowdy children; the children, emboldened, become more rowdy. Families move out, unattached adults move in. Teenagers gather in front of the corner store. The merchant asks them to move; they refuse. Fights occur. Litter accumulates. People start drinking in front of the grocery; in time, an inebriate slumps to the sidewalk and is allowed to sleep it off. Pedestrians are approached by panhandlers (Kelling and Wilson, 1982).

The theory espoused that even the small things in a neighborhood, such as abandoned property, unpicked weeds, and a broken window, would eventually lead to the disintegration of the neighborhood and eventually crime. What does a broken window have to do with Internet investigations? No we are not talking about the Windows operating system. The theory of small events and small crimes affecting the greater whole has the same effect on the Internet as it does in our own communities. The Internet is made up of various communities of interest. Social media has recently taken the lead as the most visible example. But, many Internet neighborhoods have had a few broken windows over time. Early in the Internet infancy, Usenet[21] was a popular means of communication and community building. However, it disintegrated into an often vulgar and obscene place. People using the perceived anonymity of the Internet began to post pornography, bully other users, and basically act without any moral compass to guide them. This was the real wild west of the Internet that had no sheriff to police the community. Today's Internet is no different in that sense. Certainly there are more efforts to police some areas of the Internet; however, there are more areas with broken windows. Internet relay chat, most of the social media space, and especially places like Tor's hidden services continue the "wild west" atmosphere. The problem with all of these areas is the lack of the sheriff keeping the peace. Law enforcement has been mostly absent in many Internet areas. To address the ongoing Internet crime issues law enforcement and corporate investigators need to embrace the Vere Software catch phrase "Make the Internet your regular beat."

What is needed to respond to Internet crime?

Both law enforcement and corporate investigators are constantly deluged with digital evidence issues in one form or another. The Internet continues to be a huge part of that evidence and investigative work load. So what will it take for investigators to make an effective response to Internet crimes? First of all you've taken the first step in reading this book. The other things that will make this job an easier fight are often not within the investigator's control but they include some local and national initiatives to sort out the online investigation priorities. Investigators need to not only focus on their investigations but how their communities of interests are affected by the Internet and how they can prevent them from being victims of the Internet miscreants. Investigators can:

- help their communities and business understand the need to make network and desktop security a priority;
- ensure that all cybercrime instances are reported to local law enforcement agencies;
- develop better communication among Federal, State, and local law enforcement regarding cybercrimes investigation;
- make investigations on the Internet an everyday policing routine.

---

[21]Usenet was at one time "the world's biggest electronic discussion forum," where individuals could post and response to comments and upload and download files. There was communication but it was not yet generally friendly to nontechies (Gralla, 1996).

As a national approach investigators need to encourage several things through their individual management and politicians. These include:

- Development of a national multistakeholder approach to cybercrime investigation. Use the ICAC model as a guide to developing a national approach to investigating Internet crimes and uniform standards.
- Development of an interoperable international legal framework to aid in cybercrime investigations that crosses international borders.
- The development of tools needed to deal with cybercrime/terrorism investigations.

Continuing investigative problems

Until a national approach can be developed to deal with the problems associated with investigating Internet crimes, there will be continuing issues. Investigators and their managers need to understand that from an initial investigative point of view there is no difference between cybercrime and cyber-terrorism. This is because at the first complaint the investigator usually is not going to know the person's motivation for committing the crime. The majority of online threats will continue to be cyber-crimes, most of malware and intrusion attempts although cyber-terrorism, however, will be an emerging threat. To compound these response issues will be the continuing lack of coordination of US and International law enforcement agencies. Communications technology has a growing risk from cyber threats that become increasingly sophisticated, largely global and are organized businesses. There are no geographical borders, no boundaries to the information society. Vulnerability of the nation's infrastructure is also increased as the use of communications technology becomes more prevalent.

CONCLUSION

The Internet has not changed the fact that crimes get committed and victims are created there every day. Information highlighted thus far reflects that Internet crime is as real as any committed on the street. Victims and losses are literally in the hundreds of millions. Malware attacks, followed by online scams, and phishing are probably the most prevalent type of Internet crimes. However, increasingly Internet crime is being perpetrated by "common criminals" and is no longer limited to just the techno criminal. Sex offenders are online. Gangs are using cell phones and social networking sites for criminal purposes. Mass attacks via flash mobs have been coordinated through cell phones and social media. Individuals are using the Internet to stalk, harass, and attack victims, including witnesses. Some offenders will even boast about their street crimes online. Victims, particularly corporations, are reluctant to report their victimization or the full extent of a cyber-incident.

However, no matter the location, crime needs to be reported and investigated. Internet crimes will continue to grow as we depend on the services it provides. More businesses will be victimized as they increase their online presence. What we hope to offer in this text is an opportunity for individual criminal and corporate investigators to expand their ability to respond to these crimes and offer more solutions than avoidance. The truth is that crimes committed on the Internet can be successfully investigated. Internet criminals can be found and prosecuted and victims can be gratified. What investigators need to understand is that they need to "make the Internet their regular beat."[22]

Further reading

Barwick, H. (2012, May 23). Social media is a tool for cybercriminals says Eugene Kaspersky. *Computerworld*. Retrieved from <http://www.computerworld.com.au/article/425401/cebit_2012_social_media_tool_cyber_criminals_says_eugene_kaspersky/>.

Baum, K., Catalano, S., Rand, M., & Rose, K. (2009, January). *Stalking victimization in the United States (NCJ 224527)*. Retrieved from U.S. Department of Justice website: <http://www.ovw.usdoj.gov/docs/stalking-victimization.pdf/>.

Bowker, A. (2012a, February 20). *Why does your Facebook profile have an inmate number?* Retrieved from <http://www.corrections.com/news/article/30208/>.

Bowker, A. (2012b, June 25). *Three intriguing cyber-offender questions*. Retrieved from <http://www.corrections.com/news/article/31038-three-intriguing-cyber-offender-questions/>.

Certified Forensic Computer Examiner. *History*. Retrieved from <http://en.wikipedia.org/wiki/Certified_Forensic_Computer_Examiner/>.

Computer Security Institute (CSI). *CSI 2010/2011 Computer Crime and Security Survey*. Retrieved from <http://gocsi.com/survey/>.

DesMarais, C. (2012, June 24). Another crook caught because of posting on Facebook. *PCWorld*. Retrieved from <http://www.pcworld.com/article/258259/another_crook_caught_because_of_posting_on_facebook.html/>.

Eckhart, R. (2012, March 23). Tyson's sister arrested over facebook post. *Herald Tribune*. Retrieved from <http://www.heraldtribune.com/article/20120323/ARTICLE/120329768/>.

Evans, D. (2011, July 15). *The Internet of things [Infographic]*. Retrieved from <http://blogs.cisco.com/news/the-internet-of-things-infographic/>.

Evans, J. Retrieved from <http://www.quoteland.com/author/John-Evans-Quotes/57/>.

Facebook®. Retrieved from <http://www.facebook.com/legal/terms/>.

Federal Bureau of Investigation. *Uniform crime reports*. Retrieved from <http://www.fbi.gov/about-us/cjis/ucr/ucr/>.

Gallagher, S. (2012, September 12). BlackHole 2.0 gives hackers stealthier ways to Pwn. *Ars Technica*. Retrieved from <http://arstechnica.com/security/2012/09/blackhole-2-0-gives-hackers-stealthier-ways-to-pwn/>.

Goodman, M. (2001). Making computer crime count. *FBI Law Enforcement Bulletin, 70* (8), 10−17. http://www.c-i-a.com/internetusersexec.htm.

---

[22]Trademark of Vere Software.

Gorner, J., & Meisner, J. (2012, April 26). Prosecutors say Kevin Liu was a prolific burglar who cyberstalked anyone who crossed him. Chicago Tribune. from <http://articles. chicagotribune.com/2012-04-26/news/ct-met-cyber-stalker-0426-20120426_1_prolific-burglar-cyberstalked-prosecutors>.

Gralla, P. (1996). *How the Internet works* (p. 55). Emeryville: Macmillan.

Hernandez, B. (2011, December 3). *Don't post 'I'm RICH!' on Facebook after robbing a bank.* Retrieved from <http://www.nbcbayarea.com/blogs/press-here/Dont-Post-Im-RICH-on-Facebook-After-Youve-Robbed-a-Bank-134911353.html/>.

High Technology Crime Investigation Association (HTCIA). *2011 Report on Cybercrime Investigation: A report of the International High Tech Crime Investigation Association.* Retrieved from <http://www.htcia.org/pdfs/2011survey_report.pdf/>.

Internet Crime Center (IC3). *IC3 2011 Internet Crime Report.* Retrieved from <http://ic3report. nw3c.org/docs/2010_IC3_Report_02_10_11_low_res.pdf/>.

Internet World Stats, Usage and Population Statistics. Retrieved from <http://www.internet-worldstats.com/stats.htm/>.

Kelling, G., Wilson, J. B. (1982, March). Windows: The police and neighborhood safety. *Atlantic Magazine.* Retrieved from <http://www.theatlantic.com/magazine/archive/1982/03/broken-windows/4465/2/#/>.

Korn, P. (2011, July 7). County lab keeps cyber-eye on parolees technicians scour electronic devices for evidence of violations. *Portland Tribune.* Retrieved from <http://portland tribune.com/news/story.php?story_id=130998904988341200/>.

Lardners, R. (2012, June 29). Cybercrime disclosures rare despite new SEC rule. *San Francisco Chronicle.* Retrieved from <http://www.sfgate.com/news/article/Cybercrime-disclosures-scarce-despite-new-SEC-rule-3672224.php#page-1/>.

Lenhart, A., Purcell, K., Smith, A., & Zickuhr, K. Social media and young adults (2010). *Pew Internet & American Life Project.* Retrieved from <http://pewinternet.org/Reports/2010/Social-Media-and-Young-Adults.aspx/>.

McAfee®. *McAfee Threats Report: First quarter 2012.* Retrieved from <http://www.mcafee. com/us/resources/reports/rp-quarterly-threat-q1-2012.pdf/>.

McAfee®. *McAfee Threats Report: Third quarter 2012.* Retrieved from <http://www.mcafee. com/us/resources/reports/rp-quarterly-threat-q3-2012.pdf/>.

Nakashima, E. & Warrick, J. (2012, June 4). Stuxnet was work of U.S. and Israeli experts, officials say. *The Washington Post.* Retrieved from <http://www.washingtonpost.com/world/national-security/stuxnet-was-work-of-us-and-israeli-experts-officials-say/2012/06/01/gJQAlnEy6U_story.html/>.

National Conference of State Legislatures (NCSL). *State cyberstalking, cyberharassment and cyberbullying laws.* Retrieved from <http://www.ncsl.org/IssuesResearch/Telecommunications InformationTechnology/CyberstalkingLaws/tabid/13495/Default.aspx/>.

National Gang Intelligence Center. (2009). *National Gang Threat Assessment.*

NYDailyNews.com. (2012, March 20). *Online dating sites give boot to sex offenders.* Retrieved from <http://articles.nydailynews.com/2012-03-20/news/31217130_1_spark-networks-sexual-battery-website/>.

Pinkston, R. (2011, August 10). British riots exposing social media's dark side? *CBS News.* Retrieved from <http://www.cbsnews.com/stories/2011/08/10/earlyshow/main20090575. shtml/>.

Poeter, D. (2012, September 24). New hacker collective emerges in response to anti-Islamic film. *PC Magazine*. Retrieved from <http://www.pcmag.com/article2/0,2817,2410127,00.asp/>.

Reuters. (2012, October 11). 'Shamoon' virus most destructive ever to hit a business, Leon Panetta warns. *Huffington Post*. Retrieved from <http://www.huffingtonpost.com/2012/10/11/shamoon-virus-leon-panetta_n_1960113.html/>.

Smith, J. *History of HTCIA*. Retrieved from <http://www.jcsmithinv.com/HTCIAhistory.htm/>.

Sulemanzp. (2011, November 11). Dugu virus attacked Iran's defence network!. *Info Rains*. Retrieved from <http://inforains.com/dugu-virus-attacked-irans-defence-network/>.

Symantec. (2011). Norton™'s Cybercrime Report 2011. Retrieved from <http://www.symantec.com/content/en/us/home_homeoffice/html/ncr/>.

Tech Terms. <http://www.techterms.com/>.

Traynor, L. (2012, May 3). 'Reservoir Dogs' killer Allan Bentley accused of threatening female trial witness on Facebook while behind bars. Crosby Herald. Retrieved from <http://www.crosbyherald.co.uk/news/crosby-news/2012/05/03/reservoir-dogs-killer-allan-bentley-accused-of-threatening-female-trial-witness-on-facebook-while-behind-bars-68459-30888759/>.

Vaughan, A. (2011, June 18). Teenage flash mob robberies on the rise. *Fox News*. Retrieved from <http://www.foxnews.com/us/2011/06/18/top-five-most-brazen-flash-mob-robberies/>.

Verizon. *2012 Data Breach Investigations Report*. Retrieved from <http://www.verizonbusiness.com/resources/reports/rp_data-breach-investigations-report-2012_en_xg.pdf/>.

Wortham, J. (2009, February 3). MySpace turns over 90,000 names of registered sex offenders. New York Times. Retrieved from <http://www.nytimes .com/2009/02/04/technology/internet/04myspace.html>.

Internet Criminals

2

If ignorant both of your enemy and yourself, you are certain to be in peril.
(Sun Tzu, Chinese Philosopher and author of "The Art of War," died 496 BC)

Chapter 1 introduced a working Internet crimes definition, specifically, offenses committed on or facilitated through the Internet's use. The difficulty in determining Internet crimes' true societal impact was also discussed. But what about the individuals that are committing these offenses? What do we know about them? Who exactly is the Internet criminal?

Conly (1989) was one of the first to provide an answer. She portrayed the typical computer criminal as 15−45 years old, usually male, and with an ability from highly skilled to someone with little or no technical experience. Additionally, the profile characterized these offenders as usually having no previous law enforcement contact, bright, motivated, and ready to accept technical challenges, who feared exposure, ridicule, and loss of community status. These offenders also appeared to deviate little from the accepted societal norms. They frequently justified criminal acts by viewing them as only a "game." The majority of the cases were committed by one person, however, conspiracies were starting to surface. Both government and business systems were targeted. A significant number were also "insiders," holding a trusted position in an entity, who had easy access to the victim's systems. These insiders were the first to arrive and the last to leave the office, taking few or no vacations. This profile centered on the hackers and insiders, initially the only ones committing computer crimes.

Remember this profile was created over 20 years ago, before the existence of the graphical user interface (GUI), now present on all computers. Early cybercrimes required knowledge of command line functions and frequently computer code. This profile was also created well before the Internet's massive growth or the emergence of social networking. It also predated cult hit movies like *Sneakers* (1992), *Hackers* (1995), and *The Net* (1995), which publicly exposed Internet crimes to the masses.

The unique and little understood technical skills in the 1980s are no longer needed today. Shortly after the 911 terrorist attacks, noted information security researcher and author,[1] Denning (2001) observed "...the next generation of terrorists will grow up in a digital world, with ever more powerful and easy-to-use hacking tools at their disposal." Now if one doesn't know how to do a technical task, such as hacking, a useful video tutorial can frequently be found online. YouTube® hosts instructional videos on how to hack most anything, including social media accounts on sites like Facebook®, websites, and your home WiFi network. We are now living in an era where all manner of criminal behavior, including terrorism, can be easily learned and committed with an Internet nexus. This chapter will focus on more recent attempts to profile the Internet criminal so we can "know the enemy."

Cybercrime profiling

Former FBI agent and profiler, William Tafoya[2] defined "cybercrime profiling ... as the investigation, analysis, assessment and reconstruction of data from a behavioral/psychological perspective extracted from computer systems, networks and the humans committing the crimes" (Radcliff, 2004). For our purposes the profile data is being extracted from the Internet, the largest network of all.

"Experts agree knowing more about the different skills, personality traits and methods of operation of computer criminals could help the folks pursuing these criminals" (Bednarz, 2004). There have been numerous cybercrime profiles developed over the years. Most early efforts focused on computer intrusions and hacking offenses. There are notable exceptions, such as those for cyberstalking and sexual exploitation offenders. Before delving into profile specifics it is important to understand that profiling comes in two varieties, the inductive and deductive approaches. The inductive approach assumes that individuals who committed the same crimes in the past share characteristics with individuals who are committing the same crime now. Examples of such profiles are those created for serial killers and rapists. The deductive approach uses evidence collected at the crime scene to develop a specific profile that can be used for offender identification. Understanding inductive profiles helps as the deductive approach frequently looks to them for clues in developing a more specific offender profile (Petherick, 2005).

---

[1]Denning is an accomplished author of numerous books and articles on information security and is a distinguished professor with the Department of Defense Analysis, Naval Postgraduate School. Source: http://faculty.nps.edu/dedennin/.

[2]Tafoya was an FBI special agent who worked in both the FBI Academy's Computer Crimes and the Behavioral Science Units. He served as the lead behavioral scientist on the infamous Unabomber case. His 1993 bomber profile turned out to be an uncanny match of Theodore Kaczynski, who was later arrested and convicted. Tafoya's work was also instrumental in the founding of the Society of Police Futurists International (PFI). Tafoya is now professor and director of Research at the University of New Haven. Sources: http://www.copacommission.org/meetings/hearing3/tafoya.pdf and http://www.newhaven.edu/news-events/news-releases/88175/.

Inductive profiles

As noted previously, much of the early inductive profiles focused mainly on the hacking and intrusions. Additionally, some efforts were not detailed but merely broad groupings. For instance, Kovacich and Jones (2006) indicated that early attempts placed hackers into the following three basic categories: the curious—hackers wanting to know more about computers; meddlers—hackers seeking the challenge of breaking in and finding system weaknesses; and criminals—hackers who commit these offenses for personal gain. Arkin, Kilger, and Stutzman (2004) further elaborated on the cybercriminal's motivation by adapting the Federal Bureau of Investigation's approach for examining espionage motivations for use with Internet criminals. Their acronym for these motivations was MEECES, which stands for Money, Entertainment, Ego, Cause, Entrance to social group, and Status.[3]

Cybercriminal profiles

Later attempts were much more defined and elaborate, further refining the skill level and motivations of each cybercriminal. One such hacker profile came up with eight cybercriminal subtypes (Bednarz, 2004). Shoemaker and Kennedy (2009) later developed an expanded cybercrime profile with the following 12 subtypes, again based upon skill level and motivation:

1. Kiddie (Script kiddie): This group is not technologically sophisticated and uses others' preprogramed scripts or menu-based programs. Their motivation is ego driven, usually with the intent to trespass and sometimes to invade a user's privacy. (This does not mean they are harmless as the preprogramed tools can make less sophisticated users very dangerous.)
2. Cyberpunks: This group is technologically proficient, usually young, counterculture members, and outsiders. Their motivation is also ego driven, focusing on trespass or invasion, the later of which motive is exposure. They will, however, engage in theft and sabotage but only on targets they view as legitimate. They are often responsible for many viruses, application layer, and denial of service (DOS) attacks against established companies and their products.
3. Old timers: Probably the most technologically proficient, this group's motivation is ego driven and perfecting the cyber-trespassing "art." They tend to be middle age or older, with an extensive personal and/or professional technology backgrounds, including hacking. They are the last of the "Old Guard," whose purpose was to show how good they were at overcoming defenses to gain unauthorized entry into systems. This group sometimes engages in website defacement. As they frequently knew what they were doing they usually did not cause much harm. The notable exception is the

---

[3]The FBI's origin motivations for individuals who commit espionage against their country were Money, Ideology, Compromise, and Ego, which had an acronym of MICE.

heart burn to systems administrator who has to patch the security vulnerability and check their systems to make sure there were no additional "surprises" left behind by their intrusion.

4. Unhappy insider: This profile is considered the most dangerous as these individuals are inside an organization's defenses. They can be any age and employed at any level. The major characteristic is they are unhappy with the organization and hence their motivation is revenge, oftentimes coupled with monetary gain. As a result their intent is to steal or harm the company. They may engage in extortion or exposure of company secrets. This group's criminal acts are more dependent upon direct system access as opposed to secondary access via the Internet. However, they will use Internet access to obtain tools, transfer stolen goods to their possession, or to meet other objectives.

5. Ex-insider: This is the former employee that separated from the company unwillingly through layoff or unsatisfactory performance/conduct. Again, the motivation is revenge and the purpose is to harm the company. They may use insider information to discredit the company or to overcome vulnerabilities not publicly known. If termination is not well planned and they foresee it, they may plant logic bombs or perform other destructive acts to data and/or systems.

6. Cyber-thieves: This group can be any age and do not require vast technological experience. Their motivation is profit, either stealing data or outright monetary theft. They are adept at social engineering. However, they also will use network tools (sniffing or spoofing) as well as programing exploits to get what they want. They will oftentimes get employed by a company to work from the inside, making it easier to steal. Others will work their "magic" from the outside.

7. Cyberhucksters: These are the spammers and malware distributors. They are focused on monetary gain and commercialization. They are very good at social engineering as well as spoofing. They employ spyware, tracking cookies, and even legitimate business data mines to find victims for their "products." One example of their handiwork is the pop-up banner that appears notifying the unsuspecting user that their system is infected and they need to buy the cyberhuckster's anti-virus tool, the cure for the "infection."

8. Con man: This group is motivated by monetary gain and theft is their trademark. They run the Nigerian scams but are not above phishing to commit identity and credit card theft. They are very good at social engineering and spoofing. They are harder to catch as they tend to be antonymous. Frequently, their attacks do not target specific victims, e.g., mass phishing attacks. However, some will engage in more targeted attacks on high value targets, sometimes referred to as "spear phishing."

9. Cyberstalker: This group is driven by ego and deviance. They want to invade their victim's privacy to satisfy some personal, psychological need like jealousy. Shoemaker and Kennedy (2009) also noted this group primarily

uses such tools as key loggers, Trojan Horses, or sniffers. However, as will be discussed later, this group is far more resourceful and diverse.

10. **Code warriors:** They report that this group is one of the most skilled with long histories based in technology, oftentimes with degrees. Initially, their focus was on ego enhancement and sometimes revenge. However, they have since become capitalistic, engaging in theft or sabotage. Unlike the Old Timers, who viewed their activity as an "art" they tend to look at it as a profession. They are code exploiters and Trojan Horse creators. They can be any age, but usually fall in the 30–50 age group. Additionally, they are usually socially inept and social deviants.

11. **Mafia soldier:** This group has some of the characteristics of the con man and code warriors. They are highly organized with the criminal purpose of making money in whatever manner possible. They commonly engage in theft, extortion, and privacy invasion with the goal of blackmail. Many of this group are located in the Far East and Eastern Europe, although all organized crime will likely get into this lucrative illegal enterprise.

12. **Warfighter:** Unlike the other groups, this subtype is viewed only as cybercriminal if they are fighting against you. They can be any age, but are the best and brightest any country can muster. Their motivation is infowar and they are after strategic advantages for their country and its allies and harm to their enemies. They employ all cyberweapons at their disposal, including Trojan Horses, DOS attacks, and the use of disinformation.

The above would seem to be an exhaustive list of Internet criminal subtypes. Unfortunately, Shoemaker and Kennedy's profiles neglect numerous areas of Internet criminality. For instance, none of the subtypes mention the various Internet auction frauds involving misrepresentation or nondelivery of products. They also do not cover click fraud, which involves fraudulently increasing Internet advertising revenue by manipulating the number of "clicks" generated from users accessing website ads (Grow, Elgin, & Herbst, 2006). The subtypes also do not cover Internet stock fraud, where individuals provide misleading or bogus information via the Internet to potential investors to get them to buy stock (US Securities and Exchange Commission, 2011). The ease of Internet fraud is best represented by a 16-year-old "pump and dump" scheme, in which he fraudulently hyped a stock online to drive up its value and then sold it, receiving $285,000 in ill-gotten gains (CBS News, 2009). It might be argued that these behaviors fit under one of the subtypes, such as cyberhuckster or con man. There is also no mention of such activities as illegal online gambling operations or illicit sale of pharmaceuticals. None of their subtypes match up neatly with these other cybercrime acts.

Shoemaker and Kennedy's profile also does not delve into the Internet's use by murderers. Detectives have known for years that some murders will use the Internet for research on methods to dispatch their victims. However, some murderers, more specifically serial killers, are using the Internet to hunt. Reportedly, the Internet's first serial killer, John Edward Robinson, found his post 1993 victims by trolling online chatrooms (Wiltz & Godwin, 2004). There are numerous other cases of killers meeting and luring their victims to their deaths via Craigslist (Associated Press, 2009; Kaufman, 2012; NY1 News, 2011; Snow & Kessler, 2009). One of the most notable is the unsolved serial murder case known as the Long Island Serial Killer a.k.a. the Craigslist Ripper (Fernandez & Baker, 2011). There is even a case where a police officer has been accused of online planning and communication of his intent to kidnap, rape, torture, kill, cook, and cannibalize adult women (Serna, 2012). His planning, which was thankfully interrupted by his arrest, included a computer database of 100 women containing personal information and their physical descriptions (Serna, 2012).

Cybersex offenders

Another Internet criminality overlooked by Shoemaker and Kennedy's profile is the cybersex offender. The US Department of Justice, Office of Juvenile Justice and Delinquency Prevention (1999) identified three broad cybersex offender types: (1) the dabbler (the curious with access to child pornography), (2) the preferential offender (the deviant with sexual interests involving juveniles), and (3) the miscellaneous offender (pranksters or the misguided who come into possession of child porn as a result of their own investigations). However, these categories are more specific to offenses, involving possession, distribution, and manufacturing of child pornography.

In 2000, Detective James F. McLaughlin provided a more inclusive typology. He reviewed 200 sex offenders arrested as part of a 3-year Internet law enforcement project conducted by the Keene Police Department, New Hampshire. This project targeted preferential sex offenders. From his review, he identified the following four cybersex offender categories.

1. Collectors ($n = 143$, 72%): McLaughlin considers this group made up of many "entry level" offenders, most of whom had no criminal record or had any known illegal contact with children. Collectors range in age from 13 to 65 years of age. The majority were single and living alone. Twenty-one percent were in vocations that involved contact with children. Specific occupations included: a college professor, a social worker, a camp director, an attorney, a youth counselor, school teachers, and law enforcement officers. McLaughlin observed that more individuals may be engaged in child pornography collection/trading, erroneously believing their online activities were anonymous and untraceable. He notes initially these offenders start their collection from static Internet locations (newsgroups and web pages), which do not involve real-time online interaction with other computer users. Eventually, most collectors escalate to dynamic Internet locations, involving real-time interaction with others, web-based chatrooms, and Internet relay chat. Once at the dynamic locations, these offenders also start distributing child pornography. The images in many ways become a deviant currency. Oftentimes, these offenders set up the specific file directories so they can retrieve images quickly for viewing and/or online interactions.

2. Travelers ($n = 48$, 24%): This group is made up of offenders who engage in online chats with minors and use their manipulation skills and coercion to arrange for in-person meeting for sexual purposes. Offenders in this group were 17−56 years of age. Traveler occupations included military officer, attorney, athletic director, priest, college professor, high school teacher, and a civil engineer. A majority of these offenders also collected child pornography. Travelers do not always have any criminal sex offense history. These offenders would frequently travel great distances after only chatting online a few minutes. Four traveled internationally (Canada, Holland, and Norway) and the others traveled from 10 different states. Over 50% falsely claimed they were in their teens during their online communication, with some revising the claim to something more realistic, but still false. Over 50% also sent actual pictures of themselves, many of which were nudes. Grooming communication frequently involved the offender obtaining personal information, developing trust, engaging in sexual banter, and sending pornographic images. Many maintained that they would never coerce a minor into sexual behavior, noting their conduct would be mutual. At the scheduled meetings, these offenders would show up with condoms, lubricants, photo equipment, blankets, and even Viagra®. Some offenders would send funds or bus/airline tickets to the minor to facilitate them in running away. Three of these offenders were considered to be sadistic pedophiles.

3. Manufacturers ($n = 8$, 4%): McLaughlin notes ". . .not all collectors are manufacturers but all manufacturers are collectors." The age range for manufacturers was 26−53 years. Most manufacturers were sexually involved with children or to had criminal sex offense histories. Many of these offenders had photographed children they molested years ago, were actively molesting, or were in the grooming process. In at least 50% of the cases runaway children were found being harbored in the offender's homes. Financial gain was not the motivation, with only one offender gaining less then $1,000.00. Manufacturer occupations included: professional nanny, photographer, airport worker, building superintendent, and youth music teacher.

4. Chatters ($n = 1$, 0.05%): McLaughlin included this category which is clearly based upon more information than just this study. He indicated these offenders collect child erotica (nude images) as opposed to child pornography (images depicting sex acts or lewd exhibition of genitalia area). He notes these individuals refuse to send images over the Internet, do not trust others who send them images, and warn underage persons not to do so. They are daily online as much as 12 hours more. They consider and present themselves as "teachers." Chatters will draw clear behavior lines in chatrooms, which they will not deviant from and expect others to honor. Nevertheless most will engage in cybersex and after rapport has been established escalate into phone sex. However, they are satisfied with this contact and will not want to meet the minor in the real world.

The idea that a cybersex offender's conduct is merely fantasy is not something we support, particularly as some offenders use such reasoning to rationalize their criminal conduct. However, Young (2005) presents an interesting profile with two broad online sex offender types, virtual (situational) and classic. Her profile is based upon 22 forensic interviews with suspected online sex offenders. Young recognizes the illegal conduct is serious but notes that virtual offenders are involved as experimentation, fantasy, and/or as a novelty. For Young, the virtual sex offender's online criminal behavior is more situational. They will have sexual relations with minors but juveniles are not their exclusive interest. Virtual online sex offenders start out as adult fantasy. For instance, they may begin in a chatroom called Married/Flirting and move to more suggestive rooms, such as Father/Daughter or OlderMen/Virgins. Their chat dialog is usually quick, explicit, and with little trust building or grooming. They are generally truthful about their age, name, and intentions. These offenders also tend to show remorse or shame after they are caught. The chronic online sex offender focuses on minors and has in exclusive sexual interest in juveniles. They start with teen chatrooms or other areas where minors frequent. They will go into other chatrooms, such as Father/Daughter, to trade child pornography but they realize these areas are frequented by adults pretending to be minors. Their chats are disguised, subtle, and consistent with a traditional molester's grooming techniques. They will lie about their identity as well as their true intentions. They express little or no remorse or shame at getting caught. For Young (2005), classic offenders "...exhibit a chronic and persistent pattern of sexualized behavior toward children" and as a result they "...are clearly a more serious threat to the welfare of children as they utilize the Internet, because they often have prior convictions related to sexual crimes against children on their records."

Internet harassment

Shoemaker and Kennedy subtypes frequently rely too much on software techniques by the offender, such as key loggers, Trojan Horses, or sniffers by cyberstalkers. It is true that those tools are used in some cyberstalking cases, but those high-tech tools are not present in all cases. Additionally, their subtype fails to note that cyberstalking can involve Internet communication, such as posting to a website, or the Internet as a research tool, such as on the victim or for techniques/tools. This criminality, along with cyberharassment and cyberbullying are collectively referred to as Internet harassment (Smith, 2008). These acts are defined as follows:

- Cyberstalking is the repeated use of the Internet, email, or related digital electronic communications devices to annoy, alarm, or threaten a specific individual or group of individuals (D'Ovidio & Doyle, 2003, p. 10).
- Cyberharassment involves electronic communications (e.g., email, Internet, social networking sites), absent a specific threat to the victim, e.g., continued posting unwanted, off topic, and/or unflattering comments on a social networking site, in a blog, or in a chatroom (Bowker, 2012).

- Cyberbullying is cyberharassment when both the victim and the offender are juveniles. It encompasses not only harassment activities but veiled threats (Bowker, 2012).

McFarlane and Bocij (2003) developed a useful cyberstalking topology based upon their interviews with 24 victims located in numerous countries, including Canada, New Zealand, the United Kingdom, and the United States. Their topology has the following four groups:

1. Vindictive cyberstalker: These groups threaten their victims more than the others and in the majority of cases also included offline behavior. One-third of this group had previous criminal records and two-thirds were known to have previously victimized others. Their computer literacy was rated medium to high by their victims. This group, more than any other, utilized the widest range of Internet tools, such as spamming, mailbombing, and identity theft, to harass their victims. This group was also the only to use Trojan programs. Three-quarters of this group's victims reported receiving bizarre or unclear/ unrelated comments and intimidating multimedia images and/or audio files, e.g., skull and crossbones, corpses, screams, etc. In these instances such comments were taken as evidence these stalkers had severe mental issues. Two-thirds of these victims had known their stalker before the victimization commenced. Half of the victims noted the harassment started over some trivial matter and was blown out of all proportion. One-third of the victims saw no apparent reason for the stalking. The rest of the victims acknowledged they had previously been in an active argument with their stalker.
2. Composed cyberstalker: This group was made up of stalkers who were not trying to establish any relationship with their victim. Their only apparent goal was to cause distress by constant annoyance and irritation to their victims. This group also was estimated to have a medium to high level of computer skills. These stalkers issued generalized threats to their victims. Only one in this group had a record and only one had any previous stalking history. None in this stalker group had any psychiatric history. Nevertheless, three went on to stalk their victims offline.
3. Intimate cyberstalker: This group was actually made up of two subgroups, ex-intimates and infatuates. Ex-intimates were a victim's ex-partner or ex-acquaintance. Infatuates were individuals looking for an intimate relationship with their victim. This group was characterized as trying to gain attention and/ or obtain a relationship with the victim. Additionally, victims reported this group having a wider range of computer skills than other groups, from fairly low to high. These stalkers utilized email, web discussion groups, and electronic dating sites and demonstrated detailed knowledge about their victims. The ex-intimate subgroup engaged in online behaviors ranging from trying to restore their relationship with the victim to threats on the victim's significant other or friend. In some cases the ex-intimate impersonated their victim, such as pretending to be their ex-partner in chatrooms or buying goods

online in their name. Surprising that in this subgroup there were no cases of offline stalking occurring after the cyberstalking. Infatuates were seeking to form a closer relationship with their victim, often through more intimate communication than the other subgroup. However, when their attempts were rebuffed their messages became more threatening. In one infatuate case, the offender stalked the victim offline.

4. Collective cyberstalkers: This last group involved two or more individuals stalking their victim online. This group's stalkers envisioned themselves wronged by the victim and accordingly sought to punish the victim. At times this group would recruit others to harass the victim offline. Victims ranked their stalker's computer literacy from fairly high to high. Online stalking behavior included threats, spamming, email bombing, identity theft, and intimidating multimedia to harass the victim. This group also did research on their victims. Additionally, McFarlane and Bocij realized another subgroup, corporate cyberstalking, might exist. In such cases, an organization might be criticized for a business practice and take offense. In turn, they would use harassment to discredit and/or silence the victim. This group also used identity theft to impersonate and discredit victims.

Cyberterrorism and cyberwarfare

Although Shoemaker and Kennedy's Warfighter subtype discusses acts of cyber-warfare, their profile really does not adequately address cyberterrorism. We previously mentioned the general motivation of the criminals committing crime, including the MEECES approach. The motivations for persons committing crimes on the Internet are very different than those whose intent is to commit an act of terrorism or a cyber-act of warfare. The players are also very different with varying funding and technical skill levels.

A cyberterrorists motivation is political in nature. The effect of their actions is most likely "mass disruption" as described by Rattray (2001). The intention of the cyberterrorist is not to necessarily kill anyone, but to cause disruption of services. An attack on any critical infrastructure controlled through technology can cause significant disruption to a community and force a hysterical reaction by its citizens. The cyberterrorist most likely is from an organized group but may not have extensive forethought in its application of the act.

Nelson, Choi, Iacobucci, Mitchell, and Gagnon (1999) looked at the five terrorist group types (religious, New Age, ethnonationalist separatist, revolutionary, and far-right extremist) and made some interesting conclusions in their pre-911 world. They noted that religious groups were "...likely to seek the most damaging capability level; as it is consistent with the indiscriminate application of violence that has distinguished much of their activity" (p. 10). At the time they thought the most immediate threat was the New Age or single-issue terrorist community (e.g., Animal Liberation Front), as such groups were more willing to accept disruption as a destruction substitute. They noted both Religious and New Age groups and their primary targets were located in areas with numerous high-tech targets. Additionally, both groups had the best match among desire, ideology, and environment to facilitate an advanced cyberattack. They concluded both the revolutionary and ethnonationalist separatist (ENS) groups were likely to desire the ability to launch an advanced cyberattack, but for differing reasons. For them, an advanced cyberattack offered the revolutionary group the necessary degree of control over the unintended consequences that might occur with an indiscriminate cyberattack. For the ENS group, an advanced cyberattack could serve to supplement a traditional terrorist act. Nelson et al. (1999) concluded far-right extremists were not likely to seek the advanced cyberattack capability, noting in part it was not consistent with a far-right terror psychology. Additionally, far-right groups used computer networks more often for their operations and any widespread disruption would likely also negatively affect them.

Cyberwarfare differs from cyberterrorism as it is an organized effort by a nation state to conduct operations in cyberspace against foreign nations. Included in this category is the Internet's use for intelligence gathering purposes. Cyberwar has become the little understood adjunct to cyberspace that has the potential for the greatest impact to the Internet. An all-out assault by nation states against each other would leave private citizens in its wake. The nations with the most integration of technology in their citizen's lives have the most at stake. Although emerging nations developing a technology infrastructure with a growing dependency on cellular technology could be the first to fall in any concerted broad-based cyberattack. Totalitarian regimes have found that the simple act of restricting "Tweets" can have a great effect of controlling the masses or disrupting organized activities. Interrupting the communication flow through social media could isolate a country and mask further aggressive acts. A modern example of cyberwar can be found in the alleged acts of the Russian government against their former states Estonia and Georgia (Ashmore, 2009). The Russian government allegedly used cyberattack strategies in an attempt to cripple the countries because of alleged grievances against Russia.

We will next examine some recent historical data on Internet criminals, which will hopefully provide further clues that will aid in classification and identification.

Internet Crime Compliant Center

From 2001 to 2010, the Internet Crime Compliant Center (IC3) regularly reported some characterizations of the Internet criminal. The characteristics were limited to offender gender, location, and in some reports, the method of contacting the victim. The reasons for dropping this information from the 2011 report are unknown. There is a caveat in the 2009 year report cautioning readers that information pertaining to "...perpetrator demographics represent information provided to the victim by the perpetrator so actual perpetrator statistics may vary greatly" (p. 7). Additionally, the 2009 report reflects that perpetrator gender and their residence state were reported only 38.0% and 35.1% of the time, respectively. The 2010 IC3 report, which was the last year perpetrator information was provided, reflected that nearly 75% the online crimes were committed by men. More than half resided in

California, Florida, New York, Texas, the District of Columbia, or Washington. The United States accounted for 65% of the overall reported perpetrators (if known) of online crime. The United Kingdom was next with 10.4% and Nigeria in third at 5.8%. Prior IC3 reports occasionally reported the majority of perpetrators were in contact with their victim through either email or via websites.

It is understandable that the IC3 may have decided that providing perpetrator demographics was problematic. After all, the nature of these crimes is such that the perpetrator can portray themselves to be anyone, located anywhere but where they really are located. There are anonymization (or hiding) methods that will be discussed later that offenders use on the Internet to prevent being caught. As such, it may be that IC3 concluded this information was of limited value.

One observation is noted though. For the 9 years this information was provided and it was pretty consistent. Males were reported as the perpetrator anywhere from 75% to 76%. Additionally, over half of all perpetrators were reported as living in one following states: California, Florida, New York, or Texas. Other states would appear and fall from the list but these states consistently were represented as the Internet criminal's reported location. Additionally, the United States had the dubious distinction of being the vast majority of perpetrators' home locations. Again, this is coming from complainant data and the perpetrator could be using some anonymization method to prevent being caught. But one does have to wonder why this data is consistent for each year, with no real changes. It seems unlikely that there is a grand Internet conspiracy by female criminals to make themselves male and appear to be located in the United States, in one of four particular states.

New York Police cyberstalking study

D'Ovidio and Doyle (2003) examined data gathered from all closed cases investigated by the New York Police Department's the Computer Investigation & Technology Unit (CITU) from January 1996 to August 2000, which involved aggravated harassment. They found 201 (42.8%) of these cases involved a computer or the Internet as the instrument of the offense. Of these cases, 192 were closed during the study's time frame. Case outcomes for these 192 cases revealed approximately 40% were closed with an arrest. Another 11% were closed due to insufficient evidence that a crime had occurred. The remaining cases were closed due to a jurisdictional issue, an uncooperative complaint, case transfer, or failure to identify a suspect. They then focused on the 134 cases where an arrest was made or in which a suspect was identified but not charged. They found that 80% of these cases involved males. The racial make-up of these cases was 74% white, 13% Asian, 8% Hispanic, and 5% black. The average offender age was 24 with the oldest being 53 and youngest being 10. They also found that females (52%) were more likely to be recipients of a threatening or alarming message. Thirty-five percent of the victims in aggravated harassment cases were males. Educational institutions were targeted in 8% of the cases. Private corporations and public sector agencies were targeted in 5 and 1% of the cases, respectively. The victim's racial make-up was 85% white, 6% Asian, 5% black, and 4% Hispanic. The victim's average age was 32 with the youngest victim being 10 and the oldest 62.

D'Ovidio and Doyle (2003) also found that in 92% of the cases the offender only used one cyberstalking method, which was most often email. They noted that 79% of the victims were harassed through email. The second most prevalent method was instant messaging, which was used in 13% of the cases. Chatrooms were used in approximately 8% of the cases. Message boards and websites were used in 4% and 2% of the cases, respectively. Remember that this data covered a period before social networking sites exploded on the Internet. Offenders employed newsgroups and false user profiles in only 1% of the cases. Offenders used anonymous remailers in only 2.1% of the cases. The majority of the cases involved investigations where both the offender and victim resided within the New York Police Department's jurisdiction.

McFarlane and Bocij (2003) study involved a much smaller victim set, 24, but found many of the same trends. Twenty-two (92%) of the victims were female. The most common cyberstalking method was email. In 54% of the cases, offline stalking also occurred, with six victims stalked at home, three at their worksite, and three in public places. Additionally, one victim reported they were subject to surveillance by their offender. In 33% of the cases, the offender impersonated the victim online.

Sex offenders online activities

Dowdell, Burgess, and Flores (2011) completed a study in which students as well as convicted sex offenders were given a questionnaire regarding their online activities centering on social networking sites. The study's time frame was from 2008 to 2009. Data was obtained from 466 convicted sex offenders, of which 113 were Internet sex offenders, which were defined as involving child pornography and/or travelers. The remaining 354 non-Internet sex offenders were child molestation ($n = 236$), rapist ($n = 35$), miscellaneous sex offenses ($n = 27$) (not child molestation or rape; mostly indecent exposure or voyeurism), and generic offenses ($n = 55$, no known offenses against children). Sixty child molesters also were Internet sex offenders.

They found that approximately 29% of the Internet offenders and 13% of the child molesters visited teen chatrooms. Approximately 29% of the Internet sex offenders entered chatrooms where they honestly identified themselves. Fifty-nine percent disguised their identity by name or age. Approximately 12% varied their truthfulness, sometimes being honest and sometimes lying about their identity. Roughly 63% of the child molesters provided truthful identity information in chatrooms. Approximately 37% disguised themselves, usually misstating their age. Those offenders who were both Internet sex offenders and child molesters were equally divided, 49%, between being truthful and lying concerning their identity. All offender groups preferred chatting with teenage girls. Sex offenders also preferred using MySpace® but students preferred Facebook®.

Approximately 63% of the Internet sex offenders reported initiated the topic of sex in their first online chat session. Twenty percent did so in sessions 2−6. Approximately 17% took 7 or more sessions to first approach the topic of sex. Approximately 7% of the incarcerated sex offenders and 10% of the sex offenders in the community reported having experience with an online avatar on SecondLife.[4] In comparison, approximately 6% of high school students and 4% of college students reported having a SecondLife avatar.

Capability

Clearly, the average Internet criminal is not necessarily a technology genius or the typical hacker. Today's Internet creates a situational environment where anyone with access can become the next Internet criminal. Also, the availability of highly complex tools lowers the entry level for some criminals. As a result we need to take a broader approach to classify or more importantly identify the Internet criminal. Nelson et al. (1999) initially recognized three cyberterror capability levels, simple unstructured, advanced structured, and complex coordinated. Modifying these levels, with an additional fourth level, simple structured can be useful in discussing the Internet criminal. Simple unstructured involves individuals working with little structure, forethought, or preparation. Simple structured are individuals or groups working with little structure, but with some forethought or preparation. Advanced structured groups work with some structure, but little forethought or preparation. Complex coordinated are groups or in some cases governments, working with advance preparation with specific targets and objectives. These categories help us to understand the motivations and the resources of the individual criminals. The sophistication level and the potential for larger damages increase as the perpetrator becomes more organized. Everyone, including the reader of this text starts out with a minimal level of knowledge and skill. With education we have grown in our expertise and skill. As Internet offenders educate themselves and become more active in their pursuit of criminal activity they increase their potential for harm. Additionally, if they associate with others, either loosely or through an organized structure, the level of their potential for damage exponentially expands (Figure 2.1).

At the lowest level within the simple unstructured category exists a large percentage of the cybercriminal element. This is the breeding ground for far more sophisticated action by the more organized groups. These individuals work with little structure. They are not organized for any real criminal effort and their general actions are done with very little in the way of forethought or preparation. Examples of this are the typical novice in the hacking arena. They are new to most aspects of the cyber world and spend much of their time learning about

---

[4]SecondLife is an online virtual reality, where users can create three-dimensional identities for themselves. These avatars can then work and play in a virtual community created by the user. In 2012, it was reported there were 1 million active users on SecondLife. Additionally, over $700 million a year in virtual goods transacted inside of SecondLife every year (Lacy, 2012).

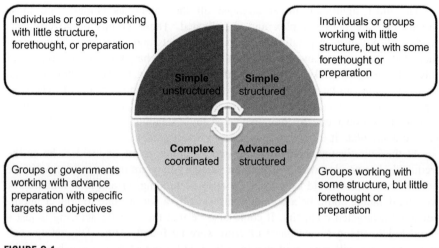

Individuals or groups working with little structure, forethought, or preparation

Individuals or groups working with little structure, but with some forethought or preparation

Simple unstructured

Simple structured

Complex coordinated

Advanced structured

Groups or governments working with advance preparation with specific targets and objectives

Groups working with some structure, but little forethought or preparation

FIGURE 2.1

Simplified perpetrator categories.

hacker techniques and tactics. In doing so they are likely to exceed their authority on a network, most likely one they are given access to as an employee. They may explore their office network and spy on others in the office. Obviously a properly configured network would not allow this and a trained network administrator with an active defense, internally and externally should identify the intruder.

The individuals identified as belonging to the simple structured category are individuals or groups working with little structure, but with some forethought or preparation. These include traditional hackers, disgruntled employees, and individuals committing crimes on the Internet. These also include the loose nit or cyber only affiliated hacking groups that associate with each other for the benefit of their egos versus the actual organized effort to hack into any company or government computer. Employees that are not happy with their current situation and plot damage or theft of company material requiring some planning and preparation are also categorized here. The online stalker (and we use this in the broadest sense here to include stalking of adults or children) is using little structure and is not an organized crime, but one that is thought out and planned.

The more complicated online threats come from the more advanced and complicated organizations. The advanced structured threat is an organized group working with some structure, but little forethought or preparation. These threats include the organized hacking group that has documented affiliations amongst its membership and generally similar philosophies that drive the group's efforts. The hacking attempts or intrusions are generally not organized, although they may individually be sophisticated in their attack. The group's individuals determine the effort more on a decentralized basis then in an organized planning from a single authority.

The most significant threat amongst all the categories comes from those threats that are both complex and coordinated. These groups or governments work with advance preparation with specific targets and objectives. This makes them the single most dangerous threat that a network has. For the investigator of Internet crimes this makes it the most difficult to investigate. The organized group or government can be involved in terrorist activity, committing acts of cyberwarfare, or collecting intelligence to support those activities. These are the most difficult to track down due to their extensive understanding of the technology and how to manipulate it to remain hidden from investigators.

As the investigator begins looking into an online crime or incident he or she frequently has no idea which perpetrator category they are investigating. A simple online fraud crime could be a front for terrorist funding, or a simple intrusion or website defacing could be a complex intrusion by a nation state to collect intelligence on a targeted company. It could also be that the website defacing is just a script kiddie trying a new piece of crimeware he found online. Ultimately each and every case will have evidence to collect and a perpetrator somewhere in the world. Internet crime victims experience harm just like any traditional crime victims suffer. Investigators have a responsibility to victims and society to follow the evidence where it leads. Some investigations may lead to nowhere and some to a successful conclusion. To cut short the investigative efforts solely on the basis of act being an Internet crime do not serve societal or justice interests.

Deductive profiling

Shoemaker and Kennedy (2009) observed that cybercrime profiling investigations involve five processes: evidence gathering, behavior analysis, victimology, crime pattern analysis, and profile development. Evidence gathering focuses on collecting all potential evidence, such as might be present in computer/network logs, on defaced websites, on social media sites, or forensically from a computer hard drive. Behavior analysis is the process of trying to obtain meaningful behavior characteristics from the evidence found. Victimology is the process of studying the victim for clues why they may have been targeted or for some kind of relationship they may have with the offender. Crime pattern analysis involves looking at the information and data from the first three stages in relationship to time and geography, and developing a working theory of who the offender might be, along with why the crime was committed. The last process, profile development, attempts to take the information and theories and create an offender profile. Frequently, this last process will look at other known profile groups, developed via the inductive approach, to bring into focus a specific offender profile. As the above reflects a knowledge of both the inductive and deductive approaches is extremely helpful in developing a useful profile that identifies the Internet criminal.

Additionally, we believe there are three general principles that pertain to identifying the Internet criminal, particularly when the offender and victim have no apparent relationship. The first principle holds that as the interaction between the offender and their victim increases, so does the potential to locate and identify the offender. The more times the offender sends an email, posts a message on a website or social networking site, etc. the more likely clues will be left behind for the investigator. Even offenders using anonymization methods, sometimes get comfortable, lazy, and make contact without adequately covering their tracks. Additionally, these clues are also not always in the form of digital evidence. An offender may inadvertently provide some piece of information, such as in an email, instant message, that gives away their identity. Take the case of cyberstalker using a bogus email or profile to communicate with their victim. As the communications continue, some will get caught in the moment and response something like "Don't you know who this is? It is Tom from work."

The second principle is as the Internet criminal creates more victims, the greater likelihood a pattern will be detected that leads to their identity. This is why it is so important that victims report the crime to law enforcement and is part of the reasoning behind the IC3 creation. As with the first principle, the Internet criminal may leave little or no evidence behind with the first few victims but get sloppy on the sixth or seventh victim and leave clues behind that lead to their location and identity. Additionally, as the Internet criminal increases their loss total with multiple victims, they increase the investigative attention. Few police agencies will devote much investigative resources to locating an Internet criminal who stole $100 from one victim. But an Internet criminal who steals $100 from say 1,000 victims, particularly if many are customers from the same financial institution, will likely result in an investigative response. As the victim tally increases, as well as the loss, so will the investigative resources devoted to finding the perpetrator(s).

The final principle is the more informed the victim, the better likelihood they will be able to assist the investigator. In cyberstalking cases, it is very important that the victim keep records of what happened when, as well as maintaining emails, instant messages, etc. By maintaining and providing this information to the investigator they can greatly assist in identifying the perpetrator. Additionally, from an online safety perspective, the more informed individuals are about the various Internet crimes, the greater likelihood they will not become victims in the first place. Obviously, this is an excellent law enforcement rationale for developing Internet safety presentations for their communities. Having an online safety initiative is less costly than conducting Internet crime investigations.

CONCLUSION

This chapter has introduced the wide diversity and variety of online criminal behaviors. All Internet crimes are clearly not all the same. Differences appear not only among the acts themselves but also the motivations and technical skills in each high-tech crime typology. Exposure to these differences helps investigators understand the reasons or motivations behind why individuals commit Internet crimes and will hopefully aid in offender identification. We also provided a simplified model for understanding these motivations. This model will assist to further understand Internet criminals and allow investigators better opportunities to identify and find those criminals.

Further reading

Arkin, O., Kilger, M., & Stutzman, J (2004). *Profiling*. Know your enemy: Learning about security threats Boston: Honeynet Project: Addison-Wesley Professional.

Ashmore, W. (2009). *Impact of alleged Russian cyber attacks a monograph*. Retrieved from <http://www.dtic.mil/dtic/tr/fulltext/u2/a504991.pdf/>.

Associated Press. (2009, April 3). "Craigslist killer" Michael John Anderson gets life in murder of Katherine Olson. *New York Daily News*. Retrieved from <http://www.nydailynews.com/news/world/craigslist-killer-michael-john-anderson-life-murder-katherine-olson-article-1.361506/>.

Bednarz, A. (2004, November 29). Profiling cybercriminals: A promising but immature science. *Network World*. Retrieved from <http://www.networkworld.com/supp/2004/cybercrime/112904profile.html/>.

Bowker, A. (2012). A victim-centered approach to supervising internet harassment offenders. *Perspectives special victim issue* (pp. 92–99). American Probation and Parole Association. Retrieved from <http://www.appa-net.org/eweb/docs/appa/pubs/Perspectives_2012_Spotlight.pdf/>.

CBS News. (2009, February 11). Pump and dump. CBS News. Retrieved from <http://www.cbsnews.com/8301-18560_162-242489.html/>.

Conly, C. (1989). *Organizing for computer crime investigation and prosecution* US Department of Justice, Office of Justice Programs, National Institute of Justice.

Denning, D. (2001). Is cyber terror next? Retrieved from <http://essays.ssrc.org/sept11/essays/denning.htm/>.

D'Ovidio, R., & Doyle, J. (2003). A study on cyberstalking: Understanding investigative hurdles. *FBI Law Enforcement Bulletin*, 72(3). Retrieved from <http://www2.fbi.gov/publications/leb/2003/mar03leb.pdf/>.

Dowdell, E., Burgess, A., & Flores, R (2011). Online social networking patterns among adolescents, young adults, and sexual offenders. *American Journal of Nursing*, *111*(7), 28–36.

Fernandez, M., & Baker, A. (2011). Long Island Serial Killer gets a personality profile. *The New York Times*. Retrieved from <http://www.nytimes.com/2011/04/22/nyregion/long-island-serial-killer-gets-a-personality-profile.html?_r=0/>.

Grow, B., Elgin, B. , & Herbst, M.. (n.d.). *Click fraud*. Retrieved from <http://www.businessweek.com/stories/2006-10-01/click-fraud/>.

Internet Crime Center (IC3). *IC3 Internet crime report* (2001 to 2011). Retrieved from <http://www.ic3.gov/media/annualreports.aspx/>.

Internet Crime Center (IC3). *IC3 2010 Internet crime report*. Retrieved from <http://www.ic3.gov/media/annualreport/2010_ic3report.pdf/>.

Kaufman, T. (2012, October 30). Jury finds stow teen Brogan Rafferty guilty on all murder charges in Craigslist killings case. *News Channel 5*. Retrieved from <http://www.newsnet5.com/dpp/news/local_news/akron_canton_news/jurors-reach-verdict-in-craigslist-killings-trial-of-stow-teen-brogan-rafferty#ixzz2B1 × 6uSIr/>.

Kovacich, G. L., & Jones, A. (2006). *High-technology crime investigator's handbook: Establishing and managing a high-technology crime prevention program* (2nd ed. Amsterdam: Butterworth-Heinemann/Elsevier.

Lacy, S. (2012, July 6). Philip Rosedale: The media is wrong, SecondLife didn't fail. *PandoDaily*. Retrieved from <http://pandodaily.com/2012/07/06/philip-rosedale-the-media-is-wrong-secondlife-didnt-fail/>.

Lasker, L., & Parkes, W. (Producers). (1992). *Sneakers* [Film]. Universal City: Universal Studios.

McFarlane, L., & Bocij, P. (n.d.). An exploration of predatory behaviour in cyberspace: Towards a typology of cyberstalkers. *First Monday*. Retrieved from <http://firstmonday.org/htbin/cgiwrap/bin/ojs/index.php/fm/article/view/1076/996/>.

McLaughlin, J. (n.d.). *Cyber child sex offender typology*. Retrieved from <http://www.ci.keene.nh.us/police/Typology.html/>.

Nelson, B., Choi, R., Iacobucci, M., Mitchell, M., & Gagnon, G. (1999). *Cyberterror: Prospects and implications* Monterrey: Center for the Study of Terrorism and Irregular Warfare, Naval Postgraduate School.

NY1 News. (2011, November 15). *Teen convicted of fatally stabbing Brooklyn Radio Reporter*. Retrieved from <http://brooklyn.ny1.com/content/top_stories/150835/teen-convicted-of-fatally-stabbing-brooklyn-radio-reporter/>.

Petherick, W. (2005). *The science of criminal profiling* New York: Barnes & Noble Books.

Peyser, M. (Producer) (1995). *Hackers* [Film]. Los Angeles: United Artists Corporation.

Radcliff, D. (Profiling Defined) (2004, March 1). *Network World*. Retrieved from <http://www.networkworld.com/research/2004/0301hackersdef.html/>.

Rattray, G. (2001). The cyberterrorism threat. In J. Smith, & W. Thomas (Eds.), *The terrorism threat and US government responses: Operational and organizational factors*. Colorado: USAF Institute for National Security Studies, US Air Force AcademyRetrieved from <http://www.au.af.mil/au/awc/awcgate/usafa/terrorism_book.pdf/>.

Serna, J. (2012, October 12). New York Police officer arrested in plot to kidnap, cook, eat 100 women. *Los Angeles Times*. Retrieved from <http://www.latimes.com/news/nation/nationnow/la-na-nn-police-officer-cannibal-women-20121025,0,6041707.story/>.

Shoemaker, D, & Kennedy, D. (2009). Criminal profiling and cyber-criminal investigations. In F. Schmalleger, & M. Pittaro (Eds.), *Crimes of the Internet* (pp. 456–476). Upper Saddle River, NJ: Prentice Hall.

Smith, A. (2008). *Protection of children online: Federal and state laws addressing cyberstalking, cyberharassment, and cyberbullying*. Congressional Research Service.

Snow, M., & Kessler, J. (2009, April 21). Med student held without bail in possible craigslist killing. *CNN*. Retrieved from <http://www.cnn.com/2009/CRIME/04/21/mass.killing.craigslist/index.html/>.

Tzu, S. Retrieved from <http://www.brainyquote.com/quotes/quotes/s/suntzu384543.html/>.

US Dept. of Justice, Office of Justice Programs, Office of Juvenile Justice and Delinquency Prevention (1999). *Use of computers in the sexual exploitation of children*.

U.S. Securities and Exchange Commission "Internet Fraud" (2011) Retrieved from <http://www.sec.gov/investor/pubs/cyberfraud.htm>.

Wiltz, S., & Godwin, G. M. (2004). *Slave master* New York, NY: Kensington Pub. Corp.

Winkler, I., & Cowan, R. (Producers). (1995). *The Net* [Film]. Los Angeles: Columbia Pictures Industries, Inc.

Young, K. (2005). Profiling online sex offenders, cyber-predators, and pedophiles. *Journal of Behavioral Profiling*, 5(1), 18.

How the Internet Works

3

I must confess that I've never trusted the Web. I've always seen it as a coward's tool. Where does it live? How do you hold it personally responsible? Can you put a distributed network of fiber-optic cable "on notice"? And is it male or female? In other words, can I challenge it to a fight?

Stephen Colbert, comedian

To many the Internet is fundamentally a confusing and mystical thing. One that touches our lives in ways few could have imaged. Everyday millions of people connect to the Internet in an attempt to be informed, maintain relationships, find new ones, and speak their minds. The Internet has been unique in history due to its ability to connect people together. It is much more than a communication method. The Internet has enabled its users to unite with others in ways that previous generations would never understand. Communication more than 30 years ago was the disconnected use of stationary technology. If you didn't want to be found you didn't answer the landline telephone. If you wanted to know the news of the world you picked up a newspaper or watched the 6 o'clock news. The Internet and its ability to communicate information in the form of complete novels to 140 characters has transformed what we think is communication. Today we are attached to our technology. Cell phones are more pervasive than computers. We are connected to the ones we love and those we have never met. The Internet intrudes into our lives at every level. Work hours are spent updating Facebook and seeing what's tweeted by Lindsay Lohan or Madonna. Home hours are spent watching movies on Netflix and surfing for deals on eBay or Craigslist. So what does this all mean for the Internet investigator? It means that everyone we know, everyone we don't know in our communities of interest, and everyone else in the connected world is online. The issue now becomes that everyone who is online is now a potential victim or suspect. To start to understand how to deal with this we have to understand the basis of the Internet and its foundations.

A short history of the Internet

The Internet before the World Wide Web (WWW or just the web) was a much different place. The Internet as we believe it to be is based on the innovations of a few bright individuals that thought connecting data on the Internet through a browsing concept was a simple change. Fundamentally browsing was a huge change. In 1989, Sir Tim Berners-Lee wrote a proposal for what would eventually become the WWW. He later helped to develop the concept of using "hypertext" to connect information. Hypertexts today are as ubiquitous as car travel. They are both used everyday and with few considering their profound societal impact. Hypertext has made the Internet available to the masses.

Prior to today's Internet there did exist a useful and diverse communication medium. Almost everyone knows that the Internet's beginnings were formed through funding of US projects under the Defense Advanced Research Projects Agency (DARPA) umbrella. The 1960s were a turbulent and dangerous time. Development of a communication method if the then Soviet Union attacked with nuclear weapons was high on the list of military projects. The projects expanded on the already suggested concept of sending packets of information between computers. This research would build the first networks and ultimately build the technology foundation we know today as the Internet. The Internet technology prior to the WWW included a variety of communications and data transfer tools that seem normal to us today. The "Cloud" is an overused term describing the use of the Internet for various storage and access to technology. This storage and other technology existed in the form of file transfer protocol (FTP), Gopher, Simple Mail Transfer Protocol (SMTP), Internet relay chat (IRC), and many others. Each was defined through a common set of protocols. Standard protocols are the basis for the Internet and its function. These protocols serve the Internet community as a common method of understanding and communication. Without standard protocols the Internet would not work or exist. These protocols exist in the Internet world as request for comments (RFC), which derive themselves from the Internet's beginning as a collaborative group across numerous disciplines. The standard bodies formed through the Internet Society as the Internet Engineering Task Force (IETF) have been effective in directing the growth of the Internet's technology. Without these protocols the Internet would not work. The advantage for the online investigator is that the protocols are published and available to us to review and understand. First and of foremost importance to the online investigator is the Internet Protocol (IP) addressing scheme.

The importance of IP addresses

The basis for Internet communication is a simple process of assigning each device attached to the Internet an address. This address allows that device to connect

IP address translation	Telephone number translation
1 2 3 - 1 2 2 - 2 1 3 - 0 1 2 Class　Network　Sub-network　Computer No	01 – 775 – 322 – 5121
• The first set identifies the type of the network (or class).	• International calling codes
• The second set identifies a specific section of network.	• Area codes
• The third set identifies a subnetwork or department within the section.	• Local prefix
• The fourth set identifies an individual, specific computer or device.	• Local numbers

FIGURE 3.1

IP address translation compared to a telephone number.

with and communicate with any other device connected to the Internet using this same addressing scheme. This addressing scheme is commonly referred to as the IP address. The most commonly used version of the IP addressing is version 4, commonly referred to as IPv4. The IPv4 address is made up of four sets of three numbers. These number sets are referred to as "octets." Each octet is made up of 256 numbers, 0−255. These 32 bits (4 bytes) of information allows for the connection of 4.3 billion devices through the Internet. The format of the IPv4 address that is commonly used is what is called the dotted decimal, e.g., **123.122.213.012**. This number is globally unique.

Let's take a look at how the IPv4 address looks and is translated. In Figure 3.1, we have a comparison of the IPv4 address and the traditional telephone numbering scheme. The traditional telephone number is similar in format (although not exactly) and an example that will help the investigator new to IPv4 understand how it functions.

As in the telephone number example there are four number sets. There is one set each for the International calling code, area code, local prefix, and the local number associated with that house. We all know now that the traditional telephone numbers are no longer just to a house. They can be to a business, mobile phone, and may even be to a fax machine. They are more in line with the IPv4 scheme, where a number is to a particular device. But for our example let's just say our number goes to a house. In Figure 3.2, we can find a location using a state, city, street, and house address as well as through latitude and longitude. On the Internet we can find a location through an IP address or a uniform resource locator (URL). Similarly in this example, the IPv4 address is broken down into those four octets that identify different parts of the address. Ultimately this leads to the individual device associated with that IPv4 address.

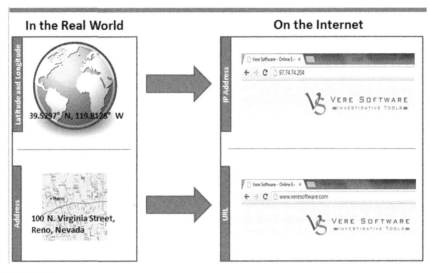

FIGURE 3.2

How we find a location.

DHCP and assigning addresses

To further confuse the situation of identifying what device is associated with an IP address, we have two ways they get assigned. The first is dynamically, which refers to the use of a pool of IP addresses that get "dynamically" assigned to a device when it requests Internet access. This is commonly done through a process called Dynamic Host Configuration Protocol (DHCP). This protocol is software running on a server, router, or other device that determines the IP addresses assignment to other devices in the network requesting access to the Internet. RFC 2131 describes this as "…automatic allocation of reusable network addresses…" Effectively for the investigator the DHCP assigns the address out of a pool of addresses to each device that connects to the network. This becomes part of the investigation trail that needs to be followed. The server or router assigning the addresses is another link in the chain of locations that may require the request of information from logs to prove what device was assigned a particular IP address at a given time (Figure 3.3).

Through the DHCP process, the addresses assigned to each device allow them individually to access the network without conflicting with another device. Devices, if assigned the same address, would not function properly on the network because information being sent to an address would not know which device to send the data, causing a conflict. Uniquely assigned addresses allow the data to

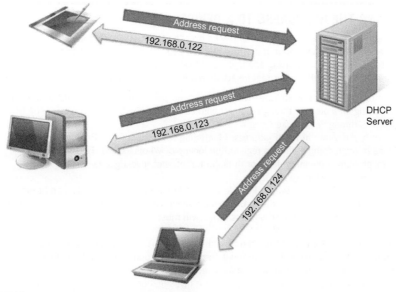

FIGURE 3.3

DHCP assignment of IP addresses.

flow to a device without this conflict. From an investigative viewpoint, this also identifies a specific device to which the address was assigned.

The assignment of an address specifically for the use of that device and that device only is called a "static" IP address. This allows the device to always have the same address when it connects to the network or the Internet. The advantage is that the device can always be found easily by other devices on the Internet looking for that device. As an example, a server providing a service such as a webpage or an FTP will also want to be found by its users. Assignment of a "static" or permanent address helps facilitate their return to that same location on the Internet. A dynamically assigned IP address would make this reconnection more difficult.

DYNAMIC DNS SERVICES

There are programs that facilitate the use of dynamically assigned addresses by an ISP to allow for public Internet resources to find a resource with a dynamic IP address. These services act as a Domain Name Server that constantly updates the DNS system with the new address for your Internet resource assigned the dynamic address. The investigator should be aware that the term "DNS" has more than one common meaning. It is used both to refer to a Domain Name Server as well as a reference to the overall Domain Name System.

TRACING THE IP ADDRESS TO A DEVICE

Tracing that individual IP address to a device over the Internet and through a network requires several steps (Keep in mind that this is a general go by as to how to trace an IP address. If the criminal is using any tools to obfuscate his address or hide his real IP address, the end results might require additional investigative actions):

1. Identify the correct IP address: This can be found potentially in the header of an email, a posting on a blog, or through a direct connection with the target by trapping the IP address through a tool like Netstat.
2. Identify the owner of the IP address: Identifying the owner of the IP address is usually done through doing a domain registration lookup or Whois lookup. This can be done through numerous online tools or through the Internet Investigators Toolkit (see Chapter 6 for further details).
3. Contact the IP address owner: Provide the IP address owner with the date and time, including the time zone and Coordinated Universal Time (UTC) the IP address was used in your investigation. The IP address owner will most likely require legal service of a subpoena or search warrant.
4. Research the information from the IP address owner: A general investigative background on the name and any address information needs to be done on the information provided by the IP owner. This information may be correct to the device used to connect to the Internet, but it may not be the target of your investigation. For instance, the device may be in a residence or business with multiple users. This information could also provide you with the wireless router that was used by another device to access the Internet.
5. Contact the owner of the device identified as accessing the Internet: The owner of the IP address will provide you with the next step in the chain of the investigation. Ensure that you have the required legal service ready when taking this next step. A simple "Knock and Talk" could also serve the purpose of identifying who accessed the Internet from the identified device at a specific location. The wireless router in question could contain logs of access and IP address assignment that may prove useful to your investigation. The logs may, if turned on, provide the investigator with device-specific information like the device network interface card (NIC) unique identifier called the media access control (MAC). The MAC address is used to identify specific devices attached to networks. However, this address is not passed through the router and will only be found at this level of the investigation (Figure 3.4).

MAC address

The last stop on the investigative journey to identifying the user of an IP address is the last router in the chain. This is most often at the business network the user is connected to or the home router used to access the Internet. This last router in the chain may contain logs of those devices connected to it that accessed the Internet. Most routers have logging but may not have the logging turned on to record the access. If the logging is turned on, the router will record the access of a device through its MAC address. The MAC address is a unique identifier assigned by the manufacturer of NICs (either the Ethernet connection or a wireless connection). The MAC address is used by the router to differentiate between devices attached to the router (Figure 3.5).

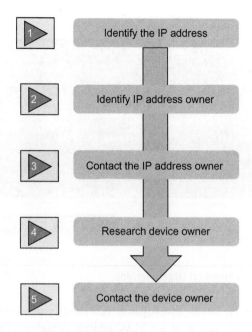

FIGURE 3.4

Device identification by IP address assignment.

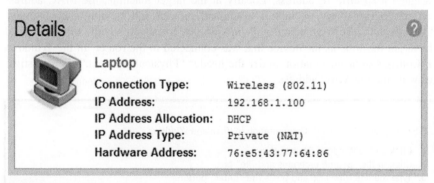

FIGURE 3.5

Example of router details of connected device.

The MAC address is six pairs of hexadecimal numbers separated by colons, broken into two sections. An example of a MAC address is 76:e5:43:77:64:86. The hexadecimal digits used in the MAC address include only the numbers 0–9 and letters A–F (see the Hexadecimal to ASCII chart in Appendix A for more details). The first section is the first three pairs of digits. This part of the MAC address is the Organizational Unique Identifier (OUI) or Vendor ID (IEEE-SA

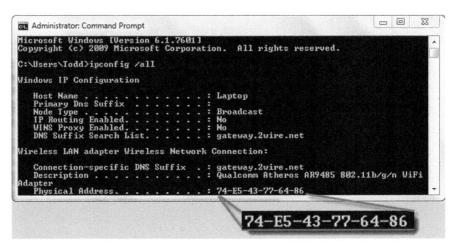

FIGURE 3.6

Identification of MAC address on target machine.

Registration Authority, 2012). Investigators can identify the MAC address manufacturer by the second section of the MAC address containing the last three digit pairs. These three hex pairs are unique to the device. The MAC address is useful during the investigation to identify the device that was attached to the router and assigned a specific IP address. Locally at the target machine, the MAC address can be confirmed by opening a command prompt and running the command "ipconfig /all." This command will provide the investigator with confirmation of the target machine as the device that was connected to the router. In the Windows IP Configuration information under the header "Physical Address," the investigator will find the MAC address.

Accessing the Windows IP Configuration in Vista and Windows 7

1. Click on the Windows Start button.
2. Click in the "Search programs and file" box.
3. Type the following **cmd** and press the "Enter" button.
4. A black console window will open. In the console window, type "**ipconfig**" and press enter. You will now see the IP address, Subnet Mask, and Default Gateway for each active network connection in your computer. If you type "**ipconfig /all**" additional information about each connection will be presented, including the connections DNS Servers and the network card MAC address (Figure 3.6).

Investigators need to be aware that the MAC address can be spoofed through various tools. This is a common technique by criminals to connect to a router without being tracked back to the specific target device by that unique number (Figure 3.7).

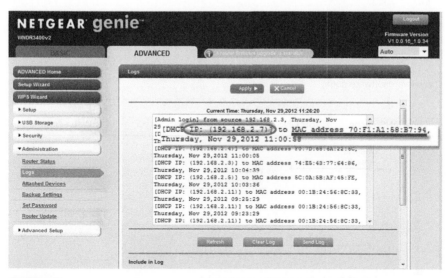

FIGURE 3.7

Identification of MAC address from a small office/home office router.

Domain Name System

In the middle of the browser request to the web server containing a webpage to be viewed is a process that identifies where in the world that webpage exists. The Domain Name System (DNS), sometimes referred to as the Domain Name Servers, is a large database of IP and URLs. The DNS is something similar to a large phone directory. The browser makes a request through the DNS system to identify the IP address of a URL. The DNS process looks up the address in its database and if it knows the IP address it passed the addresses back to the browser. If it does not know the address, it passes the request up to the next higher DNS server to assist in the identification of the IP address. The IP address when identified is passed back to the browser. The browser then makes a request to the IP address for the webpage at that address. The web server at that IP address then sends the webpage requested to the browser which then displays the webpage (Figure 3.8).

DNS records

Each DNS contains a series of records or "resource records" that describes information on each domain. These records include information about the domain so that when a request about the domain is made the correct information can be provided to the requestor. The information contained in the record includes information about the assigned IP address, any potential alias used, which DNS server

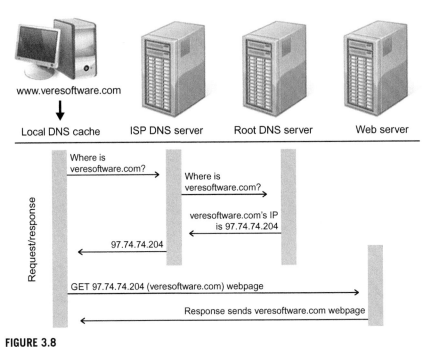

FIGURE 3.8

Domain Name System IP address lookup.

has the authoritative record about the domain mail server records and other domain records to guide the request to the right location. Getting these records use to be fairly simple with a command line lookup tool found in most operating systems called NSLookup. This tool provided the list of available records for the domain. However, recent hacking attempts of DNS servers have had any reputable DNS server administrator now refusing those requests for information. An available free tool to view the available DNS records in a single view is DNSDataView from Nirsoft (Figure 3.9).[1]

The records here provide the investigator with information as to the ownership and available locations that information may be obtained (some with further online research and some with legal service on the IP address owner) (Always keep in mind that all this work may bring you to a false address or an uninvolved party. Criminals can and do use methods to hide themselves. However, all of this still needs to be done to track down the possible leads in the investigation). In the example in Figure 3.9, we have found the following records regarding the DNS record of the domain veresoftware.com, NS, MX A SOA, and PTR. We can identify each of these Record Types using Table 3.1. Also identified with each Record Type is the Host Name and IP address associated with that record. This

---

[1]Nirsoft (www.nirsoft.com) is a maker of a variety of useful online investigative tools.

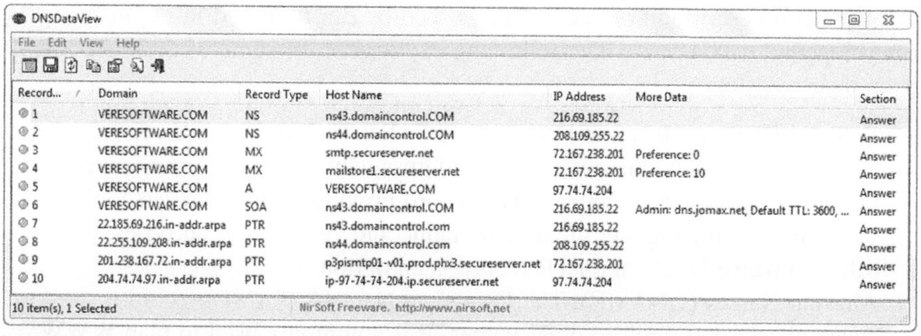

FIGURE 3.9

DNS records using DNSDataView.

Table 3.1 Domain Record Types		
Type	**Value and Meaning[a]**	
A	1	a host address
NS	2	an authoritative NS
MD	3	a mail destination (obsolete—use MX)
MF	4	a mail forwarder (obsolete—use MX)
CNAME	5	the canonical name for an alias
SOA	6	marks the start of a zone of authority
MB	7	a mailbox domain name (experimental)
MG	8	a mail group member (experimental)
MR	9	a mail rename domain name (experimental)
NULL	10	a null RR (experimental)
WKS	11	a well-known service description
PTR	12	a domain name pointer
HINFO	13	host information
MINFO	14	mailbox or mail list information
MX	15	mail exchange
TXT	16	text strings

[a]A detailed explanation of each record can be found on the Microsoft Technet Library (http://technet. microsoft.com/en-us/library/dd197499(v = WS.10).aspx).

information provides the investigator with a more complete picture of the domain and its associated connections to other servers on the Internet.

In RFC 1035—Domain Names—Implementation And Specification,[2] the document lists the various record types listed for a domain. Each of these various record types contains specific information on that aspect of the domain.

---

[2]A compilation of DNS relates RFCs can be found at http://www.zoneedit.com/doc/rfc/.

A general description of each of these records can be found in PC magazine's Encyclopedia of IT terms.[3] The following explanation of some of these records is from their website:

> Forward DNS and Reverse DNS (A and PTR): The Address (A) record associates a domain name with an IP address, which is the primary purpose of the DNS system. The Pointer (PTR) record provides data for reverse DNS, which is used for logging the domain name and verification purposes. Also called "inverse DNS," the PTR record is an option.
>
> Aliasing Names (CNAME): The Canonical Name (CNAME) record is used to create aliases that point to other names. It is commonly used to map WWW, FTP, and MAIL subdomains to a domain name; for example, a CNAME record can associate the subdomain FTP.COMPUTERLANGUAGE.COM with COMPUTERLANGUAGE.COM.
>
> DNS Name Servers (NS): The name server (NS) record identifies the authoritative DNS servers for a domain. A second NS is required for redundancy and two NS records must be in the zone file (one for the primary; one for the secondary). The secondary server queries the primary server for changes.
>
> Mail Servers (MX): The mail exchange (MX) record identifies the server to which email is directed. It also contains a priority field so that mail can be directed to multiple servers in a prescribed order.
>
> Text Record (TXT): A TXT record can be used for any kind of documentation. It is also used to provide information to the Sender Policy Framework (SPF) email authentication system.
>
> First Record in File (SOA): Start of authority (SOA) is the first record in the zone file. It contains the name of the primary DNS server, which must correspond to an NS record in the file, the administrator's email address and the length of time records can be cached before going back to the authoritative DNS server.

DOMAIN NAME SERVICE

In his testimony before the Senate Committee on Commerce, Science and Transportation, Subcommittee on Communications, on February 14, 2001, Michael Roberts, President and CEO of ICANN, said "In recent years, the domain name system (DNS) has become a vital part of the Internet. The function of the domain name system is to provide a means for converting easy to remember mnemonic domain names into the numeric addresses that are required for sending and receiving information on the Internet. The DNS provides a translation service that permits Internet users to locate Internet sites by convenient names (e.g., http://www.senaste.gov) rather than being required to use the unique numbers (e.g., 156.33.195.33) that are assigned to each computer on the Internet." Today the Internet would not work without the DNS system.

---

[3]http://www.pcmag.com/encyclopedia_term/0,1237,t = DNS+records&i=55466,00.asp.

Internet Protocol Version 6

An updated version of the IP protocol version, Ipv6 (Internet Protocol Version 6), is slowly being implemented and will eventually replace the IPv4 system. IPv6 is the next protocol version that is the basis for most communications on the Internet. IPv4 addresses started to run out in 2011. The requirement to move to a new system of addressing devices on the Internet is imperative. The effect this has on Internet investigations is significant. Investigators have had a general understanding of the IPv4 system and how to trace IPv4 addresses. IPv6 addresses are very different and require a new understanding of the IPv6 protocol. The immediate issue is the two protocols are not compatible. IPv6 is coming to a crime near you. The official launch of the IPv6 protocol occurred on June 5, 2012.

Defining IPv6

What the investigator will immediately notice is the Ipv6 addresses are much more complex and harder to remember then their Ipv4 cousins. IPv6 uses 128-bit addresses. Like IPv4, IPv6 numbers are broken into groups. IPv6 has eight groups of four numbers separated by colons (:) not periods (.) as in the IPv4 design. The four numbers in the each eight groups are hexadecimal and not numerical as in IPv4. The larger set under IPv6 provides a number of addresses that is never expected to run out. As an example, the following is an Ipv6 address: 2001:0db8:85a3:0042:0000:8a2e:0370:7334.

Translating IPv6

A single IPv6 address is defined under RFC 4291 as eight sets of four hexadecimal numbers, such as ABCD:EF01:2345:6789:ABCD:EF01:2345:6789. However, the standard allows for a variety of representations of the IPv6 address. The IPv6 address can be represented in different ways and the investigator should know these various methods to identify them in an investigation. The following Table 3.2 from RFC 5952 describe how a single IPv6 address can be represented.

In the IPv6 examples, letters are not differentiated by capital or lowercase, zeroes can be dropped and whole segments, if zero eliminated, and represented only by the colon (:) separating the segments. What this does for the investigator is provide very different looking formats for the addresses when looking at them

Table 3.2 Examples of Various IPv6 Representations

2001:db8:0:0:1:0:0:1	2001:0db8::1:0:0:1
2001:0db8:0:0:1:0:0:1	2001:db8:0:0:1::1
2001:db8::1:0:0:1	2001:db8:0000:0:1::1
2001:db8::0:1:0:0:1	2001:DB8:0:0:1::1

Table 3.3 Types of IPv6 Addresses

Address Type	Description		
Unicast	A packet is delivered to one interface.		
	Scope	**Description**	**Prefix**
	link-local	Similar to IPv4 automatic private IP addressing addresses used by computers running Microsoft Windows. Hosts on the same link (the same subnet) use these automatically configured addresses to communicate with each other.	FE80::/10
	site-local	Site-local addresses are similar to IPv4 private addresses.	FEC0::/48
	global	IPv6 unicast global addresses are similar to IPv4 public addresses. Global addresses are globally routable.	2000::/3
Multicast	A packet is delivered to multiple interfaces.		
Anycast	A packet is delivered to the nearest of multiple interfaces.		

to identify that they are IPv6 addresses. This IPv6 example would fully be represented as 2001:0db8:0000:0000:0001:0000:0000:0001 or 2001:db8:0:0:1:0:0:1.

IPv6 has three types of addresses, which can be categorized by type and scope: (Technet Microsoft). In Table 3.3, the types include Unicast (and its variations of link-local, site-local, and site-local), Multicast, and Anycast. From an investigative point of view, these address types are not initially remarkable, however, being able to identify where an IPv6 address is used can assist the investigator to determine its relevance.

The IPv6 address for your computer can be found using the command prompt and running the "ipconfig /all" command. In Figure 3.10, you can see the identified IPv6 address assigned to the system and the "link-local" IPv6 address.

Ipv4-Mapped IPv6 addresses

For the investigator's purposes, IPv4 can be mapped to IPv6 addresses under certain circumstances. This mapping is intended to aid in the migration from the IPv4 protocol to IPv6. However, this is not a direct translation of the IPv4 address to an IPv6 address. The IPv6 RFCs allow for mapping IPv4 address in the IPv6 addressing scheme. In two circumstances, RFC 4291 describes these implementations. Typically the IPv4 address is embedded in the IPv6 address. An example could be IPv4 address 97.74.74.204 mapped to an IPv6 address: 0:0:0:0:0: ffff:614a:4acc.

In hexadecimal 614a:4acc translates to the IPv4 address 97.74.74.204.

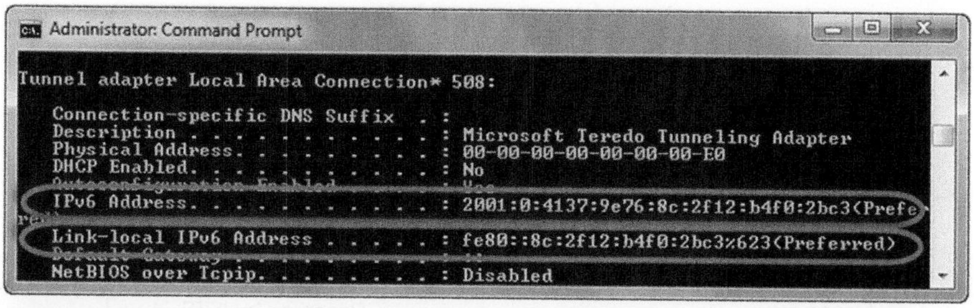

FIGURE 3.10

IPv6 address from ipconfig command.

When mapping an IPv4 address to an IPv6 address, the 128 bits of the IPv6 address are broken into three parts. The first 80 bits, or the first five segments of the IPv6 address, are zeros. The second 16 bits or the next segment in the IPv6b address is either zeros or hexadecimal FFFF. The last 32 bits or two segments of the IPv6 address is the IPv4 address (Table 3.4; Figure 3.11).

IPv6 DUID

For the investigator the DHCP Unique Identifier (DUID) is the last stop in the trail of identifying a device. DUIDs are used in the IPv6 addressed network to uniquely identify devices connected to the system. This is similar to MAC addresses use in an IPv4 router to identify individual devices. There are four types of DUIDs found within the IPv6 DHCP system to identify devices associated to the system (RFC 3315 and 6355). DUIDs are intended to remain constant over time, so that they can be used as permanent identifiers for a device. The four types are found in Table 3.5.

An example of a DHCPv6 (DHCP for IPv6) client DUID is 00-01-00-01-17-96-F9-3A-28-92-4A-3F-6C-47.

It can be broken down as in the example below:

Global Identifier	MAC Address from Ethernet Adapter
00-01-00-01-17-96-F9-3A	28-92-4A-3F-6C-47

Each DUID variation produces a unique identifier. With this one can potentially obtain the MAC address of a given device located on the machine. However, Windows appears to be maintaining the DUID over time and not reassembling a unique identifier based on hardware changes. So a direct connection to a MAC address on a hardware device might not be possible. However, from an investigative viewpoint, maintaining a unique identifier on the machine even when hardware changes are made could be extremely valuable to the investigator (Figure 3.12).

Table 3.4 IPv6 Address Space Assignment

IPv6 Prefix	Allocation
0000::/8	Reserved by IETF
0100::/8	Reserved by IETF
0200::/7	Reserved by IETF
0400::/6	Reserved by IETF
0800::/5	Reserved by IETF
1000::/4	Reserved by IETF
2000::/3	Global Unicast
4000::/3	Reserved by IETF
6000::/3	Reserved by IETF
8000::/3	Reserved by IETF
A000::/3	Reserved by IETF
C000::/3	Reserved by IETF
E000::/4	Reserved by IETF
F000::/5	Reserved by IETF
F800::/6	Reserved by IETF
FC00::/7	Unique Local Unicast
FE00::/9	Reserved by IETF
FE80::/10	Link Local Unicast
FEC0::/10	Reserved by IETF
FF00::/8	Multicast

http://www.iana.org/assignments/ipv6-address-space/ipv6-address-space.xml.

80 bits	16 bits	32 bits
0000:0000:0000:0000:0000	0000 or FFFF	97.74.74.204
::0:97.74.74.204		

FIGURE 3.11

Example of an IPv4 address mapped to IPv6.

WHERE IS THE DUID IN THE WINDOWS O/S?

For reference the online investigator can verify the DUID with a request to their digital forensic examiner. The digital forensic examiner can find the DUID on the target computer when it is secured by looking in the following Windows registry (the registry is a hierarchical database that stores configuration from settings from Windows) key on the machine: \HKEY_LOCAL_MACHINE\SYSTEM\ControlSet001\Services\Tcpip6\Parameters \Dhcpv6DUID.

Table 3.5 Types of DUIDs Found Within the IPv6 DHCP System

Type		Description
DUID-LLT	Link-layer address plus time	The link-layer address of one of the device's network interfaces, concatenated with a timestamp
DUID-EN	Vendor based on enterprise number	An enterprise number plus additional information specific to the enterprise
DUID-LL	Link-layer address	The link-layer address of one of the device's network Interfaces
DUID-UUIDs		Derived from standardized Universally Unique IDentifier (UUID) format

FIGURE 3.12

Windows IP configuration showing DUID and MAC address.

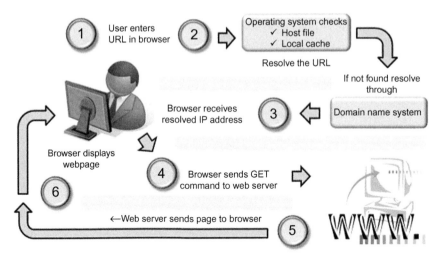

FIGURE 3.13

How a web browser actually gets a webpage to display.

The World Wide Web

The WWW or "web" is the basis for what most people think is the Internet. However, the WWW is just one of the services on the Internet. It started after the concept of Sir Tim Bernes-Lee's concept of a "hypertexting" in a browser was adopted as the preferred method of moving through the WWW. The web is a collection of publicly accessible documents (text, images, audio, video, etc.). Users view the pages via a browser (Internet Explorer, Chrome, Firefox, Opera, etc.) running on the local machine. The webpages often contain hypertext links referring to webpages or other documents. Clicking a mouse's pointer on these links calls up the referenced document or webpages. See Figure 3.13.

Uniform resource locators

The URL has become the most recognizable part of the web. An example of a fully qualified domain name is www.veresoftware.com. A domain name is commonly used now to identify companies, market to individuals, and find your favourite site on the web. A URL starts with "http://," which identifies the protocol to be used on the Internet and stands for hypertext transfer protocol. After the protocol usually comes the designator WWW, which we all know now stands for World Wide Web. Adding the WWW can be optional today because most browsers today will add the WWW. Additionally you may encounter WWW2 or WWW3 prior to a web address. These addresses and other prefixes

Table 3.6 List of Current TLDs	
AERO	JOBS
AR	MIL
ARPA	MOBI
ASIA	MUSEUM
BIZ	NAME
CAT	NET
COM	ORG
COOP	POST
EDU	TEL
GOV	TRAVEL
INFO	XXX

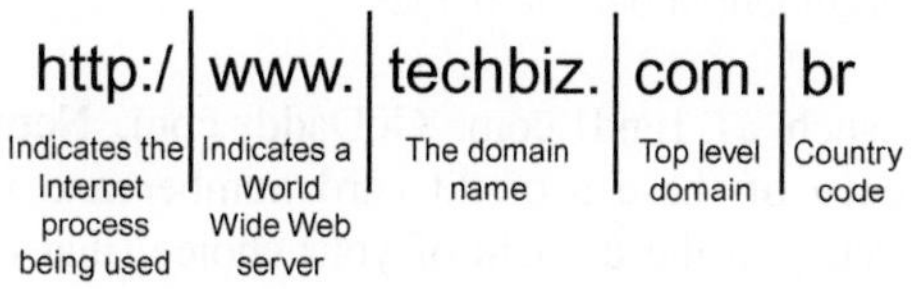

http:/	www.	techbiz.	com.	br
Indicates the Internet process being used	Indicates a World Wide Web server	The domain name	Top level domain	Country code

FIGURE 3.14

Description of the parts of a URL.

can be used by an organization to identify other web content or websites, but don't refer to any standards or Internet protocols. After identifying the protocol to be used, the domain name is the next significant part of the URL. The domain name is the registered name that identifies the location the browser will request information from on the Internet. A domain is formatted like veresoftware. At the end of the domain is the top level domain (TLD). TLDs are what the user commonly identifies as the end of the domain registration. The TLD identifies the highest level of the hierarchical structure of the URL. TLDs historically included the commonly recognized.com, .org, .mil, .edu. Over the past several years, mainly due to the increasingly diminishing English language domain availability, new TLDs have been added to the list (Table 3.6).

Country codes will appear after the TLD as a designator of the country to which the domain is registered. Country codes are by standard a two letter code at the end of the URL. Figure 3.14 provides an example of a properly formatted URL.

Domain name registration

So, how does one get a domain registered in the name of their choice? Today it is fairly simple to do. One of hundreds of domain registrars are available on the Internet. A simple search of the term "domain registrar" on Google will bring up

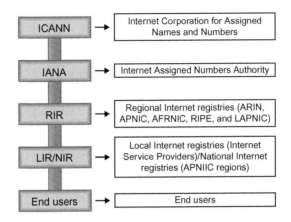

FIGURE 3.15

ICANN structure for assignment of domain names.

hundreds of results, such as 1and1.com, GoDaddy.com, Network solutions, and many others. With each of these a credit card number and the basic name and address information gets you the domain of your choice (that is if the domain you select is available). The registration of a domain name is for specified period of time from generally 1 year or more. The domain registrar submits the names to the Internet Corporation for Assigned Names and Numbers (ICANN) who is responsible for the actual assignment of Internet addresses. The investigator should be aware that any or all of this information can be falsified by the person registering a domain.

ICANN is a nonprofit organization formed under the direction of the US Department of Commerce in 1998 (ICANN 1998) to administer the domain name registration process and the DNS. ICANN has since entered into agreements with other authorities designed to assist in domain registrations for various areas around the world. The following are the five regional Internet registry (RIR) service regions:

- **RIPE**, the Europeans IP Networks
- **AFRINIC**, the African Internet Numbers Registry
- **APNIC**, the Asia Pacific Network Information Center
- **ARIN**, the American Registry for Internet Numbers
- **LACNIC**, the Latin American and Caribbean Internet Addresses Registry.

In 2000, ICANN entered into another agreement with the US Government to operate the Internet Assigned Numbers Authority (IANA). At the time, the University of Southern California had been operating the functions of the IANA through a contract with the DARPA (Figure 3.15).

Internationalized domain names

Until 2009, the characters used to register domain names were only the English language or the Latin alphabets. These conformed with the American Standard

Code for Information Interchange (ASCII). After 2009, ICAN allowed the introduction of domain names in different languages. From an investigative viewpoint, this becomes an increasingly more difficult process to identify users of international domain names (IDN) if the investigator cannot read the domain name.

Autonomous system number

Autonomous system number (ASN) is a public globally unique number used to exchange routing information between networks with assigned ASNs. These numbers are assigned to an ISP whose networks are connected to the Internet.

Other services on the Internet

As noted the Internet is not just the WWW. There are many other potential areas for an investigator to be concerned about when it comes to investigating crimes on the Internet. Located on the Internet are a variety of services not accessed through the use of an Internet browser. Each protocol listed has its RFC describing its use and they all predated the WWW. From an investigative point of view, which will be discussed later in the following chapters, each has very different approaches and problems for the investigator. Our discussion here is an introduction to several of the more commonly identified Internet protocols. These protocols can be used in an investigation as a source for identifying criminal use or as intelligence on criminal behavior.

File transfer protocol

FTP as a protocol predates the public release of the Internet by decades. FTP stands for file transfer protocol. Prior to the hyperlinks present in our current WWW, FTP was the predominate method of transferring files from a place where it was stored on a server to a user's computer. In fact FTP was designed prior to the current design of the IP addresses as we know it. File transfer is still in use as a method of transferring large files. The concept of FTP file transferring is in use in various Cloud services used throughout the Internet. The FTP protocol lets a client connect directly with an FTP server using port 20.[4] The transfer of files through this connection is directly through the IP address and/or domain (Figure 3.16).

Email or the SMTP

SMTP is the protocol for transferring electronic mail. RFC 5321 describes the protocol for the use of sending mail between mail servers also referred to as

[4]An Internet port is "...a number that indicates what kind of protocol a server on the Internet is using. For example, web servers typically are listed on port 80. Web browsers use this port by default when accessing webpages, but you can also specify what port you would like to use in the URL like this: http://www.excite.com:80. FTP uses port 21, email uses port 25, and game servers, like a Quake server or Blizzard.net, use various other ports. It is good to know what a port is, but you seldom have to specify it manually." Source: TechTerms.com. Retrieved from http://www.techterms.com/definition/port.

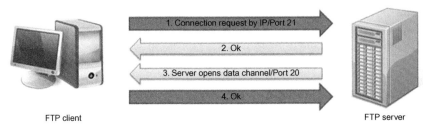

FIGURE 3.16

FTP communications between client and server.

mail transfer agents. SMTP has a dedicated well-known port number 25. It is not the protocol for collecting mail by a user. There are two typical protocols users employ to download their email. They are Post Office Protocol (POP) and Internet Message Access Protocol (IMAP). Both allow the users to collect their email from a mail server and view it locally, but do it from a slightly different manner (Table 3.7).

COMMAND LINE USE OF SMTP PROTOCOL

SMTP is such a simple protocol. Using Telnet[5] to connect to port 25 on a remote host you can type an email from the command line using the SMTP commands. This technique is usually blocked today due to hacking/phishing misuse but in the past it use to be a common way to illustrate the use of SMTP commands. The example below shows an email sent by command line from Samuel on yourmail.123.com to Lindsey on mymail.xyz.com.

```
% telnet mymail.xyz.com.25
Trying 162.21.50.4...
Connected to mymail.xyz.com
Escape character is '^]'
220 mymail Sendmail 4.1/1.41 ready at Tue, 29 Dec 2012 19:23:01 PST
helo yourmail.123.com
250 mymail Hello yourmail.123.com, pleased to meet you
mail from:< samuel@ yourmail.123.com>
250 <samuel@ yourmail.123.com>... Sender ok
rcpt to: <Lindsey@mymail.xyz.com>
250 <Lindsey@mymail.xyz.com>... Recipient ok
data
354 Enter mail, end with "." on a line by itself
Hello Lindsey, how are you?
.
250 Mail accepted
quit
221 mymail delivering mail
```

---

[5]Telnet is a program that allows a computer user to log into another computer via a text-based interface.

Table 3.7 Basic SMTP Commands

Command	Syntax	Function
Hello	HELO <sending-host>	Identify sending SMTP
From	MAIL FROM:<from-address>	Sender address
Recipient	RCPT TO:<to-address>	Recipient address
Data	DATA	Begin a message
Quit	QUIT	End the SMTP session

Post Office Protocol

POP allows a user's mail client to connect to an SMTP server that contains electronic mail items. It is the simplest of the mail protocols that uses only a few commands to connect to and accept emails from a mail server. The commands allow the users' email program to download email and delete email from the server. No other manipulation occurs between the email program and the email server.

Internet Message Access Protocol

IMAP also allows access to and the downloading of emails from a mail server. However, IMAP is more complex in that it allows the users email client to access the emails on another server as if it were locally stored. This allows the user's email client to manipulate emails stored on the server without transferring the messages between computers (Figure 3.17).

News groups, Usenet, or the Network News Transfer Protocol

Network News Transfer Protocol (NNTP) historical framework comes from Usenet, an early message transfer system. The Usenet system originally communicated over telephone connections between the servers and ultimately transformed into the Internet protocol known as NNTP. Usenet is a network of servers without a central server. Usenet has historically been a popular way to anonymously post and transfer files for exchange between users. Usenet messages look and act much like email in that there is a message format based originally on the email protocol. However, the message posting is globally to the system and viewable by everyone on the network instead of directed to a single user. Usenet messages are accessed using a "newsreader" that functions as a message reader and a tool to post messages to the system. The benefit of Usenet is the ability to read any message and post a message back to the public network. Any user connected to the Usenet system can read and post a response to the same message. The concept is like a large bulletin board where everyone can see and post a note in response to the message.

The Usenet network stores large amounts of data and this data may not remain for extended periods of time. The Usenet servers are designed to store data until it runs out of disk space. This retention process causes data to drop off the Usenet

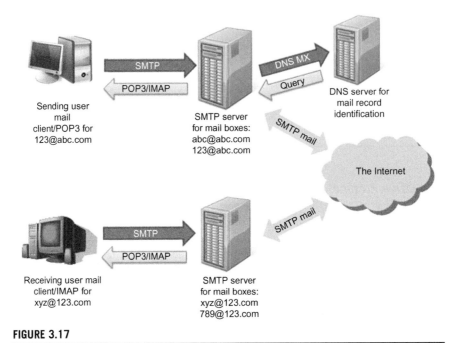

FIGURE 3.17

SMTP communications between clients.

system and be potentially unretrievable. Also, posting a file to a Usenet server may not be seen on other servers until the file is shared or "propagates" across the NNTP network. Usenet uses a hierarchy for its groups that users can download and post messages. The hierarchy is given in Table 3.8.

An example of a Usenet group is alt.sex.bondage, which discusses bondage and sadomasochism. Other private hierarchy listings can occur depending on the company or geographic location.

Chatting with IRC

Internet relay chat, or more commonly referred to as IRC, provides the user the ability to communicate through real-time text messaging. IRC is accessed through a client that gives the user access to the IRC hierarchy of servers and "channels." In these channels, the user can "chat" through written text messages with other users accessing the channel or directly with an individual member of the channel. Users can join existing channels for these communications or make their own.

Relevant RFCs

The following RFCs form the basis for the design and control of the Internet. Each RFC addresses a specific topic related to governance of the various features

Table 3.8 Usenet Hierarchy

Hierarchy	Description
comp.	Newsgroups discussing computer-related topics
humanities.	Groups discussing the humanities, such as literature and art
misc.	Miscellaneous topics that don't fit other hierarchies
news.	Groups discussing Usenet itself and its administration
rec.	Recreation topics, such as games, sports, and activities
sci.	Science newsgroups, covering specific areas
soc.	Society and social discussions
talk.	Groups discussing current events
alt.	Groups discussing any topic not defined above

of the Internet. This is not a complete list of RFCs governing the makeup of the various parts of the Internet. These can all be found at the website of the IETF at www.ietf.org.

RFC: 2131 DHCP, http://www.ietf.org/rfc/rfc2131.txt
RFC: 3315 DHCPv6, http://www.ietf.org/rfc/rfc3315.txt
RFC: 4292 IP Version 6 Addressing Architecture, http://tools.ietf.org/html/rfc4291
Guide to Mapping IPv4 to IPv6 Subnets, http://tools.ietf.org/html/draft-schild-v6ops-guide-v4mapping-00
DHCPv6, https://tools.ietf.org/html/rfc3315#page-19
Definition of the UUID-based DHCPv6 Unique Identifier (DUID-UUID), http://www.ietf.org/rfc/rfc6355.txt.pdf
RFC: 1036, Standard for interchange of USENET messages, http://tools.ietf.org/html/rfc1036
SMTP, http://tools.ietf.org/html/rfc5321
POP—Version 3, http://www.ietf.org/rfc/rfc1939.txt
RFC: 3501, IMAP—Version 4rev1, http://tools.ietf.org/html/rfc3501
RFC: 3977, NNTP, https://tools.ietf.org/html/rfc3977
RFC: 1459, IRC Protocol, http://www.ietf.org/rfc/rfc1459.txt
RFC: 2812, IRC: Client Protocol, http://tools.ietf.org/html/rfc2812
RFC: 2810, IRC: Architecture, http://tools.ietf.org/html/rfc2810

CONCLUSION

This chapter covered a description of numerous topics related to the construction of the Internet and its various parts. We discussed how IP addresses affect the process of communication between computers and how IP addresses can be used effectively to further an investigation of crimes on the Internet. We also described how various protocols have been established to describe and control the various functions of the Internet. These protocols include Internet functions for sending email, exchanging files, and using newsgroups.

Further reading

A recommendation for IPv6 address text representation. Retrieved from <http://tools.ietf. org/html/rfc5952/>.

Autonomous System (AS) numbers. (2012). Retrieved from <http://www.iana.org/assignments/ as-numbers/as-numbers.xml/>.

Contract between ICANN and the United States Government for performance of the IANA function. Retrieved from <http://www.icann.org/en/about/agreements/iana/iana-contract-09feb00-en.htm/>.

Country codes—ISO 3166. Retrieved from <http://www.iso.org/iso/country_codes.htm/>.

DHCPv6—an introduction to the new host configuration protocol. <http://ipv6friday.org/ blog/2011/12/dhcpv6/>.

DNS reference information. <http://technet.microsoft.com/en-us/library/dd197499(v=WS.10). aspx/>.

Exploring autonomous system numbers. Retrieved from <http://www.cisco.com/web/about/ ac123/ac147/archived_issues/ipj_9-1/autonomous_system_numbers.html/>.

Expressing IPv6 addresses. Retrieved from <http://technet.microsoft.com/en-us/library/ cc784831(v = ws.10).aspx/>; <https://www.ultratools.com/tools/ipv6Info/>.

File Transfer Protocol (FTP). <http://www.w3.org/Protocols/rfc959/2_Overview.html/>

Finding who is sending "bad" IPv6 traffic. Retrieved from <http://www.networkworld.com/ community/node/46069/>.

IEEE-SA—Registration Authority, Organizational Unique Identifier (OUI). (n.d.). *IEEE-SA—The IEEE Standards Association—Home.* Retrieved from <http://standards.ieee. org/develop/regauth/>.

Internationalized domain names. Retrieved from <http://www.icann.org/en/resources/idn/>; <http://www.afrinic.net/>; <http://www.apnic.net/>; <http://www.arin.net/>; <http:// www.lacnic.net/>; <http://www.ripe.net/>.

Internet Assigned Numbers Authority. Retrieved from <http://www.iana.org/domains/root/db/>.

Internet Protocol, DARPA Internet Program, Protocol Specification, September 1981. Retrieved from <http://tools.ietf.org/html/rfc791/>.

Internet Society. Retrieved from <http://www.internetsociety.org/what-we-do/internet-technology-matters/ipv6/>.

InterNIC FAQs on the domain names, registrars, and registration. (2003). Retrieved from <http://www.internic.net/faqs/domain-names.html/>.

Ipv6 Address Allocation and Assignment Policy. (2002). Retrieved from <https://www. arin.net/policy/archive/ipv6_policy.html/>.

IPv6 Address Types. <http://technet.microsoft.com/en-us/library/cc757359(v = ws.10).aspx/>.

IPv6.com. Retrieved from <http://www.ipv6.com/>.

IPv6 notation and masking basics. <http://www.tc.mtu.edu/ipv6/basics.php/>.

List of country codes. Retrieved from <http://www.ripe.net/internet-coordination/internet-governance/internet-technical-community/the-rir-system/list-of-country-codes-and-rirs/>.

Memorandum of understanding between The U.S. Department of Commerce and Internet Corporation for Assigned Names and Numbers. (1998). Retrieved from <http://www. icann.org/en/about/agreements/>.

Network News Transfer Protocol. <http://www.w3.org/Protocols/rfc977/rfc977/>

PC Magazine Encyclopedia of IT Definitions—DNS Records. <http://www.pcmag.com/ encyclopedia_term/0,1237,t = DNS + records&i = 55466,00.asp/>.

Protocol registries. Retrieved from <http://www.iana.org/protocols/>.

RFC 959—File Transfer Protocol. <http://www.faqs.org/rfcs/rfc959.html/>.

Security Tip (ST05-016) understanding internationalized domain names, Original release date: September 21, 2005. Last revised: August 6, 2008, <http://www.us-cert.gov/cas/ tips/ST05-016.html/>.

Testimony of Michael M. Roberts before U.S. Senate Committee on Commerce, Science, and Transportation, Subcommittee on Communications, February 14, 2001. Retrieved from <http://www.icann.org/en/news/correspondence/roberts-testimony-14feb01-en.htm/>.

Testimony of Michael M. Roberts President and Chief Executive Officer before the Senate Committee on Commerce, Science and Transportation Subcommittee on Communications. <http://www.icann.org/en/news/correspondence/roberts-testimony-14feb01-en.htm/>.

The Internet Engineering Task Force (IETF). Retrieved from <http://www.ietf.org/>.

The Internet Society. Retrieved from <http://www.isoc.org/internet/standards/>.

Too many options for IPv6 address configuration? Retrieved from <http://www.network world.com/community/node/55307/>.

Using NSlookup.exe. <http://support.microsoft.com/kb/200525/>.

What is a MAC address? <http://www.webopedia.com/quick_ref/what_is_a_mac_address.asp/>.

Windows command line—Nslookup. <http://www.windowscommandline.com/nslookup/>; <http://www.ietf.org/rfc/rfc1035.txt/>.

Collecting Legally Defensible Online Evidence

4

Facts are stubborn things; and whatever may be our wishes, our inclinations, or the dictates of our passions, they cannot alter the state of facts and evidence.
(John Adams, American President, 1735–1826)

Chapter 3 focused on how the Internet works and the basics of navigating its recesses for information. Investigating Internet crimes, however, requires more than just the ability or knowledge to know where to look for information. Information or more specifically evidence must not only be located but also be collected and preserved in a manner consistent with getting it admitted into the appropriate legal venue. To do otherwise negates all the investigative effort in locating it and may create a legal "house of cards," particularly if the discovered evidence was a particular case's foundation. In *Nardone v. United States* 308 U.S. 338, 341 (1939),[1] Justice Felix Frankfurter used the phrase "fruit of the poisonous tree" to describe the situation when a substantial portion of a case is built on evidence that was improperly obtained. US courts in such cases have held convictions cannot be sustained. Other countries have their own legal requirements for admitting information into evidence. As such we must be diligent that evidence found on the Internet is properly collected and preserved. This chapter will review the methods for insuring investigators do not gather Internet fruit from poisonous trees.

A few caveats are in order before we begin this review. We are not attorneys and do not play ones on television. We are not providing legal advice. We are simply providing information that will alert investigators to issues so they can plan accordingly. We strongly encourage investigators to obtain legal advice to insure collected data can be entered into evidence in whatever legal venue (administrative, civil, criminal, etc.) and jurisdiction is appropriate.

---

[1]Interestingly, this case dealt with evidence obtained through an illegal wiretap.

Defining evidence

There is a bit of confusion when we talk about the term "evidence." We believe it can take many forms, which appears to evolve with each passing technological advance. DNA evidence was unheard of until relatively recently. The terms digital or electronic evidence are also relatively new, and the terms Internet or online evidence are even more recent. But these terms reflect nothing but the form of information, not whether it can actually be admitted into evidence. Consider the following definition:

> *ESI (Electronically Stored Information). Any information created, stored, or utilized with digital technology. Examples include, but are not limited to, word-processing files, email and text messages (including attachments); voice-mail; information accessed via the Internet, including social networking sites; information stored on cell phones; information stored on computers, computer systems, thumb drives, flash drives, CDs, tapes, and other digital media.*
> **(Department of Justice (DOJ) and Administrative Office of the U.S. Courts (AO) Joint Working Group on Electronic Technology in the Criminal Justice System (JETWG), 2012, p. 12)**

In the above United States definition it does not use the term "evidence." Insa (2007) likewise noted in a European study[2] that "None of the studied countries stipulate in their legal codes a specific definition of what electronic evidence is. In all of them researchers have come across some references that are more or less specific for traditional evidence, encompassing some of those pertaining to electronic evidence" (p. 286). Hura (2011), however, references that China's new rules in criminal trials specifically address electronic evidence as follows:

> *Article 29: In examining electronic evidence, such as electronic mail, electronic data exchange, online chat transcripts, blogs, mobile telephone text messages, or electronic signatures or domain names, emphasis shall be placed on the following:*
>
> 1. *whether the electronic evidence stored on a storage medium such as a computer disk or CD has been submitted together with printed version;*
> 2. *whether the time, place, target, producer, production process, equipment for electronic evidence is clearly stated;*
> 3. *whether production, storage, transfer, access, collection, and presentation (of the electronic evidence) were carried out legally and whether individuals obtaining, producing, possessing, and witnessing the evidence affixed their signature or chop;*

---

[2]The specific countries involved in this study were Austria, Belgium, Denmark, Finland, France, Germany, Greece, Holland, Ireland, Italy, Luxembourg, Portugal, Romania, Spain, Sweden, and the United Kingdom.

4. *whether the content is authentic or whether it has undergone cutting, combination, tampering, or augmentation or other fabrication or alteration;*
5. *whether the electronic evidence is relevant to the facts of the case.*

If there are questions about electronic evidence, an expert evaluation should be conducted. The authenticity and relevance of electronic evidence should be examined in consideration of other case evidence (p. 760).

The commonality of these different jurisdictions is obtained information must meet a minimum rule before it can be admitted into a legal proceeding. Countries and their political subunits (states, provinces, etc.) have different rules or standards for admitting evidence. However, it does not end there. Even within a country different rules may apply to different venues, such as criminal proceedings versus civil proceedings. In the United States, for example, there are proceedings where the Federal Rules of Evidence (FRE) do not apply, such as extradition or rendition; issuing an arrest warrant, criminal summons, or search warrant; a preliminary examination in a criminal case; sentencing; granting or revoking probation or supervised release; considering whether to release on bail or otherwise; and where other statutes or rules may provide for admitting or excluding evidence independently from the rules (FRE Rule 1101, Applicability of the Rules). Harbeck and Yoonji (2010) also discuss the admittance of Internet-based information, such as Wikipedia entries, for use in immigration hearings, which are not governed by the FRE. Suffice to say, there can be exceptions, but for the vast majority of matters of importance, such as a civil and criminal proceedings, rules will act as gatekeepers, determining what gathered information can be presented or considered as evidence in a proceeding.

One of the initial barriers for admitting information into evidence is whether it is relevant or not to the issue at hand. If information has nothing to do with a particular issue, i.e., it isn't relevant, it can't be admitted as evidence. All countries with a common law foundation usually have this requirement. However, even countries which are not entirely common law based, such as China, require that information presented must be relevant (Hura, 2011).

The second barrier in determining whether information can be admitted into evidence often hinges on the issue of its authenticity. In the United States, this means is the evidence "what it purports to reflect" (FRE, 901). Canada has a similar definition, specifically, Section 31.1 notes "Any person seeking to admit an electronic document as evidence has the burden of proving its authenticity by evidence capable of supporting a finding that the electronic document is that which it is purported to be" (*Canada Evidence Act*, Section 31.1). Civil litigation in England and Wales allows the parties to admit a document's authenticity when it is disclosed to them, unless they serve notice that they want the issue proven at trial (Mason, 2006).

Authenticity concerns are frequently centered on whether the information has been forged or altered, either before it was collected or afterwards. This is one reason that the best evidence rule exists in many jurisdictions, which is simply that one should always present the original document whenever possible as a copy might be altered.[3] Other concerns about authenticity go right to the heart of Internet information. In 1999, one United States federal judge described Internet information in these condensing terms:

> *While some look to the Internet as an innovative vehicle for communication, the Court continues to warily and wearily view it largely as one large catalyst for rumor, innuendo, and misinformation. So as to not mince words, the Court reiterates that this so-called Web provides no way of verifying the authenticity of the alleged contentions that Plaintiff wishes to rely upon in his Response to Defendant's Motion. There is no way Plaintiff can overcome the presumption that the information he discovered on the Internet is inherently untrustworthy. Anyone can put anything on the Internet. No website is monitored for accuracy and nothing contained therein is under oath or even subject to independent verification absent underlying documentation. Moreover, the Court holds no illusions that hackers can adulterate the content on any website from any location at any time. For these reasons, any evidence procured off the Internet is adequate for almost nothing, even under the most liberal interpretation of the hearsay exception rules found in FED.R.CIV.P.807.*
>
> **(*Teddy St. Clair v. Johnny's Oyster & Shrimp, Inc.*, 6 F.Supp.2d 773, 1999)**

Subsequent court cases, such as in the landmark case of *Lorraine v. Markel Am. Ins. Com*, 241 F.R.D. 534, 538 (D. Md. 2007), have not taken such a dismal view of the admittance of Internet-based evidence (Democko, 2012). The issue of alteration at the time of collection and preservation can be addressed with good chain of custody procedures. The general issue of authenticity though requires other investigative actions. We will cover both in detail later.

Depending upon the jurisdiction and venue, information might not be entered as it is considered hearsay. Generally hearsay is information provided in a proceeding which is not presented by the person who saw, heard, or said it. In the United States, hearsay is "a statement, other than one made by the declarant while testifying at the trial or hearing, offered to prove the truth of the matter asserted" (FRE, Rule 801 (c)). In the United Kingdom, hearsay in criminal proceedings is "...a statement not made in oral evidence in the proceedings that is evidence of any matter stated" (Crown Prosecution Service, Criminal Justice Act 2003, Section 114 (1)). However, there are exceptions to when hearsay information can be presented. One of the notably ones is the business rule exception. Many jurisdictions allow business records, including computerized records, to be admitted

---

[3]Initially, the best evidence rule caused consternation for many in the early days of computer forensics as the original data was the binary information, the "0s and 1s" saved on magnetic media and not the computer printout readable by humans. Through rule changes and court decisions, computer printouts are acceptable, provided someone can establish that the source computer and its programs, which created them, is functioning properly.

into evidence if they were made in the usual and ordinary course of business. The reason being is they are most likely to be accurate and reliable for the sake of a business continuing to operate.

Some jurisdictions have legal proceedings, out of the jury's earshot, where both parties can object to evidence's admittance. If the information is admitted into evidence it can be an appeal issue, depending upon the type of proceeding. Others will allow the jury to decide the merits of each piece of evidence. For our purposes, online or Internet evidence is ESI, collected from the Internet, which has been properly collected, preserved, and for which a foundation has been laid for its admittance and/or consideration into a legal forum. Conversely, digital or electronic evidence is ESI, collected from computers[4] or electronic media, which has also met all the legal requirements for admittance and/or consideration into a legal forum.

Digital versus online evidence

Why differentiate between these two forms of ESI? They are after all "information created, stored, or utilized with digital technology." They both can be easily modified or deleted. They can both contain "metadata."[5] Additionally, they both can be quite voluminous. We differentiate the two because of the dissimilar manner in which they are collected as well how each are susceptible to modification in a different manner.

Until very recently the prevalent manner digital evidence was collected and processed was from a "dead" machine. A hard drive was imaged and all examination was done on a bit-by-bit copy of the original media. Live acquisitions of electronic data were undertaken but usually only under special circumstances. The general rule of thumb was one never examines original media.[6] Additionally,

---

[4]We use the term computer as defined by 18 USC § 1030 (e), which means ". . .an electronic, magnetic, optical, electrochemical, or other high speed data processing device performing logical, arithmetic, or storage functions, and includes any data storage facility or communications facility directly related to or operating in conjunction with such device, but such term does not include an automated typewriter or typesetter, a portable hand held calculator, or other similar device." This definition is similar to that found in many statutes within the United States and abroad.

[5]Metadata describes other data, which is contained inside a file or webpage. For instance, an image file may contain metadata that describes how large the image is, its color depth, resolution, and when it was created. It may even contain the make and model of camera that took the image as well the global positioning coordinates of where the picture was taken. Text documents may also contain information about how long the document is, who the author is, when it was written, and a short summary of the document. Webpages likewise will often include metadata in the form of meta tags. Most search engines will use this information to add pages to their search index. See Metadata Definition. (n.d.). The Tech Terms Computer Dictionary. Retrieved from http://www.techterms.com/definition/metada.

[6]This has changed somewhat with more live examinations and acquisitions taking place due to the realization that huge amounts of data might be lost if a computer is just shutdown. Additionally, the real possibility of encryption occurring upon shutdown makes imaging a "dead" computer less attractive as the first option to collect digital ESI (Shipley & Reeve, 2006).

the person collecting digital evidence also have direct access to the media containing the information, be it a computer or server. Even with the advent of remote acquisitions of data over a network, including the Internet, the examiner has some control of the target system.

Contrast such procedures with collecting online evidence. The ESI collected from the Internet is always a live acquisition. The investigator has no ability to control the original media that contains the online data. The server might not even be in the same jurisdiction, let alone the same state, province, or country, as the investigator.

Both digital evidence and online evidence are easily susceptible to modification. However, digital evidence on a hard drive or electronic media can be seized and maintained. It can be imaged and secured, allowing the investigators to use only the duplicate image for examinations. The system that contains the data can be secured. Even in a civil setting, once pertinent ESI is identified on a computer or network, it is secured until it can be provided to opposing parties with potential penalties for spoliation.

Again, contrast this to online data collection, which is merely a snapshot of what the ESI was on a particular date and time, on a website, social networking site, etc. The ESI may also only exist temporarily, such as in the case of instant messaging or chats session, and could be gone unless it is captured in some manner. Even a forensic examination might not retrieve the entire chat or instant message communication. A website might change minutes after it was first captured. The same can occur with a social networking profile. In fact, frequently the very offender who is suspected of wrongdoing has control to modify or delete the ESI completely. Depending upon the circumstances, an offender in custody could even alter a website using a mobile phone or direct a confederate to do so at their behest. In either case the offender changes ESI on the original media that is not under the control and custody of the investigator.[7]

Consider for the moment this example. A murder has occurred in a car. Police seize the car and preserve it. It is locked in storage, under police guard. The same thing occurs when police seize a computer. They lock it up and preserve it under police custody. Contrast this scenario to a murder that takes place in a park. Police do their best to capture the murder scene, taking pictures and searching for evidence, but they can't seize the park. Depending upon the circumstances, they may post a guard until they are satisfied they have collected everything, but in the end the park is not seized. They can't maintain the scene exactly as it was at the time of the murder. This is the same with online ESI. It is captured at a particular date and time, which is preserved and secured. But the original data is subject to change, just like the park which is a murder scene. Depending upon how well the investigator documented the capture of the online ESI will determine if it can be authenticated and admitted into evidence.

---

[7]In the United States, the Stored Communications Act, 18 U.S.C. 2703 (f) provides a mechanism to request ISPs preserve records pending legal action, which we will address later.

Building a foundation

Thus far we have generally discussed the legal issues of relevancy, hearsay, and authentication. Let's now focus on putting them into a useful context for the investigator tasked with gathering ESI. The first two issues are something that investigators have little control over. For instance, they can't make ESI relevant if it has nothing to do with an issue. With few exceptions, investigators have little impact on whether ESI is ruled as hearsay or not. Additionally, they can't control whether ESI ruled as hearsay can be admitted under a jurisdiction's numerous exceptions to the rules. The last issue, authentication, is impacted to a much greater extent by the investigator's actions. However, in the end authentication, like relevancy and hearsay are all argued by attorneys and decided by judges and/or juries. The investigator's task is to conduct their activities in a manner that maximizes the potential for the collected ESI to be admitted into evidence. In other words, their collection efforts must focus on gathering the "best" ESI and provide their legal authority with a good basis to argue that it should be admitted into evidence. Towards that goal, lets first turn to investigative planning, which can assist greatly in addressing all three issues. We then will follow up with some specifics in regard to authentication.

Investigative planning

Few individuals would attempt to build a house without some idea or blueprint for its construction. To do so is foolhardy as important steps may be needlessly repeated or missed, resulting in delays or worse the structure's collapse. High-tech investigations involving the collection of online ESI are no different. One must have some idea what they are investigating, be it an administrative, civil, or criminal manner and how they are going to proceed. "Documented plans focus an investigation from the start while providing a blueprint for investigators to follow" (Bowker, 1999, p. 25). A properly crafted plan will greatly aid in making sure that collected ESI can be admitted into evidence. Bowker (1999) further elaborates an investigative plan functions to:

- focus the investigative process to ensure that all litigation elements are addressed;
- limit unnecessary procedures and step duplication;
- coordinate the activities of numerous personnel on large cases;
- provide stability to the investigation if staff changes occur
- enhance communication with legal authorities by providing an outline of the investigation and identifying strengths and weaknesses in the case;
- provide a framework for the final report;
- become a training aid for inexperienced staff members.

What about online investigations in which there is no criminal violation, referred to in the United Kingdom as "open-source investigations"? (Association of Chief Police Officers in the United Kingdom, 2007). Is a plan still warranted for law enforcement conducting open-source investigations? We believe it is. *The Good Practice Guide for Computer-Based Electronic Evidence* (2007), from the Association of Chief Police Officers in the United Kingdom (ACPO Guide) notes:

> *There is a public expectation that the Internet will be subject to routine 'patrol' by law enforcement agencies. As a result, many bodies actively engage in proactive attempts to monitor the Internet and to detect illegal activities. In some cases, this monitoring may evolve into 'surveillance,' as defined under RIPA 2000. In such circumstances, investigators should seek an authority for directed surveillance, otherwise any evidence gathered may be subsequently ruled inadmissible... (p. 13).*

US law enforcement should have similar concerns, particularly as such efforts may have a chilling effect on the citizenry's First Amendment rights.[8] Benoit (2012) observed that Maryland Homeland Security and Intelligence Division (HSID) of the Maryland State Police (MSP) conducted an 18-month covert surveillance of anti-death penalty and anti-war activists in which emails were exchanged between an undercover trooper and activists, and the trooper attended various meetings. No criminal activity was detected but the investigation became public. Benoit (2012) quotes the official report as reflecting "...the surveillance undertaken here is inconsistent with an overarching value in our democratic society - the free and unfettered debate of important public questions. Such police conduct ought to be prohibited as a matter of public policy." Benoit (2012) observes that FBI guidelines address these sensitivities and have two levels of investigative activity; one called an assessment and the second a predicated investigation. Both levels require an authorized purpose. He further notes:

> *Although the Guidelines do not govern state, local, or tribal law enforcement agencies, they can be instructive. Police agencies that seek to collect information about individuals or groups who engage in protected First Amendment activities can ensure that their conduct is unrelated to the content of the ideas or expressions of the individuals or groups by documenting the purpose for their information gathering or investigative activity. By taking this action, departments can help ensure that their investigative activity is not only consistent with its law enforcement mission but also that the activities in furtherance of their objectives remain related to and in the scope of the authorized purpose. For example, a state or local agency charged with protecting a community may seek to obtain information about an upcoming protest to plan for traffic disruptions, properly allocate its resources, or protect against the commission of crimes. However, the agency should not engage in the investigative*

---

[8]In the United States the Bill of Rights, First Amendment, reflects: "Congress shall make no law respecting the establishment of religion, or prohibiting the free exercise thereof; or of abridging the freedom of speech, or of the press; or of the right of the people peaceably to assemble, and petition the government for a redress of grievances."

activity if the purpose is to discourage the protestors from lawfully exercising their rights.

Investigative components

Bowker (1999) notes that investigative plans have four components: a predication, elements to prove, preliminary steps, and investigative steps. A predication is a brief statement justifying why the investigation is being commenced. As noted above, it is very important that the particular justification be spelled out. Generally, a predication has three features: the basic allegation, the allegation's source, and date the allegation was made. Predications for open-source investigations, where there is no specific allegation, should reflect a purpose, such as community protection during a specific event, and should also include a fixed duration for the investigative activity. If a specific wrongdoing allegation is uncovered the plan can be amended to focus on the statutory elements to establish a violation. A well-written predication provides the documentation foothold for the investigative steps that follow. The next critical component is a delineation of the elements needed to establish a violation occurred. Bowker (1999) notes:

> *This component must clearly reflect what is needed to establish a criminal violation, thus focusing the investigation and providing a framework for the steps that follow. At a minimum, this component should contain all of the statutory elements and any special jurisdictional issues, such as venue and statutes of limitations (p. 23).*

The next component is a listing of the preliminary steps an investigator will employ to obtain basic background information on the victim or complainant and the suspect(s) if known. A basic Internet search, such as "Googling" for public information, is one such step. Others include online searches of public records, such as Whois and Internet registries or incorporation papers and financial reports filed with government agencies. Other steps may include reviewing agency records on prior allegations or investigations; conducting an in-depth complainant interview; and/or conducting a criminal background check of pertinent parties. Typically, preliminary step completion does not require a great expenditure of time or resources. The next part of the plan is the more specific or focused investigative steps needed to resolve and complete the investigation. They lay out the general parameters needed to establish that an infraction has occurred and each step should parallel the statutory elements of a violation. Investigative steps include:

- victims and/or witnesses to be interviewed;
- identifying and securing any legal process/authority needed for evidence collection;
- identifying ESI (digital and online) and any other evidential items (documents, weapons, contraband, etc.) to be collected and from where;
- actual collection and analysis of ESI and other items;
- suspects to be interviewed.

Following a plan will provide an outline for any final report needed to document the investigation. Plans can be tailored for civil, criminal, or administrative violations. Boilerplate plans can be created for investigations which are frequently conducted with appropriate modifications tailored to meet a current allegation. Investigators should also realize that plans can be modified as warranted based upon new uncovered information or new investigative steps needed. For instance, if one is investigating a cyberstalking case and uncovers information pointing to child pornography, the plan, and subsequent legal authority, can be modified to incorporate the elements and steps needed to establish that new allegation (civilian investigators should STOP and call law enforcement when child pornography is discovered).

Authentication

We noted previously that authentication involves proving an item is what it purports to be. It sounds simple until one considers that online ESI, such as from social media, can be easily altered, quite often easier than other digital ESI. The Internet by its very nature allows users to modify or delete data on the fly, even via mobile devices. However, online ESI can be authenticated provided proper attention is given to its collection. Chief US Magistrate Judge Paul W. Grimm noted in *Lorraine v. Markel Am. Ins. Com*, 241 F.R.D. 534, 538 (D. Md. 2007) "...the inability to get evidence admitted because of a failure to authenticate it almost always is a self-inflicted injury which can be avoided by thoughtful advance preparation" (p. 17). Investigative planning provides some of that advance preparation. This section will provide some further guidance for authenticating online ESI. However, it is by no means an exhaustive list. As Judge Grimm also observed in the above case "...courts have been willing to think 'outside of the box' to recognize new ways of authentication" (p. 36). As such we will only be providing a general outline of the "box," encouraging investigators to use their imagination and resourcefulness to provide new dimension to the authentication issue. Before commencing it is important to understand there are two basic issues with authenticating online ESI. Merritt (2012) described these two issues in describing social media evidence, which is really applicable to all online ESI. She writes:

> *Both components of social media evidence must be authenticated. The proponent must introduce evidence 'sufficient to support a finding': (1) that the original communication is what the proponent claims and (2) that the tangible download accurately reflects the original message. A plaintiff offering evidence of a defendant's blog post, for example, must offer proof 'sufficient to support a finding' that the defendant was the person who posted the information and that a screenshot of the blog accurately reflects the post. Sometimes the same evidence will accomplish both ends, but a litigant must focus on meeting both goals (p. 52).*

Let's deal with the first issue raised by Merritt that the communication is what it purports to be, namely the communication or post was created by a particular person or on the behalf of an identity. This authenticating issue can be covered under the following five broad categories: (1) content/appearance; (2) content ownership; (3) witnesses; (4) digital ESI; and (5) confession or admission.

Content or appearance relates directly to the text or other information, such as an image, contained in a communication. Is there something in the communication that reflects the author or something consistent with what the author would compose? Examples include but are not limited to the content containing:

1. a work or personal email address;
2. use of real name, known nickname, and/or screen name;
3. telephone number, address, image, or other identifying information; text contains information consistent with known communication from the author;
4. patterns or phrases regularly used by the suspected author;
5. the presence of identifying web addresses, including dates;
6. the ESI content metadata reflects potentially identifying information.

The ESI content ownership involves tracing the post or content to the location from which it was posted. In the case of a website, this would be the registered owner of the site. Identifying a post from a social networking profile could include who owns the profile and what does their profile reflect that can be associated with the owner. Additionally, an online post might contain global positioning information or that the post was made from a mobile device. The duration that the information has existed on a site may also be a method to show ownership. If the message was not at least approved by the site, why was it allowed to be maintained on the site for an extended period of time? While much of this information may be collected online, there is much in the way of identifying background information that may require legal process served on a particular Internet service provider (ISP). Information provided by the ISP may point to the actual location from which a post was made and its owner.

Finally, do not forget that it may be necessary to also secure information from the victim's or a witness's ISP as well to show content ownership. For instance, a victim receives a threatening message through their social networking account from a John Smith profile, from which there are literally thousands of profiles with the same name. They printout the post and provide a hard copy. To determine which of the John Smith profiles sent the message it might be necessary to obtain records from the victim's ISP to trace the message back to its source. Additionally, if there is some concern that a potential victim fabricated the message, the obtained ISP records may provide information to refute or verify their statement.

Obtaining a witness statement seems pretty self-evident. However, the witness must be able to articulate facts that authenticate the communication. For instance, did they see the person post the message or did they receive information from the person confirming that they posted the communication? And do they still have it?

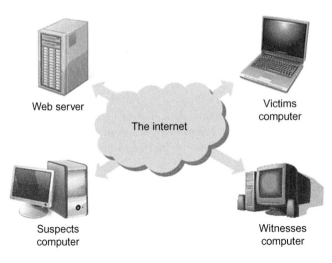

FIGURE 4.1

Possible evidence locations.

Were they a party to the communication and captured it, such as in the case of an instant message or may be they used software to record the communication live.[9] Additionally, in reviewing a communication a witness may be able to confirm that information it contains was only known by a particular person, i.e., the author. They may also be able to provide details that point to the suspect as being the message's originator. For instance, they report that they left the suspect alone at his computer on a particular date and time and information from the ISP places the message coming from his computer during the same time frame.

Digital ESI, if it can be obtained, can't be discontinued in its importance in further authenticating online ESL. If the information, in whole or part, can be traced to a computer controlled by a specific suspect this could be significant in authenticating the communication and its author. Digital ESI may also provide other information, such as a suspect's repeated access to a site or profile. This can point to circumstantial evidence that the suspect knew information was posted and took no action to remove it. Additionally, don't forget that digital ESI may also be obtained from the victim's computer or even a witness who opened the site in a browser (Figure 4.1).

It would seem obvious that a suspect's confession would be an exceptional piece of information to authenticate ESI. However, do not be content with just a general statement that they "did it." Go for details, such as is this your account, did you post this message, when, why, and from where (including which device). Even if a full confession can't be obtained, an admission of any relevant information that could tend to authenticate the ESI may be very important. For instance,

---

[9]Monitoring software used in the United States will be addressed later in this chapter.

a suspect who acknowledges that a particular profile is theirs, that they never gave account access to anyone, nor have they ever suspected their account was hacked, will have a hard later attributing a threatening post to a friend with access or a hacker.

Finally, it is important to understand that one should try to maximize the number of authentication categories addressed during an investigation. In *Griffin v. State*, 419 Md. 343, 347-48 (Md. 2011), a conviction was reversed on appeal due to authentication issues. In this case, printouts from a MySpace profile that contained threatening statements, purportedly made by the suspect's girlfriend towards a state's witness, were originally authenticated based solely on the lead investigator's testimony about the profile. The investigator noted the profile contained her picture, her birth date, her nickname, and other details. Rashbaum et al. (2012) noted that appellate court found this was insufficient due to concerns about possible fraud. They further observed the appellate court concluded other steps, such as interviewing the girlfriend, obtaining information from the respective ISP, and collecting digital ESI from the pertinent devices, would have provided proper authentication. The point here is do not stop with only one category of authentication if at all possible. Additional authentication could have included records directly from MySpace potentially including the Internet Protocol (IP) address of the users logging into MySpace.

Merritt's second authentication issue is that the tangible download accurately reflects the original message. This is the actual mechanics of collecting and maintaining online ESI and goes to the heart of chain of custody issues. One must be able to report how they collected the online ESI, including the date, time, and from where it was collected (website, blog, social networking site, file sharing interface, etc.). This is very important. Seng (2009) describes a Canadian copyright infringement case where an application for obtaining numerous ISP addressees was denied. In this case the applicant, rather than the actual investigator who developed the automated process for capturing the screenshots and ISP address, provided the data for the affidavit. The applicant simply did not have the firsthand knowledge to support the affidavit seeking the ISP order. Equally important is investigators must be able to establish that the data they collected was not changed. If a hard copy printout was made the person who printed it must be able to testify the hard copy being presented was the result of their efforts.[10] However, what about electronic copies, which are now really digital ESI? How can they be authenticated? A hash value must be calculated either during the actual collection of the data or as soon as possible after the data is saved electronically. This hash value will serve as a verification that the data has not been tampered with since its collection. The collector can then authenticate the collection, given their proper documentation of the collection, and its documented chain of custody.

---

[10]As will be discussed later hard copy printouts are really a last resort for collecting many types of online ESI, such as websites. They simply do not capture possible metadata nor do they capture embedded hyperlinks.

It is clear that investigators should have knowledge of proper procedures for collecting online ESI and be able to articulate what they did to collect the data. However, this knowledge should not be equated with a requirement that all investigators become "experts," such as delineated in FRE Rule 702.[11] Generally, investigators merely need to be able to testify to what they observed and did to collect the ESI and that the ESI they are presenting is what they originally collected.[12]

Privacy

Online ESI is publicly visible, so are there any privacy concerns or issues for the investigator? Unfortunately, this is not an easy question to answer. There are times when more than what is observed publicly needs to be obtained, such as the ISP information pertaining to an anonymous cyberstalker. Some statutes, such as the *Electronic Communications Privacy Act of 1986 (ECPA)*, limit what information law enforcement can obtain from IPS, setting various legal requirements to obtain basic subscriber information (name, location, etc.) and content (emails, social networking posts, blog posts, etc.). However, some jurisdictions have requirements for data that is collected, whether it be from public or private sources. For instance, the European Union (EU) operates under the *Protection Directive* (Directive 95/46/EC), which requires the protection of individual's personal data, including that from social media and provides standards for processing that data. Additionally, the *Fair Credit Reporting Act* (FCRA), another United States statute, places restrictions on the use of some consumer information, which can include data retrieved from social media.

We will briefly cover these statutes to expose investigators to these issues which can impact their activities no matter their location. For instance, *ECPA* covers some of the world's largest ISP and social networking sites, which are located in the United States. Additionally, many of these statutes provide civil and/or criminal penalties for their violation which heightens the need for awareness beyond just getting online ESI admitted into evidence.

---

[11]FRE 702 defines testimony of an expert witness as: "If scientific, technical, or other specialized knowledge will assist the trier of fact to understand the evidence or to determine a fact in issue, a witness qualified as an expert by knowledge, skill, experience, training, or education, may testify thereto in the form of an opinion or otherwise, if (1) the testimony is based upon sufficient facts or data, (2) the testimony is the product of reliable principles and methods, and (3) the witness has applied the principles and methods reliably to the facts of the case."

[12]Rashbaum et al. (2012) observe that the limitations of collecting archived website content may require an expert witness. Specifically, they observed "As a practical consideration, counsel should also be aware of the technological limitations of collecting archived website content, including the fact that an archived page may not include all the content as it originally appeared since content may have since been deleted, may require communication with another host for certain content, or may contain broken or redirected links. When dealing with evidence collected from the Internet Archive, counsel would be wise to consider a forensic or other expert that can provide testimony regarding these issues."

This is by no means a complete digest of privacy laws. Each jurisdiction may have its own rules. For instance, the EU's current *Protection Directive* is not followed by all European nations, with some having more stringent requirements (European Commission, 2012). The situation is no different in the United States with constitutions in 10 states (Alaska, Arizona, California, Florida, Hawaii, Illinois, Louisiana, Montana, South Carolina, and Washington) having provisions that expressly recognize a right to privacy (National Conference of State Legislatures (NCSL), 2010). NCSL also notes that six states, California, Delaware, Illinois, Maryland, Michigan, and New Jersey, passed laws prohibiting employers from requesting or requiring an employee or applicant to disclose a username or password for a personal social media account. NCSL reports California and Delaware prohibit higher education institutions from requiring students to disclose social media passwords or account information. At the end of 2012, 14 states had introduced legislation which would restrict employers from requesting access to social networking usernames and passwords of applicants, students, or employees (NCSL, 2012).

To further complicate the issue, at time of this text being written, several of these laws are under review or revision. The EU submitted on January 25, 2012, a draft revision to its data protection rules, which will not be fully implemented for 2 years (Office for Official Publications of the European Communities, 2012). Likewise, Congress is considering changes to *ECPA* (Savage, 2012). In short, this is only a starting point for the investigator, who is strongly encouraged to review his jurisdiction's laws and consult with the appropriate legal authority on these issues.

Electronic Communications Privacy Act

ECPA is actually referring to two laws, the Electronic Communications Privacy Act and the Stored Wire Electronic Communications Act. ECPA "...protects wire, oral, and electronic communications while those communications are being made, are in transit, and when they are stored on computers." There are three provisions of ECPA, which are commonly referred to as: Title I (Wiretap Act)[13]; Title II Stored Communications Act (SCA); and Title III (The Pen/Trap Statute). The below is a brief ECPA synopsis and the reader is encouraged to review the statute as well as *The ECPA, ISPs & Obtaining Email: A Primer for Local Prosecutors* (American Prosecutors Research Institute) and *Searching and Seizing Computers and Obtaining Electronic Evidence in Criminal Investigations* (U.S. DOJ).

Wiretap Act (18 U.S.C. § 2510-22)

This provision prohibits the interception of "real-time" communication (wire, oral, or electronic) by someone not a party to the communication. There are exceptions to the prohibition, such as providers engaging in actions to render their

---

[13]Wiretap procedures were initially covered under Title III of the *Omnibus Crime Control and Safe Streets Act of 1968* and as a result authorization warrants were generally known as "Title III." Title III wiretaps should not, however, be confused with Title III of ECPA.

service, court authorization, and consent. Many states also have their own version of this federal statute.

Court authorization requires a finding of probable cause and such authorization can only be granted for specific enumerated felony offenses (18 U.S.C. § 2516). Additionally, such authorization is limited to a particularly time frame, 30 days, after which the monitoring must stop or a new authorization obtained.

As noted above, one of the exceptions to interception is consent. However, there are two kinds of consent. The first is one-party consent, which is contained in the federal law and 38 state statutes. The other type is called two-party consent. This means that both parties to the communication have to consent to the monitoring for it to qualify for this exception. There are 12 states (CA, CN, FL, IL, MD, MA, MI, MO, NV, NH, PA, and WA) that require two-party consent (Reporters Committee for Free Press).

Generally, this will not impact an online investigation, unless there is a recording of real-time communication, such as might occur during undercover investigations involving instant message or chatroom interactions. In *O'Brien v. O'Brien*, Case No. 5D03-3484 (2005) a Florida appellate court ruled that computer monitoring was governed by the state's wiretap statute, which was patterned after the federal law (18 U.S.C. § 2501). In this case, software captured chats, instant messages, and web browsing by an individual without his knowledge. The trial judge in a divorce proceeding ruled the captured ESI was inadmissible as it violated state law. In short, monitoring software use, depending upon the jurisdiction and how it is used, may violate wiretap statutes.

Stored Communications Act (18 U.S.C. §§ 2701-12)

The SCA protects the privacy of a subscriber's file contents, which are stored by service providers (ISP) and subscriber records, such as their name, billing information, or IP address, maintained by the ISP (18 U.S.C. §§ 2701-12). SCA places restrictions on the release of this information and provides civil and criminal penalties for improper access to protected information. Like the Wiretap Act mentioned previously there are exceptions to these restrictions. However, these exceptions can be rather complicated, hinging on a variety of circumstances, such as whether the service provider is public or nonpublic; what kind of information is being sought (subscriber details vs. contents); whether the content has been accessed or not by the subscriber (email opened); and how long the content has been in storage unopened (less then 180 days). Compelled disclosure can occur, the method of which must be matched to the type of information requested (subscriber records vs. file content), based upon the circumstances noted above.

It is noteworthy that the legal method, i.e., a subpoena, court order, or search warrant, frequently requires a different and greater standard of proof before its issuance. The more "private" the information the greater the standard of proof must be met for the legal compulsion method. For instance, obtaining nonopened email, in storage less then 180 days, requires a search warrant, which can only be issued upon probable cause. Additionally, depending upon the compelling process, SCA may require the subscriber be notified. Deutchman and Morgan (2005) note:

> *Three types of legal process are available under the ECPA to obtain content and records information: ECPA warrants, 2703(d) court orders and subpoenas. In addition, depending upon the type of information sought, 2703(d) court orders and subpoenas may require notice to the subscriber. Generally, the more personal the information sought, e.g., email content, the higher the burden of proof for law enforcement to obtain the requisite legal process. The ECPA warrant must be supported by probable cause, the 2703(d) court order by 'specific and articulable facts,' and a subpoena typically by relevance (p. 13).*

SCA also provides a mechanism for law enforcement to request an ISP maintain records for 90 days, subject to a renewal for another 90 days (Preservation of Evidence, 18 U.S.C. § 2703(f)). This allows investigators time to obtain the proper legal compulsion method (search warrant or subpoena) without concern the records will be deleted by the provider. However, the U.S. Department of Justice (DOJ) (2009) notes there are some caveats:

> *First, § 2703(f) letters should not be used prospectively to order providers to preserve records not yet created. If agents want providers to record information about future electronic communications, they should comply with the electronic surveillance statutes discussed in Chapter 4. A second limitation of § 2703(f) is that some providers may be unable to comply effectively with § 2703(f) requests, or they may be unable to comply without taking actions that potentially could alert a suspect. In such a situation, the agent must weigh the benefit of preservation against the risk of alerting the subscriber. The key here is effective communication: agents should communicate with the network service provider before ordering the provider to take steps that may have unintended adverse effects (p. 140).*

A variable resource for ISP contact information for sending preservation requests or serving the various legal compulsion methods is maintained by SEARCH.ORG at http://www.search.org/programs/hightech/isp/. It is also worth noting that many larger ISP also provide law enforcement guides that are quite useful in understanding what records they maintain, including how long and in what format.

The Pen/Trap Statute (18 U.S.C. §§ 3127-27)
The Pen/Trap Statute provides that a government attorney may seek a court order to approve the installation of a device (pen register) that records outgoing addressing information and another device (trap and trace) to recording incoming addressing information. These devices can either be hardware or software based. The legal threshold for obtaining such an order is "...the information likely to be obtained is relevant to an ongoing criminal investigation" (18 U.S.C. § 3122(b)(2)).

These orders may authorize the installation and use of the devices for up to 60 days, which may be extended for additional 60-day periods (18 U.S.C. § 3123(c)).

Historically, these devices were used to determine who a suspect was telephoning (receiving and making calls). The devices only record the addressing information and do not capture the actual communication. However, the statute also covers communication between two computers, such as the IP addresses or Internet headers in an email (both "to" and "from" minus the subject line). The statute does not authorize the capture of the actual content of a "real-time" message, which can only be approved by a Wiretap order. A Pen/Trap order would typically be sought when it is difficult to determine where communication is originating. U.S. Department of Justice (DOJ) (2009) reflects:

> ...a federal prosecutor may obtain an order to trace communications sent to a particular victim computer or IP address. If a hacker is routing communications through a chain of intermediate pass-through computers, the order would apply to each computer in the United States in the chain from the victim to the source of the communications (p. 155).

There are of course exceptions under this statute's provisions, such as an ISP can install such a device with their consumer's consent. This statute does not prohibit an individual recording the ISP address from which they are communicating with, such as during a chat session.

EU Privacy Directive

The EU through Directive 95/46/EC of the European Parliament and Council (Directive) has established a privacy right for one's personal data. Once establishing this right, the Directive restricts how one's personal data may be collected and used and sets minimum standards for protection of the collected data. Personal data is defined under Article 2(a) as "...any information relating to an identified or identifiable natural person (data subject); an identifiable person is one who can be identified, directly or indirectly, in particular by reference to an identification number or to one or more factors specific to his physical, physiological, mental, economic, cultural or social identity." To further elaborate something as simple an email address can be personal data where it clearly identifies a particular individual (Data Protection Act, 1998, Legal Guidance).

There are two general situations where the Directive is excluded from operation. An EU state may process data in matters concerning public security, defense, state security (including the economic well-being), and in areas of criminal law. The second exception to the Directive is a "nature person in the course of a purely personal or household activity." The Directive further provides that processing of data can only occur with the data subject's explicit consent or in regards to a legitimate activity or obligation, such as performance of a contract. The Directive also provides a mechanism for a data subject to correct or have deleted erroneous information about them.

To illustrate the Directive in action, let's examine a scenario involving a social media investigation pertaining to subject's employment suitability, a legitimate purpose under the Directive. The investigation is presumably initiated with the explicit consent of the subject. The investigator identifies the subject's social media presence and proceeds to collect information from various social networking sites, some of which are located within the EU. These EU social networking sites are a "collector" maintaining data covered under the Directive. However, the investigator has now obtained data on the subject from a location in the EU. As a result, they may have become a "collector" or at least a "processor," covered under Directive's provisions, including the rules on disclosure, notifications, modifications, data security, and retention.

These provisions would at first blush seem to only apply to identities located in the EU. This is not the case and is of particular concern for non-EU businesses operating in the EU. As a result, at least in the United States, a framework had to be developed to bridge the differences, particularly in regard to data security and retention. In 2000, the U.S. Department of Commerce in consultation with the European Commission developed a "safe harbor" framework. An organization can participate in the US−EU Safe Harbor program but must comply with seven privacy principles and self-certify annually, in writing, to the US Department of Commerce that they continue to comply with those principles. The Safe Harbor Privacy Principles are as follows:

- Notice: Organizations must notify individuals about the purposes for which they collect and use information about them. They must provide information about how individuals can contact the organization with any inquiries or complaints, the types of third parties to which it discloses the information, and the choices and means the organization offers for limiting its use and disclosure.
- Choice: Organizations must give individuals the opportunity to choose (opt out) whether their personal information will be disclosed to a third party or used for a purpose incompatible with the purpose for which it was originally collected or subsequently authorized by the individual. For sensitive information, affirmative or explicit (opt in) choice must be given if the information is to be disclosed to a third party or used for a purpose other than its original purpose or the purpose authorized subsequently by the individual.
- Onward transfer (transfers to third parties): To disclose information to a third party, organizations must apply the notice and choice principles. Where an organization wishes to transfer information to a third party that is acting as an agent, it may do so if it makes sure that the third party subscribes to the Safe Harbor Privacy Principles or is subject to the Directive or another adequacy finding. As an alternative, the organization can enter into a written agreement with such third party requiring that the third party provides at least the same level of privacy protection as is required by the relevant principles.

- Access: Individuals must have access to personal information about them that an organization holds and be able to correct, amend, or delete that information where it is inaccurate, except where the burden or expense of providing access would be disproportionate to the risks to the individual's privacy in the case in question, or where the rights of persons other than the individual would be violated.
- Security: Organizations must take reasonable precautions to protect personal information from loss, misuse, and unauthorized access, disclosure, alteration, and destruction.
- Data integrity: Personal information must be relevant for the purposes for which it is to be used. An organization should take reasonable steps to ensure that data is reliable for its intended use, accurate, complete, and current.
- Enforcement: In order to ensure compliance with the safe harbor principles, there must be (1) readily available and affordable independent recourse mechanisms so that each individual's complaints and disputes can be investigated and resolved and damages awarded where the applicable law or private sector initiatives so provide; (2) procedures for verifying that the commitments companies make to adhere to the safe harbor principles have been implemented; and (3) obligations to remedy problems arising out of a failure to comply with the principles. Sanctions must be sufficiently rigorous to ensure compliance by the organization. Organizations that fail to provide annual self-certification letters will no longer appear in the list of participants and safe harbor benefits will no longer be assured (Export.gov, 2012).

As was noted at that start of this section, the EU's current *Protection Directive* is not followed by all European nations, with some having more stringent requirements. On January 25, 2012, a draft revision was made to make the protections more uniform. This new Directive will not be fully implemented for 2 years. It is beyond this text's purpose to fully explore its provisions before it has been adopted by EU states. However, there is one concept which is worth mentioning. The revised Directive strengthens a "…right to be forgotten, which means that if you no longer want your data to be processed, and there is no legitimate reason for a company to keep it, the data shall be deleted" (European Commission Justice/Data-protection, 2012). It is unclear how long ISP operating in the EU will be allowed to retain a person's record after they want it deleted. However, the implications for those conducting online investigations should be clear. The ability to collect and properly authenticate online ESI may be the only way to obtain evidence if data collectors are directed to delete it without some reasonable retention period.

Fair Credit Reporting Act (15 U.S.C. § 1681 et seq.)

In the United States, we often think of FCRA in terms of a credit check, providing a listing of outstanding financial obligations, leans, foreclosures, bankruptcies, etc. However, the FCRA encompasses more than just a "credit check" and can include information gleaned from social networking investigations. Under the FCRA (§ 603. (d)(1) Definitions; Rules of construction (15 U.S.C. § 1681a)), a consumer report is defined as

> *...any written, oral, other communication of any information by a consumer reporting agency bearing on a consumer's credit worthiness, credit standing, credit capacity, character, general reputation, personal characteristics, or mode of living which is used or expected to be used or collected in whole or in part for the purpose of serving as a factor in establishing the consumer's eligibility for: (A) credit or insurance to be used for personal, family, or household purposes; (B) employment purposes; or (C) any other purpose authorized by under Section 604.*[14]

Under the FCRA a consumer reporting agency "...means any person which, for monetary fees, dues, or on a cooperative nonprofit basis, regularly engages in whole or in part in the practice of assembling or evaluating consumer credit information or other information on consumers for the purpose of furnishing consumer reports to third parties, and which uses any means or facility of interstate commerce for the purpose of preparing or furnishing consumer reports" (FCRA § 603. (f) Definitions; Rules of construction (15 U.S.C. § 1681a)). These definitions clearly cover social networking investigations if the purpose is to collect information for a consumer report.

Employers have begun combing social networking sites to determine the suitability to hire and retain individuals. Under FCRA, an employer's investigative actions are generally excluded from the definition of a consumer report.[15] Employers finding it increasing difficult to investigate these accounts on their own frequently turn to third parties to find the information. However, a third party conducting social networking investigations on behalf of an employer does fall under the above definitions. It is therefore very important that investigators conducting such employment suitability investigations on social media understand the FCRA and its provisions. Noncompliance with the FCRA can have both criminal and civil penalties.

Mutual legal assistance

Based upon information contained in the last section, investigators may now be rethinking the wisdom of gathering online ESI if it resides in another jurisdiction,

---

[14]Along with credit and employment purposes, Section 604 includes such items as: determining "eligibility for a license or other benefit granted by a government instrumentality"; information for investors; determining capacity to make child support payments; and the requested information is determined to be legitimate business need when a business transaction is initiated by a consumer.

[15]Employers still need to be careful that their social networking investigations do not result discrimination claims based upon race, color, religion, sex (including pregnancy), national origin, age (40 or older), disability, or genetic information. Employers should also be careful that they do not violate privacy laws in their activities investigating potential or current employees' social networking profiles.

particularly if digital ESI or witness testimony is required from that jurisdiction. However, there are resources available that may be helpful if such assistance is needed within a particular jurisdiction. One of the methods for reaching out for assistance in criminal investigations is through mutual legal assistance (MLA). MLA refers to:

> ...the provisions of legal assistance by one state to another state[16] in the investigation, prosecution, or punishment of criminal offenses. Given the transborder nature of criminality, such as organized crime, trafficking in persons and drugs, smuggling in persons, and so forth, mutual legal assistance is an invaluable tool. Mutual legal assistance is usually governed by bilateral or multilateral legal assistance treaties that regulate the scope, limits, and procedures for such assistance, although domestic legislation will suffice in many cases. Treaties are often supplemented by domestic legislation in a criminal procedure code or as a separate piece of legislation. Mutual legal assistance may also be given informally through bilateral cooperation and the sharing of information between policing or judicial officials in different states
>
> **(Connor et al., chap. 14, p. 427).**

MLA can take time, particularly if prior professional relationships have not been developed through organizations, such as the High Technology Crime Investigation Association (HTCIA) or High Tech Crime Consortium (HTCC) (www.hightechcrimecops.org). Additionally, MLA is limited to universally recognized crimes and not those of a "political nature." Two major MLA are the Hemispheric Information Exchange Network for Mutual Assistance in Criminal Matters and Extradition (the "Network"), which covers all of the Americas located at http://www.oas.org/juridico/mla/en/index.html and the European Union Second Additional Protocol to the European Convention on Mutual Assistance in Criminal Matters located at http://conventions.coe.int/Treaty/en/Treaties/Html/182.htm.

For civil investigations the professional relationships developed through HTCIA (www.htcia.org) and HTCC (www.hightechcrimecops.org) can be extremely beneficial as MLA do not apply.

General guidance

There are numerous public resources for how to initially collect digital ESI from computers, many of which are from the United States.[17] Unfortunately, the specifics of collecting online ESI have been historically lacking. There were some

---

[16]State in this definition is meant imply to countries and their political subunits.

[17]The *Cyber Crime Fighting—The Law Enforcement Officer's Guide to Online Crime* (2000) (National Cybercrime Training Partnership); *Best Practices for Seizing Electronic Evidence V.3: A Pocket Guide for First Responders*, 2006 (U.S. Department of Homeland Security, United States Secret Service); and *Electronic Crime Scene Investigation: A Guide for First Responders*, Second Edition (2008) (National Institute of Justice).

early efforts to address online ESI. For instance, The National Cybercrime Training Partnership[18] distributed about 50,000 copies of *The Cyber Crime Fighting—The Law Enforcement Officer's Guide to Online Crime* in 2000 (U.S. Department of Justice, Office of Justice Programs, Bureau of Justice Assistance, 2002). This guide was noteworthy as it discussed at length not only procedures for seizing computers but also was one of the first documents to discuss steps for investigating online crimes. The guide discussed questions to ask complainants and suggested obtaining hard copy printouts or file downloads from complainants. However, it did not discuss steps for investigators to secure online data themselves. Subsequent guides, such as the Secret Services, *Best Practices For Seizing Electronic Evidence V.3: A Pocket Guide for First Responders*, focus almost entirely on computer seizure with only a brief mention of interpreting email header information. The National Institute of Justice (NIJ) (2007) *Investigations Involving the Internet and Computer Networks* does discuss very basic online ESI collection procedures, such as taking screenshots, using the "Save As[19]" command, and special software for capturing websites. Additionally, the NIJ guide mentions documentation procedures, which include making sure to note the data and time of collection and checking to insure the data was obtained. However, there is no mention of chain of custody concerns, such as securing the data or creating a hash value[20] after collection.

Why this inadequate treatment of online ESI collection? There may be several reasons. The first may be the erroneously perception that screenshots or website captures are not as important as finding digital ESI on the suspect's hard drive. This may be true if improper techniques are used which lead to admissibility issues, such as authenticity and hearsay. However, one must recognize that the evidence may sometimes only be found online and not on a suspect's computer hard drive. For instance, a screen capture may be the only recourse to gather data from a live chat session or private instant message. With the plethora of anti-forensic techniques, an examiner may be unable to retrieve the incriminating social networking post or message from the suspect's computer. As noted in the previous section, the EU's "right to be forgotten" principle may also have a negative impact on ESI being provided by an ISP.

Online ESI can be easily changed during an investigation. There also may be jurisdictional issues that make getting the data from an ISP more difficult or too time-consuming. The ACPO Guide provides the following commentary which is applicable to all jurisdictions:

---

[18]This was an early initiative between the Computer Crimes and Intellectual Property Section of the U.S. Department of Justice and the NW3C, which is now defunct.

[19]The "Save As" command allows a user to save a webpage, including the HTML coding within a Web browser. This technique will be discussed later.

[20]A hash value is the mathematical representation of a file or drive. A copy of this file can be shown to be the same as the original as long as the hash values match. If 1 bit of information is changed, the hash value will not be the same.

Evidence relating to a crime committed in the United Kingdom may reside on a website, a forum posting or a web blog. Capturing this evidence may pose some major challenges, as the target machine(s) may be cited outside of the United Kingdom jurisdiction or evidence itself could be easily changed or deleted. In such cases, retrieval of the available evidence has a time critical element and investigators may resort to time and dated screen captures of the relevant material or 'ripping' the entire content of particular Internet sites.

The second reason is the general lack of understanding of how to accomplish online ESI collection. This explanation parallels that which occurred in the late 1980s with digital ESI collection and analysis. Specifically, there were few tools to accomplish computer forensics. Those tools that did exist were not designed originally for forensics, but were adopted from other purposes. Few understood how to accomplish digital ESI collection and analysis. As time went on forensic tools were created specifically for digital ESI collection and analysis. With the development of these tools specific procedures came into existence that guided their further development and their proper use. Currently dealing with online ESI is where the field was with digital ESI in the late 1980s. There are few properly designed tools for this specific purpose. Most tools still used were developed for other purposes. A few agencies, such as the Internet Crimes Against Children (ICAC) Task Forces (TF), have developed standardized investigative methods for online ESI. However, this is unique in the law enforcement community. The vast majority of law enforcement agencies have no standard methodologies in place for the collection and analysis of online evidence. Just like what occurred with computer-based ESI, investigators are learning to adapt and develop to meet the challenge of collecting online ESI. Shipley (2007) notes:

Current law enforcement investigative methodologies for the Internet are varied and many. Some agencies have dedicated the necessary resources to conduct investigations and still many others have ignored the Internet and the crime conducted there, either out of ignorance or negligence. No standard process currently exists to guide an investigator, at any level within the government (local, state or federal), military or those investigating the Internet for a corporation. This has caused a lack of understanding among those assigned these tasks, and have caused the development of a variety of practices within this community. To add to the lack of consistent practices, the lack of specialized tools in this area has driven the adoption of tools specifically designed for other purposes. These tools have sometimes provided the investigator with insufficient support for best evidence practices. However, investigators ever adapting to their changing world, proceeded ahead and have put many criminals in prison based on their ability to collect evidence from the Internet with tools not designed for evidence collection.

A good starting point for developing procedures is the four principles noted in the ACPO Guide. Although, written primarily for computer-based digital ESI, the

ACPO Guide is one of the few resources which actually discusses collecting online ESI. The guide also discusses undercover online investigations and open-source investigation, which is proactively patrolling the Internet for evidence of crimes. Additionally, these principles are useful for online ESI, as they stress that data must not be changed; those accessing data should have a certain level of competency; and that documentation and chain of custody are important considerations. These are all key components to making sure online ESI can be admitted as evidence. Also, these four principles summarize nicely concepts found in other public resources on electronic data collection.[21] Finally, although noted for law enforcement, the evidence collection procedures for criminal law are universally more stringent than those in any other proceeding. As such, anyone serious about getting their online ESI admitted as evidence in any legal forum must strongly consider the following ACPO Guide principles:

> *Principle 1: No action taken by law enforcement agencies or their agents should change data held on a computer or storage media which may subsequently be relied upon in court.*
> *Principle 2: In circumstances where a person finds it necessary to access original data held on a computer or on storage media, that person must be competent to do so and be able to give evidence explaining the relevance and the implications of their actions.*
> *Principle 3: An audit trail or other record of all processes applied to computer-based electronic evidence should be created and preserved. An independent third party should be able to examine those processes and achieve the same result.*
> *Principle 4: The person in charge of the investigation (the case officer) has overall responsibility for ensuring that the law and these principles are adhered to. (p. 4).*

Early in the digital evidence process development, the NIJ Technical Working Group on Digital Evidence (TWGDE) produced the document *"Electronic Crime Scene Investigation, A Guide for First Responders,"* which outlined a four stage process for dealing with digital evidence. Those four stages were collection, examination, analysis, and reporting of the digital evidence.[22] Shipley (2007) narrowed the focus for online ESI to three steps: collection, preservation, and its presentation. There may be occasions where analysis may be needed, such as examining metadata. However, using the best collection procedures feasible will

---

[21]The only caveat is other law enforcement guides frequently stress officer safety as an additional factor or principle in seizing digital ESI.

[22]This process was later enhanced with the Abstract Digital Forensics Model which increased the stages to 9. However, several of the new additional steps, such as returning evidence, are not applicable to online ESI. See http://www.utica.edu/academic/institutes/ecii/publications/articles/A04A40DC-A6F6-F2C1-98F94F16AF57232D.pdf.

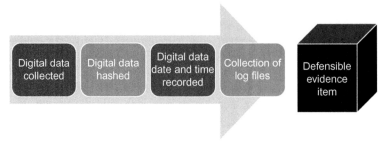

FIGURE 4.2

Detailed proper online ESI collection steps.

facilitate such additional steps if needed. Shipley (2007) describes these three basic steps as follows:

Collection: Includes the actual capture of content viewed by the user. This can be a webpage or items on a webpage, such as image files, music files, or documents. It can also be instant message conversations or chat conversations using a variety of applications designed for that purpose.

Preservation: Includes the treatment of this digital evidence using the concepts and principles learned from computer forensics when dealing with digital evidence (Figure 4.2).

a. Don't change the evidence if possible.

b. Collect the evidence in a verifiable manner.

c. Maintain a proper chain of custody of the evidence.

Presentation: Means the actual viewing offline of the evidence in a manner simulating its real-time collection. This could include viewing chat logs or video files of the websites visited or the real-time chat sessions.

CONCLUSION

This chapter provided an overview of online ESI. The focus was not to make investigators legal experts. However, we hopefully provided the general knowledge to gather the "best ESI" to ensure any legal authority has a good basis to argue that it should be admitted into evidence. We firmly believe that with proper planning investigators will go a long way to insure, in Judge Grimm's words, there are no "self-inflicted injuries" with regard to authentication. We cannot stress enough that today's legal environment mandates that investigators: (1) don't change the evidence, if possible; (2) collect it a verifiable manner; and (3) maintain a proper chain of custody. This book's remaining chapters will provide in-depth techniques based upon these legal mandates to insure online ESI can be admitted into any legal forum.

Further reading

Adams, J. (n.d.). BrainyQuote.com. Retrieved from http://www.brainyquote.com/quotes/quotes/j/johnadams134175.html/.

Association of Chief Police Officers in the United Kingdom. (2007). *The good practice guide for computer-based electronic evidence.* Retrieved from http://www.7safe.com/electronic_evidence/ACPO_guidelines_computer_evidence.pdf/.

Benoit, C. (2012). Picketers, protesters, and police the first amendment and investigative activity. *FBI Law Enforcement Bulletin.* Retrieved from http://www.fbi.gov/stats-services/publications/law-enforcement-bulletin/august-2012/picketers-protesters-and-police/.

Bowker, A. (1999). Investigative planning creating a strong foundation for white-collar crime cases. *FBI Law Enforcement Bulletin, 68*(6), 22−25.

Canada Evidence Act. OAS—Organization of American States: Democracy for peace, security, and development. N.p. (n.d.). Retrieved from http://www.oas.org/juridico/mla/en/can/e/.

Connor, V. M., Rausch, C., Albrecht, H., & Klemencic, G. (2008). *Mutual legal assistance and extradition. Model codes for post-conflict criminal justice.* Washington, DC: United States Institute of Peace.

Crown Prosecution Service Hearsay. (n.d.). Legal guidance: The Crown Prosecution Service. Retrieved from http://www.cps.gov.uk/legal/h_to_k/hearsay/.

Data Protection Act. (1998). *Legal guidance.* Retrieved from http://www.ico.gov.uk/upload/documents/library/data_protection/detailed_specialist_guides/data_protection_act_legal_guidance.pdf/.

Deutchman, L., & Morgan, S. (2005). *The ECPA, ISPs & obtaining E-mail: A primer for local prosecutors.* Alexandria, VA: American Prosecutors Research Institute, Retrieved from <http://www.ndaa.org/pdf/ecpa_isps_obtaining_email_05.pdf/>.

Democko, B. (2012). Social media and the rules of authentication. *University of Toledo Law Review, 43*(Winter), 367−405.

Electronic Communications Privacy Act of 1986. (ECPA). (n.d.). *IT.OJP.GOV home.* Retrieved from <http://www.it.ojp.gov/default.aspx?area=privacy&page=1285/>

Electronic Crime Scene Investigation: A Guide for First Responders, Second Edition. (2008). Washington, DC: U.S. Dept. of Justice, Office of Justice Programs, National Institute of Justice. Retrieved from < https://www.ncjrs.gov/pdffiles1/nij/219941.pdf>.

EUR-Lex—31995L0046—EN. (n.d.). *EUR-Lex.* Retrieved from <http://eur-lex.europa.eu/LexUriServ/LexUriServ.do?uri=CELEX:31995L0046:en:HTML/>.

European Commission Justice/Data-protection. (2012, February 20). *How does the data protection reform strengthen citizens' rights?* Retrieved from http://ec.europa.eu/justice/data-protection/document/review2012/factsheets/2_en.pdf/.

European Commission. (2012). *Commission proposes a comprehensive reform of data protection rules to increase users' control of their data and to cut costs for businesses-press release.* Retrieved from http://europa.eu/rapid/press-release_IP-12-46_en.htm?locale=en/.

Export.gov. (2012). U.S.−EU safe harbor overview. *Export.gov—Home.* Retrieved from http://export.gov/safeharbor/eu/eg_main/.

Fair Credit Reporting Act, 15 U.S.C. § 1681 et seq.

Federal Rules of Evidence (FRE). (2011). Washington: U.S. G.P.O.

Griffin v. State, 419 Md. 343, 347-48 (Md. 2011).

Harbeck, D., & Yoonji, K. (2010). Is the Internet "Voodoo"?: Evidentiary weight of Internet-based material in immigration court. *Connecticut Public Interest Law Journal, 10*(I), 3—12.

Hura, D. (2011). China's new rules on evidence in criminal trials. *International Law and Politics, 43,* 740—765.

Insa, F. (2007). The admissibility of electronic evidence in court (A.E.E.C.): Fighting against high-tech crime results of a European study. *Journal of Digital Forensic Practice,* 285—289.

Investigations involving the Internet and computer networks. (2007). Washington, D.C.: U.S. Dept. of Justice, Office of Justice Programs, National Institute of Justice. Retrieved from < https://www.ncjrs.gov/pdffiles1/nij/210798.pdf>.

Lorraine v. Markel Am. Ins. Com, 241 F.R.D. 534, 538 (D. Md. 2007).

Mason, S. (2006). *Proof of the authenticity of a document in electronic format introduced as evidence.* Pittsburgh: ARMA International Educational Foundation, Retrieved from http://www.mnhs.org/preserve/records/legislativerecords/docs_pdfs/Proof_of_authenticity_of_a_document.pdf/.

Merritt, D. (2012). Social media, the sixth amendment, and restyling: recent developments in the federal law of evidence. *Touro Law Review, 28,* 27—54.

National Conference of State Legislatures (NCSL). (2010). *Privacy protections in state constitutions.* Retrieved from http://www.ncsl.org/issues-research/telecom/privacy-protections-in-state-constitutions.aspx/.

National Conference of State Legislatures (NCSL). (2012). *Employer access to social media passwords.* Retrieved from http://www.ncsl.org/issues-research/telecom/employer-access-to-social-media-passwords.aspx/.

O'Brien v. O'Brien, Case No. 5D03-3484. Northern District of Florida (2005).

Office for Official Publications of the European Communities (2012). *Proposal for a Regulation of European Parliament and of the counsel on the protection of individuals with regard to the processing of personal data and on the free movement of such data (General Data Protection Regulation).* Luxembourg: Office for Official Publications of the European Communities.

Pen/Trap Statute (18 U.S.C. §§ 3127-27).

Rashbaum, K., Knouff, M., & Murray, D. (2012). Admissibility of non-U.S. electronic evidence. *Richmond Journal of Law and Technology, XVIII*(3), 58—76.

Reporters Committee for Free Press. *Can we tape?* Retrieved from http://www.rcfp.org/taping/.

Savage, C. (2012). Panel approves a bill to safeguard e-mail. *The New York Times,* p. 7.

Seng, D. (2009). Evidential issues from pre-action discoveries: *Odex PTE LTD v. Pacific Internet Ltd. Digital Evidence & Electronic Signature Law Review, 6,* 25—32.

Shipley, T. (2007). Collecting legally defensible online evidence. *Vera Software.* Retrieved from <http://veresoftware.com/uploads/CollectingLegallyDefensibleOnlineEvidence.pdf/>.

Shipley, T., & Reeve, H. (2006). *Collecting evidence from a running computer: A technical and legal primer for the justice community* Sacramento: SEARCH, The National Consortium for Justice Information and Statistics, Retrieved from http://www.search.org/files/pdf/CollectEvidenceRunComputer.pdf/.

Stored Communications Act (SCA) (18 U.S.C. §§ 2701-12).

Tech Terms Computer. http://www.techterms.com/.

Teddy St. Clair v. Johnny's Oyster & Shrimp, Inc., 706 F. Supp. 2d 773 (S.D. Texas 1999).

U.S. Department of Justice (DOJ). (2009). *Searching and seizing computers and obtaining electronic evidence in criminal investigations.* Silver Spring, MD. Retrieved from <http://www.justice.gov/criminal/cybercrime/docs/ssmanual2009.pdf/>.

U.S. Department of Justice (DOJ) and Administrative Office of the U.S. Courts (AO) (Joint Working Group on Electronic Technology in the Criminal Justice System (JETWG)). (2012). *Recommendations for electronically stored information (ESI) discovery production in federal criminal cases.* Washington, DC. Retrieved from http://www.fd.org/docs/litigation-support/final-esi-protocol.pdf/.

U.S. Department of Justice, Office of Justice Programs, Bureau of Justice Assistance. (2002). *The National White Collar Crime Center: Helping America fight economic crime.* Washington, DC. Retrieved from <https://www.ncjrs.gov/pdffiles1/bja/184958.pdf/>.

U.S. Department of Justice, Office of Justice Programs, National Institute of Justice. (2001). Electronic crime scene investigation: An on-the-scene reference for first responders. Washington, DC. Retrieved from <https://www.ncjrs.gov/pdffiles1/nij/187736.pdf/.>

Wiretap Act (18 U.S.C. § 2510-22).

Documenting Online Evidence

> The guy who knows about computers is the last person you want to have
> creating documentation for people who don't understand computers.
> **Adam Osborne (1939–2003, American Author and entrepreneur, who introduced the
> world's first portable computer)**

Documenting online evidence, as described in Chapter 4, is legal requirement. Screenshots or digital camera shots alone are no longer valid documentation methods for online investigations. Authentication is a legal hurtle that must be overcome to getting online ESI admitted into any legal proceeding. The bits and bytes we find on the Internet are no different than those we are familiar with when found on a hard drive or a cell phone we physically possess. Internet data exists on a hard drive or memory storage space somewhere in the world. The difference between traditional digital forensic collection and Internet evidence collection is the methods available to us to document the data. In this chapter, we will discuss those methods and procedures that can be used and introduce various tools that can make this process verifiable and authenticated.

Process for documenting online ESI

Documenting Internet ESI involves understanding the various protocols in use and ensuring that you are collecting the information that the protocol makes available. We discussed in Chapter 3 how the Internet and its various protocols work. Understanding these protocols is critical for investigators to comprehend the importance of the processes discussed in this chapter. In Chapter 4, we outlined a basic process to consider when collecting Internet ESI to maximize its admittance as evidence. Using that format we will discuss specifically what procedures need to be conducted to accomplish those processes.

Collection

Collection is the basic function of documenting Internet evidence. Collection includes the actual gathering of the data of interest as well, if possible, the metadata surrounding that data. Metadata is information that describes the source data. It can include various time stamps, author information, the program used to make the code or many other file-specific pieces of information. The process begins with identification of the data to be gathered, its protocol determination, collection methodology and location identification.

Internet ESI collection processes can be broken into two types: (1) those conducted from the investigator's office equipment (i.e., from his desktop or laptop) and (2) those collections conducted in the field on the victim's or witness's computer. Always, online ESI collection requires some forethought on the investigator's part regarding the method, the process, and its validity. Online ESI collection can require the inclusion of your agency's or company's digital forensic examiners. Consultation with the digital forensic examiners may be required before collecting digital evidence in a particular case. The following collection tools and processes describe how the Internet investigator can collect online ESI in an effective and valid method. Decisions to use these methods should include consultation with agency or company policy on digital evidence, agency or corporate legal and technical advisers and management acknowledgment of these methods.

Identification

Identification of the items to be collected comes from the investigator's understanding of the case facts. If a complaint received is about data found on a website the investigator needs to get clear and concise information as to the website involved in the complaint. This includes the complete website (URL) address involved in the complaint. If the complaint is about an auction site posting the complete details about the site, auction item name or number, seller and any relevant information regarding the sale are needed. If the complaint is about a chatroom, the details of the specific chat program used, the chatroom involved and the suspect's username and chat details need to be collected.

INVESTIGATIVE TIP

Interviewing the Cybercrime Victim

Internet Access

1. Who is your Internet service provider (ISP)?
2. What kind of Internet service do you have?
   a. Dial up
   b. DSL (Digital Subscriber Line)
   c. Cable
   d. Wireless
3. Where did this occur? (your home, work, school, etc.?)
4. What are your email addresses?
5. Who owns the computer you used? (you, your employer, school, parents, etc.)
6. Did you access the Internet through a network? (employer, school, etc.)
7. Did you access the Internet through a wireless network and is so where?

Chat-Related Crimes
1. What was the chat service where this occurred?
2. What was the date and time this occurred?
3. What is the chatroom(s) name where this occurred?
4. What is your screen name or nickname in this chatroom? What is the suspect's screen name or nickname? Do you know their real name?
5. Did the chatroom have an operator or moderator and if so, what is their screen name or nickname? Do you know their real name?
6. Did you recognize anyone else in the chatroom and if so, what is their screen name or nickname? What about their real name?
7. Did you save or printout out a copy of the conversation?
   a. If you saved it, can you provide a copy to us? (If possible, try to observe them saving it.)
   b. If they printed it out, try to get the original hard copy.

Newsgroup-Related Crimes
1. What is the newsgroup's complete name?
2. Do you access newsgroups via software or through a website?
3. Did you save the posting to a computer?
   a. Can you provide an electronic copy? (If possible observe them saving it).
   b. If not, did you print a copy of the posting and can we have the original hard copy?
4. Is this newsgroup available directly from your ISP?
5. Which newsgroup service do you use?
6. Which computer server did you use to access this newsgroup? What is the name of the posting?

E-mail-Related Crimes
1. Do you have the email(s) address of the person who sent the email, including the header information? (For a discussion about email headers and their collection see Chapter 8.)
2. Did you still have the email(s)? Where?
3. Can you provide an electronic copy to us? (Ask to observe the copying.)
      (This copy needs to include the header information.)
4. Do you have a printed copy of the email and may we have the original?
5. Is your email software- or web-based?

Social Networking-Related Crimes
1. What is your profile name and which email account is associated with it?
2. Where was the post made, your shared area or another user's area?
3. What profile name made the post?
4. Who else may have seen the post and what is their profile name (real name)?
5. Was the message sent to your profile and if so do you still have it? (It may be very important to get access to this message, which will point to the originating profile.)

Protocol/application determination

Identifying the protocol used provides the investigator with an understanding of the requirements needed to collect that particular type of Internet data. These include but are not limited to:

a. HTTP (Hyper Text Transfer Protocol)
b. SMTP (Secure Mail Transfer Protocol)
c. FTP (file transfer protocol)

   d. IM (instant message)
   e. P2P (peer to peer)
   f. IRC (Internet relay chat).

   Protocol identification is determined quickly based on the initial interview with the victim. The victim should know where on the Internet they were victimized, i.e., a chatroom, threatening emails sent to them, or an auction site with a known URL. The collection process for each different protocol determines the approach the investigator needs to take to collect the data. The investigator needs to be aware that specific applications used by the victim may cause difficulty in the collection process. The application used in the victim's allegation may often be required to complete any further assessment or evidence collection. The reason is that many of the application manufacturers use proprietary coding to prevent easy access to the program, log files, and other potentially useful data.

Collection methodology

Once the first two steps are completed the investigator needs to develop a collection methodology. This critical third step lays out a plan and identifies tools/procedures for its successful execution. The plan for collecting Internet evidence includes several factors not just identifying details of the target location and going there. Prior to actually going to the Internet offense location investigators need to consider the following:

1. Collection of target intelligence
   a. After the victim interview collection of suspect information can be accomplished through basic research on search engines. The investigator should attempt to locate any other Internet references on the target (See Chapters 12 and 14 for further details). Other mentions of the suspect's real name, username, screen name, or email address can provide a better perspective of the target's intentions. Also consider searches on other information, such as telephone/cell numbers, business names, or any other specific information. These efforts can also provide the investigator with additional potential victims or associates or avenues for identifying the target.
2. Determine the tools required to document the type of protocol used on the target (multiple protocols might be in use).
   a. Tools will be dictated by the protocol.
   b. Simple video recording or snapshots of the protocol may be the only valid options to collect the data from the target site.
   c. Some protocols may require the investigator to collect the storage container of the data on the victim's computer such as a Microsoft Outlook PST (email personal storage file) which contains the email. We will discuss further in Chapter 8 how email collection can be accomplished effectively by the Internet crimes investigator.

d. Determine if the investigator has access to commercial tools designed for the collection of evidence from the Internet.

e. Identify inexpensive or freeware tools that can assist with the collection of data from the Internet. Be aware that just because its free on the Internet does not mean it is safe to use. Many free Internet tools can come with spyware or adware that could compromise an investigation.

3. Determine if undercover activities will be required to further the investigation.

  a. Refer to agency/company policy for undercover operation initiations.

  b. Assume the victim's or co-conspirator's identity, with proper approval or prepare an undercover identity.

  c. Prepare undercover computer.

  d. Prepare online documentation tools for collection process.

4. Estimate resources needed

  a. How much time will be needed to properly collect the online ESI?

  b. How much data storage will be required?

INVESTIGATIVE TIP

Basic Internet Searches

You are looking for information on a suspect, named John Hammerbeer, with an email address of burgerscigarsbeer@gmail.com. He also uses the telephone 216-337-xxxx. Here are some tips for doing an Internet search:

1. If your investigation is centered on a specific area such as social networking site, search the directory, or listing for profile information. This may give you more information than the victim or witness provided to facilitate other searches. Focus on the name and email address, key pieces of information for such member directories.

2. When using your Internet search engine, keep your terms simple to start. For instance, don't combine all of the information into one mega-search. Consider searching these following terms:

  a. Search the name, particularly as it is rather unique. If you search only by the last name you will get not only hits that maybe be John Hammerbeer but also Tim or Alice Hammerbeer. Placing quotes around the name, such as "John Hammerbeer" will give you only hits where it appears as John Hammerbeer. However, you will not get hits where the entry appears such as John E. Hammerbeer. You also will not get an alphabetical entry that appears, such as might be in telephone directory, i.e., Hammerbeer, John. Try varying your search to see if you get additional hits.

  b. Search by the email may also be helpful as it is rather unique. Try searching the full email. Be aware that after the @ symbol will point to the ISP, which could be an employer, school, or in this case a provider that has a social networking (Google+). This gives you some more information about your suspect and other places to search. Also try searching with everything before the @ symbol, as some users may use numerous email accounts and posting with a very similar account name, such as burgersbeercigars@hotmail.com or burgerbeercigars1@gmail.com.

  c. Search the telephone number. You may find it associated with other postings or websites. Follow up and check out these other sources for additional search terms. Note the area code. Search the area code to where it is located, in this case it is Cleveland, Ohio.

> 3. Okay, you search the name John Hammerbeer and it turns out there are individuals in 10 states with that name. Now is time to combine your search terms. We know that the area code above is associated with numbers from Cleveland, Ohio. Try combining the name and area as "John Hammerbeer" + "Ohio" or "John Hammerbeer" + "Cleveland, Ohio."
> 4. Okay, you have tried your favorite search engine. Consider the same steps with other search engines, as they may have different results.
> 5. For additional tips, search for tips for configuring Internet search terms and check out your search engine's help page. A great investigative resource is also *Google hacking for penetration testers*, 2nd edition by Johnny Long (Syngress, 2008). It provides an in-depth look at how to form Google searches to gain the most information.

Collection methodology's importance cannot be overstated. If the investigator attempts to collect online ESI with improper tools they may miss important data, such as metadata, that could have been gathered. Probably more problematic is attempting to gather online ESI with a tool that just can't accomplish the task at all, such as the use of personal computer-based tools in some online gaming environments. Additionally, some investigators may not adequately consider the time needed for some online ESI collection. They allot a small window right before lunch or at the end of the day, when the task is best accomplished in a larger time frame, particularly when chain of custody is of importance. After all, law enforcement does not go to a crime scene, execute a search warrant, start gathering evidence, only to stop and come back after lunch. Plan to collect online ESI data so that it can be done with as little interruption as possible. Obviously, some scenarios, such as those involving undercover online operations, will require uninterrupted operations, which can be accounted for by good planning and forethought. The point is one must consider these issues so that the proper collection methodology is used for the Internet crime being investigated.

Location identification

Locating where something is physically on the Internet is more art than science. It requires finding both the Internet location and the physical address. The Internet location is the website address or URL and IP address, or email account. It can lead you to the service provider for the email account such as Gmail or Hotmail. Tracing the IP address from the URL or the email can provide the investigator with the leads required to identify the target. Tracing IP addressing will be discussed at length in Chapter 8 and is one of the basic skills of the Internet investigator. Locating the actual physical location of the IP address involves tracing it, serving legal service on ISP that own that address and investigations of the target identified by the ISP and the location(s) associated with the target.

Preservation

Preservation of Internet ESI is based on the standards law enforcement already uses when it deals with digital ESI. This includes segregating the data and hashing that data set. In the digital forensics field this is done by forensic examiners who image (make a complete bit for bit copy) of the acquired data into a unique evidence file. This allows the investigator to then use a tool to hash the single data set. Commonly used in digital forensics are tools such as EnCase®, FTK Imager®, ProDiscover®, X-Ways or the open source DD command, to make these data sets. However, tools commonly adopted for use as Internet investigative tools do not generally allow for this kind of collection. The investigator can copy the data into a folder and then use one of the available tools for forensic imaging to acquire the data in a logical image file. These tools will then provide a hash value for the data set and provide the authentication of the data collected. To overcome these issues the investigator can purchase a commercial product such as WebCase® by Vere Software (2013) or follow a standard methodology for documenting and authenticating their data collection. We will be discussing in detail hashing and its importance to the Internet investigation later in this chapter under the section Authenticating the Collected Evidence.

Presentation

Presenting collected Internet ESI is not as easy as easy as printing an email and producing it in court (although a printed email can be authenticated by the sender). Internet evidence in its native form is just electronic bits and bytes. Presenting this kind of information requires the evidence to be viewed in its native form on a computer in a browser or an application designed to view the particular protocol, e.g., IRC. Compilation of the information is best done in some form of HTML formatted report to allow for linkage to images, webpages, and videos as collected during the investigation. Building an HTML page with the attachments can often be difficult for average users. Searching online for a free HTML builder can make the process much easier.

Tools/techniques for documenting Internet evidence

Tools for documenting online ESI have historically been those found on the Internet intended for other purposes and adopted by investigators for collection purposes. A good example of this has been the taking of snapshots of webpages, or portions of pages, relevant to the investigation. Many tools have been available for accomplishing this task. One of the early adopted tools was Techsmith®'s SnagIt (TechSmith, 2012). SnagIt was an early on favorite of Internet investigators because of its easy use and its ability to save images in multiple formats. Techsmith® also makes the popular program Camtasia (TechSmith, 2012) for recording video of screens on a computer. Camtasia has also has been popular with investigators primarily due to its availability and support. Additional tools required for the Internet investigators include those designed to collect protocol-specific information. IRC and various chat programs require applications that can interact with the protocol from that program. A good example of that is Skype™, currently owned by Microsoft®. Skype™ is a well-accepted chat/video messaging

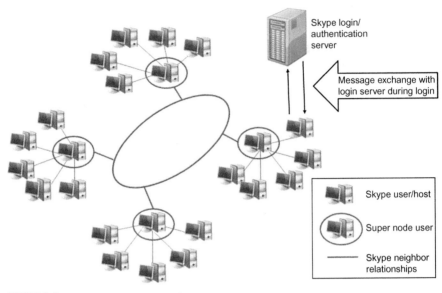

Skype login/
authentication
server

Message exchange with
login server during login

Skype user/host

Super node user

Skype neighbor
relationships

FIGURE 5.1

How Skype works.

program built around a hybrid peer-to-peer[1] concept and client/server[2] concept (Singh & Schulzrinne, 2005). Investigating a case involving Skype™ would generally include using Skype™ in some fashion to attempt to identify or contact the suspect. Additionally, Skype™ proprietary program encrypts its communication tunnel requiring use of its tool for the investigation (Figure 5.1).

Save As

Capturing a webpage can be done simply in your favorite browser by using the "Save As" function found in Windows Internet Explorer, Mozilla's Firefox, or Google's Chrome. Simply select the "single file" in Internet Explorer or the "complete" function in Firefox or Chrome to collect a full copy, which includes the source code to copy the file to your investigative machine (see Chapter 13 for further details). This process only captures the current page being viewed and not an entire website. From a documentation point of view the investigator is collecting what he sees and not what a tool determines is important.

---

[1]"Peer to peer is from user to user. Peer to peer implies that either side can initiate a session and has equal responsibility." http://www.pcmag.com/encyclopedia_term/0,1237,t=peer-to-peer&i=49053,00.asp.

[2]"Client/server describes the relationship between two computer programs in which one program, the client, makes a service request from another program, the server, which fulfills the request." http://searchnetworking.techtarget.com/definition/client-server.

Pictures and video

Documenting what you see on the Internet can simply be done through camera shots, screenshots and/or video recording. These tools will not capture source code, like Save As. However, they nevertheless are important to show what the site looked like to the investigator at the time of capture. Additionally, there are cases where the Save As feature will not work, such as capturing an instant message. The use of digital cameras is sometimes required, such as when capturing a message or chat in a gaming console environment. As mentioned above investigators have also been using various screen capture tools for collecting Internet evidence. Tools such as MWSnap[3] easily allows the investigator to capture portions of a screen or the entire desktop during the evidence collection process. Other screenshot capture tools include HoverSnap,[4] Greenshot,[5] and LightScreen.[6] All of these tools will capture screenshots. However, they also have options that are important for authentication purposes. Specifically, they have features that allow the user to name the image and to include the date and time of creation to be included in the file name.[7] Additionally, they allow screenshots to be taken quickly, in succession, and to be saved in an investigator-selected folder (Figures 5.2).

Tools such as Camtasia or CamStudio allow the investigator to video record anything they are investigating on the Internet. This can include a chat session, lengthy websites, or even videos playing on a website so they are viewed in the context they are playing on the website. CamStudio is an open source tool available for download from http://camstudio.org/. CamStudio's operation is very simple. Click the red start button and the tool asks you what window to record and it begins recording. Click on the pause or stop button to stop recording. CamStudio also allows the user to include the system date and time in the file name and permits the user to sequentially save the files in an investigator-selected folder. One additional feature allows the investigator to include and show a date and time stamp in the recording being made. Again, these are great features for investigators concerned about authentication and chain of custody issues. One caveat to using some of these tools is they will not capture the audio portion, particularly if the system has no microphone. This can be remedied with the use of a digital recorder (Figures 5.3).

Hashing evidence

Hashing as previously discussed is the digital fingerprinting of a set of data. In this case that data is the ESI we collect. We can ensure the data is not changed later by using a hashing tool such as Quick Hash (http://sourceforge.net/projects/quickhash/)

---

[3]http://www.mirekw.com/winfreeware/index.html.
[4]http://www.snapfiles.com/get/hoversnap.html.
[5]http://getgreenshot.org/.
[6]http://lightscreen.sourceforge.net/.
[7]Note that these tools use the system date and time for the file name. If the system date and time are incorrect that value will be placed in the file name.

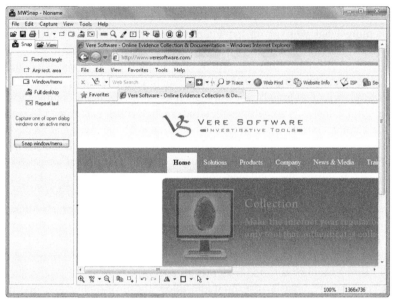

FIGURE 5.2

MWSnap screen capture tool.

FIGURE 5.3

CamStudio video capture tool.

that can hash an individual file or a directory and then produce a report of the files hashed. The hashes listed can then be added to your investigative report detailing your actions. The hash values can be provided with the evidence items on a CD or DVD and validated by the opposing counsel by running their own hashing program against the files. Copies of the files can be shared and discussed with parties, with the hash values ensuring they are not altered. This allows for authentication of the files and leads to their introduction in legal proceedings (Figure 5.4).

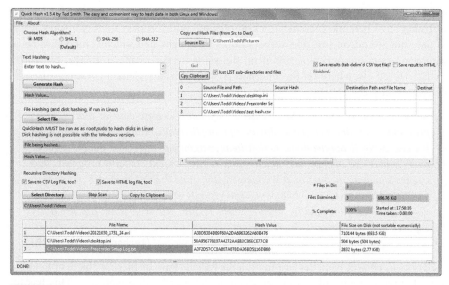

FIGURE 5.4

Quick Hash tool.

Collecting entire websites

The process of documenting entire websites is not a trivial matter. Many discussions can be found on this topic and numerous tools can be found to assist the investigator in this process. We will discuss several here and the pro's and con's of collecting entire websites from an evidentiary viewpoint. We will discuss further in Chapter 13 the makeup of a website in more detail. Look ahead to that chapter for a better understanding of websites protocols.

Website collection can easily be done by the investigator who has access to the server containing the data. However, that is not the case when the investigator is looking at website over the Internet. The investigator observes the Internet website through the interpretation of a web browser. Whether the Investigator is using Microsoft's Internet Explorer, Mozilla's FireFox or Google's Chrome, the browser interprets the data found on the server containing the website of interest. Collecting the website depends on the browser's ability to interpret the data, the security found on the web server, and the ability for the tools to access the web server data and document what it finds there. Additionally, an investigator should be aware that how a website is presented on his computer can be effected by the cookies previously stored there by a website. Prior to making any assumptions about the data on a website the investigator should clear the collection machines web cache and cookies to ensure a correct and current view of the site.[8] Modern websites have become increasingly complicated and webpages and websites refer to data not stored on just one server. Links to images and videos embedded on a webpage are commonly not stored on the same server as the webpage, but links to data stored elsewhere on the Internet. Also, webpages contain a variety of code versions that include active content.

> *Active content is a type of interactive or dynamic website content that includes programs like Internet polls, JavaScript applications, stock tickers, animated images, ActiveX applications, action items, streaming video and audio, weather maps, embedded objects, and much more. Active content contains programs that trigger automatic actions on a Web page without the user's knowledge or consent.*
>
> *Web developers use active content to visually enhance the Web page or provide additional functionality beyond basic HTML. All Web users are regularly exposed to active content.*

(Techopedia.com, 2012)

Tools to collect websites are many and varied. Few of these website collectors are effective in their collection and documentation of entire websites. This has to do with the active content and the fact that data on websites is hosted at these other locations on the Internet and not just the server the website is hosted. Website downloaders commonly have issues with Flash, Javascript, and common gateway interface (CGI). They also will not download any server side code such as php, asp.net, databases, etc. This is because the hosting server prevents access to these kinds of server side operations.

Other issues when downloading a website can include copyright and robot.txt rule violations. Copyright marks on the Internet on websites and elsewhere are as enforceable as any copyright mark found in the real world. Robot.txt files are found on websites and tell webcrawlers, such as Google and Bing, whether or not the site authorizes the sites to be crawled by their bots. Of course this can be easily circumvented because the file is just a polite method of saying please don't crawl my site. It is not any actual block to the site and most crawlers can be set to ignore the Robot.txt file. A review of the sites Terms of Service (ToS) might be required by the investigator before making any attempt at crawling a website. This might be important information to know, even if you ignore the ToS on the site, when you testify about your data collection methods. Here is an example of what can be found in the Robot.txt file:

User-agent: *
Disallow: /

The term User-agent: * refers to all robots (if you only wanted to stop Google from crawling the site you could add Googlebot) and the term Disallow says what not to search. In our example it is everything on the website. Common tools for conducting

---

[8]For details on clearing your browser cache and cookies go to http://www.wikihow.com/Clear-Your-Browser's-Cache and http://www.wikihow.com/Clear-Your-Browser's-Cookies.

website collections include free tools such as HTTrack and Wget and commercially there are tools like Offline Explorer™ from Metaproducts™ (www.metaproducts.com) and Teleport Pro from Tenmax (http://www.tenmax.com). Each of these tools assists the Internet investigators collect data from websites. They all have various settings included in their formats that allow the investigator to collect from a single page to numerous pages within the targeted URL.

INVESTIGATIVE TIP

Using Wget

Wget is a command line tool that allows the investigator to collect a website's data.

Setup Wget

Create directory for Wget C:\wget

   Download Wget from http://www.gnu.org/software/wget/ to the C:\wget directory.

Run Wget from the Command Prompt

Open a command prompt by clicking on the windows and typing "cmd" in the search box. You could also go to the Windows Start Button|All Programs|Accessories|Command prompt to get to the command prompt.

   Set "Path" to run Wget from command prompt by typing in the command prompt "path C:\wget;%path%." This tells Windows to look in the folder c:\wget for the command.

   In the command prompt type the following command:

Wget —mirror —p —html-extension —convert-links www.examplewebsite.com

The following is an explanation of the commands (Figure 5.5):

--p	Get all images, etc. needed to display HTML page.
--mirror	Make a mirror copy of the website.
--html-extension	Save HTML documents with.html extensions.
--convert-links	Make links in downloaded HTML point to local files.
www.examplewebsite.com	Add the targeted website to copy here in place of the example.

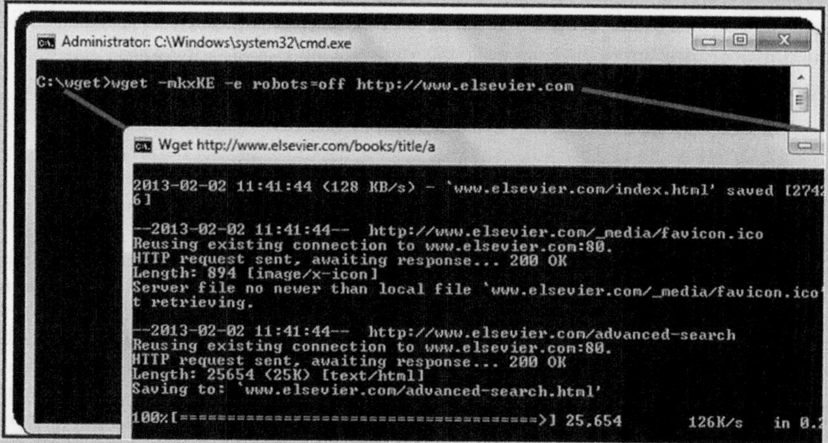

FIGURE 5.5

Wget command line tool for downloading a website.

Authenticating the collected evidence

Authentication of online ESI requires the investigator document the "fingerprint-ing" of the data collected. Investigators in the digital forensic process do this same procedure through hashing. Hashing is taking the data set collected[9] and applying a mathematical algorithm to the data set and getting a numerical value. This numerical value, hash value, or simply hash, is unique to that data set. Several different types of hashing algorithms exist. Most commonly used in the collection and authentication of digital files are the hashing algorithms Message-Digest Algorithm (MD5) and Secure Hash Algorithm (SHA) SHA-1.[10]

INVESTIGATIVE TIP

Hashing Defined

The algorithm creates a numeric representation of the data set and displays it as a 16-character hexadecimal value; i.e., a 128-bit checksum. The odds of two computer files with different contents having the same MD5 hash value is roughly 10 raised to the 38th power or a one followed by 38 zeros (1 in 100,000,000,000,000,000,000,000,000, 000,000,000,000)

Hashing can be accomplished with various tools. A quick search of the Internet will find various free hashing tools the investigator can run against their collected data sets to identify and document their collection process. Most of these tools are fairly simple to use and require the investigator to simply point to tools to the file and the tool will produce a numerical value such as:

60e46aeaed758964902dd7ae99858f03
MD5 hash example

This numerical value will change when as little as a single bit from the origi-nal data set has been altered. This way the receiver of the data can validate that the data has not changed once it is received from the investigator. The receiver can run the same algorithm against the data set and obtain the same hash value. A different value means something was changed.

---

[9]Data sets collected include not only Save As files, website capture, and screen shots but also images taken with digital cameras of screens or digital audio recordings.

[10]Message-DigestAlgorithm (MD5) is an algorithm developed by Professor Ronald L. Rivest of MIT. (Source: Information Security Information—SearchSecurity.com. (n.d.). Retrieved from http://searchsecurity.techtarget.com/definition/MD5). SHA-1 was actually the first algorithm developed in cooperation with the National Institute of Standards and Technology (NIST) under the category called Secure Hash Algorithm (SHA). However, there was a flaw found in this algorithm in 2005. This has lead to numerous improvements in the value, with the most recent being called SHA-3, which was announced on October 2, 2012. (Source: Requirement, L. (n.d.). NIST.gov—Computer Security Division, Computer Security Resource Center. Retrieved from http://csrc.nist.gov.)

Input	Hash function	Hash output	
There	MD5	60e46aeaed758964902dd7ae99858f03	
Their	MD5	ad5faa0fe33faa81ae236749fd8485ac	
They're	MD5	209d716312a73015f73dbc7f14091537	

FIGURE 5.6

Example of hashing differences.

Hashing for authentication is unique because that single bit of data that is changes causes not just a slight variation in differences but a significant change in the value produced. As shown in Figure 5.6, the various spellings of there, their, and they're all produce a very different output. Using this kind of hashing can ensure that the investigator's data when produced during any legal proceeding can be properly validated by any parties reviewing the data and checking the hash value against the one listed in the investigator's report.

INVESTIGATIVE TIP

Common Tools for Documenting Internet Evidence

Commercial Tools
- SnagIt, www.techsmith.com
- Camtasia, www.techsmith.com
- Microsoft Internet Explorer, www.microsoft.com
- WebCase, www.veresoftware.com.

Free Tools
- MWSnap, www.mirekw.com/winfreeware/index.html
- Camtudio, www.camstudio.org/
- HoverSnap, www.snapfiles.com/get/hoversnap.html
- Greenshot, www.getgreenshot.org/
- LightScreen www.lightscreen.sourceforge.net/
- Hash tool, www.digitalvolcano.co.uk
- HTTrack, http://www.httrack.com/
- Quick Hash, http://sourceforge.net/projects/quickhash/
- Wget, http://www.gnu.org/software/wget/
- WinWGet, http://www.cybershade.us/winwget/.

Prior to using any the free applications, read the software's ToS to ensure that you are complying with the software's agreement. Purchase of the software may be required for government or commercial use.

Validation of online evidence collection tools

Tool validation is a standard process in the digital forensics field. Validation is done by comparing a tool's output against a known data set. Within the data set are known files and artifacts that can be used to benchmark the tool's collection and analysis efforts. Tool validation allows the investigator to report their familiarity with their tool's operation and the level of its output accuracy.

However, validating tools in the Internet investigations arena is a horse of a different color. We have learned the data on the Internet is (1) not under the investigator's control and (2) has a high potential to change, making tool validation methods normally conducted by digital forensic personnel impossible for the Internet crime investigator. Live Internet investigation does not lend itself to validation in the same manner as the digital forensic tools. The "known" data set has to be located somewhere within the control of the investigator.

However, all is not lost. Tool validation can still occur with some care and planning. A website can be set up specifically for validation purposes. The website should contain known artifacts that are documented and that can be later identified in the tool's collection process. By doing this the investigator can validate the contents of the collection.

Webcase®

WebCase® is a tool designed by retired law enforcement to assist investigators in the collection of Internet information in a legally defensible and reportable manner. WebCase® was designed specifically to assist the Internet investigator overcome several common problems. These issues include:

- The amount of training time required to make an individual competent and confident enough to investigate crimes occurring online.
- The lack of tools specifically designed for online investigations.
- Proper evidence handling procedures for Internet ESI.
- Secure storage of Internet ESI.
- Undercover identity management.
- Internet-based suspect management.
- Usable and understandable reporting.

The WebCase® user interface (Figure 5.7) is intended to assist the online investigator record and store online investigations. WebCase® provides the investigator with an easy to use format, with an initial case interface to assist the investigator add required data. The case format allows the investigator, new to WebCase®, to add the required initial information needed to properly identify a case, including agency-/company-specific information and the addition of an agency or company logo for the reporting application. The investigator utilizes the evidence collection screen to record and manage online investigative activity. The saved data is hashed and stored in a secured environment within the tool. Reports based on the evidence collected can then be published in HTML and burned to CD/DVD for distribution.

FIGURE 5.7

WebCase® collection interface with Whois.

INVESTIGATIVE TIP

Example Collecting Evidence Using WebCase®

Set up a New Case

- **a.** Complete the case information.
- **b.** Include in the case a complete fictitious undercover identity.
- **c.** Include a fictitious suspect or target.

Collect a Webpage

- **a.** Click the "Collect Evidence" button and proceed to the evidence collection panel.
- **b.** Start the TCP/IP and Keystroke logging.
- **c.** Launch Internet Explorer.
- **d.** Navigate to the page to be collected.
- **e.** Save the Domain registration/geo-location for the page.
- **f.** Archive the target page.
- **g.** Take a thumbnail of the target page.
- **h.** Collect the HTML of the target page.
- **i.** Verify your collections by right clicking on the collected items in the "Collected Items" box.
- **j.** Exit to Investigations Management screen by clicking "Done."
- **k.** Open the case and Click 'Generate an Evidence Report."
- **l.** Click View report.
- **m.** Burn completed report to CD.

Video Record a Website
  a. Set up a new case.
  b. Complete the case information.
  c. Include a fictitious suspect or target.
  d. Click the "Collect Evidence" button and proceed to the evidence collection panel.
  e. Start the TCP/IP and Keystroke logging.
  f. Launch Internet Explorer.
  g. Navigate to the page to be collected.
  h. Save the Domain registration/geo-location for the page.
  i. Click "Start Video/Screen Capture" button.
  j. Click "Record" button to start video evidence collection.
  k. Review website by slowly paging and scrolling through site.
  l. When complete click "Stop" to end recording.
  m. Complete evidence comments and file name.
  n. Click "Done."
  o. Verify evidence collected.
  p. Exit to Investigations Management screen.
  q. Open the case and Click "Generate an Evidence Report."
  r. Click View report.
  s. Copy the report to a separate folder.

Field collection of online ESI

Field collection of online ESI is an often overlooked investigative function. The reason has been that simplified collections processes have often been ignored in lieu of complete digital forensic collections. However, in many situations this might not be practical and resources for the complete forensic image collection may not be possible. Shutting down a live computer may make a threatening instant message irretrievable. Seizing a victim's or witness's computer is very disruptive and a bit heavy handed to retrieve a couple threatening emails or messages from a suspect. For non-cybercrime cases, such as a car vandalism, police do not seize the car nor do they search the victim's home. Why would police seize or search a victim's computer to recover a few bytes of data the compliant is willing to provide? Investigator must also be aware that a complete forensic examination, depending upon an agency's workload, can take several weeks or months. Waiting for this examination may needlessly delay the investigation. So what's the investigator to do? Well, collect the evidence! Internet ESI in the field is most likely going to be found on a victim's or witnesses' computer. The decision to conduct field collection depends on the case, the collection environment, such as an on or off computer, the victim or witness's cooperation and the investigator's ability to properly effect the collection.

Making an online evidence field collection USB device

Using tools on a USB device, on a running Windows computer systems, allows for the investigator to access the live computer with minimal intrusion or changes to the computer system. The most significant change is likely to be a new entry in the Registry,[11] which occurs when an investigator plugs a USB device into the computer. However, turning on a dead system will significantly make more changes to data on the drive than accessing a live system. This is due to the processes involved in the startup of the computer commonly referred to as the "boot" process. The boot process during the Windows startup changes numerous operating system files needed to start the operating system. However, this process does not change the user-created files on the system. From the investigator's point of view they are documenting user accessible files and things observed through their victim's web browser. Investigators must consider the effects of these changes, in view of the case, the victim or witness's cooperation and the investigator's ability to properly effect the collection. For instance, if a victim reports that they have the saved communication and merely need to turn on their computer to retrieve it, than it likely makes sense to turn on the computer and capture the ESI. The investigator knows what he or she needs to retrieve. Contrast this scenario, with a missing child or murder case, where the investigator has no idea what evidence is on the computer or what might be destroyed by turning on the computer in a Windows environment. The file dates and times of its last shutdown might be relevant to the investigation. Booting the system might affect the retrievable operating system data. Again, investigators should consult their respective agency or company policy on digital evidence as well as agency or corporate legal and technical advisers on accessing an on versus off computer.

If the investigator properly sets up a USB device, it can be used to document certain types of information from a victim or suspect's computer. The general type of information to be documented are emails, chats, or other things resident temporarily only on the victim's or witnesses' computer. Using the following tools, the investigator can make a collection USB device capable of documenting ESI on the victim or witnesses' computer. Tools required to build the USB collection device include an USB device, sufficient in size to collect the requisite data and tools necessary to capture ESI in a variety of formats.

To begin, we suggest first using PortableApps to build your USB tool kit. The PortableApps.com Installer (http://portableapps.com/apps/development/portableapps.com_installer) quickly and easily allows the investigator to build a field portable USB collection device. Using PortableApps installer the investigator can install applications that can accomplish functions necessary for good collection processes. We include the following suggestions but the

---

[11]Windows registry is... "a repository for hardware and software configuration information." (Sheldon, 2004, p. 159) It can contain what software has been installed, how recently some programs have been used, user passwords, and what devices have been accessed by the system. For instance, every time a new USB device is plugged into a Windows computer that device will be recorded in the registry. The device's type, including its serial number, will be recorded in the registry.

investigator may find additional valuable tools based on his own training and experiences. Most if not all of these tools are available from portableapps.com. Others can be found at pendriveapps.com. These tool's usefulness is not limited to the field. They can be used in the office for agencies with limited resources. One caveat is in order. Prior to using any of the applications you install, read the software's ToS to ensure that you are complying with the software's agreement. Purchase of the software may be required for government or commercial use.

1. System information for Windows (SIW) portable (http://www.gtopala.com/SIW): This program allows the investigator to collect information on the system that evidence is being collected. SIW produces a report that can be added to the investigator's collection documentation.
2. NotePad2 portable (http://www.flos-freeware.ch/notepad2.html): This application provides the investigator with a small program for note collection or copying, pasting and saving text from programs such as email headers.
3. IrfanView portable (http://www.irfanview.com/IrfanView portable): This tool allows the investigator to view image files.
4. Lightscreen portable (http://lightscreen.sourceforge.net/Lightscreen): This screen capture utility allows the investigator to take screenshots of the victim's or witnesses' computer. This program can be set to save files with the system date and time included in the file name.
5. CamStudio portable (http://sourceforge.net/projects/portableapps/files/CamStudio%20Portable/) allows the investigator to video record anything on the screen related to the investigation on the victim or witnesses' computer. The program can be set to save the files with the system date and time included in the file name. Additionally, it has a time stamp feature, allowing the data and time to be included in the recording.
6. Checksum control portable (http://sourceforge.net/projects/checksumcontrol/): This is an easy to use MD5 hashing tool to allow the investigator to hash the collected evidence.
7. Forensic imager (http://www.accessdata.com/support/product-downloads AccessData): produces a forensic imaging tool that can be run from a thumb drive. The Forensic Tool Kit Imager Lite allows the investigator to make targeted forensic collection of data from a victims/witnesses' hard drive. Included in the collection process is a hash of the data collected.

INVESTIGATIVE TIP

How to Set up and Use PortableApps
1. Start with a new USB thumb drive or one that has been formatted and wiped.
2. Download the PortableApps platform from the website PortableApps.com.
3. Run the downloaded file by double-clicking it.
4. Select the root of your thumb drive as the installation location.
5. Click Install.

6. Upon the completion of the installation navigate to your USB drive through Windows Explorer.
7. Double-click on the program "StartPortableApps.exe."
8. The PortableApps icon will appear in the system tray of the computer.
9. The PortableApps menu will also appear. If the PortableApps menu doesn't appear click the tray icon.
10. In the PortableApps menu click the "Apps" button. To add additional applications click on "Get more Apps" button.
11. An installed application will launch and present a list of the available that you can install.
12. Select the listed PortableApps for inclusion on your thumb drive and download each to your computer.
13. Each App is downloaded through the program and will automatically install onto the thumb drive.
14. Once the installation is complete all the installed applications will appear in PortableApps menu list.
15. Once installation is completed you can take this device to another computer and use all of these programs. Upon plugging in the device to another computer, it may Autorun, and the PortableApps menu will appear. Be patient because before the program will start the system must first recognize the USB device. If Autorun feature is disabled, you will have to repeat steps 6 and 7, noted above. You can also just access the programs directly from the device without using the PortableApps menu (Figure 5.8).

FIGURE 5.8

Recommended PortableApps installed on investigators USB device.

Why use FTK imager?

Many of those reading this, particularly those with a digital forensic background, maybe wondering why include FTK Imager as part of a USB Tool Kit. It is after all a commercial forensic imaging software tool distributed by AccessData Corporation It is a forensic tool designed specifically for the preview of hard drives and making forensic images. Why would an Internet investigator be involved in making forensic images?

The portable version of this tool, FTK Imager Lite, can be used to make a targeted collection of data from a victim/witnesses' computer that will not be generally examined further by digital forensic lab examiners. Its use is generally done to collect specific targeted data on the victims/witnesses' computer that has been identified for the investigator. For example, the victim reports they have been saving all the threatening chat messages to a folder/directory called Threats under My Documents. The option to use this tool depends on the circumstances presented and the need to acquire the evidence in a timely fashion. The investigator should ensure that they have consent to conduct the evidence acquisition and conduct the collection according to the facts know at the time.

FTK Imager Lite is a free download that can be found on AccessData's website at http://accessdata.com/. However, registration is required to download the installation file. Once the file is downloaded double-click on the installer to install the program on your investigative USB device. After you have installed FTK Imager Lite, click on the FTK Icon on the USB device to open FTK Imager. Click "File" in the top tool bar and select "Add Evidence Item," this will open a pop up box. Select the Logical Drive radial button and select "Next." The select "C" drive for the local machine or other logical drive letter where the evidence to be acquired is and click open and then "Finish."

In the tool you will now see on the left side, the drive letter selected. Click on the + sign to open it for viewing. Keep clicking on the + signs to open up the folders of the computer. This view allows you to see the folders and in the right panels you can click and view files. Browse to the folder location of the evidence acquired and in the right pain select the item and right click on the file. Select "Add to Custom Content Image (ADI)." The selected file will appear in the lower left panel "Custom Content Sources." Repeat this for every file or folder to collect. To make a forensic image of the selected items click "Create Image" in the lower right corner of the "Custom Content Sources" pane. Select the "Add" button and complete the case information. Select "Next" and identify the investigators USB drive to send the image to. Add a file name and select finish. Select the "Start" button to begin acquisition of the data. You can verify the files in the image by adding the image as an evidence item. You can then go through the various folders to review the files the image contains.

Field process for using the investigative USB device

The investigator in a field situation can document evidence as the victim or witness presents the information during the investigation on a Windows-based computer. The following is a general process to use during field investigations (The Appendix C also has a sample worksheet which can be used to document information, noting times/dates, tools used, etc.):

1. Obtain written permission from the victim or witness to access their computer and run applications to document the evidence.
2. Note the computer's state, on or off, and document the date and time of the system, as well as the actual date and time.
3. Insert the USB device in the targeted Windows system, and document the time.
4. Start the PortableApps program on the USB device.
5. If not previously done make an evidence folder on the USB device with the case number/name for the investigation.
6. Start the SIW portable application and save the HTML report regarding the system to the evidence folder on the investigative USB device.
7. Start the desired program to document the information on the victims/ witnesses' Windows-based computer.
8. Save the collected system information to the evidence folder on the investigative USB device.
9. Examine your USB drive to make sure you have captured everything and hash the saved files with the PortableApp hashing program.
10. Properly eject the USB device with the evidence. *It is very important that you properly eject the USB device as failure to do so may ruin your device as well as destroy your data.* Find your device under My Computer, right click the device, and select "Eject." You should see a message that it is save to eject. Document when you ejected the tool. (Note: If you are using PortableApps, the menu has a feature to eject the device as well.)
11. Upon returning to the office, the investigator should burn the collected files to CD/DVD for adding to the evidence file.

Collection from Apple Macintosh

Apple Macintosh computers may not have the market share size of Microsoft Windows but they are still a significant area of potential evidence collection. The Internet investigator should be prepared to deal with the potential for collecting evidence from Apple computers.

Apples in the field

The collection from Apple Macintosh computer is not as easily done using the listed methods. There are currently no portable applications designed for the collection and documentation process in the field. However using the same concepts for the Windows machines we can build a portable collection device on a thumb drive for use on a Macintosh computer. The Apple Macintosh OS X user can find the PortableApps to use at FreeSMUG (www.freesmug.org). The following apps can be used by the investigator on newer Apple Macintosh computers. The directions for adding them to a thumb drive can be found on the FreeSMUG website.

1. Portable Gimp http://www.freesmug.org/portableapps:gimp/
   This program allows the investigator to take screenshots of the evidence to be collected.
2. Abiword http://www.freesmug.org/portableapps:abiword/
   This program is a word processor that can allow the investigator to keep notes and copy data on the screen into a text document.
3. Portable VLC OS X http://www.freesmug.org/portableapps:vlc
   This program allows the investigator to take video of the screen of the evidence to be collected.

Apple office collection

Apple computers are becoming regular additions to office networks. Investigators may have at their disposal an Apple computer for conducting their Internet-based investigations. The following tools can be employed by the investigator to aid in his documentation and screen capture of evidence from the Apple Macintosh. Capturing the screen on an Apple Macintosh is as simple as pressing the Command (Apple) key + Shift + 3. Hold each key until you hear the sound of a picture being taken. A new icon on the local desktop will appear called "Picture 1." There are other tools available that can also be added to the computers applications. Here are some tools that can assist the investigator document Internet evidence from their Apple office system:

Free tools

1. Capture Me http://www.chimoosoft.com/products/captureme/
   Capture Me is a free tool that allows the user to save the files in various formats. This is its single biggest advantage over the built-in Apple tools.
2. Jing http://www.techsmith.com/download/jing/
   Jing is a free tool from the makers of Snagit that allows for the capture of screenshots and video on both Mac Windows systems.

Commercial tools

1. LittleSnapper http://www.realmacsoftware.com/littlesnapper/
   LittleSnapper is a commercial tool for taking screenshots and video on Apple computers.
2. Camtasia:Mac http://www.techsmith.com/camtasia.html
   Camtasia:Mac is a tool to video record the screen on Apple computers.
   Table 5.1 is a comparisons of the various collection concepts for each protocol.

INVESTIGATIVE TIP

Make a Quick Video of the Macintosh Screen with a Built-in Tool

Click on Application folder.

Click on open Quick time player.

Click "File" and "New Screen recording."

Press the record button on the Screen Recording box.

Press "Start Record" button.

To stop press the stop button.

File is saved in the video folder on the local machine.

INVESTIGATIVE TIP

I didn't bring my investigative USB device to the scene. What can I do?

There are several features built in to most operating systems that could help you document the evidence on the victim's computer. Here are a few options to aid the investigator.

Windows (all flavors)

Print Screen Function: Open the screen to which you want to take a snap shot and press the Print Screen Key (PrtSc or Print Screen). To save it open an application, on the system such as Paint (found in the accessories) or Word and paste the item into the tool. Select "Save" and save it to the systems desktop for later retrieval.

Windows 7 and 8

Snipping: To access, click Start button. In the search box, type Snipping Tool, and then, in the list of results, click Snipping Tool. Snipping tool will allow you to capture entire screen, open Window, or a specific area. (http://windows.microsoft.com/en-US/windows7/Use-Snipping-Tool-to-capture-screen-shots)

Macintosh

(Source: http://www.applegazette.com/mac/how-to-take-a-screenshot/)

Desktops/Laptops

Screen: Command and Shift-3. Saves it to a file on the desktop.

Area shot: Command-Shift-4, then select an area, and it saves it to a file on the desktop.

iOs devices (i-Pads/i-Phones/iPod Touch)

Screenshot: Push Home Button and Power Button simultaneously. Saves image to Photo Gallery.

Android

Phones (4 or later): (Source: http://www.techlicious.com/how-to/how-to-create-screenshots-on-your-phone-and-computer/)

Hold down volume and power keys at the same time.

Samsung: Hold down Home Button and Power Keys at the same time.

Other

Skitch: This program is frequently already installed on Macintosh and iOs Devices and allows you to take screenshots. It also may be installed on Android and some Windows systems. Look for the pink heart icon. It may also be found in the applications folder. (Source: http://evernote.com/skitch/)

Digital camera: If all else fails take a camera shot of the screen with a digital camera or your cell phone.

Table 5.1 Quick Tool to Protocol Comparison

Tool Option	Protocol	Cons
Hard copy printout Digital camera/video Screenshots or video captures	HTTP (websites) SMTP (email) FTP (file transfer protocol) IM (instant message) P2P (peer to peer) IRC (Internet relay chat)	All: Do not capture hyperlinks or metadata. Depending on the method, can be very time consuming (screenshots vs. video captures). Hard copy printouts can be voluminous and a printer has to be present. Additionally, hard copies must be scanned to be easily transmitted electronically. Digital cameras require proper lighting and/or resolution. Screenshots/video captures require the presence of program or software capability
Save As	HTTP (websites)	Requires one page at time to be saved as a result time consuming to capture entire website. Can't be used to capture other protocols.
Website capture	HTTP (websites)	May not capture all data. Requires additional checking to insure proper data collection. Can't be used to capture other protocols.
Program-specific feature	Program/protocol specific	Investigator must be aware of how feature operates and where to locate data that is created. May still have to use other methods to collect data.

Organizing your online ESI

Internet evidence collection and documentation does not lend itself easily to be put into a document report. The most common way to produce this kind of collected evidence is to simply burn the files to a CD or DVD and turn them over to your supervisor or legal counsel. Organization of the files is important and documenting the location on the disk and reference to the contents helps the user understand the evidence and makes the collected evidence easy to understand.

Folders should include:

Report
 Image files

Video files
Webpages
Other

When saving file a good naming convention for saving the file is the case number, the investigator's name or badge number, the date and the evidence item number. As an example:

10022013_0894_20131001_001
Date-Badge#-Case#-Evidence Item#

A consistent naming convention lets the collecting investigator understand when the evidence was collected and what case the evidence is from. It also helps the reader later identify and differentiate between the evidence items. Included in the folders should be a document containing the hash values for each of the evidence items. The collected items in the folder would look something like:

Case # 10022013

- -----Report
  ---------10022013_0894_20131001_Report.doc
- ----------Image files
  ------------------------10022013_0894_20131001_001
  ------------------------10022013_0894_20131001_002
  ------------------------10022013_0894_20131001_003
  ------------------------10022013_0894_20131001_004
- ----------Video files
  ------------------------10022013_0894_20131001_005
  ------------------------10022013_0894_20131001_006
- ----------Webpages
  ------------------------10022013_0894_20131001_007
- ----------Other
  ------------------------10022013_0894_20131001_008
  ------------------------10022013_0894_20131001_009

The investigative report

The Internet investigations report is no different than any other investigative report. It includes the initial cause for conducting the investigation and the Internet ESI. It also includes the methods used to collect and document the online ESI found. The report should also reflect the hash values of the collected ESI. Included in the report should also be the authority the investigation was conducted and reference any appropriate investigative statute or policy. If the e-investigation was conducted in an undercover capacity the policy and authority for such operations should be noted as well. (Refer to Chapter 10 for further discussion on model policies). Included in this section of the report should be the investigator's undercover identity (if the investigation is complete ensure the report is not for wide dissemination), documentation of any contacts with the target of the investigation and any information regarding the target as identified during the investigation.

INTERNET INVESTIGATIONS REPORT FORMAT

Case Number:_____   Date:_____

Investigator:_____   ID #:_____

Case Type: _____

Victim:_____   Target:_____

Evidence:_____

_____

_____

Evidence collection method: The investigator used the following tools to document the collection of the evidence collected in the Internet during this investigation:

- SnagIt
- WebCase
- Internet Explorer

Targeted Internet Protocols and Identifying Information:

1. Websites:
   a. www.......com
2. IRC:
   a. Username bob1234 on
   b. IRC Server xxxxx
   c. IRC channel "cardz"

Identified Target(s):

1. Bob Smith

Details:
This investigation is about Internet content found at the following URL http://www........com hosted by a hosting service provider XXXXXX which appears to be hosted in the United States.

The domain is registered to:

The content on the URL appears to be....

Conclusion: Brief description of the violations and evidence supporting they occurred.

Making a report with links in Microsoft Word is fairly straight forward. Open a new document in Word and type the report. The references can then be linked simply by highlighting the text to requiring the link. Select the "Insert" tab and then select "Hyperlink" to a webpage or other page within the document. The links can be to the evidence items in a separate folder which can include images taken or video files. Repeat this until you have all the hyperlinks you need. Using HTML to make a similar report is a little more complicated than making links in a Word document.

CONCLUSION

This chapter was designed to provide the reader with a basic understanding of how and why Internet evidence is documented. It also provided some of the basic tools adopted for this purpose or designed intentionally for documenting Internet ESI the investigator might encounter. The tools and methods mentioned in this chapter are designed on the premise that digital evidence on the Internet is still digital evidence and needs to be handled in a manner consistent with the process of traditional digital evidence collection. We encourage that before anyone uses these tools on a real case they try them out and get used to how they function and operate. We also strongly encourage users to take the extra step and validate the tools they intend to use. By doing so, they prepare themselves in case anyone questions their methods or tools used to collect online ESI.

Further reading

AccessData. (n.d.). e-Discovery, Computer Forensics & Cyber Security Software|AccessData. Retrieved from <http://www.accessdata.com/>.

Active Content. 2012. Retrieved from <http://www.techopedia.com/definition/4847/active-content/>.

Abiword—FreeSMUG. (n.d.). *Welcome to online free open source software Mac user group—FreeSMUG*. Retrieved from <http://www.freesmug.org/portableapps:abiword/>.

CamStudio—Free Screen Recording Software. (n.d.). *CamStudio—free screen recording software*. Retrieved from <http://www.camstudio.org/>.

Capture Me—Screen Capture Software for Mac OS X. (n.d.). *Chimoosoft—Freeware and shareware software for Mac OS X*. Retrieved from <http://www.chimoosoft.com/products/captureme/>.

Download Jing, Free Software for Screenshots and Screencasts. (n.d.). *TechSmith—Screen capture and recording software*. Retrieved from <http://www.techsmith.com/download/jing/PortableGimp.app/.

EnCase Forensic—Computer Forensic Data Collection for Digital Evidence Examiners. (n.d.). Retrieved from <http://www.guidancesoftware.com/encase-forensic.htm/>.

Free Portable Software USB Flash Drive Applications|Pendriveapps. (n.d.). *Free portable software USB flash drive applications|pendriveapps.* Retrieved from <http://pendriveapps.com/>.

FreeSMUG. (n.d.). *Welcome to online free open source software Mac user group—FreeSMUG.* Retrieved from <http://www.freesmug.org/portableapps:gimp/>.

Giles, C., Sun, Y., &Council,I. Measuring the web crawler ethics. In: *Proceedings of the international world wide web conference 2010* (*WWW 2010*). pp. 1101–1102. Retrieved from <https://clgiles.ist.psu.edu/pubs/WWW2010-web-crawler-ethics.pdf/>.

Greenshot—A free and open source screenshot tool for productivity. (n.d.). Retrieved from <www.getgreenshot.org/>.

HoverSnap Freeware download and reviews from SnapFiles. Retrieved from <http://www.snapfiles.com/get/hoversnap.html>.

How to Capture Screenshots on Your Phone and Computer—Techlicious. (n.d.). *Home—We make tech simple—Techlicious.* Retrieved from <http://www.techlicious.com/how-to/how-to-create-screenshots-on-your-phone-and-computer/>.

How to Clear Your Browser's Cache (with screenshots)—wikiHow. Retrieved from <http://www.wikihow.com/Clear-Your-Browser's-Cache/>.

How to Clear Your Browser's Cookies (Windows or Mac)—wikiHow. (n.d.). Retrieved from <http://www.wikihow.com/Clear-Your-Browser's-Cookies...>.

How to Take a Screenshot|Apple Gazette. (n.d.). *Apple gazette—Your ultimate guide to thinking differently.* Retrieved from <http://www.applegazette.com/mac/how-to-take-a-screenshot/>.

HTTrack Website Copier—Free Software Offline Browser (GNU GPL). (n.d.). Retrieved from <http://www.httrack.com/>.

Information Security Information- SearchSecurity.com. ((n.d.)). Retrieved from <http://searchsecurity.techtarget.com/definition/MD5/>.

Lightscreen. (n.d.). Retrieved from <http://www.lightscreen.sourceforge.net/>.

Long, J. (2008). *Google hacking for penetration testers.* Burlington, MA: Syngress Pub..

MD5 Hash. (n.d.). Digital Volcano. Retrieved from <www.digitalvolcano.co.uk/>.

Microsoft Corporation. (n.d.). Explorer. Retrieved from <http://www.microsoft.com/>.

Mirek's Free Windows Software. (n.d.). MW Snap. Retrieved from <http://www.mirekw.com/winfreeware/mwsnap.html/>.

Offline Browsing, Stream Downloading and Productivity Software—MetaProducts Systems. (n.d.). Retrieved from <http://metaproducts.com/>.

Osborne, A. Retrieved from <http://www.brainyquote.com/quotes/quotes/a/adamosborn200906.html/>.

PortableApps.com—Portable Software for USB, Portable and Cloud Drives. (n.d.). *PortableApps.com.* Retrieved from <http://portableapps.com/>.

Portable VLC OS X—FreeSMUG. (n.d.). *Welcome to online free open source software Mac user group—FreeSMUG.* Retrieved from <http://www.freesmug.org/portableapps:vlc/>.

Quick Hash GUI|Free Security & Utilities software downloads at SourceForge.net. (n.d.). Retrieved from <http://sourceforge.net/projects/quickhash/>.

Requirement, L. (n.d.). *NIST.gov—Computer security division, computer security resource center.* Retrieved from <http://csrc.nist.gov>.)

Screenshot & Website Capture For Mac—LittleSnapper. (n.d.). *Realmac software—Creative software for Mac &amp iPhone.* Retrieved from <http://www.realmacsoftware.com/littlesnapper/>.

Scrivano, G. (n.d.). GNU Wget. The GNU Operating System. Retrieved from <http://www. gnu.org/software/wget/>.

Sheldon, B. (2004). Forensic Analysis of Windows Systems. In E. Casey (Ed.), *Handbook of computer crime investigation: Forensic tools and technology pp. 133–165*. San Diego, CA: Academic Press.

Singh K., & Schulzrinne, H. (2005). Peer-to-peer Internet telephony using SIP. In: *Proceedings of the international workshop on network and operating systems support for digital audio and video (NOSSDAV '05). ACM*. New York, NY, pp. 63–68. http:// doi.acm.org/10.1145/1065983.1065999.

Skitch|Evernote. (n.d.). *Evernote|Remember everything with Evernote, Skitch and our other great apps*. Retrieved from <http://evernote.com/skitch/>.

Skype. (n.d.). *Free Skype Internet calls and cheap calls to phones online*. Retrieved from <http://skype.com/>.

Software for Computer Forensics, Data Recovery, and IT Security. (n.d.). Retrieved from <http://www.x-ways.net/>.

Software for Screen Recording and Video Editing (n.d.). *TechSmith—Screen capture and recording software*. Retrieved from <http://www.techsmith.com/camtasia.html/>.

Technology Pathways—Computer Forensics, Digital Discovery, Auditing, Incident Response. (n.d.). Retrieved from <http://www.techpathways.com/>.

TechSmith—Screen Capture and Recording Software. (n.d.). Retrieved from <http://www. techsmith.com>.

Tennyson Maxwell Information Systems, Inc.—Downloads. (n.d.). Retrieved from <http:// www.tenmax.com/company/downloads.htm/>.

The Web Robots Pages. Retrieved from <http://www.robotstxt.org/>.

Use Snipping Tool to capture screenshots. (n.d.). *Microsoft windows*. Retrieved from <http://windows.microsoft.com/en-US/windows7/Use-Snipping-Tool-to-capture-screen-shots/>.

Vere Software—Online Evidence Collection & Documentation. (n.d.). Retrieved from <http://www.veresoftware.com/>.

Welcome to online Free Open Source Software Mac User Group—FreeSMUG. (n.d.). Retrieved from <http://www.freesmug.org/>.

Using Online Investigative Tools

6

It's not the tools that you have faith in—tools are just tools. They work, or they don't work. It's people you have faith in or not. Yeah, sure, I'm still optimistic I mean, I get pessimistic sometimes but not for long.
Steve Jobs (1955–2011, American Businessman and founder of Apple)

Tools for the investigator are no different on the Internet than in the real world. Tools allow the investigator to understand and act within the environment and document what he sees within that environment. The tools available for his use are sometimes complicated and require a greater understanding of the tool's effects on the environment. Effectively using a tool will help the investigator not only collect online ESI but possibly ascertain the motivations or intentions behind the person who created the data. The tools and websites described in this chapter will aid the investigator in identifying when, how, and where offenders have added ESI to websites as well as data found ancillary to the offender as recorded by third party websites. This chapter will explore some of the tool options that the Internet investigator has to assist in his evaluation of the Internet and its potential for finding online ESI data that is evidence of criminal or civil violations.

Investigative toolbars

One of the most useful developments in online investigations was the creation of toolbars specific to investigator needs. These toolbars have been designed around the needs of average Internet investigators and provide them with direct access to resources to enable them to quickly further their investigations. Two such examples of these toolbars are *SEARCHinvestigative Community Toolbar* by SEARCH. org and the *Internet Investigators Toolbar* by Vere Software. Both of these toolbars are free, available for download, and can be installed on the investigator's choice of browsers, such as Explorer, Firefox, or Chrome. These toolbars provide various drop-down menus that give access to numerous investigative utilities and sites on the Internet. The SEARCH toolbar can be downloaded at http://searchinvestigative.ourtoolbar.com/. The Vere Software Toolbar can be downloaded from their website at www.veresoftware.com (Figure 6.1).

Vere Software Investigative Toolbar

Of the two, we like Vere Software Investigative Toolbar because along with some of the same basic features of SEARCH's toolbar, it also includes options for searching anonymously and is solely focused on Internet investigations tools. The SEARCH.org tool includes forensic references not usually germane to the Internet investigator. The Vere Software Investigative Toolbar provides resources for assisting in securing the investigator's computer for Internet investigative activities. As such we will focus on navigating the features of Vere Software Investigative Toolbar. This toolbar allows easy access for the investigator directly from the browser to useful sites, such as Internet Protocol (IP) tracing tools and websites to search for people. Investigators can easily track IP addresses or search the various parts of the web. The toolbar also provides WebCase® the *Online Evidence Tool* users, access to Vere Software's online training and forums associated with WebCase®. Downloading this toolbar can be done from the Vere Software website at www.veresoftware.com (Figures 6.1 and 6.2).

From left to right on the toolbar are the available resources for the investigator. The first drop down allows the investigator to access information about the toolbar. The next block gives the investigator quick access to the Bing search engine. The next drop downs are tools that provide the investigators access to the most used websites to assist them in their Internet investigations. We will discuss some of the more common sites. We won't discuss them all because as everything on the web, things change frequently. Some sites change their locations and some sites just disappear.

IP Trace

The IP Trace drop down provides the investigator with access to Internet resources that assist in the investigation and identification of IP addresses. The first resources include tools to identify the domain ownership of IP addresses included ARIN, DNS Stuff, Network Tools, and Central Ops. The next resources

FIGURE 6.1

Snapshot of SEARCH.org toolbar.

FIGURE 6.2

Internet Investigators Toolbar.

are to assist the investigator trace emails and identify the sender of an email. The remaining resources help to identify the geolocation of IP addresses (Figure 6.3).

The web links to ARIN, DNS Stuff, Network Tools, and Central Ops are tools that allow the investigator to determine information about the ownership of domain addresses and IP addresses. Each of the websites provides some of the same basic information such as the Domain registration information. Each site presents other options for identifying additional information about the domain name or IP address. The investigator uses these sites to identify ownership, addresses, and telephone numbers associated with domains and IP addresses. With this information one can begin an investigation into a targeted domain or IP address.

The email tracing features provide the investigator with links to websites to assist in tracing emails. Spamcop is a great resource for identifying how to access email headers on various email programs. The email tracing references allow the investigator to cut and paste the email headers into the website, which parses out the IP addresses and other information in the header. The remaining sites, IPChicken, MaxMind, and InterentFrog, are used to geolocate an IP address. Geolocation is the locating of a physical location associated with the IP address. Now, for the investigator this does not necessarily mean the actual location of the suspect. It often only means the city. In some circumstances it can mean a physical address, but this is generally where the server of an Internet service provider (ISP) is that uses the IP address.

Web Find

The Web Find drop down provides the investigator with access to Internet resources that assist in the investigation and identification of people and businesses on the Internet. The first resources under "Find People" include numerous resources to research people on the Internet. The next section is resources to

FIGURE 6.3

Internet Investigators Toolbar IP Trace drop down.

search social media sites. The following sections include business search resources, sites to search for similar images, and sites to research telephone numbers (Figure 6.4).

The Web Find resources include five general categories of online resources: Find people, Social Networking site searches, Find Business Information, Search Similar Images, and Search Phone Numbers. Each of the categories contains several different resources for the investigator. The Find People category has numerous sites of interest to the investigator. Each site has a variety of information and can individually provide the investigator with a start to identifying additional information on the target. Collecting information from multiple sites can provide a clearer picture of the target, their family members, and even addresses. Some of the sites include:

1. ZabaSearch: This site is a search engine that means it indexes information and does not store it. Zaba search indexes only information on people that is found on the Internet and collated. They collect information from various places on the web, including phone directories, public records, and social networking sites.

2. Pipl: This site searches multiple search engines and produces what they call information from the "Deep web." The site is able to identify large amounts of data and produces it on an easily to follow manner. The identified data is linked to its source and quickly reviewable.

FIGURE 6.4

Internet Investigators Toolbar Web Find drop down.

Website Info

This drop down provides the investigator with access to Internet resources that assist in website investigation and identification. The resources include websites to identify information on specific sites, including archived information found on the Internet about those websites.

The Website Info resources include five general categories of online resources: Find Information on websites, Find Old Webpages, WebServer Information, Safe Surfing Checks, and Translate a website or text. Each of the categories contains several different resources for the investigator. The Find Information on websites has several sites of interest to the investigator to ascertain website information. The Find Old Webpages links provide resources to identify what a webpage looked like in previous iterations. WebServer Information links give the investigator access to several resources to determine the communication between the investigator's browser and the webpage and servers he is connected. Also in this section are resources to help check websites for malware, translate websites and a tool to save videos from websites (Figure 6.5).

Internet service provider

The ISP drop down provides access to one of the most important Investigative resources on the Internet, the SEARCH ISP list. This resource provides a list of the legal contacts for Internet Service Providers and various websites to expedite the service of subpoena, court orders, and search warrants. The ISP list was originally started by James Nerlinger, who still maintains the Computer Forensic Investigators Digest (CFID) list server, as a service to the forensic community. In 2005, Todd G. Shipley, then the Director of the SEARCH High Tech training program, arranged to take over the list to continue its existence as a resource. The High Tech training staff at SEARCH has continued to update the list to provide the digital forensics community with a much needed resource. The information is updated as newer information is identified and shared with SEARCH. Additionally on the site can be found the publically available law enforcement guides for various ISPs and popular social media sites (Figure 6.6).

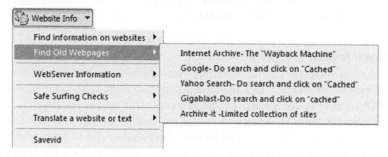

FIGURE 6.5

Internet Investigators Toolbar Website Info drop down.

FIGURE 6.6

ISP drop down—access to SEARCH ISP list.

FIGURE 6.7

Internet Investigators Toolbar Secure drop down.

Secure

The Secure drop down provides access to Internet resources that assist in securing the investigator's computer systems. The resources include websites to help the investigator identify potential security breaches in the computer they use to access the Internet. These tools can assist in determining the need for updating and securing investigative machines (Figure 6.7).

Additional toolbar functions

On the toolbar there are several other functions available to the Internet investigator that may be of interest. This includes a button to identify the current outward facing IP address as recognized by the browser. This allows the investigator to quickly identify what IP address he is using that is exposed to the Internet. Additional buttons include a tool to identify the speed of the Internet connection and one to allow the investigator access to a proxy website to allow temporary hiding capabilities for the investigator. Included in the toolbar is also access to Vere Software's training material, including videos on WebCase® and other documents.

The Internet Investigators Toolkit

Specifically built for the online investigators needs, the *Internet Investigators Toolkit* is a quick desktop application that allows you to obtain information about web ownership and domain information. The Toolkit is a compact Java tool that enables quick assessment, from the online investigator's desktop, of information about websites and other online activities. The tool is free to law enforcement investigators and can be downloaded from the Vere Software website www.veresoftware.com (Figure 6.8; Table 6.1).

All of the tools in the Internet Investigators Toolkit are common utilities found on various websites regularly used to conduct online investigations. Each of these programs has the option to save the results into a document file to allow the recording of the information later in the investigator's report. Let's take a look at each of the tools and what function they serve in the Internet investigation.

Whois

Whois serves the Internet investigator as the basic tool for identifying the domain registration of a website. Domain registration, if legitimate, can provide the investigator with the next step in the identification of a website owner. Commonly we can find tools such as those on the Internet Investigators Toolbar that serve the

FIGURE 6.8

Internet Investigators Toolkit.

Table 6.1 The Internet Investigators Toolkit's features

Whois	Provides domain registration information lookup
MX	Provides mail server records lookup
Netstat	Provides information and statistics about protocols in use, along with current TCP/IP network connections
Ping	Determines whether a specific IP address is accessible. It works by sending a packet to the specified address and waiting for a reply. Ping is used primarily to troubleshoot Internet connections
Resolve	Is a utility that resolves a host URL to an IP address, or an IP address to a server which hosts that IP address
Traceroute	Traces and records the route a packet travels from your computer to an Internet host. It shows how many hops the packet requires to reach the host, and how long each hop takes
TCP/IP	Shows the current configuration of the user's network connections
Stats	Shows certain information about the user's computer, including: • Microsoft Windows version • hard drive label and serial number • active TCP/IP connections • interface lists • IPv4 and 6 routing tables • persistent routes
WebCase	Opens WebCase if the user has a licensed copy installed or takes the user to the Vere Software homepage
About	Provides the tool's version number and the manufacturer's information
Exit	Closes the tool

same function. The domain registration for a website can detail significant information as to the operation of the website and the person or company that owns it. Table 6.2 details the type of information that is found in the domain registration of a website.

MX function

MX serves as a tool to identify the mail server records of an email address. It researches the email address provided and returns the following records as shown in Figure 6.9.

The MX records include three specific pieces of important information about the domain investigated (Table 6.3). They are:

www.veresoftware.com	canonical name = veresoftware.com
veresoftware.com	MX preference = 10, mail exchanger = mailstore1. secureserver.net
veresoftware.com	MX preference = 0, mail exchanger = smtp.secureserver.net

Table 6.2 Domain Registration Explanation

Domain Registration Information	Explanation of the Domain Registration
Registered through: GoDaddy.com, LLC (http://www.godaddy.com)	Internet domain registrar
Domain name: VERESOFTWARE.COM	Domain name
Created on: 21-Feb-07 Expires on: 21-Feb-13 Last updated on: 30-Nov-11	Dates the domain name was registered, when the domain registration expires and when the domain information was last updated
Registrant: Vere Software 4790 Caughlin PKWY #323 Reno, NV 89519 United States	The person or company listed as the registrant along with the registered address
Administrative contact: Shipley, Linda linda@veresoftware.com Vere Software 4790 Caughlin PKWY #323 Reno, NV 89519 United States Tel.: + 1 8884324445; fax: +1 5623723257	The listed administrative contact for the domain along with the administrative contacts address and telephone numbers
Technical contact: WebMaster, Webmaster info@veresoftware.com Vere Software 4790 Caughlin PKWY #323 Reno, NV 89519 United States Tel.: + 1 8884324445; fax: +1 5623723257	The listed technical contact for the domain along with the technical contacts address and telephone numbers
Domain servers in listed order: NS43.DOMAINCONTROL.COM NS44.DOMAINCONTROL.COM	The Domain servers that contain the start of authority (SOA) records for the domain

Netstat

Netstat serves as a tool to identify the real-time connection of IP addresses between two computers. What this means during the Internet investigation is that during chat sessions certain chat program functions allow the user to send documents or pictures between two people communicating through the chat program. When this occurs the two chatters make a direct connection between their computers through their IP addresses. (Chat programs will be further explained in

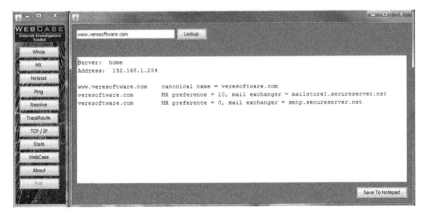

FIGURE 6.9

Internet Investigators Toolkit MX record lookup.

Table 6.3 MX Record Return Explanation

Record Name	Record	Explanation
canonical name =	veresoftware.com	Proper name for address
MX preference =	10	The priority by which the mail agent handling the mail routes the mail to a particular server. Mail is routed to the server with the lowest number
mail exchanger =	mailstore1.secureserver.net	Server location to actually route the mail

Chapter 15.) Netstat is a program when running that can capture this traffic and record the incoming IP address of the target of the investigation (Figure 6.10).

Ping

Ping is utility to identify if a particular IP address is accessible through the Internet (or intranet). Ping sends a series of packets to the specific address and waits to see if there is a reply from the computer behind the IP address. In the networking world, Ping was commonly used to identify problems in a network. Today many servers and computers on the Internet ignore the requests thinking that it might be a hacking attempt (Figure 6.11).

Resolve

Resolve serves as a tool to enter a web address, such as www.veresoftware.com, and identifies the corresponding IP address that represents that URL:

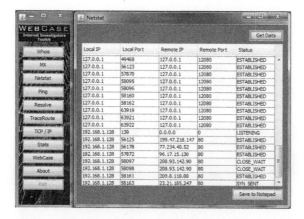

FIGURE 6.10

Example Netstat capture of IP addresses.

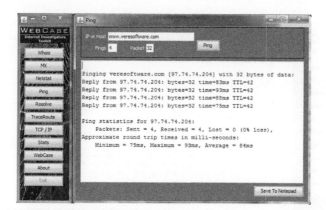

FIGURE 6.11

Example Ping of an IP address.

97.74.74.204. It will also do the reverse, turning an IP address into a URL. This program provides the investigator further information as to the potential owner of an IP address (Figure 6.12).

Traceroute

Traceroute identifies the route a packet travels from the IP address of your computer to another IP address. The Traceroute tool records each hop, or server it goes through, as it travels across the Internet and the time each hop takes to move to the next. This can be informative as to possible paths an email of packet may have travelled, but because of the Internet's make-up it can only provide the path

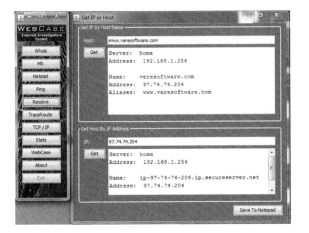

FIGURE 6.12

Example of Resolve function.

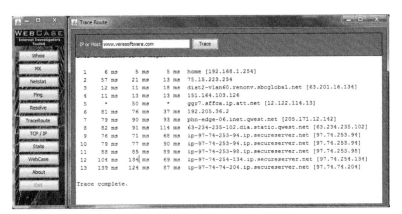

FIGURE 6.13

Example of Traceroute.

at that time the Traceroute was run and not the path a previous packet took, or will take in the future (Figure 6.13).

TCP/IP function

The TCP/IP function identifies the current configuration of the investigators network connections. This includes IPv4 and IPv6 addresses of the local machine, its MAC address, the machines default gateway (the router address of the device they access the Internet through and other connection information) (Figure 6.14).

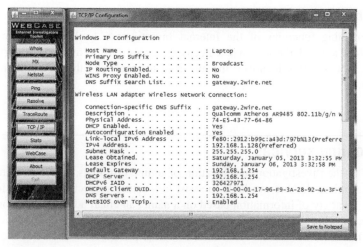

FIGURE 6.14

Example TCP/IP data collection.

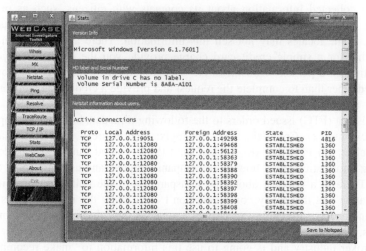

FIGURE 6.15

Example of the Stats function.

Stats function

The Stats tool documents certain information about the computer that it is run on. This includes identifying information about the computer, including the Microsoft Windows version, the hard drive descriptive information as provided through the operating system, active TCP/IP connections, and other routing information (Figure 6.15).

Other buttons

The remaining functions of the Internet Investigators Toolkit are buttons that open WebCase®, if the user has a licensed version on the machine it is running on. The About button identifies the maker of the tools and the Exit button closes the tool.

Paid online services

To add in the investigation and location of online criminals, there are numerous pay for services that are available to assist in locating suspects. These services all provide a variety of information based on a name, an email address, telephone/cell number, or other descriptive personal identifying information. These services are unique to the United States based on the limited privacy laws. Most of the information recorded comes from various purchased databases and then are collated with other databases to form a picture and background of an individual or company. The database information is often purchased from government agencies that sell the collected information about its contacts with citizens, such as property records or marriage records. Of course this is individual to each state and its regulations. Some locales may not sell this information. There are many online services that for a simple credit card charge provide you the information you are requesting on a person or business. No background on the purchaser is normally required other than to complete the request and provide a credit card number.

Be aware that the time this book is being written, the Federal Trade Commission (FTC) issued orders to the following nine data brokerage companies: (1) Acxiom, (2) Corelogic, (3) Datalogix, (4) eBureau, (5) ID Analytics, (6) Intelius, (7) Peekyou, (8) Rapleaf, and (9) Recorded Future. The orders are seeking information about how these companies collect and use data about consumers. There is a concern about the transparency in the collection of consumer information and that many consumers don't even know the information is being sold, and/or have the ability to correct erroneous data that is contained in these records. The FTC is currently in the process of studying privacy practices in the data broker industry and is going to use this information to "make recommendations on whether, and how, the data broker industry could improve its privacy practices" (FTC, 2012).

Much of this increased scrutiny is no doubt due to apparent inaccuracies or incomplete information maintained by some in the data broker industry. The situation is aggregated when erroneous information cannot be corrected or purged easily by consumers. The increased FTC scrutiny will likely increase the quality of these records. It, however, may limit the ability to get access to these records in the future. The caveat for the Internet investigators is to only use records maintained by data broker company as a starting point. For instance, if a data broker record was to reflect an individual had a criminal record, the original source of that information should be sought, such as the court maintaining the conviction information. Relying solely on data broker records without independent inquiry could result in inaccuracies or investigative missteps.

One of the greatest strengths of using large data broker services, such as Lexis-Nexis or TLO, is they frequently have the ability to point out patterns in the data, reflecting relationships between individuals and/or companies, that might be overlooked if using individual investigative resources. This can be very important in tying together parties involved in criminal acts that literally span the Internet and the world.

Lexis-Nexis®

Lexis-Nexis is one of oldest, largest, and respected data brokers. It was originally founded in Ohio in 1973 through the collaborative efforts of a Jerome Rubin and Donald Wilson on behalf of the Mead Corporation (Miller, 2012; UPI, 2006). Initially it was focused on legal documents and journalism, which were made available online, over telephone lines via a dedicated terminal the size of a washing machine (Miller, 2012). As record management digitalization grew so did Lexis-Nexis researching capabilities. The company reports providing its customers with access to billions of searchable documents and records from more than 45,000 legal, news, and business sources (LexisNexis, 2013). Additionally, they note they have a "...comprehensive collection of over 36 billion public records for comprehensive information on individuals and businesses—including names, addresses, places of employment, cellular and unpublished phone numbers, licenses, property records, and much more" (LexisNexis, 2013).

Lexis-Nexis provides a variety of online investigative products, including those targeted to serve law firms, corporate legal, government, corporations, and the media. There are two pricing options, transactional and flat rate. Transactional pricing falls under two plans, hourly and per search, both of which operate as "pay as you go." Flat rate pricing has two plans, Volume Bonus and Authorized User. Each of these flat rate plans has pricing based on a monthly fixed commitment usage in exchange for discounted rates (LexisNexis Pricing Plans, 2013).

TLO®

TLO® was founded in 2009 by Hank Asher, an innovative and colorful technical entrepreneur of over 25 years. TLO was not Asher's first entry into the database brokerage business. He had developed Database Technologies, which he sold in 1999 and later Seisint, which he sold to Lexis-Nexis, in 2006. Asher named TLO®, which stands for "The Last One", as an indication that it would be his last business venture, which it was as he died in 2013. At the time of his death, Asher was reportedly the largest financial donor in the history of the National Center for Missing and Exploited Children and provided TLO® child protection software at no charge to law enforcement in 40 countries (Gale, 2013).

TLO® notes there are "no sign-up fees, no monthly minimums, no long-term contracts required." It also has two fee structures, either flat rate or transactional structure (TLO®—General Pricing, 2013). TLO® provides the ability to search for information on individuals or businesses. Search reports include the following:

- Individuals: Names, Aliases, and SSNs; Bankruptcies, Foreclosures, Liens, Judgments, and Criminal History; Current and Historical Addresses; Phone Numbers including Listed and Unlisted Landlines, Cell Phones, and Utilities Data; Relatives, Neighbors and Associates; Assets including Property and Vehicles; Licenses including Professional, Driver's, and Email addresses and Social Networks.
- Businesses: Current and Previous Employees, Officers, and Directors; Assets Bankruptcies, Liens, and Judgments; UCC Filings; Current and Historical Phones, Addresses, and DBAs; Branches, Subsidiaries, Parent Companies, and Headquarters (TLO® People Searches & Business Searches, 2013).

CONCLUSION

This chapter was designed to provide the reader with a basic understanding of some of the tools available to the Internet investigator for identifying and recording evidence found on the Internet during an investigation. Discussed were basic tools and resources the investigator can employ to assist during an investigation. As with any tools employed during Internet investigations, the investigator should become familiar with the concepts and output of the tools prior to use. Process and tool validation are also important and should be conducted before employing during real investigations.

Further reading

FTC to Study Data Broker Industry's Collection and Use of Consumer Data. (2012, December 18). *Federal Trade Commission.* Retrieved from <http://www.ftc.gov/opa/2012/12/databrokers.shtm>.

Gale, K. (2013). TLO's Hank Asher: A one of a kind technology pioneer, dead at 61. *South Florida Business Journal.* Retrieved from <http://www.bizjournals.com/southflorida/blog/2013/01/tlos-hank-asher-a-one-of-a-kind.html?page=all/>

Internet Investigators Toolbar. (2013). *Vere Software.* Retrieved from <http://www.veresoftware.ourtoolbar.com/>.

LexisNexis. (2013). Public record search tool, LexisNexis. *Business solutions & software for legal, education and government.* Retrieved from <http://www.lexisnexis.com/en-us/products/public-records.page/>.

LexisNexis Pricing Plans. (2013). *Business solutions & software for legal, education and government.* LexisNexis. Retrieved from <http://www.lexisnexis.com/gsa/76/plans.asp/>.

Miller, S. (2012). For future reference, a pioneer in online reading. *Wall Street Journal*. Retrieved from <http://online.wsj.com/article/SB10001424052970203721 704577157211501855648.html?KEYWORDS=lexisnexis/>

Request for Comments: 5321 Simple Mail Transfer Protocol. Retrieved from <http://tools. ietf.org/html/rfc5321/>.

SEARCH. (2013). *SEARCHinvestigative toolbar download*. Retrieved from <http:// searchinvestigative.ourtoolbar.com/>.

TLO®—General Pricing. (2013). *Investigative research & risk management tools—TLO®*. Retrieved February 7, 2013, from <http://www.tlo.com/general_pricing.html/>.

TLO® People Searches & Business Searches (2013). *Investigative research & risk management tools—TLO®*. Retrieved from <http://www.tlo.com/reports.html/>.

UPI (2006). *Lexis-Nexis founder Don Wilson dies*. Retrieved from United Press International.

Vere Software—Online Evidence Collection & Documentation. (2013). *Vere Software Internet Investigator's Toolbar*. Retrieved from <http://veresoftware.com/>.

Online Digital Officer Safety

7

Man is a tool-using animal. Without tools he is nothing, with tools he is all.
Thomas Carlyle (Scottish Philosopher, 1795−1881)

Digital officer safety

Conducting Internet investigations is not without computer security problems. Anyone going online should take basic precautions to prevent the problems associated with viruses, spyware, and/or other malware (Figure 7.1). This chapter will not deal with undercover situations which will be discussed at length in Chapter 10. Instead, it will prepare the new investigator with the various tools needed to ensure successful investigations by limiting exposure to Internet dangers.

All products mentioned in this chapter are property of their respective companies. This is not an exhaustive list of potential software applications available in each category, but merely suggestions for the investigator who is new to online investigations. We have found the noted products useful in safeguarding your investigative computer from compromise by either a virus or other malware.

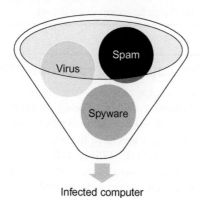

FIGURE 7.1

Infected computer.

The intent of this chapter is to provide the investigator with some consideration for the various protective utilities available. Obviously, tool installation will depend on the investigator's administrative control over the operating system used for online investigations. Many government-owned computers require the user to obtain permission to load any additional software onto an agency-owned system and require administrative access to do so. In most cases, an agency's IT department will be protecting their system and the attached computers will have many of these same application types. These suggestions are for the investigative computer not generally attached to an agency's network or behind existing firewalls. The online investigator needs to be aware of the potential Internet threats in order to help protect against data leakage, loss, and potential system compromise. The online threats to an investigator continue to be those commonly reported, such as viruses, malware, and other malicious code and external attempts to access your computers. Each of the thousands of threat types can be protected against if the investigator understands the requirements and the tools to do so. It is important for the investigator to protect his system to keep viruses and other threats from spreading to other agency-controlled systems. It is also important to protect the validity of the investigation conducted and ensure that any Internet electronically stored information ultimately collected is protected from these potential threats .

INVESTIGATIVE TIP

Software Installation

Before you download any software to your computer, be sure to read the instructions. Additionally, make sure that any software installed is compatible with the system's version of the Windows operating system. Some software may not be compatible with older Windows versions. Also, be aware some software calls back to its owners' or company's website. Many applications have "update" functions that call "home." The investigative computer user may not want to allow these functions to occur depending on the software package used. However, some investigative tools may not function correctly if blocked by the user. Finally, be aware of copyright restrictions. For instance, some "free" protective applications are only for personal use and a license must be purchased for commercial purposes.

Online investigative computer protection process

Protecting your investigative computer is a continuing process that requires constant attention. Generally, government and corporate systems are protected by an Information Security section that has mandates to protect the network from intrusion. Federal agencies and certain contractors have to comply with the Federal Information Security Management Act of 2002 (FISM) (OBM, 2010). This United State legislation ... "defines a comprehensive framework to protect government information, operations and assets against natural or man-made threats" (Rouse, 2011). The US Department of Homeland Security ... "exercises primary responsibility within the executive branch for the operational aspects of Federal agency cybersecurity with respect to the Federal information systems that fall within FISMA" (FISMA, 2013).

In general, FISMA does not exempt the undercover use of computers or the investigative needs of investigators (OBM, 2010). A federal agency's consideration of this chapter's recommendations needs to take FISMA into account.

Security protocols may include certain restrictive functions that can prevent the Internet investigator from successfully accessing areas on the World Wide Web or other protocols to conduct required research and investigations. This is obviously a necessary function within large-networked environments. The Internet investigator may be required to have a machine or machines that are outside of the organizational network to prevent any contamination of the network through accessing websites. These machines would also allow the accessing of Internet protocols such as IRC, P2P, or newsgroups that would normally not be allowed in a networked environment. Legislative mandates and organization policy will dictate the approach the Internet investigator takes in this regard. Setting up the investigative computer will be of course also depend on its purpose. The investigator should prepare their computer with the tools required for the investigation. Having additional ports[1] open that are unnecessary for the investigation's purpose may put the computer at risk.

Additionally, separate machines for accessing the Internet along with a separately purchased Internet access account may be required. This provides the Internet investigator the ability to have access to IP addresses that do not return to the organization. This prevents anyone that does research on the investigator's IP addresses from immediately being able to identify their organization. Purchase of such "clean" accounts should not be done with a credit card that comes back immediately to the organization either. There could be a possibility that the organization's information is tied to the account or the IP address if a static IP is used.

> **INVESTIGATIVE TIP**
> **Exposing Agency Credit Card**
> You might say that this could never occur. While teaching an online investigations course to a state agency that won't be named, an instructor ran the IP address obtained through an IP lookup for the public facing IP address in the class. Not thinking anything about doing this because it was a classroom setting, a look of shock came over the host's face. On the break, he approached the instructor and advised that Internet account being used in the class was their undercover account. The static IP address when run came back to the state agency. They had used a government credit card to obtain the account and the Internet Service Provider added agency identifying information to the Domain registration.

The question that is bound to be raised by many of you is which operating system should an investigator use for their investigative machine. Specifically, is a Windows-based system, a Linux or a Macintosh system more secure? There are more viruses and other malware out there that target Windows-based systems. However, Macintosh systems also can be attacked by malware and this trend is

---

[1] A Port is a "logical connection place" specifically referring to the Internet protocol TCP/IP.

growing. Linux is not generally a system used by new users. Windows machines have a larger share of the market, including among government agencies. As a result, more folks are accustom to their use. Additionally, vendors, aware of this larger market share, provide more programs, including those that can be used for investigative purposes, for Windows-based systems. As such, the question becomes not only which system is more secure but which system can be made secure and provide more options for the online investigator. In the end, both operating systems can be attacked. We are providing procedures that may seem to have a Window's bias. In reality, these protective measures should be employed regardless of which operating system an individual or agency decides is the best investigative option and value for them.

The process of protecting your online activities will depend on your current computer configuration and the protection you already have employed. We can break the process down into two main categories and then into subsections of each of the two main sections. These two main sections include basic preparation and protection of the investigative computer and continuing security maintenance for keeping the investigative computer secure. The following are the steps for each:

1. Basic preparation and protection
   - Firewall installation and updates
   - Antivirus program installation and updates
   - Spyware detection software installation and updates
   - Installation of browsers and browser updates
   - Blocking cookies
   - Configuring the system's operating system and making sure it is up to date
   - Preparing system backups.
2. Continuing security maintenance
   - The potential for using encryption
   - Operating system updates
   - Browser updates
   - Software updates, tools, system, antivirus, anti-spyware programs, etc
   - Keeping the system clean
   - Testing the security of the system
   - Regular or programmed backups. (See figure 7.2).

Basic investigative computer protection

Protecting the investigative computer is sometimes overlooked or not given the required attention. An investigator's priority can be to get online, collect the evidence, research the bad guy, and solve the crime. However, not doing the basics in protecting one's self from Internet dangers is no different than a policeman going to work without a bullet resistant vest and gun. The following sections are intended to outline some basic procedural steps in securing the investigator's computer.

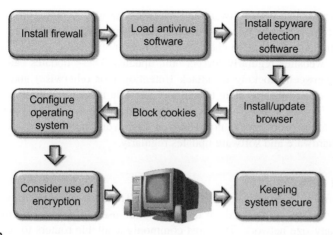

FIGURE 7.2

Online investigative computer protection process.

Firewall installation

One of the most important aspects of controlling, wanted or unwanted, traffic to and from your computer is through a firewall's use. The Information Assurance Technology Analysis Center defines a firewall as:

> ... *"is an application (or set of applications) that create a barrier between two domains, in whatever way 'domain' is defined (i.e., physical domain, logical domain, virtual domain). All firewalls enforce an ingress control policy that is based, at least in part, on traffic filtering. Many firewalls provide other security features, but these are not necessary for an application(s) to be deemed a firewall. In all cases, the purpose of the firewall is to protect entities in one domain from threats originating in another domain"* (pg. 6).

Firewalls can be either software or hardware and provide a barrier between computers or networks and untrusted areas, such as the Internet. Firewalls can also be set up between networks inside an organization, creating an additional barrier between sensitive information and the rest of the organization's network. Firewalls operate as gatekeepers, allowing only approved communication to occur with the protected area. As gatekeepers, they can prohibit communication with predetermined malicious websites or blacklisted URL. Additionally, they can check packet traffic for malicious code or activity and stop it from reaching the protected area. They also operate to prevent communication from occurring from inside protected areas that should not be happening, such as the transmission of confidential data or communication being attempted beyond approved protocols. If you do not install firewalls, your system may be compromised by viruses or other attacks and cease to function properly. Firewalls are therefore clearly an essential tool in controlling what happens to your computer while conducting online investigations.

You should have both software and hardware firewalls running in place. They protect against different things and each has their strengths/weaknesses. When setting them up, make sure to check the box to be notified for updates; otherwise, check their websites regularly for periodic updates. These updates can mean the difference between blocking an attack (intentional or otherwise) and having to restore to a clean machine state to halt any possible intrusion. Often the software programs will alert when a new version is available, but don't rely on the vendor's tool to provide update notifications. Plan your investigative schedule to check for hardware and software updates regularly.

Hardware firewalls

Hardware firewalls come in a variety of types. There are commercially available systems that can cost thousands of dollars and are used by network administrators to control any size network. The most commonly available routers for general use are the types that connect to the average Small Office/Home Office (SOHO) network. They are small, easily configurable routers which contain firmware that allow for simple user configuration. They are specifically intended for SOHO use with DSL or cable modem connections. Most have a wireless capability installed as a feature on the router which allows the use of a laptop, or other device, anywhere within the range of the wireless router. Range from which a device can connect through the wireless function depends greatly on the make and model of the firewall. Routers also allow the investigator to distribute their broadband Internet connection between multiple computers. Putting together a SOHO network allows your investigative team to back up computer's files on networked computers or storage devices in case an infected machine needs to be restored. Additionally, routers often have features that can be of potential use to the online investigator such as logging (Figure 7.3).

The logging feature can assist the investigator in the identification of attempted, or successful, intrusions into their investigative system or network. The logs can also identify when investigative systems accessed the Internet and potentially where on the Internet the systems went. Each router and its configuration are different. Be sure to read the manufacturers' manual to identify individual device features. At a minimum, the following common steps should be considered for router security:

1. Enable encryption: Current SOHO routers generally have Wired Equivelent Privacy (WEP) (an older hackable encryption system), Wi-Fi Protected Access (WPA) preferable, or WPA2 encryption. Ensure you turn on the encryption and use a strong password/passkey; otherwise, anyone with a wireless card could connect to your wireless access. If available, choose WPA-PSK (pre-shared key) and use a strong password/key.
2. Change the service set identifier (SSID)/disable broadcast: If you enable the wireless function, the default SSID (or wireless name for your access point) for your router needs to be changed to something unique to your system and

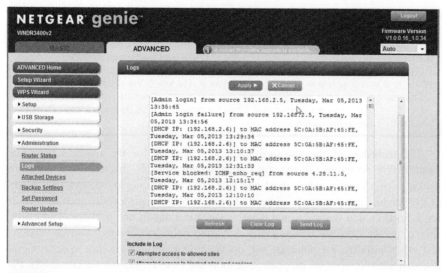

FIGURE 7.3

Example of router log.

does not identify the organization. The default SSID name makes it easier for hackers to identify and exploit your system. Disable the SSID broadcast so it cannot be seen. This will make your system stealthier and harder to discover. Simply turning off this function can prevent attack issues from the wireless feature.

3. Remote management: Turn off remote management. Sometimes called Wide Area Network (WAN) Management. This feature lets you change the router's settings from the Internet. It's an excessive risk and one that does not need to be taken.

4. Change the access password to your router: The default password for your router can probably be found on the Internet. Select a strong password of at least eight characters, using a combination of letters, numbers, and symbols. The password selected should not be a word easily found in the dictionary.

5. Disable Universal Plug and Play on the router.

6. Media Access Control (MAC): A good security option is MAC addressing. This ties hardware device addresses for each computer to a specific network subnet address (as assigned by your router) associated with your machine in order to validate the devices. It prevents unauthorized access to your network by unknown hardware.

7. Ping: Uncheck any options that allow the router to respond to a ping command from the Internet. No need to let anyone know your router is online.

> ## DEFAULT PASSWORDS
>
> Most hackers know the default passwords for commonly sold routers and it has become a known exploit. Those that don't know them can find them on websites, such as Routerpasswords.com and just look them up. A strong password is at least 8–12 characters, including letters, numbers, and symbols. The longer the password the better! Do not use words found in the dictionary or common names. These can make a brute force attack to crack the password successful. Store the password in a safe place in case changes need to be made to the router.

The inclusion of the software mentioned here is for the reader's use. The authors have no interest in the software referenced in this chapter. Many software packages of a similar nature exist and new products are deployed regularly. Many of the vendors provide applications that provide blended protection, such as including a firewall, anti-malware, and data backup functions in one package. The reader should use the software mentioned as a starting point and research current versions and other software for potential use on the investigative computer system. Good research sites for reviews on protective tools are CNET (http://www.cnet.com), PC World (http://www.pcworld.com), and SC Magazine (http://www.scmagazine.com). These sites routinely evaluate, compare, and publish the results on protective software and hardware. Be careful with "free" versions of anything. Most of them come with some adware or tracking software which could expose an investigator.

Software firewalls

The Windows operating systems since Windows XP SP2 (Service Pack 2) have each come with a built-in software firewall. If you use them, ensure that you have the latest version and updates installed. There are also many commercial software firewalls that offer different features and functionality than the Windows firewall. Often the use of something other than the Windows firewall is a matter of preference. If you use another commercial firewall, be sure to check its compatibility with Windows firewall. The Windows firewall may need to be turned off to allow the proper operation of the added firewall. Often the Windows operating systems do

> ## INVESTIGATIVE TIPS
> **Commonly Used Software Firewalls For Stand Alone or SOHO**
> *Freeware Versions:*
> Zone Alarm, http://www.zonelabs.com
> Comodo Firewall, http://www.comodo.com
> Outpost Free Security Suite, http://free.agnitum.com/
>
> *Combination of Firewall and Antivirus Programs:*
> Bitdefender, http://www.bitdefender.com
> Kapersky, http://usa.kaspersky.com
> Norton, http://www.symantec.com
> Trend Micro, http://trendmicro.com

not operate well when two software firewalls, or antivirus programs, are running at the same time. Be sure to disable the Windows firewall before loading any other firewall to prevent any conflict between the software firewalls. Firewalls should obviously be configured to prevent malicious intrusion into the investigative system. However, they should not be set so restrictively that individuals can't access certain sites, such as social networking sites, that may be needed for investigative purposes.

Malware protection

Protecting your investigative computer from malware is another required basic step toward protecting your Internet investigations systems. A running antivirus application will help to prevent viruses and other potential attacks from compromising the investigator's equipment and evidence collected. Antivirus application manufacturers provide products that assist the user in the prevention of computer virus infections. Generally, these products involve two techniques for detecting virus. The first and most prevalent technique uses antivirus signatures, which are ... "a string of characters or numbers that makes up the signature that anti-virus programs are designed to detect. One signature may contain several virus signatures, which are algorithms or hashes that uniquely identify a specific virus" (Janssen, 2013). Antivirus software searches for these signatures on the hard drive and removable media (including the boot sectors of the disks) and Random Access Memory. If it finds a virus signature, it quarantines the file, with the anticipation of removing it from the system. The application vendor updates their virus signature database, which their software periodically checks for updates. The pitfall to this detection method is its vulnerability to a "zero-day threat." For instance, a newly created virus's signature takes time to be discovered and uploaded to the database. If the signature is not in the database, the antivirus application will not identify the virus if its only detection is through signatures.

Another method is heuristic analysis. In this approach, the antivirus software allows a suspected program to run in a controlled environment on the system before allowing it run on the user's system (see Investigative Tips, Virtual Machines and Sandboxes in this chapter). If the suspected program performs any functions that are associated with malware, the antivirus application stops the program and notifies the user (Security News, 2013). The problem with this technique is it can lead to false positives. Because of these issues, many vendors have applications that blend the two approaches together.

INVESTIGATIVE TIP

Possible Conflicts of Antivirus Software

Beware that a common problem with virus applications is their incompatibility with each other. Installing multiple virus applications on the same computer can cause unexpected problems. Before installing any new virus program, uninstall any existing program first so that there is no conflict between the programs.

Be sure to update the programs (and their virus definitions) periodically. Setting the program to check for updates that you can manually install is a good idea. Set up a policy within the investigative team environment about when to do full system scans; otherwise, the programs may not provide you with the complete protection they can offer. Some of the programs require a system reboot and can run the antivirus program for hours to ensure a hard drive is virus clean. This is best down at night so as not to impact investigations. It is not recommended that these tools do automatic update installations. This prevents an update from forcing a reboot during the middle of an investigation. During set up of the software, ensure to select *not* to update automatically.

INVESTIGATIVE TIPS

Commonly Used Antivirus Software:

Avast (www.avast.com): This program updates frequently, sometimes 2–3 times a day when a lot of changed viruses are going around. It also automatically updates itself multiple times a day.

AVG (www.grisoft.com): AVG updates more often than most commercial virus programs but is an effective antivirus program.

Bitdefender (www.bitdefender.com): One of their products not only has anti-malware features but also includes a firewall to monitor Internet and Wi-Fi connections.

Norton Antivirus (www.symantec.com): Symantec, maker of Norton Antivirus, is a major player in the antivirus community. Their product has been a standard for computer users for many years.

McAfee VirusScan (www.mcafee.com): McAfee is another mainstay in the antivirus community.

LavaSoft (www.lavasoftusa.com): Lavasoft made the original Adware removal program and has branched out into general antivirus support.

Malwarebytes (www.malwarebytes.org): Another popular malware protection software.

Spyware protection

Spyware has become one of the most pervasive Internet threats and has become a common method to attack a computer. The simple act of accessing a website can result in the spyware installation. Besides tracking and reporting back on a user's Internet history, some can capture personal data and login credentials. Some monitoring software, deployed covertly as spyware, can take and transmit screen shots and even activate a user's webcam. Hyppönen (2012) recently described the capabilities of malware, known as Flame, to include keyloggers, screengrabbers, and the ability to turn on the microphone of an infected computer. Spyware therefore represents a serious data leakage threat. Additionally, spyware infestations can slow a computer to a crawl, with numerous pop-up ads, and browser redirects to malicious websites, which further compromise security. Infections can get so bad that sometimes the only recourse is to reformat the hard drive to remove the offending programs.

As with virus protection, you should update the programs/definitions periodically and do full manual scans; otherwise, the programs are as worthless as if they were never installed. Installing and using the listed software will remove most malware and keep a system clean. Most of the listed software offers the same functions. Running them all on the same machine would undoubtedly cause conflicts on the investigative machine. The investigator needs to review the software that best suits their needs and install only the needed tools for the investigation.

INVESTIGATIVE TIPS

Commonly Used Anti-Spyware Programs

Spybot (www.safer-networking.org). A freeware program that helps to protect you from spyware. This program is also available as a portable application at portableapps.com.
SpywareBlaster (http://www.brightfort.com/spywareblaster.html): A freeware program that helps to protect you from spyware.
Microsoft Windows Defender (www.microsoft.com).
Microsoft Security Essentials: It's currently free as long as you validate your Windows operating system with genuine Windows. Defender comes standard on Windows since Vista. It doesn't work with earlier versions of the OS (http://windows.microsoft.com/en-us/windows/security-essentials-download).
McAfee Site Advisor (www.siteadvisor.com): This is a free plug-in program for both IE and Firefox that lets you know if you're on an unsafe site with spyware.
Rootkit Revealer (www.microsoft.com/technet/sysinternals/Security/RootkitRevealer.mspx): This free program from Microsoft scans for a very nasty category of spyware called rootkits. Rootkits are a very stealthy form of spyware written to hide within the operating system.
Webroot (www.webroot.com): Webroot makes a series of security and antivirus products to protect computers.

Installing and updating browsers

A browser is an application that provides a method for users to access and interact with text documents, graphics, and other computer files on the World Wide Web. Three of the most popular browsers are Microsoft's Internet Explorer, Mozilla's Firefox, and Google's Chrome. It is very important to keep the browser updated and when appropriate to move to a more recent version.

Internet Explorer (microsoft.com/downloads): Internet Explorer is the web browser that comes standard with Windows Operating System. The current version of Internet Explorer that is available from Microsoft is version 10. This version is much better at protecting the online user than previous versions.

Firefox (www.mozilla.com/). Firefox is a free, open source Web browser for Windows, Linux, and Mac OS X. It offers customization options and various features including pop-up blocking, tabbed browsing, privacy and security measures. The Firefox user interface is designed to be easily customizable by adding "extensions." Firefox is one of the most popular browsers and has many extensions to expand its functionality.

Chrome (https://www.google.com/intl/en/chrome/browser/): Chrome is a browser produced by Google that is simple and fast. It was recently rated as the

Table 7.1 Useful IE, Firefox, and Chrome Extensions

Extension	Internet Explorer	Firefox	Chrome
WOT http://www.mywot.com/	Yes	Yes	Yes
Fiddler http://www.fiddler2.com/	Yes	Yes	Yes
Dom Inspector https://addons.mozilla.org/en-US/firefox/addon/dom-inspector-6622/		Yes	(Similar tool built in)
DebugBar http://www.debugbar.com/	Yes		
Search Engine Security http://www.zscaler.com/resourcestools.php	Yes	Yes	Yes
Hide My Ass (proxy service) http://www.hidemyass.com/software/proxy-browser-extension/		Yes	Yes
IPv4 to IPv6 Converter http://tejji.com			Yes
Screen Capture (by Google) https://chrome.google.com/webstore/detail/screen-capture-by-google/cpngackimfmofbokmjmljamhdncknpmg?hl = en			Yes
Disconnect https://disconnect.me/			Yes

best overall browsers (Mediati, 2012). It allows for the addition of extensions to add third-party functionality. For the investigator, it also has a built-in "Developer" function that allows the user to easily access the source code of a webpage and view its various parts.

Useful browser-investigative extensions

A browser extension extends the usefulness of a browser. Many companies have developed these add-on software extensions for specific function for the user. A search for "extension" and your browser of choice will provide the investigator with a significant number of options. In Table 7.1, we provide a small list of tools that could be useful to the investigator.

Blocking cookies

The purpose of cookies is to identify website users and prepare customized Web pages when the user returns. A website using cookies may ask the user to complete certain information about themselves or simply record information about their computer and their incoming Internet address. This information is saved in a "cookie," sent through your browser, and then stored on your computer. The next time you go to the same website, your browser will send the cookie previously downloaded to the Web server. This Web server can then use this previous information to present you with custom Web pages, such as "Hello Bob, thanks for returning to our web site".

Cookies really personalize a user's browsing experience. The type of cookies that accomplishes this are called, First-party cookies. These cookies do record your viewing on a particular website. However, they do not follow your browsing beyond that particular website. Some websites will not allow your browser to function properly unless you allow first-party cookies. The problem comes in with what are called "third-party cookies." These cookies are not placed on your computer by the site you are actually visiting. As you explore a website and access different pages, the data on those pages may come from other website servers. These other website servers, which you never actually visited, place their own cookies on your machine. These third-party cookies report back to these other servers your browsing habits, even though you never actually visited them. Third-party cookies can be disabled. To make matters a bit more complicated, cookies can also be set to be either session specifically, which only operate during the browsing sessions, and persistent cookies, which remain after the browsing session ends (Gibson, 2005).

Selecting block all cookies in your browser setting prevents first-party cookies from being placed on your machine, which can adversely affect access to some sites. Browsers can be adjusted to selectively block third-party cookies. Reportedly, Firefox 22 will automatically block third-party cookies (Keizer, 2013). Other browsers require you to make the change yourself. With Internet Explorer, it is not as simple as just going to Tools > Internet Options > Privacy Settings and moving the bar up to most restrictively. Doing so will restrict first-party cookies too. Instead select the Advanced tab. This allows the user to permit first-party cookies but block third-party cookies. Do not select the option enabling session cookies as that will also permit third-party cookies to be installed. Google Chrome is much easier. Select settings and then Privacy. Under Cookies, select "Block third-party cookies and site data". Obviously, these various options can change as browsers are updated. The important thing to understand is to look for options that block third-party cookies (Figure 7.4).

Windows operating systems and application changes
Disable file sharing
File sharing for computers running Microsoft Operating systems allows other computers on a network to access your computer. According to Microsoft's support website, Windows XP computers by default has file sharing enabled. When the file sharing is enabled, anyone with access in the network and proper permissions can access the shared files. If you do enable it to share between two or more computers, be sure to enable tight permission to afford only access by authorized persons. Also make sure you have a strong password. A strong password is at least 8 + characters of random letters, numbers, and symbols. Never open up more folders than you need and *never* share the c:\ (root) drive.

Windows updates
Make sure you have patched all critical Windows exploits. You can check at the following Microsoft website for those updates:

http://www.update.microsoft.com/

FIGURE 7.4

Internet Explorer advanced privacy settings.

Enable automatic checking and manually check often for critical updates.

If you use Microsoft Office, Word, Outlook, or Express here's the link for critical patches:

http://office.microsoft.com/en-us/

INVESTIGATIVE TIPS

Don't Forget Your Mobile Devices

Cooney (2012) recently wrote that the General Accounting Office had found "... the number of variants of malicious software aimed at mobile devices has reportedly risen from about 14,000 to 40,000 or about 185% in less than a year." It should be no surprise that criminals are attacking cell phones and other mobile devices. Investigators therefore need to utilize the same protective measures noted in this chapter for their mobile devices. Keep up with all system and application updates. Insure these devices have strong passwords and the data they contain are fully encrypted. Many of the vendors noted also provide protective utilities, such as antivirus and firewalls for mobile devices. For additional tips for mobile device security, check out Cooney's article at http://www.pcworld.com/article/2010278/10-common-mobile-security-problems-to-attack.html.

Cloning or image the investigator's computer

Cloning a hard drive refers to making a copy of the working system as not only a backup, but as a clean copy that can be used to overwrite the existing system with a clean unaltered or infected system. The technique of cloning the drive is copying the data on the investigators drive to the exact same position on another hard drive or the clone. This is a common technique applied by Information Technology personnel and System Administrators during the general maintenance of computers under their control. This gives the investigator the ability to put a new copy of the system back on the investigative machine if it has been compromised by malware or hackers. Similarly, imaging refers to a process of copying the data on the investigators hard drive but taking that same data the clone makes and placing it into a large file. This file can be stored on another drive with other image copies of the investigator's computer hard drives.

So how does the investigator do this? There are many programs out there to assist the investigator to accomplish this task. In the Investigative Tips Sidebar, Commonly Used Cloning Utilities, we provide several free and commercially available tools to accomplish this task. Each of these tools helps the investigator through a process of copying the investigative computer hard drive either to another hard drive or to an image file.

INVESTIGATIVE TIPS

Commonly Used Cloning Utilities

Free Cloning Tools

    Redo Backup, http://redobackup.org/

    DriveImageXML, http://www.runtime.org/driveimage-xml.htm

    HDCLone, http://www.miray.de/products/sat.hdclone.html#free

Commercial Cloning Tools

    Acronis, http://www.acronis.com/

    XXClone, http://www.xxclone.com/index.htm

    Disk Copy, http://www.easeus.com/disk-copy/

INVESTIGATIVE TIPS

Virtual Machines and Sandboxes

A more advanced method an investigator might consider to safeguard their computers when conducting Internet investigations is the use of virtual machines or tools called sandboxes. Each of these provides a certain level of protection that can prevent intruder access or malicious code from penetrating the investigative system.

1. Virtual machines: A virtual machine allows one computer to act as multiple computers, all sharing the same hardware on an individual computer. The virtual machine is a large software file which implements an operating system. The virtual machine is separate from the system that is the host. This allows it to share the hardware of the host, but not the software. Basically, it is a computer running within a computer. The benefit to the investigator is that if the system is attacked or compromised, the investigator simply turns it off and starts another clean, uninfected system.
2. Sandboxes: The term Sandbox in reference to computers refers to the separation or segregation of running applications within an operating system. When a program that hasn't been approved to run on the system tries to run or install itself, the host computer system makes a "sandbox" to run the program in so as not to allow it to contaminate the entire computer.

    Both of these options are good tools for the Internet investigator to implement in his computer setup process. Each of them takes an additional understanding of computers and software implementation and may be beyond the basic investigator's ability.

Keeping your investigative computer secure
Encryption

Encryption of your working files is a recommended practice for the online investigator. Encryption prevents the unauthorized access of sensitive information. However, investigators new to using encryption should practice with the encryption tool they decide to use before ever using it on real case files. Once encrypted, if you lose the key, you have lost the files. An additional issue is that backups need to be made on a regular basis if encryption is employed. A significant limitation of encryption is not its implementation but the electromechanical devices it is stored on. If an encrypted hard drive fails, the investigator may never get the data back.

INVESTIGATIVE TIPS

Commonly Used Encryption Programs

Commencing with Windows 2000, Windows XP Professional, and Windows Server 2003, there is a built-in security feature allowing users to encrypt individual files or folders, through Encrypting File System. Several Windows flavors, commencing with Windows Vista (Ultimate and Enterprise), allow for full-disk encryption, through Bit-Locker. Additionally, the following programs are available for the investigator interested in using encryption:

TrueCrypt, www.truecrypt.org
    TrueCrypt is a free open source encryption program.
Best Crypt, www.jetico.com
    Best Crypt makes several good products.
PGP, www.pgp.com
    PGP is the standard others compare to when making encryption decisions.

Keeping your system clean

Your operating system needs regular maintenance to keep working at its peak efficiency. The Windows operating system and your browser store many bits of information that over time can affect the computer's functioning. Periodically, purge your browser's Internet cache, history, and cookies. A simple Google search will locate step-by-step cleaning procedures for any particular browser in use.

Windows has also two tools that are very useful for helping to optimize your Windows system. Both tools are located in Start Menu/Accessories/System Tools. There you will find Disk Cleanup and Disk Defragmenter. Both are tools that should be used on a regular basis to maintain the performance of your system.

There are many third-party products to assist you in keeping your system running smoothly. These tools will locate cache, cookies, history, temporary files, etc. and delete it from your computer. Some tools also include "wiping" functions that not only delete the information but also make it impossible to recover.

> **INVESTIGATIVE TIPS**
> **Commonly Used Cleaning Programs**
> CCleaner, http://www.piriform.com/ccleaner
> CCleaner is one of the better all-around Windows cleaning tools. It is updated regularly and new features are added.
> Fix-it™ Utilities, https://www.vcom.com/
> Another good product to help keep your system running.

Testing your security

Now that your computer is secured, it's time to test its defenses. Shields Up!! and Leak Test by Gibson Research Corporation (https://www.grc.com), test your investigative system to determine its security level and how much information it may be leaking. To check how stealthy your machine is on the Internet, go to www.grc.com. Use the Shields Up test to check your investigative system for open ports and other potential security risks. If interested in further information about securing computer systems, the author Steve Gibson's site (www.grc.com/SecurityNow.htm) is a good one to explore and learn about additional things to do in order to secure your computer. Other web locations for testing your system are:

> www.dslreports.com/tools and omicron.hackerwhacker.com/freetools.php.
> Both sites have various tools to test the security of your investigative computer system.

> **INVESTIGATIVE TIPS**
> **Other Protection Measures to Consider**
> You are looking for criminals on the Internet, don't be a victim yourself. It's best to avoid the trap if possible rather than solely depending on antivirus software.
>
> 1. Don't open emails without running a virus scan first.
> 2. Don't download files and execute them. Run a virus scan on the file first.
> 3. Don't click on links within the text of an email or open email attachments. Scan all attachments.
> 4. Be wary of freeware products. Many can contain adware or malware. Virus scan them first.
> 5. Update vulnerable software with the latest security patches (like Adobe Reader and Java Runtime Environment).
> 6. Scan files for viruses.
> 7. Regularly create new restore points to help recover after a possible infection.
> 8. Don't just click a hyperlink. Hover over your mouse over the link and check for consistency between the link and the destination.

> **INVESTIGATIVE TIPS**
> **Lowering Your Online Presence**
> The Internet provides numerous resources for the investigators to find information about their suspects. However, those same resources can also be used by criminals to find out information about us and our loved ones. One step to help limit exposure is not to post

personal information online in the first place. Too many in law enforcement post personal information on social networking media for the world to see. Investigators should periodically log out of their social media profiles. While logged out, they should check their profiles to see how much of their data is publicly available due to lax privacy/security settings. However, one's exposure is not just limited to what an investigator may erroneously post. One investigator found that their local church had posted his name, his wife's name, and their minor children's names and their home address on the church's website. Selling one's home will sometimes result in the realtor posting the owner's name with the property. They are endless examples of where individual's identifying information bleeds onto the Internet. As was indicated in Chapter 6, there are also numerous data brokerage companies collecting, selling, and disseminating personal information. Investigators should therefore routinely run basic Internet searches on themselves to see what online information is readily available that pertains to them. Where information exists, steps can be taken to remove it. Some steps such as contacting the website owner and asking the information be removed can be rather simple. Some companies also provide opt out requests on their websites. Other databases require written requests, sometimes mailed to the company. Even after data is removed, it can return and the process has to be periodically repeated.

CONCLUSION

This chapter has provided the Internet investigator with a guide to securing their investigative computer. The tools references provided here are a guide only and not the absolute software required. The investigator should look to the comments made here as a continuing process. Follow the process and you will help to ensure that you are protected. Don't follow the process and you can be assured that you will be vulnerable. The current crop of malware and virii is indiscriminate in their application. The Internet investigator will always be at risk when going online. However, using the guidance provided in this chapter can assure the investigator will be better prepared to defend against the growing threats presented by investigating crimes on the Internet.

Further reading

Ad-Aware Free Antivirus and Antispyware, Protection from Virus, Spyware & Malware, Top Internet Security for Windows. (n.d.). *Lavasoft*. Retrieved from <http://www.lava-softusa.com/>.

Antispyware, Antivirus, Endpoint Protection & Mobile Security. (n.d.). *Webroot*. Retrieved from <http://www.webroot.com>.

Antivirus Software, Firewall, Spyware Removal, Virus Scan: Computer Security. (n.d.). *ZoneAlarm*. Retrieved from <http://www.zonelabs.com>.

Antivirus Software Internet Security & Cloud Security. (n.d.). *Trend micro USA*. Retrieved from <http://trendmicro.com>.

Avast! Download Free Antivirus Software or Internet Security. (n.d.). *Avast!*. Retrieved from <http://www.avast.com>.

AVG, Antivirus and Internet Security, Virus Protection. (n.d.). *AVG*. Retrieved from <http://www.grisoft.com>.

Backup Software for Data Backup and Disaster Recovery in Windows and Linux. (n.d.). *Acronis*. Retrieved from <http://www.acronis.com>.

Basic Digital Officer Safety. (n.d.). *Vere software*. Retrieved from <www.veresoftware.com>.

Bitdefender Antivirus Software. (n.d.). *Bitdefender antivirus software*. Retrieved from <http://www.bitdefender.com>.

Carlyle T. (n.d.). *BrainyQuote.com*. Retrieved from <http://www.brainyquote.com/quotes/quotes/t/thomascarl399446.html>.

CCleaner—PC Optimization and Cleaning—Free Download. (n.d.). *Piriform*. Retrieved from <http://www.piriform.com/ccleaner>.

Chrome Browser. (n.d.). *Google Chrome browser*. Retrieved from <https://www.google.com/intl/en/chrome/browser/>.

Cogswell, B., & Russinovich, M. (n.d.). *RootkitRevealer. Microsoft Corporation*. Retrieved from <www.microsoft.com/technet/sysinternals/Security/RootkitRevealer.mspx>.

Cooney, M. (2012, September 21). 10 Common mobile security problems to attack. *PC World*. Retrieved from <http://www.pcworld.com/article/2010278/10-common-mobile-security-problems-to-attack.html>.

Default Router Passwords—The Internet's Most Comprehensive Router Password Database. (n.d.). Retrieved from <http://routerpasswords.com/>.

DOM Inspector 2.0.13. (n.d.). *DOM Inspector 2.0.13*. Retrieved from <https://addons.mozilla.org/en-US/firefox/addon/dom-inspector-6622>.

Download Free Firewall Software From Comodo. (n.d.). *Comodo*. Retrieved from <http://www.comodo.com>.

DriveImage XML Backup Software—Data Recovery Product. (n.d.). *Runtime software*. Retrieved from <http://www.runtime.org/driveimage-xml.htm>.

Encryption Software, Symantec. (n.d.). *Symantec*. Retrieved from <http://www.pgp.com>.

Endpoint, Cloud, Mobile & Virtual Security Solutions. (n.d.). *Symantec*. Retrieved from <http://www.symantec.com>.

Federal Information Security Management Act (FISMA). (2013). Retrieved from <www.dhs.gov/federal-information-security-management-act-fisma>.

Fiddler Web Debugger—A Free Web Debugging Tool. (n.d.). *Fiddler web debugger*. Retrieved from <http://www.fiddler2.com>.

Fix-it™ Utilities. (n.d.). *Avanquest*. Retrieved from <https://www.vcom.com>.

Free Hard Disk Copy/Clone Software for PC & Server Hard Drive. (n.d.). *EaseUS*. Retrieved from <http://www.easeus.com/disk-copy>.

Gibson, S. (2005). *Misfortune cookies. Gibson Research Corporation*. Retrieved from <http://www.grc.com/cookies.htm>.

Gibson Research Corporation. (n.d.). Retrieved from <https://www.grc.com>.

Hackwhacker Firewall Test, Security News, Free Security Scan. (n.d.). *Hackwhacker.com*. Retrieved from <http://omicron.hackerwhacker.com/freetools.php>.

Hyppönen, M. (2012, September 4). *Flame is lame? Not so much. SC Magazine*. Retrieved from <http://www.scmagazine.com/flame-is-lame-not-so-much/article/254684>.

Information assurance tools report (7th ed.). (2011). Herndon, Virginia: Information Assurance Technology Analysis Center. Retrieved from <http://iac.dtic.mil/csiac/download/firewalls.pdf>.

Internet Explorer—Microsoft Windows. (n.d.). *Microsoft Windows.* Retrieved from <http://windows.microsoft.com/en-us/internet-explorer/download-ie>.

IP Blacklist Check and Monitor. (n.d.). *Adminkit.net.* Retrieved from <http://www.admin-kit.net/>.

IT Security News and Security Product Reviews. (n.d.). *SC magazine.* Retrieved from <http://www.scmagazine.com>.

Janssen, C. (2013). What is a virus signature?—Definition from techopedia. *Techopedia Information Technology and Business Meet.* Retrieved from <http://www.techopedia.com/definition/4158/virus-signature>.

Jetico. (n.d.). *Jetico software.* Retrieved from <http://www.jetico.com>.

Kaspersky Lab US, Antivirus & Internet Security Protection Software. (n.d.). *Kaspersky lab.* Retrieved from <http://usa.kaspersky.com>.

Keizer, G. (2013). Firefox to auto-block third-party ad cookies by summer. *Computerworld.* Retrieved from <http://www.computerworld.com/s/article/9237105/Firefox_to_auto_block_third_party_ad_cookies_by_summer>.

Malware Bytes. (n.d). Retrieved from <http://www.malwarebytes.org>.

McAfee, Antivirus, Encryption, Firewall, Email Security, Web Security, Risk & Compliance. (n.d.). *McAfee.* Retrieved from <http://www.mcafee.com>.

McAfee SiteAdvisor Software—Website Safety Ratings and Secure Search. (n.d.). *McAfee.* Retrieved from <http://www.siteadvisor.com>.

Mediati, N. (2012, September 19). Web browser showdown: Which windows app is really the best? *PC World.* Retrieved from <http://www.pcworld.com/article/2009768/web-browser-showdown-which-windows-app-is-really-the-best.html>.

Microsoft Security Essentials—Microsoft Windows. (n.d.). *Microsoft Windows.* Retrieved from <http://windows.microsoft.com/en-us/windows/security-essentials-download>.

Microsoft Update. (n.d.). *Microsoft.* Retrieved from <www.update.microsoft.com/windowsupdate>.

Miray Software—HDClone—Hard Disk Copy, Hard Disk Backup, Hard Disk Rescue!. (n.d.). *Miray software.* Retrieved from <http://www.miray.de/products/sat.hdclone.html#free>.

Mozilla Firefox Web Browser—Free Download—mozilla.org. (n.d.). *Mozilla Firefox web browser.* Retrieved from <http://www.mozilla.com>.

OD. (n.d.). *Critical start.* Retrieved from <http://www.criticalstart.com>.

Office of Budget and Management, (OBM) Office of the President, Clarifying cybersecurity responsibilities and activities, M-10-28 (July 6, 2010). Retrieved from <http://www.whitehouse.gov/sites/default/files/omb/assets/memoranda_2010/m10-28.pdf>.

Outpost Security Suite Free—The first Free Complete Internet Security Suite. (n.d.). *Agnitum.* Retrieved from <http://free.agnitum.com>.

PCWorld—News, tips and reviews from the experts on PCs, Windows, and more. (n.d.). *PC World.* Retrieved from <http://www.pcworld.com>.

Product Reviews and Prices, Software Downloads, and Tech News. (n.d.) *CNET.* Retrieved from <http://www.cnet.com>.

Proxy2k. (n.d.). *Company2k.* Retrieved from <https://company2k.net>.

Redo Backup Bare Metal Restore Solution GUI Backup Open Source GPL Recovery. (n.d.). *Redo backup and recovery.* Retrieved from <http://redobackup.org>.

Rouse, M. (2011). What is Federal Information Security Management Act (FISMA)?. Definition from WhatIs.com. Information Security Information, News and Tips—SearchSecurity.com. Retrieved from <http://searchsecurity.techtarget.com/definition/Federal-Information-Security-Management-Act>.

Safe Browsing Tool, WOT (Web of Trust). (n.d.). *WOT (Web of Trust)*. Retrieved from <http://www.mywot.com>.

Security News. (2013). *"Heuristic Virus Definition" PC Tools*. Retrieved from <http://www.pctools.com/security-news/heuristic-virus-definition>.

Security Now. (n.d.). *Gibson Research Corporation*. Retrieved from <http://www.grc.com/SecurityNow.htm>.

Security Solutions for Mobility, Cloud Apps and Social Media. (n.d.). *Zscaler*. Retrieved from <http://zscaler.com>.

Speed Tests and Problem Diagnosis Tools, DSLReports.com, ISP Information. (n.d.). *DSLReports home: Broadband ISP reviews news tools and forums*. Retrieved from <http://www.dslreports.com/tools>.

Spybot—Search & Destroy from Safer-Networking Ltd. (n.d.). Safer-Networking Ltd. Retrieved from <http://www.safer-networking.org>.

SpywareBlaster®, Prevent Spyware and Malware. Free download. (n.d.). *BrightFort*. Retrieved from <http://www.brightfort.com/spywareblaster.html>.

Tactical Panda IT Services—Spoofstick. (n.d.). Tactical panda IT services. Retrieved from <http://www.tacticalpanda.co.uk/spoofstick.html>.

The App Maker, Tejji. (n.d.). *Tejji*. Retrieved from <http://tejji.com>.

The Encrypting File System. (n.d.). *Resources and tools for IT professionals TechNet*. Retrieved from <http://technet.microsoft.com/en-us/library/cc700811.aspx>.

TrueCrypt—Free Open-Source On-The-Fly Disk Encryption Software for Windows 7/Vista/XP, Mac OS X and Linux. (n.d.). *TrueCrypt*. Retrieved from <http://www.true-crypt.org>.

Wilson, D. (n.d.). *How to remove your personal information from Google and the Internet*. Retrieved from <http://www.wilsonsecurityagency.com/Remove%20Your%20Personal%20Information.pdf>.

Windows® Defender from Official Microsoft Download Center. (n.d.). *Microsoft Corporation*. Retrieved March 10, 2013, from <http://www.microsoft.com/en-us/download/details.aspx?id=17>.

XXCLONE, A New Way of Cloning the Windows System Disk. (n.d.). *XXCLONE*. Retrieved from <http://www.xxclone.com/index.htm>.

How to disable simple file sharing and how to set permissions on a shared folder in Windows XP. Retrieved from <http://support.microsoft.com/kb/307874>.

Help protect your files using BitLocker Drive Encryption. (n.d.). *Microsoft Windows*. Retrieved from <http://windows.microsoft.com/en-us/windows-vista/help-protect-your-files-using-bitlocker-drive-encryption>.

What's the difference Between BitLocker Drive Encryption and Encrypting File System?. (n.d.). *Microsoft Windows*. Retrieved from <http://windows.microsoft.com/en-us/windows-vista/whats-the-difference-between-bitlocker-drive-encryption-and-encrypting-file-system>.

Tracing IP Addresses Through the Internet

8

Everybody should want to make sure that we have the cyber tools necessary to investigate cyber crimes, and to be prepared to defend against them and to bring people to justice who commit it.
Janet Reno, Former Attorney General of the United States

Tracing IP addresses

Internet Protocol (IP) addresses provide the basis for online communication, allowing devices to interface and communicate with one another as they are connected to the Internet. As was noted in Chapter 3, IP addresses provide investigators a trail to discover and follow, which hopefully leads to the person(s) responsible for some online malfeasance. In Chapter 5 and 6, we discussed different tools that investigators can use to examine various parts of the Internet, including identifying the owners of domains and IP addresses. In this chapter, we are going to discuss tracing an IP address and the investigative advantages of this process. We have covered the tools to help us trace IP addresses in previous chapters, but here we want to walk through the process of identifying the IP to trace and who is behind that address.

Online tools for tracing an IP address

Tracing IP addresses and domains is a fundamental skill for any Internet investigator. There are many resources available on the Internet to assist in this process. Of primary importance are the entities responsible for the addressing system, namely, the Internet Assigned Number Authority (IANA) and its subordinate bodies the Regional Internet Registries (RIR). In addition to IANA and RIR, there are a multitude of other independent online resources that can assist the investigator in conducting basic IP identification.

IANA and RIR

Starting at the top is IANA. According to their website they are "...responsible for the global coordination of the DNS Root, IP addressing and other Internet protocol resources." What this means to the investigator is that they manage and assign the top level domains, that is, .com, org, mil, edu. (see Table 3.6 for additional examples) and coordinate the IP addresses and their allocation to the RIR. IANA established the RIR to allocate IP address in geographical regions.

The RIR system evolved over time, eventually dividing the world into the following five regions:

1. African Network Information Centre (AfriNIC) for Africa, http://www.afrinic.net/
2. American Registry for Internet Numbers (ARIN) for the United States, Canada, several parts of the Caribbean region, and Antarctica, https://www.arin.net/
3. Asia-Pacific Network Information Centre (APNIC) for Asia, Australia, New Zealand, and neighboring countries, http://www.apnic.net/
4. Latin America and Caribbean Network Information Centre (LACNIC) for Latin America and parts of the Caribbean region, http://www.lacnic.net/en/web/lacnic/inicio
5. Réseaux IP Européens Network Coordination Centre (RIPE NCC) for Europe, Russia, http://http://www.ripe.net/

Each site has a search "Whois" function that allows the investigator to identify IP registration information. IANA and the RIR are the official registrars and owners of the domain records and IP addresses. An investigator wishing to verify the owner of an IP can use the RIR to locate the records.

Internet commercial and freeware tools

There are also many Internet sites to look up IP and Domain registrations. Some provide the basic registration information and other sites combine additional tools that enable the investigator to identify an IP's physical location. The following websites, mentioned in Chapter 6, are easily accessible from the Vere Software Internet Investigators Toolbar, and are important utilities for the investigator:

DNS Stuff (http://www.dnsstuff.com/tools/tools): This website has been around for a number of years. It offers both free and pay options for assisting in IP addresses identification and other online information.
Network-Tools.com (http://network-tools.com): Another website with a simple user interface to assist in IP tracing.
CentralOps.net (http://centralops.net/co/): This is another website that assists with your IP tracing. One of its features, Domain Dossier, does multiple lookups on an IP address or domain.

In some circumstances, the investigator may look up a domain or and IP address with these commercial tools and find the address concealed by the commercial registrar. In these cases, the investigator may need to go to the commercial registrar's site and use the Whois search located there to determine the domain registration records. Each of the mentioned websites presents the domain

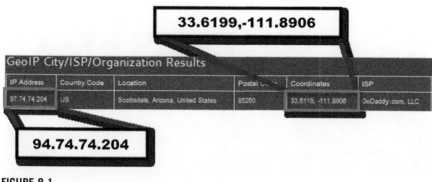

FIGURE 8.1

Maxmind demo search for IP address.

registration information in a slightly different manner and may have additional tools useful to the investigator. Experience with each will provide the investigator with a better understanding of each site's features.

Geolocation of an IP address

Geolocation in general refers to the identification of the real geographical area of an electronic device, such as a cell phone, IP addresses, WiFi, and MAC addresses. Now that being said that does not mean an IP address can be traced directly to a house. Geolocation particularly for IP addresses is not an exact science. Unlike cell phones that can be traced via their GPS coordinates or cell tower triangulation, IP addresses use a common database of address locations maintained by different companies. One of the most commonly used databases is maintained by Maxmind, Inc. which can be found at www.maxmind.com. Maxmind provides a free service to geolocate an IP address to a state or city. Purchasing their services can give the Internet investigator access to a more precise location, up to and including physical addresses. There are other online services that provide geolocation identification of IP addresses such as IP2Location.com. Some investigative tools, such as Vere Software's WebCase, include access to the Maxmind database as a feature of its domain lookup. On Maxmind's website you can use their demo function to identify an IP addresses location. An example of a Maxmind search for the geolocation of IP address 97.74.74.204 is shown in Figure 8.1.

Along with identifying the geolocation of the address as Scottsdale, Arizona, website provides the latitude and longitude based on this location and the Internet Service Provider (ISP) hosting the IP address, in this case GoDaddy.com LLC.

FIGURE 8.2

Bing Maps search for specific latitude and longitude.

TOOLS AND TIPS

Map the IP Address

With the latitude and longitude of an IP address provided through Maxmind, you can enter data into Google Maps, Bing Maps, or any of the online mapping programs to translate those coordinates into a physical location on a map (Figure 8.2).

Using geolocation to identify an IP address may get you close or it may not. What the geolocation will tell you is the identified location of the IP address. The databases get this information from a variety of sources including ISP) and self-reported data. Most often, the Geolocation will give you a general idea of the server location hosting the IP address and not the physical location of anyone committing a crime. However, this information does provide verification of ISP ownership of an IP address, which can further the investigation, including referrals to the appropriate local agency for assistance. Be aware that geolocation can identify an IP address if known, but this address may be to an ISP or could be a Tor exit node (see Chapter 9 for further information on Tor) and not actually related to the target.

Digging deeper into IP tracing—what the DNS tells us

The basics of IP tracing are finding out who owns a domain or who is registered to an IP address. Once that is found out, you contact the ISP for further information (usually through some means of legal service). But what other things can you find out about an IP address online without an attorney? Let's take a look at some of the things available to us that can be traced from a domain or an IP address through the DNS records.

DNS records

The Domain Name System (DNS) is a service on the Internet that translates the Uniform Resource Locators (URLs) or domain names into an IP address. Domain names are alphabetic making them easier to remember. The Internet, however, is based on IP addresses and communicates using that number sequence. The DNS in its simplest form is a big telephone book. Computers use it to look up the location of the server to which the IP address is located. So what other potential information is available to the investigators on the DNS?

Using the online website CentralOps.net, we can identify additional information about a domain. As an example we have used www.veresoftware.com to search under "Domain Dossier" and selected the "DNS records" search. With that search, we are returned with a variety of additional information on the domain and the records contained on the DNS server (Table 8.1).

The "type" of record gives us certain additional information on the domain:

- CNAME stands for "Canonical Name" record:
  CNAME is a type of DNS record that identifies the domain name as an alias of another. This tells the investigator whether or not there are other services running on that domain (such as an FTP or a web server running on different ports) on a single IP address. Each of these services will have its own entry on DNS (such as ftp.veresoftware.com and www. veresoftware.com).
- SOA stands for "start of authority" record:
  This DNS entry specifies authoritative information about a DNS zone (DNS zones may be a single domain or several), including the primary name server, the email of the domain administrator, the domain serial number, and several timers relating to refreshing the zone.

Table 8.1 CentralOps.net DNS Records Search for www.veresoftware.com

Name	Class	Type	Data	
www.veresoftware.com	IN	CNAME	veresoftware.com	
veresoftware.com	IN	SOA	server:	ns43.domaincontrol.com
			email:	dns.jomax.net
			serial:	2007112000
			refresh:	28800
			retry:	7200
			expire:	604800
			minimum ttl:	86400
veresoftware.com	IN	MX	preference:	0
			exchange:	smtp.secureserver.net
veresoftware.com	IN	NS	ns43.domaincontrol.com	
veresoftware.com	IN	NS	ns44.domaincontrol.com	
veresoftware.com	IN	A	97.74.74.204	

- MX stands for "mail exchange" record:
  The DNS record maps the domain researched to the mail exchange servers registered to that domain.
- NS stands for "name server" record:
  This record identifies the authoritative name servers for the domain.
- A stands for "address" record:
  This DNS record identifies the IP address assigned to the domain researched.

So how can that be useful in your investigations? With the DNS records, we can identify the server that provides email service to the domain. This is the MX record. This record can provide us a lead to additional domains used or operated by the domain of interest. The CNAME can give potentially additional services running on an IP address. The NS record can give you further information about the upstream ISP that services the domain being researched.

TOOLS AND TIPS

So How Do We Ultimately Determine IP Address Assignment?

- Search the IP address through a domain identifying tool, such as Network Tools.
- Upon identifying the company that is assigned the IP address, determine the proper legal compulsion method to obtain the records being sought prior to contacting them (see Chapter 4).
- Beware the ISP may attempt to notify the target about your actions without an order from a court stating not to identify the account holder. Additionally, if the ISP believes that the account is being used for criminal activity, they may close the account. If you have an ongoing investigation, this may hinder your ability to track the suspect.
- Use the legal contact information available from the SEARCH.org website, or, click the "ISP" button on the Internet Investigators Toolbar.
- Contact the company that is assigned the IP address in question and obtain records, with appropriate legal procedures. From their records, determine the identity of the person using the IP address at the date and time in question.

Tracing emails

Email is as ubiquitous as any of the IPs we have discussed. Other than the World Wide Web, this is one of the most used tools for communication. It is commonly employed for everything from personal communications to business use. Unfortunately, it is also a favorite tool for threats and harassment by criminals and stalkers. This section will explain the basic parts of an email and how to effectively identify the sender or identify the pieces of the email that can further the investigation through additional follow-up.

We previously discussed the protocol in Chapter 3 that routes email, the Simple Mail Transfer Protocol (SMTP). The email itself has several features that are unique and make identification possible. These features provide initial clues which may not identify a specific person or sender without additional investigative steps. To start email addresses, have the standard familiar format of the username, the @ symbol, the domain name used by the user and the top level domain associated with the domain name. For example:

username@domain (e.g., todd@veresoftware.com)

The email we see in our email program generally shows only the sender, the receiver, and the subject line. As we discussed in Chapter 3, there is a significant amount of data in the unseen headers of the email that gives the investigator important information that can be useful in possibly establishing an email's sender's identity. We know that in general an email travels from a sender's computer to their mail service to recipient's mail service, where it resides on a mail server (computer that stores and delivers mail). Each next time the receiver logs into his or her account, the mail reader retrieves the message to his or PC/workstation. As the email travels through the Internet, from email server to email server, it gathers data from each processing server. Each of these servers gives the investigator an idea of how the email traveled from sender to receiver. In Figure 8.3, we have shown the process of the email traveling through the Internet.

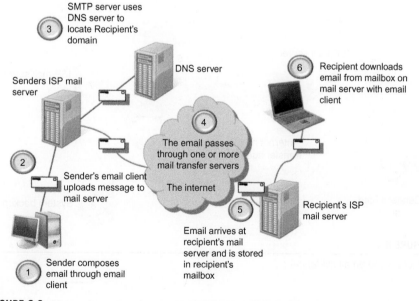

FIGURE 8.3

How email works.

Where is the evidence?

So if we are talking in general about where evidence could be, it could be in numerous places along that path (Figure 8.4). However, that does not mean a copy of the email will exist on each location when you attempt to locate it. Depending on the jurisdiction, records of the email transfer may not be required to be kept by government regulations. In the United States, there are no specific record retention requirements for tracking email. Each service provider sets its own standards for logging information. What we can generally identify are the copies of a previously sent email messages that may be stored at accessible locations. Those accessible locations include:

- The sender's device[1]
- The sender's mail server
- The recipient's mail server
- The recipient's device.

A record of the email transmission (date, time, source, and destination) can reside in these same locations. Accessing these records can be done through the sender's device or through a forensic examination of the device. Before

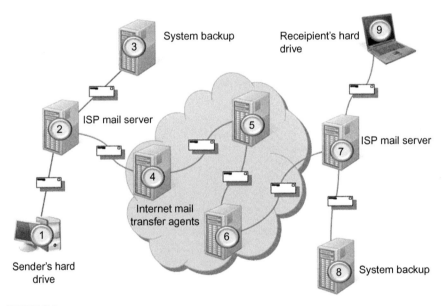

FIGURE 8.4

Where is the email evidence?

---

[1]Devices can be computers, tablets, or cell phones, or anything that can be used to send or receive email.

accessing data, be aware there are different legal requirements in play. Accessing data that resides on the sender's device requires consent or a traditional search warrant. However, in the United States, data that resides on a server requires compliance with the Stored Communications Act (SCA) (see Chapter 4). Of course, accessing any of the records requires the proper legal authority which can include consent, a subpoena, or search warrant. Additionally, depending on the laws in the investigator's country, other legal options for access may be available.

Viewing email headers

To determine the sender of an email, an investigator needs the email's header information. An email header is the information added to the beginning/top of the electronic message. Normally, email clients and web services only show an abbreviated form of the header. Email headers are created by the email servers that process the messages. Adding information depends on the email protocol used. Not every server adds detailed information to the header as it passes through the server. Viewing the email headers is different for each email program or service. In Chapter 4, we discussed using Spamcop from the Internet Investigators Toolbar to identify the specifics of accessing email headers for different email services and tools. From the Spamcop website, we can easily identify how to access full email headers to be reviewed for identifying information.

The information commonly displayed are the abbreviated headers. We normally see in an email:

> From:
> To:
> CC:
> Subject:
> Date:

For the investigator, the identifying information is the "From" line which is the email address the message purportedly came from, the "To" line which is where the message was sent, and the "CC" line is where other email addresses receiving the message are included. Is this information enough to properly trace an email? The answer is it certainly no. There is more information which can be used to effectively identify email movement through the Internet.

The full header provides the investigator with significantly more data with which to determine the veracity of the email as well as its origin. What the full headers can help the investigator identify are:

- Who sent the email
- Which network it originated from
- Which email servers processed it

INVESTIGATIVE TIPS

Accessing Headers in Common Web Mail Services

Google Mail
1. Open the message you want to view the headers.
2. Click the down arrow next to the "Reply" link.
3. Select "Show Original" and a new window will open with the full headers.

Windows Live Mail
1. Right click on the message.
2. Select "View Source".
3. A new window with the full headers and HTML source of the email will open.

Yahoo! Mail
1. Click Actions dropdown.
2. Select "View Full Headers".
3. A new window with the full headers will open.

- Miscellaneous information:
  - Time stamps
  - Email client
  - Encoding information.

The investigator needs to also understand that not all the information in the header is useful to the investigation. Let's take a look at what the typical full email header can contain:

- The originator fields:
- *From:, Sender:, Reply-To:*
- Date:
- Received:
- X-Originating-IP:
- Message-ID:
- X-Mailer:
- X-MIMEOLE:

Headers are comprised of lines of information called header fields. Each field contains a field label, followed by a colon ":" and then the field body. The headers are "generally" layered bottom-to-top. For the investigator this means we start at the bottom of the full header and read up to determine how it traveled through the Internet mail services. The first field is on the bottom and subsequent fields added on top, in the order they are written by the mail server they were transferred through (Figures 8.2 and 8.3). In the full header, there are several header fields we can use to trace emails:

1. Sender's email address.
2. Email server information which includes the Message-ID. The SMTP relay information, which includes the sender's IP address or initial SMTP server's IP address.

3. Common in SMTP servers is the additional information not standard in the protocol. These fields are added to the header by the SMTP server and are unique to the server. They are easily identified as any field starting with an "X". In the SMTP standard, anything beginning with a "X" is nonstandard and has no direct translation in the standard.

A commonly used nonstandard field has been one called "X-Originating-IP". The "X-Originating-IP" has been used by SMTP servers to store the originating IP address of the email's sender. This field can identify the IP address assigned to the sender by their ISP for that session.

Another field of interest is the Message-ID. Every email sent through an SMTP server is assigned a unique ID by the originating SMTP email server. This Message-ID can identify the originating SMTP server from which the investigator can obtain logs (of course this is an issue of timeliness as the server may not retain the records for long periods of time). If the investigator provides this message-ID to the corresponding ISP, it can aid in locating the records needed to identify the sender. For the ISP it is easier, and usually faster, to search email server logs for the Message-ID then to find IP addresses associated with the email. The Message-IDs look very similar to email addresses, for example:

192809895-1238802958-cardhu_decombobulator_blackberry.rim.net-1937758735-@bxe1280.bisx.prod.on.blackberry

The information to the left of the "@" symbol is the unique identifier and the server it came through. The information to the right of the "@" identifies the domain to which the email server assigning the Message-ID belongs.

The Date Field in an email can come from different sources. The date and time can be from the sender's computer, or the date and time can be from the initial email server the message was sent through. These dates and times can possibly determine the sender's general location by time zone if the information comes from their system clock. However, this must be interpreted cautiously, because this depends on the email service used.

Time differences

We mentioned briefly earlier that strict reliance on dates and times stamps should be done at the investigator's peril. Knowing where the time stamp came from is sometimes difficult and should not be totally relied on as coming from the sender. The reason is the investigator will rarely have all the information required to know what email program was used to send the email and the SMTP server settings that passed the email on through the Internet. The sender could employ a "Send Later" feature to throw the receiver off and make them believe the email was written and sent at a time different than when it actually was composed.

Even Microsoft recognizes that differences in time stamps can occur within Outlook. On Office.com, they have the following reference about this fact:

How time stamps appear in messages:

NOTE: You might notice cases where the sent time is after the received time. This delay might be caused by a difference between the system clocks on the sender's computer and on your email server.

Header information translation

Every email header is different and has its own unique identification. In the following tables, we take a look at an email sent from a Yahoo email account to a Google (Gmail) account. We first have to login to and access the receiving Gmail account. Once we open the received email in Gmail, we click on the dropdown arrow on the right side of the email nest to the "reply" arrow. This opens up several options including "Show original". Selecting "Show original" opens the header in another window (Figure 8.5).

Table 8.2 has the complete header we extracted from the email sent to the test Gmail account. Table 8.3 provides a detailed explanation of the header information reflected in Table 8.2. The complete header has several areas of interest to the investigator. We can break the header into five areas of interest:

1. The servers the email passed through
2. Encrypted mail header
3. The traditional To, From, Subject, and Date lines
4. Mail transfer program information
5. Nonstandard information added by servers and email programs

Remember that the email servers stamp the "received" information from the bottom up in the header. In Table 8.4, we break out the raw data in Table 8.2

FIGURE 8.5

Gmail account accessing full headers.

Table 8.2 Example Header from Yahoo Email to Gmail

Delivered-To: testgmailaccount@gmail.com

Received: by 10.49.15.197 with SMTP id z5csp55241qec;
    Sun, 24 Feb 2013 12:24:27 -0800 (PST)

X-Received: by 10.236.162.197 with SMTP id y45mr16233991yhk.110.1361737467542;
    Sun, 24 Feb 2013 12:24:27 -0800 (PST)

Return-Path: <testyahooaccount@yahoo.com>

Received: from nm26.access.bullet.mail.mud.yahoo.com (nm26.access.bullet.mail.mud.
yahoo.com. [66.94.237.91])
    by mx.google.com with ESMTPS id a27si13288213yhn.132.2013.02.24.12.24.27
    (version = TLSv1 cipher = RC4-SHA bits = 128/128);
    Sun, 24 Feb 2013 12:24:27 -0800 (PST)

Received-SPF: neutral (google.com: 66.94.237.91 is neither permitted nor denied by best
guess record for domain of testyahooaccount@yahoo.com) client-ip = 66.94.237.91;

Authentication-Results: mx.google.com;
    spf = neutral (google.com: 66.94.237.91 is neither permitted nor denied by best guess
record for domain of testyahooaccount@yahoo.com) smtp.
mail = testyahooaccount@yahoo.com;
    dkim = pass header.i = @yahoo.com

Received: from [66.94.237.127] by nm26.access.bullet.mail.mud.yahoo.com with
NNFMP; 24 Feb 2013 20:24:26 -0000

Received: from [66.94.237.121] by tm2.access.bullet.mail.mud.yahoo.com with NNFMP;
24 Feb 2013 20:24:26 -0000

Received: from [127.0.0.1] by omp1026.access.mail.mud.yahoo.com with NNFMP; 24
Feb 2013 20:24:26 -0000

X-Yahoo-Newman-Property: ymail-3

X-Yahoo-Newman-Id: 968415.26467.bm@omp1026.access.mail.mud.yahoo.com

Received: (qmail 55713 invoked by uid 60001); 24 Feb 2013 20:24:26 -0000

DKIM-Signature: v = 1; a = rsa-sha256; c = relaxed/relaxed; d = yahoo.com; s = s1024;
t = 1361737466; bh = qwi0 + QrpLlhGpEVETzboOXvvDxVGRXmYMTrUSv0peL8 = ;
h = X-YMail-OSG:Received:X-Rocket-MIMEInfo:X-Mailer:Message-ID:Date:From:Subject:
To:MIME-Version:Content-Type; b = 13CKqrHzBlBA17dE7 + 2T/
HS1QEk0sDAHBlO1NQ1FCNIuDZYYsVFTktrzyHV/3/
QSOeNnk8gLqofZj0 + MBzKzlAG + 4oPUKrYGwqsiF2ufhj/
kRLdORZ + hF + j56lnPV + e1uLUnr4i2iS2Ei3ScK + yRtfKJivjbY76jl2hsdL9jLqk =

DomainKey-Signature:a = rsa-sha1; q = dns; c = nofws;
    s = s1024; d = yahoo.com;   h = X-YMail-OSG:Received:X-Rocket-MIMEInfo:X-
Mailer:Message-ID:Date:From:Subject:To:MIME-Version:Content-Type;b = RiLBl0Box/
DViNyFivNHcESpQunKLGEYtJUG0vhpW1F18nXcLSc4Y4oNmF/
Ko4l0 + oxOnOeOQAHXa2Coz7HNC1RiNSklxkoMmDom6SXg/
gKJtKaHrzEwRyyjkxQZmb3do + ePaObBJ4G50aS65j/DytTiotQbcTKnKslteE9HhGk = ;X-
YMail-OSG: 7cqc6isVM1kJzx4ley5DeT1ZT.xzbruV5C.MlBV9T28FYZh
    mmmqcaH_nyQ_a.QJW4Hom8M35yydPvDNwPXyjHDlRtTzyHepGAV8cBmlN.yX
    ZsjUW9jHBTRIAyZBts52CF_RcL9Q_aOabKlQbc3y0jYQzNjexZXuVSdDkWnA
    vH8go3GRcXdJM4U2HJaQEqSQbxXFYKHCksZ7uKrB4Gkx57a7LZTBsUkrp4pC

(Continued)

Table 8.2 (Continued)

SMWQho3fNIH5RtBbEAmppqMdcQhlJwUofuXGKFdqTaA_07p4.K7lcasK_yo6
93z6qCrIMVvvou6H7_3RW5DV5DGgsdQLpnZavRc.SYWrRbFmc1iW.4MkiREq
5GLkMNaYHxZHuo2FgWiVWMoUk51rf8BDtb2VqAdgLDebVfN.E_KzQBOk5CBK
EVWdq_S0aSmOu5.xJUQ15n4Uu.ID7A7Wywxg5ihR7Ejqrgau_zzJhMg--Received:
from [209.78.21.148] by web180903.mail.ne1.yahoo.com via HTTP; Sun, 24 Feb 2013
12:24:26 PST

X-Rocket-MIMEInfo: 001.001,VGVzdCBFbWFpbAEwAQEBAQ--

X-Mailer: YahooMailClassic/15.1.2 YahooMailWebService/0.8.134.513

Message-ID: <1361737466.90408.YahooMailClassic@web180903.mail.ne1.yahoo.com>

Date: Sun, 24 Feb 2013 12:24:26 -0800 (PST)

From: Todd Shipley <testyahooaccount@yahoo.com>

Subject: Test email from Yahoo to Gmail

To: testgmailaccount@gmail.com

MIME-Version: 1.0

Content-Type: multipart/alternative; boundary = "-1576899772-1434694979-
1361737466 = :90408"

---

and provide the path the message took through various SMTP servers
(Table 8.5). One can see that the first documented record of our email example
moving through an email server is by a Yahoo server in line #1. Of particular
note is that the sender's IP address 209.78.21.148 in line #1 is correctly identified and belongs to the ISP used by the sender to log into their online email
account. Escalating through the hops the email paths shown in numbers 2–5,
Yahoo hands off the message amongst its own servers and in hop #6 passes the
email off to Google. In the last hop #7, Google passes the email off to the
user's account. Looking at the time stamps this all occurs in a matter of seconds. In that short period of time, seven servers touched the email, passing it
on to the recipient. Note that the Yahoo servers are using UTC time (old
Greenwich Mean Time) to stamp the email; however, Google translates the
time into the local Pacific Standard Time. When the user looks at the email at
the receiving or sending end, their email program translates the time into the
local time zone. Table 8.3 breaks down the additional elements found in the
header.

Another email header

If we look at another email header, this time one sent through Yahoo to Gmail,
but via the user's desktop application Microsoft Outlook, we see similar actions
through the Mail Transfer Agents (MTAs) (Table 8.6).

Table 8.3 Email Header Explanation from Yahoo to Gmail

Header Name	Header Value	Explanation
Delivered-To	testgmailaccount@gmail.com	Account email sent to
X-Received	by 10.236.162.197 with SMTP id y45mr16233991yhk.110.1361737467542; Sun, 24 Feb 2013 12:24:27 -0800 (PST)	Server in Google Mail system that received the email
Return-Path	<testyahooaccount@yahoo.com>	Email address of sender
Received-SPF	neutral (google.com: 66.94.237.91 is neither permitted nor denied by best guess record for domain of testyahooaccount@yahoo.com) client-ip = 66.94.237.91;	Refers to Sender Policy Framework (SPF), an email validation system to prevent spam by attempting to verify sender IP (Table 8.4)
Authentication-Results	mx.google.com; spf = neutral (google.com: 66.94.237.91 is neither permitted nor denied by best guess record for domain of testyahooaccount@yahoo.com) smtp.mail = testyahooaccount@yahoo.com; dkim = pass header.i = @yahoo.com	Email server checked DKIM header and correctly identified sender's email service as valid
X-Yahoo-Newman-Property	ymail-3	Yahoo mail server version
X-Yahoo-Newman-Id	968415.26467.bm@omp1026.access.mail.mud.yahoo.com	Yahoo mail assigned ID number for this email
DKIM-Signature	v = 1; a = rsa-sha256; c = relaxed/relaxed; d = yahoo.com; s = s1024; t = 1361737466; bh = qwi0 + QrpLlhGpEVETzboOXwDxVGRXm YMTrJSv0peL8 = ; h = X-YMail-OSG:Received: X-Rocket-MIMEInfo:X-Mailer:MessageID:Date:From: Subject:To: MIME-Version:ContentType;b = 13CKqrHzBlBA17dE7 + 2T/HS1QEKOsDAHBIO1NQ1FCNluDZYYsvFTktrzyHV/3/ QSOeNnk8gLqotZj0 + MBzKzIAG + 4oPUKrYGwqsiF2ufhj/ kRLdORZ + hF + j56InPV + e1uLUnr4i2iS2Ei3ScK + yRtfKJivjbY76ji2hsdL9jLqk =	Encrypted DKIM header
X-YMail-OSG	7cqc6isVM1kJzx4ley5DeT1ZT.xzbruV5C.MIBY9T28FYZh mmmqcaH_nyQ_a. QJW4Hom8M35yydPvDNwPXyjHDIRtTzyHepGAV8cBmlN. yXZsjUW9jHBTRIAyZBts52CF_RcL9Q_aOabKIQbc	Unidentified Yahoo YMail function

(Continued)

Table 8.3 (Continued)

Header Name	Header Value	Explanation
	3y0jYQzNjexZXuVSdDKWnAVH8go3GRcXdJM4U2HJaQEqSQbxXFYKHCksZ7uKr B4Gkx57a7LZTBsUkrp4pCSMWQho3fNIH5RtBbEAmppqMdcQhlJwUofuXGKFdq TaA_07p4.K7IcasK_yo693z6qCrlMvwou6H7_3RW5DV5DGgsdQLpnZavRc. SYWrRbFmc1iW.4MkiREq5GLkMNaYHxZHuo2FgWiVWMoUk51rf 8BDtb2VqAdgLDebVfN.E_KzQBOk5CBKEVWdq_S0aSmOu5.xJUQ15n4Uu. ID7A7Wywxg5ihR7Ejqrgau_zzJhMg--	
X-Rocket-MIMEInfo	001.001,VGVzdCBFbWFpbAEwAQEBAQ--	Explanation Unknown
X-Mailer	YahooMailClassic/15.1.2 YahooMailWebService/0.8.134.513	Email program used to send email; in this case, Yahoo's classic mail service
Message-ID	<1361737466.90408.YahooMailClassic@web180903.mail.ne1.yahoo.com>	Message-ID added by Yahoo
Date	Sun, 24 Feb 2013 12:24:26 -0800 (PST)	Date of the email
From	Todd Shipley <testyahooaccount@yahoo.com>	Sender's email address
Subject	Test email from Yahoo to Gmail	Subject line of the email
To	testgmailaccount@gmail.com	Recipient's email address
MIME-Version	1.0	Multipurpose Internet Mail Extensions (MIME) version
Content-Type	multipart/alternative; boundary = "-1576899772-1434694979-1361737466 = :90408"	Content type of email which is used by the email program to know how to understand and display the email

Table 8.4 Path Email Took Through Various SMTP Servers

Hop	From	Through Which Server	With What Protocol	Time in UTC
7		10.49.15.197	SMTP	2/24/2013 12:24:27 -0800 (PST)
6	nm26.access.bullet.mail. mud.yahoo.com 66.94.237.91	mx.google.com	ESMTPS[a]	2/24/2013 12:24:27 -0800 (PST)
5	66.94.237.127	nm26.access. bullet.mail.mud. yahoo.com	NNFMP[b]	2/24/2013 20:24:26 -0000
4	66.94.237.121	tm2.access.bullet. mail.mud.yahoo. com	NNFMP	2/24/2013 20:24:26 -0000
3	127.0.0.1	omp1026.access. mail.mud.yahoo. com	NNFMP	2/24/2013 20:24:26 -0000
2		qmail 55713 invoked by uid 60001		2/24/2013 20:24:26 -0000
1	209.78.21.148	web180903.mail. ne1.yahoo.com		2/24/2013 12:24:26 PST

[a]*ESMTPS refers to the encryption layers used in the email. See RFC 3848:ESMTP and LMTP Transmission Types http://rfc-ref.org/RFC-TEXTS/3848/chapter1.html#d4e439556.*
[b]*NNFMP according to several Internet resources stands for "Newman No-Frills Mail Protocol". However, nothing specific from Yahoo can be found that supports that. Yahoo also does not publish any material on its internal handling of email.*

Table 8.5 Received-SPF Header Explanation

Received-SPF: pass	A permitted sender
Received-SPF: fail	Is not designated as permitted sender
Received-SPF: softfail	Is not designated as permitted sender
Received-SPF: neutral	Is neither permitted nor denied
Received-SPF: none	Not designate permitted sender
Received-SPF: permerror -extension:foo	Uses mechanism not recognized by this client
Received-SPF: temperror	Error in processing during lookup

Table 8.6 Example Header from Yahoo Email to Gmail Using Outlook

Delivered-To: testgmailaccount@gmail.com

Received: by 10.49.15.197 with SMTP id z5csp127114qec;
    Mon, 18 Feb 2013 18:50:36 -0800 (PST)

X-Received: by 10.66.52.79 with SMTP id r15mr41491157pao.46.1361242236401;
    Mon, 18 Feb 2013 18:50:36 -0800 (PST)

Return-Path: <testyahooaccount@yahoo.com>

Received: from nm6.access.bullet.mail.sp2.yahoo.com (nm6.access.bullet.mail.sp2.
yahoo.com. [98.139.44.133])
    by mx.google.com with ESMTPS id o3si22639630paz.263.2013.02.18.18.50.35
    (version = TLSv1 cipher = RC4-SHA bits = 128/128);
    Mon, 18 Feb 2013 18:50:36 -0800 (PST)

Received-SPF: neutral (google.com: 98.139.44.133 is neither permitted nor denied by
best guess record for domain of testyahooaccount@yahoo.com) client-
ip = 98.139.44.133;Authentication-Results: mx.google.com;
    spf = neutral (google.com: 98.139.44.133 is neither permitted nor denied by best
    guess record for domain of testyahooaccount@yahoo.com) smtp.
    mail = testyahooaccount@yahoo.com;
    dkim = pass header.i = @att.net

Received: from [98.139.44.96] by nm6.access.bullet.mail.sp2.yahoo.com with NNFMP;
19 Feb 2013 02:50:35 -0000

Received: from [67.195.22.118] by tm1.access.bullet.mail.sp2.yahoo.com with NNFMP;
19 Feb 2013 02:50:35 -0000

Received: from [127.0.0.1] by smtp113.sbc.mail.gq1.yahoo.com with NNFMP; 19 Feb
2013 02:50:35 -0000

DKIM-Signature: v = 1; a = rsa-sha256; c = relaxed/relaxed; d = att.net; s = s1024;
t = 1361242235; bh = zDR8VzuSnPALPI2Oe0w4idEjFWbQmVNUfwUuop1dpk0 = ;
h = X-Yahoo-Newman-Id:X-Yahoo-Newman-Property:X-YMail-OSG:X-Yahoo-SMTP:
Received:From:To:Subject:Date:Message-ID:MIME-Version:Content-Type:X-Mailer:
Thread-Index:Content-Language; b = zJ6IwoUheNqzLrPKXzAzh25v/
6hiSU5MQSoB5MRNBOatvsCJEYRFMegqEEXMM8TxQmhEQp/
BvRBTykTjZ + aVgVcZyZBRJ9owG/hsRXmOl9jGlc + 1VOqDP0rQkpk/
TruVlkp5i4LQLIXcwMxzm6VD + QDekG3CkS3uk4Jua3LrSHQ =

X-Yahoo-Newman-Id: 739883.27524.bm@smtp113.sbc.mail.gq1.yahoo.com

X-Yahoo-Newman-Property: ymail-3

X-YMail-OSG: JLThjqoVM1lOm4wlt7jk.KDJFl0WnQIXguxMhWNboTRHyEQ
    1J8yrK68QHDPUdtpDaJ8rhi_6Lm6RiT8qZmyN5u0LxSobBgQLCmOXpsuG.VW
    H05DsSSQTMF6vJmQA5DoPhvKw0oOyUc7h9f18rDo5BESykTCdd2lpRCquoRx
    rDX9h16_fggb9okkodkSMhaHpLOTOXgF0t9wQ_FAnA8qXLh3RBRkjVnAvK1r
    O0pU_GxpX9tJuaAolBehXj3C2bVVMB0t8sZla08felznFdrmHJiSHq3eWLlp
    _jbHWtNnspUThlEdggEnWyz1se6yCfN0hxuDwGjcvx_CeZPAaoacLwBkMmcP
    K9qxZPG4xQWWZthxd7RJFfQ2KgjBmtj3LOD4cEhsVi35pnaNOFHAWwmJ5p2R
    S.tg0zT3aZZgmMR_DxLki9.oC9FWy9Fhr6A--

X-Yahoo-SMTP: epBFhb6swBDqEduYvn.LxJxG.wQ.d6_TLI6Cmny3

Received: from Laptop testyahooaccount(toddshipley@209.78.21.184 with login)
    by smtp113.sbc.mail.gq1.yahoo.com with SMTP; 18 Feb 2013 18:50:35 -0800 PST

(Continued)

Table 8.6 (Continued)

From: "ATT" <testyahooaccount@yahoo.com>
To: "Todd Shipley" <testgmailaccount@gmail.com>
Subject: Yahoo to Google Email
Date: Mon, 18 Feb 2013 18:50:38 -0800
Message-ID: <002d01ce0e4b$e6724e70$b356eb50$@att.net>
MIME-Version: 1.0
Content-Type: multipart/alternative;
boundary = "---- = _NextPart_000_002E_01CE0E08.D854B3C0"
X-Mailer: Microsoft Outlook 14.0
Thread-Index: Ac4OS9/suTp1w2JJS/Krzk1m1OaP3w = =
Content-Language: en-us
X-Antivirus: avast! (VPS 130218-0, 2/18/2013), Inbound message
X-Antivirus-Status: Clean

INVESTIGATIVE TIPS
Why a Server Hop Matters

When investigating email headers, the investigator identifies various MTAs that handle the email and pass it to the next server. Each of these is a potential source of information and evidence of the email's movement through the Internet. However, the evidence may not reside there long. Additionally, the evidence in the hops indicates something useful for possibly fulfilling the statutory requirements of some crimes. For instance, some crimes, particularly federal statutes, need an interstate nexus. A Threatening Interstate Communications, 18 U.S.C. § 875 violation requires that the communication crossed state lines. Identifying each of the server IP addresses and their associated owners may go a long way to establishing such legal elements.

In Table 8.8, we can see that the first record of anything through our email servers is by Yahoo in line #1. What is different in this example is the sender's IP address is correctly identified as well as the name of the computer sending, which is "Laptop". The name of the computer used to prepare the example as given in Tables 8.6 and 8.7 is verified by the system information page from that computer as shown in Figure 8.6. Looking at Table 8.8, we can escalate through the hops the email paths show in numbers 2–4. It shows Yahoo passing the email amongst its own servers, and in hop #5, Yahoo finally passes the email off to Google. In the last hop #6, Google passes the email off to the user's account. Looking at the time stamps this all occurs in a matter of seconds. In that short period of time, six servers touched the email, passing it on to the recipient. The investigator should be aware that the servers either stamp the times with the local time of the server or use UTC time (old Greenwich Mean Time) as the time used to stamp the

Table 8.7 Email Header Explanation from Yahoo to Gmail Through Outlook

Header Name	Header Value	Explanation
Delivered-To	testgmailaccount@gmail.com	Account email sent to
Received	by 10.49.15.197 with SMTP id z5csp127114qec; Mon, 18 Feb 2013 18:50:36 -0800 (PST)	Google email server passing email
X-Received	by 10.66.52.79 with SMTP id r15mr41491157pao.46.1361242236401; Mon, 18 Feb 2013 18:50:36 -0800 (PST)	Server in Google mail system that received the email
Return-Path	<testyahooaccount@yahoo.com>	Email address of sender
Received	from nm6.access.bullet.mail.sp2.yahoo.com (nm6.access.bullet.mail.sp2.yahoo.com. [98.139.44.133]) by mx.google.com with ESMTPS id o3si2263963Opaz.263.2013.02.18.18.50.35 (version = TLSv1 cipher = RC4-SHA bits = 128/128); Mon, 18 Feb 2013 18:50:36 -0800 (PST)	Yahoo email server passing email
Received-SPF	neutral (google.com: 98.139.44.133 is neither permitted nor denied by best guess record for domain of testyahooaccount@yahoo.com) client-ip = 98.139.44.133;Authentication-Results: mx.google.com; spf = neutral (google.com: 98.139.44.133 is neither permitted nor denied by best guess record for domain of testyahooaccount@yahoo.com) smtp. mail = testyahooaccount@yahoo.com; dkim = pass header.i = @att.net	Refers to SPF, an email validation system, to prevent spam by attempting to verify sender IP (see Table 8.5)
Received	from [98.139.44.96] by nm6.access.bullet.mail.sp2.yahoo.com with NNFMP; 19 Feb 2013 02:50:35 -0000	Yahoo email server passing email
Received	from [67.195.22.118] by tm1.access.bullet.mail.sp2.yahoo.com with NNFMP; 19 Feb 2013 02:50:35 -0000	Yahoo email server passing email
Received	from [127.0.0.1] by smtp113.sbc.mail.gq1.yahoo.com with NNFMP; 19 Feb 2013 02:50:35 -0000	Yahoo email server passing email
DKIM-Signature		

	v = 1; a = rsa-sha256; c = relaxed/relaxed; d = att.net; s = s1024; t = 1361242235; h = zDR8 VzuSnPALPl2Oe0w4idEjFWb QmVNUfwUuop1dpk0 = ; h = X-Yahoo-Newman-Id:X-Yahoo-Newman-Property:X-YMail-OSG:X-Yahoo- MTP:Received: From:To:Subject:Date: Message-ID:MIME-Version:Content-Type:X-Mailer:Thread-Index:Content-Language; b = zJ6lwoUheNqzLrPKXzAzh25v/6hiSU5MQSoB5MRNBOatvsCJEYRFMe gqEEXMM8TxQmhEQp/BvRBTykTjZ + aVgVcZyZBRJ9owG/hsRXmOl9jGlc + 1VOqDP0rQkpk/TruVlkp5i4LQLlXcwMxzm6VD + QDekG3CkS3uk4Jua3LrSHQ =	Encrypted DKIM header
X-Yahoo-Newman-Id	739883.27524.bm@smtp113.sbc.mail.gq1.yahoo.com	Yahoo mail assigned ID number for this email
X-Yahoo-Newman-Property	ymail-3	Yahoo mail server version
X-YMail-OSG	JLThjqoVM1IOm4wlt7jk.KDJFl0WnQIXguxMhWNboTRHyEQ1J8yrK68QHDPUdtpDaaJ8rhi_ 6Lm6RlT8qZmyN5u0LxSobBgQLCmOXpsuG.WWH05DsSSQTMF6vJmQA5DoPhvKw 0oOyUc7h9f18rDo5BESykTCdd2lpRCquoRxrDX9h16_fggb9okkodkSMhaHpLOTOX gF0t9wQ_FAnA8qXLh3RBRkjVnAvK1rO0pU_GxpX9tJuaAolBehXj3C2bVVMB0t8 sZla08felznFdrmHJiSHq3eWLlp_jbHWtNnspUThIEdggEnWyz1se6yCfN0hxuDwGjcvx _CeZPAaoacLwBkMmcPK9qxZPG4xQWWZthxd7RJFfQ2KgjBmtj3LOD 4cEhsVl35pnaNOFHAWwmJ5p2RS:tg0zT3aZZgmMR_DxLki9.oC9FW y9Fhr6A--	Unidentified Yahoo YMail function
X-Yahoo-SMTP	epBFhb6swBDqEduYvn.LxJxG.wQ.d6_TLI6Cmny3	Unidentified Yahoo SMTP function
Received	from Laptop testyahooaccount(toddshipley@209.78.21.184 with login) by smtp113.sbc. mail.gq1.yahoo.com with SMTP; 18 Feb 2013 18:50:35 -0800 PST	Yahoo email server receiving the email from the login IP address of 209.78.21.184 and the device name used to send the email "Laptop"
From	"ATT" <testyahooaccount@yahoo.com>	
To	"Todd Shipley" <testgmailaccount@gmail.com>	Sender's email address

(Continued)

Table 8.7 (Continued)

Header Name	Header Value	Explanation
		Recipient's email address
Subject	Yahoo to Google Email	Subject line of the email
Date	Mon, 18 Feb 2013 18:50:38 -0800	Date of the email
Message-ID	<002d01ce0e4b$e6724e70$b356eb50$@att.net>	Message ID added by AT&T (Yahoo)
MIME-Version	1.0	MIME version
Content-Type	multipart/alternative; boundary = "----=_NextPart_000_002E_01CE0E08.D854B3C0"	Content type of email which is used by the email program to know how to understand and display the email
X-Mailer	Microsoft Outlook 14.0	Identifies email program used to receive the email at the user's desktop
Thread-Index	Ac4OS9/suTp1w2JJS/Krzk1m1OaP3w = =	Microsoft Outlook Message-ID
Content-Language	en-us	Language used in email
X-Antivirus	avast! (VPS 130218-0, 2/18/2013), Inbound message	Antivirus program Avast used to scan inbound messages
X-Antivirus-Status	Clean	Antivirus program declaration that email is "Clean" of any malware

Table 8.8 Path Email Took Through Various SMTP Servers

Hop	From	Through Which Server	With What Protocol	Time in UTC
6		10.49.15.197	SMTP	2/19/2013 2:50:36 AM
5	nm6.access.bullet.mail.sp2.yahoo.com 98.139.44.133	mx.google.com	ESMTPS	2/19/2013 2:50:36 AM
4	98.139.44.96	nm6.access.bullet.mail.sp2.yahoo.com	NNFMP	2/19/2013 2:50:35 AM
3	67.195.22.118	tm1.access.bullet.mail.sp2.yahoo.com	NNFMP	2/19/2013 2:50:35 AM
2	127.0.0.1	smtp113.sbc.mail.gq1.yahoo.com	NNFMP	2/19/2013 2:50:35 AM
1	Laptop 209.78.21.184	smtp113.sbc.mail.gq1.yahoo.com	Login	2/19/2013 2:50:35 AM

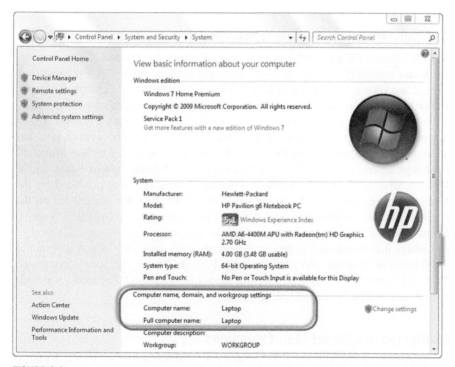

FIGURE 8.6

System page in Windows 7 showing computer name.

Table 8.9 Standard Internal Header Information from an Microsoft Exchange Server

Microsoft Mail Internet Headers Version 2.0

Received: from exchfe02.ad.xxx ([10.10.xxx.xx]) by exch10.ad.xxxi with Microsoft SMTPSVC(6.0.3790.3959);

    Fri, 22 Nov 2011 10:29:13 -0800Received: from KMBT59C636.ad.agi ([10.10.x.xx]) by exchfe02.ad.xxx with Microsoft SMTPSVC(6.0.3790.3959);

    Fri, 22 Nov 2011 10:29:13 -0800

    To:bbxxx@xxxx.com Subject:Message Sender:hxxx@xxxx.com From:hxxx@xxxx.com

    Reply- To:hxxx@xxxx.com X-Mailer:KONICA C550 Date: Fri, 22 Nov 2011 10:29:13

    -0800Message-Id:<4 7 A3043 8.50C.00206B59C636.hxxx@xxxx.com> MIME-Version: 1.0

Content-Type:multipartlmixed; boundary = "KONICA_MINOLTA_Internet_Fax_Boundary"
Content-Transfer-Encoding:7 bit Return-Path: hxxx@ xxxx.com

email. When the user looks at the email at the receiving or sending end, their email program will generally translate the time into the local time zone, that is, Mon, 18 Feb 2013 18:50:38 -0800 (-0800 is 8 h after UTC or Pacific Standard Time).

A Microsoft Outlook header translation through an exchange server

Not all headers we may need to look at go through the Internet. Email headers are found internally in popular email networks such as Microsoft Exchange servers. If we take a look at the header fields from a common Microsoft Exchange Outlook email, we can identify other interesting information about the email. Table 8.9 reflects a unique situation. The email chain starts from a printer. A document is scanned on the printer that is attached to the systems network (and has an assigned email address on the network), and gets processed by the Microsoft Exchange server. As a result, this email contains a separate header based on the IP from RFC 5322 Internet Message Format. This header was produced by the Konica printer, which sent the email. Table 8.10 lists the definition of the Outlook header information as defined by Microsoft from their website. Ultimately, the message ends up in the user's mailbox that it was addressed to and where it is transferred to the local storage of the user. Our header is found in the Microsoft Outlook Personal Storage File (PST) on the user's computer. Table 8.11 provides a listing of standard header information translation for definitions found in RFC's 5321, 5322, and 2045.

Multipurpose Internet Mail Extensions

We previously discussed the mail transfer program protocol SMTP in Chapter 3. It is the standard protocol for sending email through the Internet. However, it does have limitations. The largest limitations are due to the size of the email that

Table 8.10 Outlook Header Information Translation

Conversation Topic:	The topic of the conversation thread of the Outlook item
Sender Name:	The display name of the sender for the Outlook item
Received By:	The display name of the true recipient for the mail message
Delivery Time:	No definition found
Creation Time:	The creation time for the Outlook item
Modification Time:	A *Date* specifying the date and time that the Outlook item was last modified—Read-only
Submit Time:	No definition found
Importance:	The relative importance level for the Outlook item
Sensitivity:	Indicates the sensitivity for the Outlook item
Flags:	A mail item with a flag marked through the user interface
Size:	Indicates the size (in bytes) of the Outlook item

Table 8.11 Translation of Standard Header Information

Standard Header Information Translation	Field Explanation from RFC 5322 and 2045
Microsoft Mail Internet Headers Version 2.0	This header is added by Microsoft Outlook.
Received: from exchfe02.ad.xxxi ([10.10. xxx.xx]) by exch10.ad.xxxi with Microsoft SMTPSVC(6.0.3790.3959); Fri, 22 Nov 2011 10:29:13 -0800	The "Received:" field contains a (possibly empty) list of tokens followed by a semicolon and a date-time specification. Each token must be a word, angle-addr, addr-spec, or a domain. Further restrictions are applied to the syntax of the trace fields by specifications that provide for their use, such as [RFC5321].
Received: from KMBT59C636.ad.xxx ([10.10.x.xx]) by exchfe02.ad.xxx with Microsoft SMTPSVC(6.0.3790.3959); Fri, 1 Feb 2010 11:40:23 -0800	When the SMTP server accepts a message either for relaying or forfinal delivery, it inserts a trace record (also referred to interchangeably as a "time stamp line" or "Received" line) at the topof the mail data. This trace record indicates the identity of the host that sent the message, the identity of the host that received the message (and is inserting this time stamp), and the date and time the message was received.
To:bbxxxxx@xxxx.com	The "To:" field contains the address(es) of the primary recipient(s)of the message.
Subject:Message	The "Subject:" field is the most common and contains a short string identifying the topic of the message.

(Continued)

Table 8.11 (Continued)

Standard Header Information Translation	Field Explanation from RFC 5322 and 2045
Sender:hxxx@xxxx.com	The "Sender:" field specifies the mailbox of the agent responsible for the actual transmission of the message.
From:hxxx@xxxx.com	The "From:" field specifies the author(s) of the message, that is, the mailbox(es) of the person(s) or system(s) responsible for the writing of the message.
Reply-To: hxxx@xxxx.com	When the "Reply-To:" field is present, it indicates the address(es) to which the author of the message suggests that replies be sent.
X-Mailer: KONICA C550	Implementors may, if necessary, define private Content-Transfer-Encoding values, but must use an x-token, which is a name prefixed by "X-", to indicate its nonstandard status, for example, "Content-Transfer-Encoding: x-my-new-encoding".
Date: Fri, 22 Nov 2011 10:29:13 -0800	The origination date specifies the date and time at which the creator of the message indicated that the message was complete and ready to enter the mail delivery system.
Message-Id: <4 7 A3043 8.50C.00206B59C636.hxxx@xxxx.com>	The "Message-ID:" field provides a unique message identifier that refers to a particular version of a particular message. The uniqueness of the message identifier is guaranteed by the host that generates it (see below). This message identifier is intended to be machine readable and not necessarily meaningful to humans. A message identifier pertains to exactly one version of a particular message; subsequent revisions to the message each receive new message identifiers.
MIME-Version: 1.0	A MIME-Version header field, which uses a version number to declare a message to be conformant with MIME and allows mail processing agents to distinguish between such messages and those generated by older or nonconformant software, which are presumed to lack such a field.
Content-Type: multipartlmixed; boundary = "KONICA_MINOLTA_ Internet_Fax_Boundary"	A Content-Type header field, generalized from RFC 1049, which can be used to specify the media type and subtype of data in the body of a message and to fully specify the native representation (canonical form) of such data.

(Continued)

Table 8.11 (Continued)

Standard Header Information Translation	Field Explanation from RFC 5322 and 2045
Content-Transfer-Encoding: 7 bit	A Content-Transfer-Encoding header field, which can be used to specify both the encoding transformation that was applied to the body and the domain of the result. Encoding transformations other than the identity transformation are usually applied to data in order to allow it to pass through mail transport mechanisms which may have data or character set limitations.
Return-Path: hxxx@xxxx.com	The "Return-Path:" header field contains a pair of angle brackets that enclose an optional addr-spec.

can be sent and its inability to deal with non-ASCII characters. This has been overcome with an additional set of protocols that describe how to send larger messages and attachments. This protocol is commonly referred to as MIME. MIME stands for Multipurpose Internet Mail Extensions. MIME allows the inclusion of non-ASCII characters and non-English languages, multiple fonts, and of course multimedia objects such as images, audio, and video (Brodkin, 2011).

MIME has become the standard protocol for allowing the addition of media as in pictures and video into an email. How does this occur you might ask? Well, the protocol uses an encoding method known as base64 to convert the nontext items, binary data, such as videos, or pictures into text. This then allows the standard SMTP to more easily transmit the data. Upon receipt, your email program unencodes the base64 data into a file we can understand again. MIME uses the Content-Type field to help it determine if the data needs to be encoded. Table 8.12 provides an explanation for common MIME Content-Types (Figure 8.7).

Looking at little X

We already mentioned that header entries beginning with an X are nonstandard and applied by a user's email program or an email server or MTA that it passes through. The X lines in the header are intended to provide additional information to aid in the sending of the email through various servers. To understand some of the X lines in an email header, we have put together a short list in Table 8.13 of commonly encountered X lines you might see when tracing an email header. Many of these can be found in various RFCs including RFC 2076.

Table 8.12 Content-Type Explanation

Content-Type	Description
application/octet-stream	Used where the message is an unknown type and contains any kind of data as bytes
application/xml	Used for application-specific xml data
x-type	Used for nonstandard content type
image/jpeg	Used for images
multipart/related	Used for multiple related parts in a message
multipart/signed	Used for multiple related parts in a message including signature
multipart/mixed	Used for multiple independent parts in a message

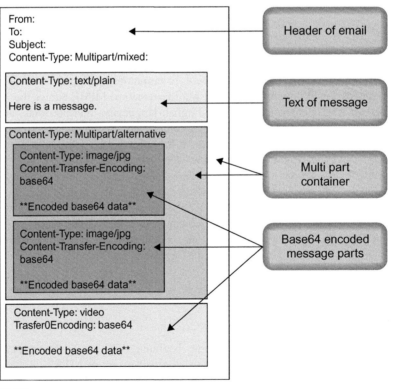

FIGURE 8.7

MIME email analysis.

Table 8.13 Common X Header Explanations

Header	Explanation
X-Apparently-To	Intended receiver of the email
X-Antivirus	Antivirus tool used to check email
X-Antivirus-Status	Status of the email according to the antivirus tool as Clean or Spam
X-Complaints-To	Where to direct your complaints you have about an email you received
X-Confirm-Reading-To	Create an automatic response for read messages
X-Errors-To	The address to send an email to for any errors encountered
X-Ymail-ISG	Yahoo Incoming Spam Guard
X-Mailer	Program used to send the email
X-Notifications	Explanation Unknown
X-Originating-IP	IP address of ISP used by sender
X-PMFLAGS	Additional information used with Pegasus Mail
X-Priority	Priority of email being sent
X-Received	MTA receiving email (does not necessarily mean the last server in the line
X-Sender	Additional information about the sender of the email
X-Spam-zzz	Where zzz is any number of different spam tags relating to the Spam filter on the email server. Some of these include Checker-Version, Level, Report, and Status
X-UIDL	Used with emails distributed over POP
X-Yahoo-Newman-Property	Explanation Unknown
X-Yahoo-Newman-Id	Yahoo internal mail transfer protocol ID
X-Ymail-OSG	Yahoo Outgoing Spam Guard

THINGS TO KNOW

Sender IP information in an email header is often controlled by the MTAs first processing the email. Historically to prevent spam, these MTAs would pass through the sender's IP address. This assisted the receivers of an email trace back the email to the sender. This was commonly added as the header X-Originating-IP. Changes to the way some of the large ISP companies process email have started to appear. Google no longer adds the sender's IP address in their headers. As of mid-December 2012, Microsoft has started adding a new line to its headers titled X-EIP and has removed the X-Originating header. The X-EIP header appears to be an encoded IP address, but to date has not been translated. Controlling spam has become a significant issue and one that has affected the method by which the investigator traces an email.

INVESTIGATIVE TIPS

Email from Other Sources

Email is such a prolific tool that it is available not just on computers but also on cell phones, gaming devices, tablet devices, and social media sites. Headers sent from these devices can also provide the investigator with specific header information about the sender and the location or device sent from. This can provide another potential source of digital evidence for later collection and review by digital forensic investigators.

Android Phone Email:

Email sent from an Android phone can be potentially identified through the email headers through the Content-Type header. The Content-Type header may have "com.andriod.email" in the text. The Message-ID may contain "email.android.com". The first "Received:" line will most likely contain an IP address assigned to the cell phone's service provider.

iPhone Email:

Email sent from an iPhone can be potentially identified through the email headers through the Content-Type header. The Content-Type header may have "text/plain; charset = us-ascii". An "X" header X-Mailer may contain the text "iPhone Mail". The first "Received:" line will most likely contain an IP address assigned to the cell phone's service provider.

Nook Tablet devices:

Email sent from a Nook Tablet can potentially be identified through the email headers Message-ID which may contain "email.android.com".

Facebook email:

Emails sent from a Facebook account may be identified from the account sender which will be the Facebook account followed by @facebook.com. The first received line may also include the text "helo = www.facebook.com" and the DKIM header may have a reference to facebook.com also. There may possibly be an "X-Originating-IP" header containing an IP belonging to facebook.com.

Faking an email and hiding its sender

So we have looked at the real header, but what can be done to hide the real sender of an email. There are several things the sender can do to hide their location from the receiver. A few of those methods include:

1. Anonymous remailers/ open relays: SMTP mail servers on the Internet that allow anyone on the Internet to forward email. These have become increasingly difficult to find because most of them have been closed due to their misuse by spammers.
2. Email on anonymous networks: Anonymous email sent through the Tor or I2P networks. Tor and I2P both offer access to email through their anonymized networks (www.torproject.org and www.i2p2.de).
3. Forging email headers: Sender uses controlled SMTP server to send email with altered email.
4. Anonymous email accounts: Email accounts with no requirement for inputting real identifying information about the sender. Most of the larger email services including Google, Yahoo, and Microsoft Live allow the suspect or the investigator to create fictious accounts.

5. Fake mail generators/disposable and temporary accounts: Web-based services that let the sender input any return email address. Searching the Internet will find numerous sites that provide this service. Most of these advertise they keep no records of the IP addresses connecting with the email server as a way to assure their customer's privacy.

Each of these methods adds to the difficulty the investigator will have in identifying the IP address of the suspect or possibly make it entirely impossible to trace. Identifying the actual IP address may include legal service on multiple IP addresses or undercover contact with the target.

Collecting email from a web-based system

Email collection from a web-based service can be an effective evidence collection technique for the investigator. Both criminal investigators and civil investigators can properly collect the web-based email in support of their investigations. Examples of collection possibilities include documentation of a victim's threatening emails or a civil investigator conducting client collection of emails in response to a litigation hold request. Regardless of the reason given to the proper authority for the investigator to collect the email, such as permission or by court order, the investigator can collect emails stored on a remote server belonging to a web-based email provider.

Collecting email from web-based accounts can be accomplished fairly easily with a proper understanding of the mail protocols used. Email from a web mail account can be done by using a local email client (one installed on the investigator's workstation or laptop) like Outlook from Microsoft or a free client like Zimbra from VMWare. Using one of these local email clients, the investigator can set up his connection to the web-based email service and synch his client with the web-based service. Each of the web-based email services has slightly different connection parameters. The investigator needs to research the connection parameters prior to conducting the collection. This will ensure the collection is conducted without issues. Prior to the collection, the investigator needs to have the proper legal authority established and obtain the login usernames and passwords for the account to be acquired. Logging into the web-based email service, such as Google, may also require compliance with certain security features like their notification of an unrecognized computer. This can require the collection of a text message from the account holder's cell phone.

Mail protocols

SMTP is the protocol used for transmitting email across the Internet. We discussed this protocol in Chapter 3. Along with the SMTP protocol are the protocols for accessing the user's mail transfer servers. These protocols are:

- Post Office Protocol (POP)
- Internet Message Access Protocol (IMAP)

Both POP and IMAP are used for communication between a user's email program and the user's mail transfer server. Each protocol allows the email user to download their email to a local device for later or off-line review. The functions of the protocols are different and require specific setup on the mail transfer server as well as the local device to accept the mail through these processes.

Conducting email collection from web-based services should be done through the use of IMAP and not POP. While POP is an effective tool for personal synchronization of email and access to that email, it does not effectively allow for complete collection of web-based email. IMAP was designed to allow for complete control and synchronization of SMTP email accounts on an email server. While IMAP is the best method for collecting the email, POP may be the only alternative depending on the email service. Yahoo as an example does not allow desktop access through IMAP. We discuss how each method is accomplished below.

Investigator's email collection options

The investigator has several options available to collect email from a MTA. The investigator can provide legal service to the mail hosting company and wait for their response. This may be the only option if access externally from the web is not available. If the investigator has external access to the email account with the appropriate permission and account access information, there are some other options for collecting the email. Each option requires an understanding of the protocol and the requirements of the MTAs (the MTA in these cases usually refers to a web-based accessible email service, that is, Gmail, Yahoo mail, or Live mail). We are going to discuss two of the easiest options for the investigator to access the mail account externally or from the user point of view. The first is a free method, Zimbra by VMware, and the other uses a reasonably common email program, Outlook by Microsoft. Both of these tools provide the investigator the ability to collect email from mail transfer services. Both programs are desktop tools that give the user the ability to collect the emails from a specific account that the investigator has access to. The access requires that the investigator has the legal authority and the username and password to the account.

To accurately collect the email from the MTA, the investigator in most cases will have to login to the account and set up the account to allow for the transfer of the mail using either POP access or IMAP. Depending on the accessed email service, additional features may need to be invoked to allow for the collection of all folders. In Gmail, additional steps are required to collect the chats saved in the account. The investigator needs to change the setting to have the chat viewable in the mailbox. Also in Gmail, contacts and calendar events require a separate export of those items as they are not in the mailbox which has an IMAP access connection. The investigator can document the settings of the account and any changes he makes by taking screen shots of the access process, using the tools noted in Chapter 5. Each of the Internet email programs have different settings and should be researched prior to conducting the email collections. Common with any of the collection methods is that they are using the Internet and any latency it may have as well as the email servers containing the data to be collected. What this means to the investigator is that when the synchronization of the account begins between the method selected and the email account, the time involved in the collection can be a few minutes with small amounts of data to hours for accounts with large numbers of emails.

INVESTIGATIVE TIPS

Always there are exceptions to every rule. In the case of downloading email from web-based services, it is Yahoo. Yahoo mail collection can be a little different depending on the service being provided by Yahoo. Yahoo has free access accounts and paid email accounts. The free services are generally only accessible by the POP3 protocol. The pay accounts have the option of accessing the account through IMAP. Some reports by Yahoo users on the Internet have related they have accessed their free accounts by IMAP access, but Yahoo states they do not support that protocol for free accounts. There are third party utilities that purport to connect through the IMAP protocol, but validation by the investigator should occur prior to implementing any utility during an investigation.

Zimbra Desktop email collections

Zimbra Desktop is an email program from VMWare, the makers of virtual machine technology. Zimbra Desktop is part of a suite of email service programs provided as Open Source and pay for products. The Zimbra family of products includes server-based programs as well as the desktop program we are going to discuss here. Zimbra Desktop is a simple to use and install program that allows the investigator to easily capture email from an online mail service. Here are the steps:

Zimbra Desktop installation:

1. Download Zimbra Desktop from the Zimbra website www.zimbra.com.
2. Install Zimbra Desktop on local machine.
3. The first screen will ask for the investigator to add an email account. Select the type of email to collect.
4. Under Add New Account add the account name, email address, and password. Select "Check Messages:" to "manually" and check "Sychronize all calendars" and "Synchronize all contacts and groups".
5. Click "Validate and Save".

Some additional notes for setting up specific accounts:

a. Setting up a Yahoo account may require additional validation processes.
b. Gmail accounts require you to change the Gmail account settings to accept IMAP connections. In addition, the folders within the Gmail account need to be made visible to the IMAP function. Under the "Label" tab in the settings function select the "Show in IMAP" for each folder to collect and select

FIGURE 8.8

Adding new account to Zimbra.

"show". This makes the folders visible in the folder tree on the left side of the screen and downloadable.

Setting up new accounts in Zimbra Desktop: (Figure 8.8).

The Add New Accounts function in Zimbra Desktop allows you to easily add new accounts. The selections include:

- Yahoo! Mail: You can set up Yahoo! Mail, Yahoo! Mail Plus, Yahoo! Small Business, Ymail, or Rocketmail accounts.
- Gmail: Your Gmail account must be set up to allow IMAP access. You must log into the target Gmail account and enable IMAP in the "Labels" tab under the settings. Check all the items to "Show" and check the box for each item to "Show in IMAP".
- Other POP/IMAP accounts: You must have complete settings information in order to set up POP/IMAP access. You can obtain such information from the target's service provider or research it on the Internet.

Once the account is added select the account and right click to select "Send/Receive".

Once the synchronization is complete, the investigator can verify that the email was collected by comparing the number of emails in the online account to the number held in the synchronized account in Zimbra. The investigator can then use the Zimbra email client to export the messages out in a compressed file as an evidence container. In Zimbra click on the "Preferences" tab and an option under the targeted user account will appear called "Import/Export". Click this and a new field will appear on the right. Under "Export" select "Advanced Settings"

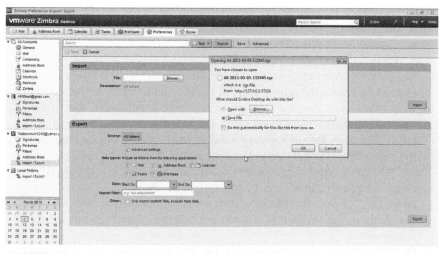

FIGURE 8.9

Zimbra Desktop saving email from online account.

and include all the data types required. Set the data range and leave the "other" box blank. Click the "Export" button and a box to save the data will appear. Zimbra saves the data in a compressed .tgz file to the location you select. This evidence container can then be hashed to provide a unique identifier for the file. After email collection is completed, the investigator needs to access the account and return the settings to their original state. The investigator can use Zimbra to review the email after the emails are saved separately as an evidence item (Figure 8.9).

Using Outlook for email collections

Using Microsoft Outlook for web-based email collections requires setting up Outlook to access the email account. The investigator needs to research online the exact account access settings prior to conducting the collection. Simply doing a Google or Bing search on the email server and "IMAP Account Settings" will provide the setting information needed. The following steps can be used in Outlook to set up a new account for collection:

1. Create a new email account by clicking on "Tools", then "E-mail Accounts".
2. Add a new email account and click "Next".
3. Select IMAP and click "Next".
4. This window asks for specific connection information. The investigator should have already researched the specific connection requirements for the email service to be accessed including:
   a. Your name: This is the user's account to be accessed.
   b. Email address: The user account's complete email address.

    c. Incoming mail server: The incoming mail server for the email service.

    d. Outgoing mail server: The outgoing mail server for the email service.

    e. Username: The user's account username.

    f. Password: The user's password.

5. At this point, don't click on the "Next" button; click on the "More Settings" button to compete the proper setup of the account to allow for the collection.

6. Under the "More Settings" box, there are specific options unique to the web-based email service from which the investigator will be collecting email. The prior research should indicate what exactly will be required for the particular email service you are collecting from. As an example, under the "Outgoing Server" tab the box titled "My outgoing server (SMTP) requires authentication" may be required to be checked. Additionally, under the "Advanced" tab, the setting for the "incoming server" and the "outgoing server" ports may need to be changed to meet the service access requirements.

7. Once the settings are correctly input, the investigator can click "OK" and Outlook will test the connection. If the connection is good two green check marks will appear, if not an error notice will appear advising the investigator to correct the settings.

8. Outlook will connect to the email service with the input account information and settings and begin to download the folder structure and then the emails. This however is not the end of the setup process for the collections using Outlook. Because the services are online and the email is accessible through the Internet Outlook does not automatically download complete files and their attachments. Depending on the version of Outlook, the investigator is using the investigator needs to go to "Send/Receive Groups" and go to the account and select "Edit".

9. In the "All Accounts" window, each folder option needs to be changed. The investigator needs to be selected and the "Download complete item including attachments" radio button selected individually for the folders to be collected. Select "OK" when completed. This will allow all the email to be saved into the Outlook account previously setup by the investigator.

10. Once the downloading of the account information is complete (this can take several hours even for small accounts), the investigator can go to the Outlook storage location for the version used during the collection and copy the Outlook PST file into evidence.

    Once the synchronization is complete, the investigator can verify that the email was collected by comparing the number of emails in the online account to the number held in the synchronized account in Outlook. The investigator can then use the Outlook email client to export the messages out in a Microsoft Windows PST file as an evidence container. The PST file is the common storage file for email in Outlook. This PST can then be hashed to provide a unique identifier for the file.

After the email collection is completed, the investigator needs to access the account and return the settings to their original state. The investigator can use Outlook to review the email after the PST is saved separately as an evidence item.

INVESTIGATIVE TIPS

Other Investigative Techniques for Identifying Targets on the Internet

Identifying the target of an investigation through IP addresses is a standard tool of the Internet investigator. But, if one can't get the correct IP address, or identify the target's ISP, what can the investigator do? Well the investigation doesn't end just because the target has hidden himself. Granted it makes it much more difficult, but finding them can occur. Remember, the more often the suspect(s) engages or interacts with their victim(s) or repeats their illegal conduct the more likely you as the investigator will be given additional clues that will lead to their identification and apprehension. In later chapters, we will discuss proactive investigations and specific things the investigator can employee to identify targets. IP addresses are still the corner stone of any of these processes.

Relevant RFCs related to IP tracing

The following Request for Comments (RFCs) reflects the standard protocols that guide the formation, sending, movement through the Internet, and receiving of emails. Each of the references provide the investigator with a variety of information that is unique to emails and the use. Becoming familiar with the underlying email protocols will provide the investigator with a solid foundation of how the email system works. It will also enable the investigator to easily identify and parse through an email's header to identify where and when it was produced. To locate the RFCs, the investigator can go the Internet Engineering Task Force (IETF) website at http://www.ietf.org/rfc.html and using the search function can find the listed RFC.

Message Format
- RFC 2822 Internet Message Format
- RFC 3464 Extensible Message Format for Delivery Status Notifications

SMTP—Simple Mail Transfer Protocol
- RFC 821
- RFC 1652 SMTP Service Extension for 8 bit-MIMEtransport
- RFC 1869 SMTP Service Extensions
- RFC 1870 SMTP Service Extension for Message Size Declaration
- RFC 1985 SMTP Service Extension for Remote Message Queue Starting
- RFC 2034 SMTP Service Extension for Returning Enhanced Error Codes
- RFC 2476 Message Submission
- RFC 2554 SMTP Service Extension for Authentication
- RFC 2821 Simple Mail Transfer Protocol

- RFC 2920 SMTP Service Extension for Command Pipelining
- RFC 3030 SMTP Service Extensions for Transmission of Large and Binary MIME Messages
- RFC 2645 ON-DEMAND MAIL RELAY (ODMR) SMTP with Dynamic IP Addresses
- RFC 2852 Deliver By SMTP Service Extension

MIME

- RFC 822 Standard for the Format of ARPA Internet Text Messages
- RFC 2045 Multipurpose Internet Mail Extensions (MIME) Part One: Format of Internet Message Bodies
- RFC 046 Multipurpose Internet Mail Extensions (MIME) Part Two: Media Types
- RFC 2047 Multipurpose Internet Mail Extensions (MIME) Part Three: Message Header Extensions for Non-ASCII Text
- RFC 2048 Multipurpose Internet Mail Extensions (MIME) Part Four: Registration Procedures
- RFC 2049 Multipurpose Internet Mail Extensions (MIME) Part Five: Conformance Criteria and Examples

POP3—Post Office Protocol, Version 3

- RFC 1939 Post Office Protocol—Version 3

IMAP4—Internet Message Access Protocol, Version 4

- RFC 2683 IMAP4 Implementation Recommendations
- RFC 3501 Internet Message Access Protocol—Version 4rev1

CONCLUSIONS

This chapter provided methods by which one can trace an IP address and emails. Tracing an IP address is a basic function of the Internet investigator. Understanding the process required to locate the IP address and determine its origin is fundamental to the successful completion of an investigation. We have attempted to cover the basic skills necessary to accomplish these basic processes. Familiarity with the information in this chapter will give the investigator a solid foundation for investigating crimes committed on the Internet, particularly in how to identify those responsible for their commission.

Further reading

AFRINIC (n.d.). *African network information centre*. Retrieved from <http://www.afrinic. net/>.

APNIC—Home. (n.d.). Asia-Pacific Network Information Centre (APNIC). Retrieved from <http://www.apnic.net/>.

ARIN. (n.d.). American Registry for Internet Numbers (ARIN). Retrieved from <https://www.arin.net/>.

Brodkin, J. (n.d.). The MIME guys: How two internet gurus changed e-mail forever. *Network World—Network World*. Retrieved from <http://www.networkworld.com/news/2011/020111-mime-internet-email.html?page=1>.

Common Internet Message Header Fields. (n.d.). *People.dsv.su.se*. Retrieved from <http://people.dsv.su.se/~jpalme/ietf/mail-headers/mail-headers.html/>.

DNSstuff. (n.d.). *DNS tools, manage monitor analyze, DNSstuff*. Retrieved from <http://www.dnsstuff.com/tools/tools/>.

FortÃ©. (n.d.). Internet message headers—quick reference. *Tieto- ja sÃ¤hkÃ¶tekniikka Tampereen Teknillinen Yliopisto*. Retrieved from <http://www.cs.tut.fi/~jkorpela/headers.html/>.

Free Online Network tools—Traceroute, Nslookup, Dig, Whois lookup, Ping—IPv6. (n.d.). *Free online network tools*. Retrieved from <http://centralops.net/co/>.

How Base64 Encoding Works—About Email. *About email—find free email, email program support, spam help and tips*. Retrieved from <http://email.about.com/cs/standards/a/base64_encoding.htm/>.

Internet Assigned Numbers Authority. (n.d.). Internet Assigned Numbers Authority. Retrieved from <http://www.iana.org/>.

IP Address Geolocation to Identify Website Visitor's Geographical Location. (n.d.). *IP address geolocation*. Retrieved from <http://IP2Location.com/>.

LACNIC. (n.d.). Latin America and Caribbean Network Information Centre (LACNIC). Retrieved from <http://www.lacnic.net/en/web/lacnic/inicio/>.

MaxMind—IP Geolocation and Online Fraud Prevention. (n.d.). *MaxMind—IP geolocation and online fraud prevention*. Retrieved from <http://www.maxmind.com/>.

Reno, J. (n.d.). *BrainyQuote.com*. Retrieved from <http://www.brainyquote.com/quotes/quotes/j/janetreno315534.html/>.

Request for Comments (RFC) Pages. (n.d.). *Request for comments (RFC) Pages*. Retrieved from <www.ietf.org/rfc.html/>.

RIPE Network Coordination Centre. (n.d.). Réseaux IP Européens Network Coordination Centre. Retrieved from <http://www.ripe.net/>.

Setting Up POP/IMAP Accounts. (n.d.). *Zimbra*. Retrieved from <http://www.zimbra.com/desktop/help/en_US/Zdesktop/z-Setting_up_POP_IMAP_accounts.htm/>.

SPF: RFC 4408 (n.d.). *SPF: Project overview*. Retrieved from <http://www.openspf.org/RFC_4408#header-field/>.

Traceroute, Ping, Domain Name Server (DNS) Lookup, WHOIS. (n.d.). *Traceroute*. Retrieved from <http://network-tools.com/>.

Understanding the Information Contained in an E-mail Header. (n.d.). *Computer hope's free computer help*. Retrieved from <http://www.computerhope.com/issues/ch000918.htm/>.

Working Unseen on the Internet

9

You know, it's really strange now with the Internet, with everyone having an unsolicited, anonymous opinion.
Jeff Daniels, American Actor

Internet anonymity

Being anonymous on the Internet is a technique used by many. It simply means an author's actions or messages are not revealed to others. It is not just a criminal's practice but a technique used by anyone trying to prevent others from identifying who they are and what they do online. The idea of being anonymous in one's writing is not a twenty-first century concept. Benjamin Franklin signed fictitious names and even created entire personas to get his letters published by his printer brother. One of Franklin's fictitious profiles was Silence Dogood, a purportedly, middle-aged widow (Public Broadcasting Service, 2002).

Internet users under totalitarian regimes deploy anonymity techniques to prevent their governments from identifying those who would use online free speech to change their situation. These techniques also can be used to circumvent Internet restrictions or filtering. Others trying to prevent their activities being known can use these methods to hide from stalkers. The simplest online anonymity technique is the use of a false name or a pseudonym. Common in emails or in chat rooms, individuals sometimes use fictitious names to conceal their identity.

However, using online anonymity methods is not without possible legal ramifications, particularly if one violates civil and/or criminal statutes. One can't assume someone's real identity, even to engage in legitimate online discourse, without facing possible civil action if not criminal penalties. This is particularly the case if the discourse is contrary to the real person's views. Additionally, using anonymity methods only makes it more difficult, but not impossible to catch someone engaging in criminal behavior. Once a person crosses the legal boundaries with their online behavior, anonymity serves as only an obstacle, not a complete barrier, to possible discovery and prosecution. Criminals are frequently more apt at using online hiding techniques than law enforcement or corporate investigators. They also need not be concerned with breaking laws, let alone administrative polices or procedures, in connection with using anonymity techniques. However, investigators have to be concerned with how their online actions, including the use of anonymity methods, may violate the law or negatively impact their cases and/or agency.

Responsible use

In 1999, the federal law enforcement agencies in the United States came together to form the Online Investigations Working Group (Working Group),[1] to provide some general guidance for investigators conducting online investigations. The result was 11 principles,[2] five of which focus on issues considering anonymity and/or working undercover online.[3] These pre-911 principles imposed no new restrictions on agents' conduct but did create two new procedural rules for agents or agencies to follow, concerning online undercover facilities (a consultation requirement with US Department of Justice (USDOJ)) and appropriating online identities (concurrence requirement from USDOJ). The principles were for federal agencies and not specific to state law enforcement, with the exception of highlighting concerns over local investigations with international connections. They were developed with the concept that agents were to follow their respective agency's internal rules, regardless of whether they were working online or in the real world. For instance, if they were permitted to work covertly in the real world than they could likewise work covertly online. Additionally, if there were a set of

---

[1]The Working Group was created approximately 2 years before 911 and the realignment and creation of the Department of Homeland Security. With that in mind, the Working Group had representatives from: the Justice Department (Criminal Division): (Computer Crime and Intellectual Property Section, Organized Crime and Racketeering Section, Terrorism and Violent Crimes Section, Child Exploitation and Obscenity Section, Office of International Affairs, the Tax Division, the Environment and Natural Resources Division, the Antitrust Division, the Civil Rights Division, the Office of Legal Counsel, the Inspector General's Office, the Attorney General's Advisory Committee, the Executive Office for United States Attorneys, and the Office of Policy Development); the Federal Bureau of Investigation; the Drug Enforcement Administration; the Immigration and Naturalization Service; the United States Marshals Service; the Treasury Department, Office of the Undersecretary for Law Enforcement, the Internal Revenue Service; the US Secret Service; the Bureau of Alcohol, Tobacco, and Firearms; the US Customs Service, the Federal Law Enforcement Training Center, the Financial Crimes Enforcement Network (FinCEN); the Department of Defense, the US Postal Service, the Inspectors General through the President's Council on Integrity and Efficiency, and the Food and Drug Administration.

[2]They are formally known as "Online Investigative Principles for Federal Law Enforcement Agents" (November 1999). It is noteworthy that document has the following footer advisement posted on each page: "Property of the United States Government, Contains Sensitive Law Enforcement Information; Distribution Limited to Law Enforcement Personnel." It was initially released, somewhat redacted, to the Electronic Privacy Information Center (EPIC) in 2004. It is now available online in its entirety from Public Intelligence at http://publicintelligence.net/the-department-of-justices-principles-for-conducting-online-undercover-operations/.

[3]The other six principles covered were approving Internet research, use of online services to communicate, use of software tools, prohibiting access to restricted online sources or facilities without legal authority, online activity by agents during personal time, and investigations where data and/or witnesses are located in foreign country.

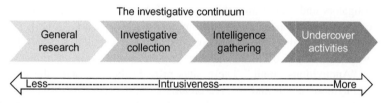

FIGURE 9.1

The investigative continuum.

rules that were to be followed for covert work in the real world, those same rules were to be followed to the extent possible, in an online environment. As the need arises, we will discuss those pertinent principles in this chapter and the next.

For now it is important to understand that the discussion of online anonymity techniques is not to provide a method to bypass agency or corporate rules on how investigations are to be conducted. Toward that objective, investigators need to consider how their investigative duties fall on an investigative continuum from least to more intrusive. The investigative continuum consists of general research, investigative collection, intelligence gathering, and undercover activities (Figure 9.1).

Additionally, it is important to understand that while conducting each of these activities, one maybe disclosing who they are or who they work for online, hence the possible need to use anonymity methods. Will that disclosure hamper their investigation? Will identification have a chilling effect on someone's legitimate right, for instance, the presence of law enforcement in a public online debate on gun control? However, is such surveillance, even covertly, justified by the law? Could online identification and presence negatively impact one's agency or company? For instance, someone visiting a pornographic website to document another employee's unauthorized access to that website, will just as likely leave identifying information, with that website, as the first employee. If that information becomes public, is it to be viewed merely as one bad employee and an investigation, or that the entire agency or company is visiting a pornographic website. Investigators need to consider the ramifications of their online activities before they engage in them. Using anonymity techniques as an investigator are only justified if the overall online activity is clearly authorized.

Common methods to gain web anonymity

The most common method for an investigator to gain a level of Internet anonymity is through the use of a free email account. The most commonly used email addresses are the big service providers, Google's Gmail, Microsoft's live.com, and the tried and true AOL. The investigator can obtain multiple accounts in their personas to use for a variety of purposes. Free account and trial memberships on various websites can assist with building the persona. Familiarity with these sites can help investigators understand how they work so when an investigation of this type of site occurs they will have an understanding of what to look for.

Investigators can also use anonymous or disposable email services through various websites. Many of these services can be found with a simple Google Search of "Anonymous email." These sites provide the user with the ability to send an anonymous email and receive email for short periods of time, such as a registration requirement at a website. Some sites will also forward email received at the anonymous account to any account the user selects. These sites differ from the above free email services as one does not have to register with the service. Additionally, the user's IP address information is frequently not maintained as long as one of the free email accounts noted above. For instance, when one registers for a free email account, the IP address from where they are accessing the account is frequently maintained indefinitely. Whenever a user accesses the account, the free email service provider will also maintain a record of that IP address. However, with an anonymous service that IP address information, although collected, is only maintained for a very short time. For instance, Guerrilla Mail will delete logs after 24 hours.

Both free and anonymous accounts are obviously used by criminals who give false names and other information to commit extortion, death threats, or stalking through the Internet. Criminals also use free accounts to aid in their theft of computer accounts and to receive anonymous payments, such as untraceable digital cash (E-Gold, Bitcoin, etc.). The Achilles' Heel for discovering who is behind the account is the IP address information collected when one registers and/or accesses the account. The free accounts maintain this information longer than the anonymous accounts. However, one can't use the same anonymous accounts indefinitely. If one creates a free account with bogus information or even an anonymous account from their home computer, that IP address may be discovered, particularly if someone does something illegal.

The low-tech solution is not to create or access the account using one's own Internet Service Provider. Criminals know this and will use cybercafes and/or free Wi-Fi hot spots like Starbucks or McDonalds or any number of others to access these accounts, adding another layer of anonymity to their crimes. Many communities now even offer free Wi-Fi services throughout their city. If someone traces the IP address it will come back to the cybercafe or the free Wi-Fi hot spot. The next sections of this chapter will deal with more advanced methods of concealing your IP address.

INVESTIGATIVE TIP

Common Anonymous Email

Anonymouse.org, http://anonymouse.org/anonemail.html
Guerrilla Mail, http://www.guerrillamail.com/
Jetable, http://www.jetable.org/en/index
Mailinator, http://www.mailinator.com/
Send Anonymous Email, http://www.sendanonymousemail.net/

What your computer can reveal about you

In the last chapter, we discussed how to check your investigative system for potential attack points. We even recommended some websites that you can use to check your security. What we haven't discussed is exactly what your investigative system can reveal about who you are and what system you are using. So for the purposes of this section, let's ask ourselves a question. What does your computer tell other computers about you?

What your browser reveals (http requests)

Web browsers, like Internet Explorer, Firefox, or Chrome, are tools designed to allow a user to access resources on the World Wide Web. To facilitate this access, the web browser has to communicate with a server on the Internet that contains the data that you are seeking. This communication is a standard protocol designed to let both sides agree to exchange data. Your browser sends data to the web server and requests the page you've asked for. It contains details on browser needs and what it will accept back from the server. It reveals the browser type, its version, and the browser's capabilities. The communication can also reveal software installed on the investigator's computer, potentially sites you have visited, your Internet Service Provider, and even IP address (Figure 9.2).

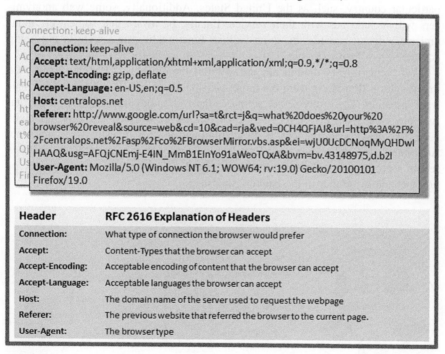

FIGURE 9.2

Example of browser headers and their explanation.

Anonymizing your surfing

For the investigator, there are several web-based methods to anonymize your browsing. The first option to consider is the use of a proxy via a website. A proxy is an agent authorized to act for another. These web anonymizers simply act as a go between the investigator's browser and the website that is being investigated. (We will discuss the use of a proxy server, aka proxy firewall or application level gateway, later in the chapter) There are numerous free and pay websites that can act as proxy. These sites should be tested out so that you are aware of their functionality before using them during an investigation. Some of the websites allow you to browse successive webpages and some do not. Others will not allow you to conduct certain investigations, such as peer-to-peer (P2P) cases or complete downloads. Some web anonymizers could retain information of the investigator's browser and IP address. Sometimes, web anonymizers, such as Anonymouse.org (http://anonymouse.org/anonwww.html), do not allow you to choose your originating IP address. You get whatever IP address is available, which may or not be an issue for your investigation. Others, such as Hidemyass. com (http://www.hidemyass.com/proxy/) and Newipnow.com (http://www.newip-now.com/), will allow you to pick from a range of various IP addresses. However, even this range may limit your choices to those originating from a particular country, such as the United States. Additionally, some web anonymizers will include ads with their service. Finally, be aware that some web anonymizers will not provide the same look or functionality, as a website not being accessed via a proxy (Figure 9.3).

Web anonymizers though are not without their benefits. Besides hiding the investigator's IP address from the target website, these sites can also prevent malware infection. The proxy server acting as the web anonymizers is the server that runs any code from the target page. So if the target webpage has any malicious code the proxy can prevent it from running on the investigator's machine. Additionally, by redirecting your Internet traffic through the anonymizing services secure servers, your online identity is protected. These servers often use encryption technology similar to the banking industry.

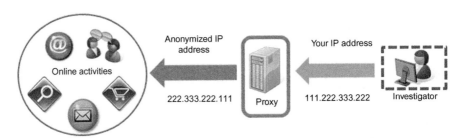

FIGURE 9.3

How proxying websites work.

Another method for hiding your activities while on the Internet is through the use of Virtual Private Networks (VPN). VPN's also act as a go between your browser and the website you want to access. However, they have the added benefit of encrypting all the communication between your browser and the website. Some of the same limitations that apply to web anonymizers also apply to VPNs. Many of the web anonymizers also provide VPN for a fee.

The pay version of Anonymizer found at www.anonymizer.com is an example of a VPN. This program hides your computer's IP address from the Internet and provides an encrypted tunnel (Secure Sockets Layer (SSL)) between your computer and Anonymizer's servers. SSL is the same encryption you see when you do banking or other secure business over the Internet. It also reduces spam and tracking. You can easily toggle the program on and off. Some sites don't like it (i.e., Google) because they think you're a hacker doing a denial of service attack. A simple search for VPN services online will provide a number of available services that can suit the investigator's needs.

THE GOOD AND THE BAD OF ANONYMIZATION
The Good: Freedom of speech, anticensorship, and anonymous tips.
   The Bad: Bypassing Internet use policy, abusing organization resources, and preventing filters from monitoring activities.
   The Ugly: Spam, piracy, information and identity theft, cyber-stalking, and hiding terrorist activities (Figure 9.4).

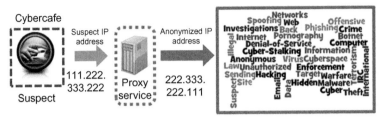

FIGURE 9.4

Criminal use of multiple layers of anonymity.

Using proxy servers with your own network

When investigating Internet crimes the investigator needs to consider how much information that he presents to servers and webpages that he may be examining. Hiding oneself on the Internet used to be the hackers' purview. However, technology changes and so has the ability to easily implement the same techniques hackers use to hide themselves during your investigations. There are many techniques for eluding identification on the Internet. Proxies have been used for years for this purpose. They act as a go between your network and the one you are investigating. A proxy server acts on your behalf and forwards to the server you are looking at any requests you make. The server you are investigating only sees the "proxy." Proxy servers, also known as a proxy firewall, aka, Application Level Gateway, can be a hardware device or software application. A proxy server used in a normal network helps to prevent a hacker from obtaining internal addresses and details of that private network. It is an intermediary device that indirectly connects two systems and, as a result, allows these systems to communicate directly. In your own network, proxy servers can be used as a device to protect the network from unauthorized access and help to secure a network against outside attack. Proxy services are not limited to just hardware devices or applications. They can also be available as an Internet service.

Free online proxy servers

You can find proxy servers on the Internet that can be used during an investigation. Public proxy servers can be found at various websites such as Free Public Proxy Servers List http://www.proxies.by. Certainly, use of any "free" service on the Internet for an investigation comes with certain risks. You don't know who owns the server, nor do you know if the owner is monitoring traffic coming and going on the proxy server. Investigators using these servers need to understand these potential risks when conducting an investigation through these servers. One of the issues with using free proxy servers is that they are very transient in nature. Most come and go fairly quickly as a service. One day that IP address has a proxy server and the next day it is gone. As a hiding method, this can be very useful to the criminal as well as the investigator. Changing the IP addresses of the proxy servers used makes the user far more difficult to find. Finding these "free" proxies is as simple as searching Google for the term "free proxy." Many sites maintain these lists for a variety of uses and not just for use by criminals. Persons in countries that don't allow free and unabated access to the Internet, or those trying to prevent a repressive government from finding postings on a blog, use these proxies.

So how is this different than a web-based anonymous service? Well, a web anonymizer is a website that offers the proxy services for your web browsing. This communication uses an application protocol, specifically, Hypertext Transfer Protocol (HTTP). Internet Explorer, or any other browser or tool will use HTTP. The free proxy servers on the Internet are servers that can be connected to by various tools to reroute your Internet traffic. This can be your browser, but it can also be, an Internet Relay Chat (IRC) client or any other Internet tool that allows the user to set up a proxy connection through another server. This routes the tool's traffic through the IP address of the proxy server thus hiding the tool's Internet traffic. In Figure 9.5, you can see that the Local Area Network (LAN) settings are rerouted through the IP address listed as the proxy.

To Tor or not to Tor

The Onion Router (Tor) is a significant tool in the "I need to hide on the Internet" world (Figure 9.6). Tor was developed from a concept originally written about by the US Navy. According to the Tor website, "Tor protects you by bouncing your communications around a distributed network of relays run by volunteers all around the world: it prevents somebody watching your Internet connection from learning what sites you visit, and it prevents the sites you visit from learning your physical location" (Tor Project Anonymity Online).

Your browser normally makes a call out through your Internet Service Provider to servers on the Internet. These servers easily identify who you are by your IP address so they can communicate back with you. This exposure of your IP address is what can tell the target who you are and possibly where you are in the world. The Tor network in its simplest description strips that information out and only provides the end user with an IP address belonging to the Tor network and not you. Thus you have effectively hidden from the end website you are visiting or target user that you may be communicating with through the Internet (Please note this is an over simplification of the process and exact details of how the Tor network works can be found on the project website). The current Tor Browser bundle installs its own browser version that does not allow the user to change the proxy settings in the browser. You can still use the installed "Vadalia" (like the onion) package to proxy your own browser through the Tor network, although the Tor project no longer recommends this practice.

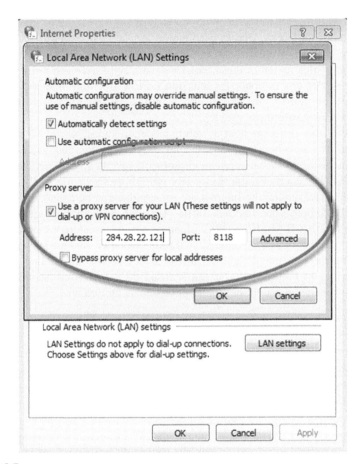

FIGURE 9.5

LAN setting tab showing proxy settings in Internet Explorer.

Using Tor during online investigations is much easier now than in the past. This is due to the increase in most users' Internet bandwidth, the constant upgrading and improving of the Tor software and its easy integration into the popular browsers. So how does the investigator implement Tor during their investigations? Well, the simplest method is to use the Tor network to hide browsing activity. If you are investigating a webpage or website, we know that there is certain information that our browser tells that server or website about who we are and potentially where we are. Our browsers can reveal our IP addresses, what kind of browser we are using, and its version. We can use Tor to prevent a suspect webpage from identifying us.

Using Tor in your investigations is as easy as downloading it and installing the Tor browser. Go to the Tor project website (www.torproject.org) and download the current Tor Browser Bundle Windows installer. Click on the

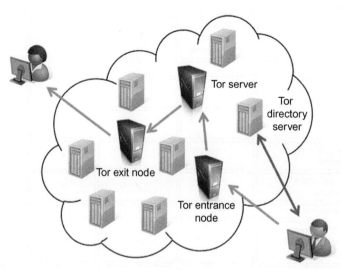

FIGURE 9.6

Tor network.

executable file and the Tor project installs. Previous versions of Tor required setting the proxy settings in your browser to use the Tor network, but this is all done automatically during the installation of the latest Tor browser bundle.

The Tor project has a page you can go to that will verify that you are using the Tor network properly or you can go to one of the websites on the Internet that grabs your IP address like http://whatismyipaddress.com/ to identify what IP address you are exposing to the world.

We are now ready to go online and start our investigation without being identified. Things to note here. The online application being used by the Tor network in this configuration is the Tor browser. If you send an email to the target from your normal email client on your desktop, use another browser, instant messaging, or use P2P software you will potentially expose who you really are by your IP address. To use any other applications through the Tor network you need to set them up to use the Tor proxy settings.

Other things to consider if you are not using the Tor Browser Bundle is that your browser set up needs to turn off the running of scripts, ActiveX, and cookies. Also block pop-ups. But you say "I can't access all the good content on the Internet". Correct, you can't but then the end user can't identify you either through holes in these protocols. Each of these features enhance our web surfing experience, but they also require a code be downloaded through your browser and run on your machine. This can allow for the code to default to a port in use that is not being redirected to the Tor network, thereby exposing who you are. This may not be important in all the cases you work, but be aware of it. If you lock down your browser and don't get the content you want, you can always relax the

	Better website anonymizers	Better VPNs/proxies	Tor	Tails
Hides IP address	✓	✓	✓	✓
Allows user to select "source" IP location	✓ i	✓	✓	✓
Allows surfing to multiple sites	✓ iii	✓	✓	✓
Allows downloading from websites visited		✓	✓	✓
Works with numerous internet protocols		✓ iv	✓ v	✓
Encrypts traffic		✓ vi	✓ vii	✓ viii
Allows use of windows based internet evidence collection tools	✓	✓	✓	
No data is saved to local investigative computer				✓
Requires installation of software on local investigative computer		✓ ix	✓	✓
Cost to user	✓ x	✓ xi		

i Some of the websites have an option to do this but most do not.
ii Some VPN's/Proxies have an option to do this but most do not.
iii Free Website anonymizers may not continue to protect user after multiple links to different websites.
iv User must set other Internet tools to use proxy/VPN settings.
v User must set other Internet tools to use Tor Socks settings.
vi Encryption is between user's computer and server through the VPN connection.
vii Tor transmissions are encrypted until they data exit the last Tor node before delivery to the receiver.
viii Tor transmissions are encrypted until they data exit the last Tor node before delivery to the receiver.
ix Most VPN's require some software to be installed.
x Some websites have pay for service versions.
xi See viii above

FIGURE 9.7

Comparison of Internet hiding tools.

controls and go back and look at the site. You know at least the risks and can make a decision based on the needs of your investigation (Figure 9.7).

Tor's hidden web services

Gormley (2011) wrote a short article which described how drugs were blatantly being sold on the Internet and members of Congress were very concerned and demanding an investigation. Selling drugs on the Internet is nothing new. The place on the Internet "openly" selling drugs was on the Tor network through the

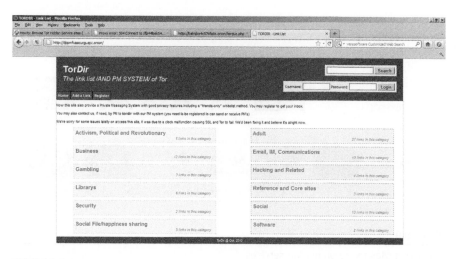

FIGURE 9.8

TorDir hidden services site.

use of Tor's "Hidden Services" function. The "Silk Road" is an online market open for the sale of goods and named after the ancient road used to bring goods from the Orient to the West. (The person behind the Silk Road hidden service was arrested by the FBI as this book was going to print. Goldstein 2013). For the power users, the Tor network's hidden services are probably nothing new. For the average online investigator though, you may have heard of Tor and may have even tried to use it. But were you aware that webpages can be concealed within the Tor network? Have you ever seen a ".onion" domain name? Hidden services were introduced to the Tor network in 2004. They are run on a Tor client using special server software. This "hidden service" uses a pseudo top-level domain of ".onion". Using this domain, the TOR routes traffic through its network without the use of IP addresses. To get to these hidden services, you must be using the Tor network.

How do you find sites using these hidden services? Well there is not a real "Google" for finding these sites, but there are lists of the addresses that can be found on the Tor network such as the Core Onion at http://eqt5g4fuenphqinx.onion/.

Core.onion, according to its hidden services site, has been in the network since 2007. Once on the Tor network and after accessing the Core.onion, you will find a simple directory to start exploring hidden services on the Tor network (Figure 9.8).

TorDir is another directory of hidden services. It gives you access to a variety of sites that offer instant messaging services, email, items for sale, social media—type sites, and marketplaces, all concealed through the Tor network. In the markets, a variety of things are for sale, and many appear on their face to be illegal. You can find sites for the purchase of illegal drugs, pornography, including sites with descriptive names indicative of child pornography and downloads for

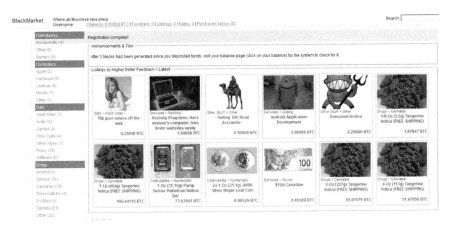

FIGURE 9.9

Example of sites found on hidden services.

hacked versions of various software. File sharing also looks to be popular and can be found in several .onion sites (Figure 9.9).

Users of IRC can find similar hidden services on Tor. The Freenode website at http://freenode.net/irc_servers.shtml gives clear instructions on how to access Freenode IRC servers on Tor's Hidden Services.

Tor is not the only anonymization service on the Internet. Ip2 is another anonymizing network that is becoming increasingly popular, which has its own "eeepsites" similar to the hidden services offered in Tor that a user can post content to like a website. Hidden services on both the Tor network and Ip2 are going to increasingly become a location that will be misused by criminals. It will also become a place on the Internet that investigators will need to become familiar with if they are to further their online investigations.

Tor and tails

Investigators that have a significant need to hide their computing system and ensure that they won't be recovered can use a tool like the Amnesic Incognito Live System (Tails). Tails is a bootable DVD or USB drive that implements the Tor project. Tails uses the Debian Linux operating system. Using a bootable DVD or USB bypasses a computer's operating system, with all programs being run from the DVD or USB, and loaded into the machine's Random Access Memory (RAM). In this way data is not saved to the computer's hard drive, even unintentionally.

Tails' advantage is that the system uses the binaries on the DVD or USB that have been solely designed to prevent any possible exposure of the user to others on the Internet. The bootable DVD or USB drive implementation runs on its own operating system and has a solid implementation of the Tor project's network.

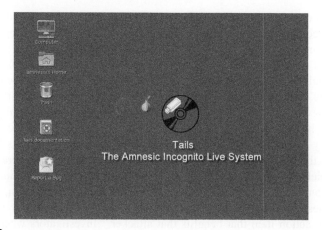

FIGURE 9.10

Screenshot of tails.

This helps to ensure that the system used cannot be identified from someone wishing to identify the computer used. The downside of using Tails is none of the Windows-based collection tools previously noted will work (Figure 9.10).

INVESTIGATIVE TIP

Evidence Collection in Tails

There are some programs built into Tails as part of the Debian-based Linux distribution that can be used to collect evidence. The important thing to remember in using these programs is to save all files to your desktop and transfer them to your USB device before you shut down the program. Otherwise, the files created will be lost when the system is shut down. Two basic tools are GIMP and Open Office. Locate GIMP and start the program. After it has loaded, select File and Create, which will provide an option to capture a screenshot. After capturing a screenshot, save it to the desktop. Open Office can be used to capture text. Locate the program and open it. Capture text or make notes as you would in any word-processing program. Again, save the created file to your desktop. You also can still use the "Save As" feature in the built-in browser, which is Firefox. Again, whatever you capture or create should be saved to the desktop and moved to a USB device.

Tracking criminals who use anonymous methods to hide

We have discussed many tools to use to hide ourselves online. We know our investigative targets can do the same thing. So how is it that we can track those who use these kinds of services for criminal purposes? There are many different things that can be done mechanically to track criminals online. What the investigator needs to know at the start is that a knowledgeable criminal maintains their security and use of the technology to prevent identification and will be harder to locate and identify than those that are not as diligent. One of the best methods of identifying people online is the same tactic that hackers have used for years, social engineering. In the context of Internet investigations, social engineering is the act of manipulating people to do something or reveal information.

This kind of tactic has long been the criminal's mainstay. A simple but effective ruse could be faking a telephone call to the target stating your calling from the company's "Help" desk. The criminal asks the target for assistance with an issue. During this conversation the criminal gets the target to reveal his login and password as he is helping work through a computer problem on the network. This seems overly simple and unlikely, but it is how many famous hackers like Kevin Mitnick got the right information to allow access to networks they were attacking. Kevin Mitnick has said that "Social engineering is using manipulation, influence and deception to get a person, a trusted insider within an organization, to comply with a request, and the request is usually to release information or to perform some sort of action item that benefits that attacker." Investigators when trying to identify those using anonymization need to be thinking in the same terms. Get the criminal to reveal certain things about themselves that they would not normally do. Security-conscience targets are probably less likely to do this; however, everyone makes mistakes.

CRIMINALS USING ANONYMIZATION

If you ask Hector Xavier Monsegur, aka Sabu, about what whether or not using anonymization is a good thing, you might get a loud "Yes." As a member of the LulzSec hacking group, an offshoot of Anonymous, he regularly protected his identity through the use of the Tor. According to articles about his arrest he logged into a channel on IRC one time without using Tor and revealed his actual IP address. The FBI was able to use this information to identify who he was and charge him with crimes related to his hacking. The lesson on both sides is that when anonymization tools are used they can effectively hide your activity, both criminal and investigative. However, one slip and your real identity can be revealed. For law enforcement, this can ruin months of work and the potential prosecution of the targets.

Tools for catching the hiding Internet target

The basics of catching a target hiding on the Internet require that there be some interaction in most cases. That interaction could be trading an email, communicating in a chat room, or getting them to visit a website or social media page. In each of these situations, there are things that could be implemented that might help to reveal usable information about the target. The investigator has to remember though that the information identified online may be an IP address that is hidden behind a proxy or other hiding technique. Identifying the real IP address used by the target could lead to identifying the real person who is the target of the investigation. You can easily identify if the target is using the Tor network by checking the IP address you have through the publicly available list of exit nodes used by the Tor network. The Tor networks' last server on its network is called the "exit node." This is the last computer server in the Tor chain that is identifiable by the investigator in the network. You can identify this IP address by going to the Tor Project website, www.torproject.org, and checking around on their project portal pages. They have a public list of the exit nodes for research purposes.

We can start with the simplest of the tools for identifying a target and that is an email. We spent some time in Chapter 8 talking about IP addresses and tracing them to their source. Reading an email header, if not spoofed, can give the investigator a direction to locate the target. Other effective techniques that can be used are tools like those from ReadyNotify.com or AnonymousSpeech.com. These websites offer tools that add content to the email, or documents attached to the email, that when opened by the target can track the target's IP address. Each of these services will identify the receiver's IP address. There are limitations with their usage. Some email tools like Microsoft Outlook require that the attachment be accepted to allow for the tracking tool to work.

More proactive methods

There are some more proactive methods of identifying anonymous users on the Internet. Two companies have tools that can add in this more technical method. This is far beyond the basic level but is worth mentioning hear for the basic investigator to know that with the right skills and technology most targets can be found. The Gamma Group, a British company, sells its software to governments solely for criminal investigations. Its product FinSpy, part of the FinFisher product suite, is a proactive tool used to identify, track, and monitor targets on the Internet. Details on the tool are limited publicly but some reports identify that it is being deployed around the world in various investigations.

Another tool designed specifically to assist in the identification of Internet users of anonymous technology is ACAV by Vere Software. Under a grant from the USDOJ, Vere Software and their partner, the University of Nevada, Reno's Computer Science and Engineering Department, developed a tool called ACAV. ACAV was designed to assist state and local law enforcement investigators identify criminal users of anonymization. Both of these companies reportedly release their tools only to law enforcement investigators.

THE HEWLETT-PACKARD LESSON

In 2006, Hewlett-Packard investigators were called to task by the government for the techniques they used to ferret out an insider who was leaking sensitive information. One of the techniques used was web bugs via ReadyNotify.com. McMillian (2006) article notes: "When the question of whether web bugs are legal has been tested in the United States, courts have tended to focus on whether this type of technology violates federal wire tapping laws," says Chris Jay Hoofnagle, senior staff attorney with the Samuelson Law, Technology and Public Policy Clinic at the University of California, Berkeley. Hoofnagle says "State courts could take up the issue of web bugs, considering the existence of anti-hacking laws in states such as California. California law prohibits certain uses of computer resources without the permission of the user, and nobody knows for sure whether HP's actions would violate this law or similar statutes in other states."

None of the HP investigators got in legal trouble for use of web bugs. However, several did get into legal hot water for how they used the technique called pretexting to convince telephone companies to provide confidential information. In one case, the investigator used the target's own Social Security number, thereby committing identify theft, to convince the telephone company to provide the confidential information. One result of this case was the passage of the Telephone Records and Privacy Protection Act of 2006, which prohibits pretexting to buy, sell, or obtain personal phone records, except when conducted by law enforcement or intelligence agencies.

The bottom line as always is seek legal advice for your investigative procedures before you use them (Figure 9.11).

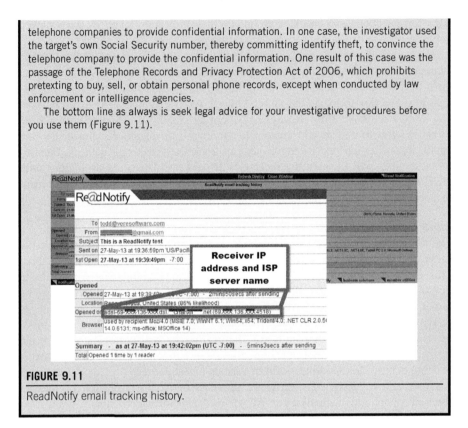

FIGURE 9.11

ReadNotify email tracking history.

Other methods of identifying Internet users can be through web bugs, or web beacons, designed especially for embedding in a webpage. This is already a common practice within the marketing community. Google Analytics is a commonly used web bug inserted into a webpage to track users. This same concept can be used to trac

k and identify a target during an investigation. These can be web beacons, which are small objects embedded in the webpage, that when loaded by the user's browser make a call back to a server controlled by the owner. Tynan (2013) notes there were more than 1,300 tracking companies following users through these techniques.

Another method that can be used to track users by their IP address is through the review of server logs from websites. The website owner with access to the server can identify users' IP addresses when they click the website on the server. Investigators can set up a web server with an undercover website designed for the investigation and use this as a method to track users browsing to the undercover website.

PRINCIPLE 7 ONLINE UNDERCOVER FACILITIES

At the start of this chapter, we noted that Online Investigations Working Group (Working Group) had provided 11 principles concerning online investigations. Principle 7 deals with the creation of an undercover website, in part creating a consultation requirement for federal law enforcement. Principle 7 also notes several areas of concern for federal law enforcement in this area. One area is the website administrator versus law enforcement role. Principle 7 reflects: "Law enforcement agents may not circumvent the statutory restrictions on government access to information simply by covertly becoming a service provider. Thus, while law enforcement agencies may use the system provider's authority to manage or protect the system, they may not use the system administrator's legal powers to gather evidence normally obtainable only through procedures required by Electronic Communications Privacy Act (ECPA). To avoid legal complications, agencies should consider taking steps to separate the responsibility for administering the online facility, to which one legal framework applies, from its criminal investigative function, to which a different legal framework applies" (p. 37).

These principles were created in 1999. However, it would behoove any investigator especially, those from federal agencies, to consult with their legal authority if they are planning to create an undercover website.

CONCLUSION

In this chapter, we discussed the use of anonymization as tools for the investigator as well as for the criminal. Anonymization can be an effective method for the investigator to secure their computing systems and their actions on the Internet. Each tool discussed has its own advantages and disadvantages, and investigators need to carefully consider their tool selection and how they are implemented. The use of anonymization by criminals does not halt an investigation. There are methods by which the investigator can track users of anonymization on the Internet. It can make an investigation more complicated and requires more effort on the part of the investigator, but it does not stop the investigation itself. Clearly, understanding anoymization techinques and how they are used by criminals is become an important skill for the online investigator.

Further reading

About freenode IRC Servers. (n.d.). *Freenode IRC servers*. Retrieved from <freenode.net/irc_servers.shtml>.

Anonymizer—Online Privacy, Security, and Anonymous Surfing Solutions. (n.d.). *Anonymizer, Inc*. Retrieved from <https://www.anonymizer.com/>.

Anonymous VPN, Proxy & Torrent Proxy Services. (n.d.). *TorGuard*. Retrieved from <http://torguard.net/>.

Architecture of the World Wide Web, Volume One. (2004). *World wide web consortium (W3C)*. Retrieved from <http://www.w3.org/TR/webarch/>.

Benjamin Franklin. Wit and Wisdom. Name that Ben, PBS: Public Broadcasting Service. (2002). *PBS*. Retrieved from <http://www.pbs.org/benfranklin/l3_wit_name.html/>.

BTGuard—Anonymous BitTorrent Services. (n.d.). *BTGuard*. Retrieved from <http://btguard.com/>.

Certified Email with Delivery Receipts, Silent Tracking, Proof-of-Opening History, Security and Timestamps. (n.d.). *ReadNotify.com*. Retrieved from <ReadyNotify.com>.

Daniels, J. (n.d.). *BrainyQuote.com*. Retrieved from <http://www.brainyquote.com/quotes/quotes/j/jeffdaniel434329.html/>.

EPIC—Wiretapping. (n.d.). *EPIC—Electronic Privacy Information Center*. Retrieved from <http://epic.org/privacy/wiretap/onlineprinpt1.pdf/>.

Fast VPN and Anonymous Proxy—Privacy, now and cheap—Proxy.sh. (n.d.). *Proxy.sh*. Retrieved from <https://proxy.sh/>.

FinSpy Agent—Gamma International (UK) Limited Software Informer. (n.d.). *Gamma International (UK) Limited Software Informer*. Retrieved from <http://finspy-agent.software.informer.com/>.

Free Proxy—Surf Anonymously & Hide Your IP Address. (n.d.). *Hide my ass! free proxy and privacy tools—surf the web anonymously*. Retrieved June 10, 2013, from <http://www.hidemyass.com/proxy/>.

Free Public Proxy Servers Lists HTTP, HTTPS Secure Tunnel Connect IRC, SOCKS, CGI PHP Web, Transparent Anonymous Elite High Anonymous, Standard, Non-standard Ports. (n.d.). *Free public proxy servers lists*. Retrieved from <www.proxies.by/>.

Garsiel, T., & Irish, P. (2011, August 5). How browsers work: Behind the scenes of modern web browsers—HTML5 Rocks. *HTML5 Rocks—A Resource for Open Web HTML5 Developers*. Retrieved from <http://www.html5rocks.com/en/tutorials/internals/how-browserswork/>.

Goldstein, J. (2013, October 2). Arrest in U.S. Shuts Down a Black Market for Narcotics - NYTimes.com. The New York Times - Breaking News, World News & Multimedia. Retrieved from <http://www.nytimes.com/2013/10/03/nyregion/operator-of-online-market-for-illegal-drugs-is-charged-fbi-says.html?_r=0>.

Gormley, M. (2011, June 5). Senators target internet narcotics trafficking website silk road. *Breaking news and opinion on the Huffington Post*. Retrieved from <http://www.huffingtonpost.com/2011/06/05/senators-internet-narcotics-_n_871466.html/>.

I2P Anonymous Network—I2P. (n.d.). *I2P Anonymous Network—I2P*. Retrieved from <www.i2p2.de/>.

Jetable.org—Home. (n.d.). *Jetable.org—Home*. Retrieved from <http://www.jetable.org/en/index/>.

Jones, K. (2007, June 29). Lessons learned from HP's pretexting case. *InformationWeek, Business Technology News, Reviews and Blogs*. Retrieved from <http://www.informationweek.com/lessons-learned-from-hps-pretexting-case/200001776/>.

KPROXY—Free Anonymous Web Proxy—Anonymous Proxy. (n.d.). *KPROXY—Free Anonymous Web Proxy*. Retrieved from <http://www.kproxy.com/>.

Leyden, J. (2012, March 7). The one tiny slip that put LulzSec chief Sabu in the FBI's pocket. *The Register: Sci/Tech News for the World*. Retrieved from <http://www.theregister.co.uk/2012/03/07/lulzsec_takedown_analysis/>.

Li, B., Erdin, E., Güneş, M. H., Bebis, G., & Shipley, T. (2011). An analysis of anonymizer technology usage. *Traffic monitoring and analysis third international workshop, TMA 2011, Vienna, Austria, April 27, 2011: proceedings* (pp. 108–121). Berlin: Springer.

Mailinator—Let Them Eat Spam!. (n.d.). *Mailinator—Let Them Eat Spam!* Retrieved from <http://www.mailinator.com/>.

McMillian, R. (2006, October 6). Web bugs trained to track your E-Mail. *PCWorld—News, Tips and Reviews from the Experts on PCs, Windows, and More.* Retrieved from <http://www.pcworld.com/article/127444/article.html/>.

Mitnick, K. (n.d.). *BrainyQuote.com.* Retrieved from <http://www.brainyquote.com/quotes/quotes/k/kevinmitni469455.html/>.

NewIPNow.com—Change IP On Demand. Private proxies and More. (n.d.). *NewIPNow. com.* Retrieved from <http://www.newipnow.com/>.

Ninja Cloak: Fast, Free, Anonymous Web Browsing (n.d.). *NinjaCloak.com.* Retrieved from <http://www.ninjacloak.com/>.

Proxify® Anonymous Proxy—Surf the Web Privately and Securely. (n.d.). *Proxify®.* Retrieved from <https://proxify.com/>.

RFC 2616: IETF HTTP/1.1 RFC. Retrieved from <http://tools.ietf.org/html/rfc2616/>.

RFC 2965: IETF HTTP State Management Mechanism RFC References. Retrieved from <http://tools.ietf.org/html/rfc2965/>.

RFC 4229: HTTP Header Field Registrations. December 2005 (contains a more complete list of HTTP headers). Retrieved from <http://tools.ietf.org/html/rfc4229/>.

Send Anonymous Email. (n.d.). *Send Anonymous Email.* Retrieved from <http://www.sendanonymousemail.net/>.

Send Anonymous Email, Anonymous Domain and Anonymous Hosting. (n.d.). *Anonymous Speech.* Retrieved June 9, 2013, from AnonymousSpeech.com.

The Department of Justice's Principles for Conducting Online Undercover Operations, Public Intelligence. (n.d.). *Public Intelligence.* Retrieved from <http://publicintelligence.net/the-department-of-justices-principles-for-conducting-online-undercover-operations/>.

Tor Project Anonymity Online. (n.d.). *Tor Project Anonymity Online.* Retrieved from <https://www.torproject.org/>.

TorrentPrivacy—Hide your Personal Activity in P2P world. (n.d.). *TorrentPrivacy.* Retrieved from <https://torrentprivacy.com/>.

Tynan, D. (2013, March 21). Web trackers are totally out of control. *ITworld.* Retrieved from <http://www.itworld.com/it-management/349218/web-trackers-are-completely-out-control/>.

Vere Software—ACAV. (n.d.). *Vere Software—Online Evidence Collection & Documentation.* Retrieved from <http://veresoftware.com/index.php?page = ACAV/>.

VPN Service, from the Leaders in VPN Private Internet Access VPN Service. (n.d.). *Private Internet Access.* Retrieved from <https://www.privateinternetaccess.com/>.

WebRTC 1.0: Real-time Communication Between Browsers. (n.d.). *World Wide Web Consortium (W3C).* Retrieved from <http://www.w3.org/TR/webrtc/>.

WebWarper: Saving Traffic, Antivirus, Acceleration, Anonymizer, Optimization of Sites. (n.d.). *WebWarper.* Retrieved from <http://webwarper.net/>.

What Is My IP Address Lookup IP, Hide IP, Change IP, Trace IP and more. (n.d.). *What Is My IP Address.* Retrieved from <whatismyipaddress.com/>.

Wong, G. (2006, October 5). Ex-HP chairman Dunn, others charged in leak case—October 4, 2006. *CNNMoney.* Retrieved from <http://money.cnn.com/2006/10/04/news/companies/hp_california/index.htm?cnn = yes/>.

Covert Operations on the Internet

10

Some of the bravest and the best men of all the world, certainly in law enforcement, have made their contributions while they were undercover.

Thomas Foran, Former United States Attorney

Covert operations on the Internet

Covert operations on the Internet and online undercover work are becoming an increasingly important task for the Internet investigator. Being undercover on the Internet is significantly different than doing the same activity in the real world. Think about it for a moment. Is there any way in the "real world" a 40-year-old male cop could successful impersonate a 13-year-old female to catch a sex offender? Only with the advent of the Internet are such investigations possible. Although the contact may not be in person, the skills are very similar. This chapter will help to outline the process to establish a properly configured undercover persona and use that identity during your Internet investigations.

Working covertly on the Internet is not a function of simply making a Hotmail account and sitting in a chatroom. Unfortunately online undercover investigative training, even for law enforcement, is not always provided. Tetzlaff-Bemiller (2011) noted that law enforcement personnel training for targeting sexual predators is not consistent across all units or agencies. To maximize effectiveness and to insure cases are not lost due to the use of improper techniques, there needs to be consistency in the content and frequency of undercover Internet investigation training.

Additionally, investigators and their employers have to develop effective policy, skills, and operation planning techniques to conduct covert and online undercover operations. So what is the purpose of working covertly on the Internet? Covert operations, like all investigative activities, are either proactive or reactive. They include:

- General intelligence gathering, including establishing information sources, identifying locations and web presence of questionable activities, and mapping online and social relationships/networks.
- Seeking out and identifying illegal behavior and establishing a crime has occurred.

- Establishing motives for crimes.
- Identifying relationships between targets, victims, and other subjects.
- Establishing whether the illegal activity constitutes a criminal enterprise and identifying the structure of that enterprise, including its leadership and assets.
- Providing location information of the targets, relationships, and victims.
- Disproving possible alibis of both targets and victims.
- Plan for and communicate with suspects/targets.

The traditional purpose of undercover activities is to gain the trust of an individual while acting as someone else to learn something useful to your investigation. Working undercover on the Internet has the same purpose. Only the location has changed. The Internet has numerous areas that can provide the undercover investigator with opportunities to find additional information related to their investigation. We have previously discussed these locations, each of which has its own protocols with unique methods of identifying, collecting, and presenting usable information. Common among all of these is the development and planning process prior to going online. Additionally, Internet investigators going undercover have to prepare their identity as any other undercover operative. Besides the investigative planning steps noted in Chapter 4, Internet undercover operations also include:

1. Clearly identifying the purpose: This is singly the most important part of the process. Is the purpose to establish the elements of a crime that has already occurred or it to be proactive and to stop a crime before it has been completed? Maybe the purpose is general intelligence gathering or "open source investigations," which were discussed in Chapter 4. Whatever the purpose, it must be specifically defined to keep the investigation focused.
2. Identify the means: What undercover persona (emails, profiles, etc.) needs to be developed? This will be dictated by the area which is the investigation's focus. Is the investigation centered on chatroom activities or on IRC channels? Is it a P2P investigation? All of these locations require different means to go undercover. Additionally, it is also necessary to identify the needed offline communication methods, such as undercover cell phones and postal addresses, while maintaining the undercover personas.
3. Define time resources: What days and hours will you be online? This answer will likely be dictated by your undercover persona. You can't pretend to be a minor if you are online when you are supposed to be in school or asleep. You also create difficulties if you are pretending to be located in one area, such as Europe, but are regularly online consistent with someone located in a Pacific Standard Time zone. How long will you be undercover in an online area before you conclude it is time to adjust your persona or location or altogether discontinue the activity?
4. Identify documentation requirements: How are you going to document your undercover activities? Up until this point we have talked about capturing websites and taking screenshots. However, documenting undercover activity online involves capturing not only the target's activities but also your

interactions with them. Also, don't forget to consider any legal requirements that may exist for how you record your activities. For instance, recall in Chapter 4 we noted there are 12 states (CA, CN, FL, IL, MD, MA, MI, MO, NV, NH, PA, and WA) which require two-party consent to record a communication, unless some legal process is met. Deciding how you are going to meet that requirement is important if you have to record a telephone or Skype communication with your target. Additionally, undercover investigations in a gaming environment will likely require digital video capabilities to capture the interactions with targets. As such, a special area or room may be needed.

5. Plan for the unexpected: Undercover investigations occur in real time and you have to expect the unexpected. What if your target, a sex offender, wants to meet you as minor, in half an hour? How will you handle it? Will you be able to marshal the manpower needed in a moment's notice or will you need to come up with a reasonable excuse why that can't happen. Brainstorming "what-if" scenarios as well as training and experience will help you be prepared for the unexpected.

"On the Internet no one knows you are a dog" (Fleishman, 2000)

Working undercover online requires the investigator to act as someone else. The process of building an undercover background to use on the Internet can be from the simple to the complex. Simple can include merely creating a fake Gmail account. More complexity can be actually building a persona and supporting information about the identity. The investigation will always dictate the level of persona required. Each investigator should plan ahead for this purpose. This can be done by building a variety of personas. Some of these will be a general use tools such as throwaway email addresses. These can be used and dumped if the case is over or the account has been compromised during the course of its use. The building of a more complete persona can be simply preparing a personal background for the identity.

Internet operations and policy considerations

Undercover online operations are becoming more common, but management control still needs to be in place to ensure compliance with agency/company policy, local regulations, and the law. The first issue to resolve is does my agency/company have a policy regarding "Undercover Operations"? The reason for policy is to ensure not only compliance with company direction and the law, but to give the investigator the boundaries by which they can conduct undercover operations on the Internet. When considering the policy, the investigator should identify whether or not the investigation falls within the jurisdiction of the agency or company. The investigator needs to insure that their actions never exceed their authority. Even though the Internet is essentially an open book, there are some legal limits to your investigations. Additionally, the policy needs to ensure that the investigators actions do not violate federal, state, or local laws regulating undercover investigations.

Other policy considerations include how an agency or a company selects personnel for conducting undercover operations. Historically, undercover personnel in the real world have been selected based on their skills in dealing with people. A good "talker" or someone that can BS very well, outgoing, and aggressive was a good candidate for undercover work. On the Internet those same skills, along with a technology savvy background, are the kind of talents required to successfully investigate crimes online in an undercover capacity. The persons assigned to this kind of work should be volunteers and not personnel chosen because a slot needs to be filled. Persons selected for undercover work should not only possess the above skills but be interested in the work to safeguard the program's integrity. Assigning disinterested personnel could have a detrimental effect on the program.

Some undercover assignments, even on the Internet, can be stressful and result in the possibility the investigator may develop mental health issues or concerns. Child abuse and pornography investigations are the most obvious. Wolak and Mitchell completed a 2009 study involving 511 agencies, whose employees work with Internet Crimes Against Children (ICAC) Task Force. Online survey responses were solicited from the participants. They found that about half of the survey participants were concerned about the psychological impacts of work exposure to child pornography. Thirty-five percent of ICAC Task Force participants had seen problems arising from work exposure to child pornography. The study also reported:

> Survey participants noted that undercover investigations in which personnel pose as minors also create difficulties for some personnel because of their sexually explicit content. 'Those that engage in undercover chat operations or those that work cases involving communication between adults and children are exposed to material that I believe can be just as harmful ...' (pg. 9—10)

Any stressful situation can cause mental health concerns if not monitored or identified by supervisors governing the investigations. The investigator needs to be aware of this as a problem and should pay attention to themselves and coworkers in an attempt to identify potential issues. From a policy concern, the agency or company should have guidelines for how to deal with investigators' stressful situations from working undercover. This is particularly true for any law enforcement investigation dealing with the constant viewing of child pornography, not to mention the audio that unfortunately is present with many of the moving images. As noted above, frequently portraying a minor or deviant online to communicate with sex offenders, even without child pornography as a factor, can have a detrimental impact on an investigator's mental well-being.

Some of the things the policy should address are there any preassignment screening conducted? One area noted by Wolak and Mitchell was the need for open communication with new staff about the nature of child exploitation investigations and what may be encountered by the investigator. They also noted an inquiry might be warranted to determine if the potential investigator might be particularly troubled by these investigations, for instance being a victim of abuse or currently having children themselves. Additionally, openly discussing potential negative effects on the investigator and what may be done to alleviate stress should be covered. Other policies to consider are regular screening and conducting post assignment screenings. Such proactive measures can aid in the identification and prevention of problems encountered by an employee during undercover Internet operations.

Jurisdictional considerations are another area that the investigator should be aware of and have references to in their policy. In the United States, some Internet crimes may share joint jurisdiction, with one legal entity having stricter penalties that might be more appropriate for the crime. Certain crimes lend themselves better to state and local jurisdictions versus federal prosecution. At other times a federal prosecution is a better course of action. Operational policy should provide guidance on the best possible options for the investigator's case. The investigator also needs to be aware of their jurisdiction's legal requirements for these cases. Some state statutes have elements that require there actually be a "real" victim and not just an undercover law enforcement investigator acting as one. As always the facts of the case should dictate involvement of different investigative and prosecutorial jurisdictions. The key for the investigator is to know and use all available legal resources.

Corporate investigators have their own concerns when it comes to jurisdiction, in particular when crossing international boundaries. For the investigator, these can cause significant issues they need to consider. Many countries have very different laws regarding, privacy, how Internet crimes can be prosecuted and how to deal with employee terminations based on internal investigations related to employee's Internet actions. Clearly policy guidelines need to be vetted by the agencies or company's legal authority.

GET CONNECTED!

Investigating online sexual exploitation of children is a resource intensive law enforcement activity. Going undercover, particularly when other agencies are working cases, may result in duplication and a waste of resources. It is also not unheard of to have one sex offender communicating simultaneously with several undercover investigators in different jurisdictions in an attempt to have illicit relations with a minor. As a result, there is a need to coordinate these cases and for investigators to be able to communicate with one another. In the United States, ICAC Task Forces were created to help federal, state, and local law enforcement agencies enhance their investigative responses to offenders who use the Internet to sexually exploit children. Funded by the US Department of Justice, Office of Juvenile Justice and Delinquency Prevention, the ICAC program consists of a national network of 61 coordinated task forces representing over 3,000 federal, state, and local law enforcement and prosecutorial agencies. The ICAC program provides training and guidelines on how to properly conduct these online investigations to its member agencies. For a state or local law enforcement agency seeking to become a member go to https://www.icactaskforce.org/Pages/TaskForceResources.aspx.

Additionally, in May of 2006, the US Department of Justice initiated Project Safe Childhood (PSC), a unified and comprehensive strategy to combat child exploitation. This program combines law enforcement efforts, community action, and public awareness. The five essential components of PSC are (1) building partnerships, (2) coordinating law enforcement, (3) training PSC partners, (4) public awareness, and (5) accountability. Law enforcement seeking to become a PSC partner should contact their local US Attorney's Office.

Other countries frequently have their own programs. In Canada, the Royal Canadian Mounted Police (RCMP) operates Integrated Child Exploitation (ICE) Teams, whose objective is to work... "in conjunction with the RCMP Tech Crime Unit, is to identify and assist child victims of sexual abuse, identify those responsible for the abuse and to lay appropriate criminal charges for the assaults, creation of the images and their distribution."

In short, these cases are too important, to go it alone. Reach out and get connected to other law enforcement agencies in your area working these cases. You will be better trained and better prepared to investigate these online cases.

Ethics during undercover operations

Obviously the investigator conducting online investigations and those conducting undercover operations must follow a code of ethics that can define proper procedures. Investigators must follow all state, local guidelines and federal laws. But there are several other sources that the investigator should look to for guidance. The High Technology Crime Investigation Association (HTCIA) has a code of ethics and core values that if followed can give a proper foundation for conducting investigations, regardless of their type, i.e., criminal or civil. Additionally groups like the International Association of Investigative Specialists have membership code of ethics that drive the investigation of digital evidence. The High Tech Crime Consortium (HTCC) also has as its first goal... "To endorse high ethical standards and best practices in the investigation, acquisition and examination of digital evidence." Additionally, HTCC is a partner in the Consortium for Digital Forensic Specialists, which is working to consolidate the digital forensic field around common standards and ethics.

HTCIA CORE VALUES

1. The HTCIA values the Truth uncovered within digital information and the effective techniques used to uncover that Truth, so that no one is wrongfully convicted!
2. The HTCIA values the Security of our society and its citizens through the enforcement of our laws and the protection of our infrastructure and economies.
3. The HTCIA values the Integrity of its members and the evidence they expose through common investigative and computer forensic best practices including specialized techniques used to gather digital evidence.
4. The HTCIA values the Trusted network of forensic and investigative professionals within private and public businesses including law enforcement who share our values and our vision.
5. The HTCIA values the Confidentiality of its membership and the information, skills, and techniques they share within the association.

Some areas that are not generally described in ethics statements are the not so obvious, such as offensive behaviors when conducting Internet investigations. We are not referring to offending someone, but the act of going on the offensive. The investigator again has to understand his role in the investigation and what he can and cannot legally do during the investigation. When do his actions cross the line from investigating a crime to potentially perpetrating one himself? This has been the age old problem with undercover operations and investigators' interaction with the criminals. In fact, J. Edgar Hoover, the first director of the Federal Bureau of Investigations, resisted allowing his agents to work undercover against the Mafia, believing that although some criminals would be caught, some of his agents might be corrupted as well (New York Times, 1981).

Traditional investigators working undercover are always on guard to ensure that their actions don't cross the line from observer to active participant, either as a follower or leader. On the Internet, there are other things that could ethically cross that similar line. An investigator in general, without proper legal authority, should never be sending virus, Trojan, or worms to a suspect or any other type of file that would disrupt, delay, or destroy another person's computer system. This is not to say that at certain times and under the requisite legal authority that this cannot be done, but in general some of these actions are not acceptable. Additionally, investigators must never send actual child pornography images or other digital contraband to a target.

One real concern in online undercover cases in the United States is the issue of entrapment. In *U.S. v. Poehlman*, 217 F. 3d 692 (Court of Appeals, 9th Circuit 2000) an appellate court overturned Mark Poehlman's conviction, which originated as an Internet sting investigation. Poehlman was a retired Navy man, who was also a cross-dresser and foot-fetishist. He had posted to "alternative lifestyle" discussion groups. His posts were initially rejected. Eventually, one woman, "Sharon," responded to his posts and they began their online relationship. "Sharon" however was an undercover agent.

Sharon advised Poehlman that she had three female children aged 7, 10, and 12 and she needed a "special mentor" for them. After several emails, Poehlman finally understood she was looking for a sex teacher for her children, and he graphically responded how he would "instruct" them. Eventually, Poehlman traveled from Florida to California to meet Sharon and to have sex with her female children in a hotel. After meeting with "Sharon" he was shown some child pornography, which he examined and indicated he always looked at little girls. He was then directed to an adjunct room containing the "children." Much to his surprise the room contained Naval Criminal Investigation Special Agents, FBI agents and Los Angeles County Sheriff's Deputies and he was arrested.[1]

The Ninth Circuit indicated that examining an entrapment defense requires the following questions be asked: (1) Did government agents induce the defendant to

---

[1]He was also convicted in California state court for attempted lewd acts with a minor. He completed his 1-year prison sentence and was charged federally 2 years after his release from state custody.

commit the crime and (2) Was the defendant predisposed to commit the crime? If the answer to the first question was "yes" a conviction could still be upheld if the answer to the second question was also "yes".

The Ninth Circuit found that Poehlman was interested in a relationship with "Sharon." However, it was only after she made future communication dependent upon him agreeing to serve as sexual mentor to her children did he finally agreed to play the role she had in mind for him. The Ninth Circuit found it was clear that the government had induced Poehlman to commit the crime based upon the communication between Poehlman and "Sharon."

The Ninth Circuit then focused on whether Poehlman was predisposed to commit the offense before he had any contact with government agents. Based upon all the communications and facts of the case, the Ninth Circuit concluded that the government had not met its burden to prove he was … "predisposed to demonstrate any preexisting propensity to engage in the criminal conduct at issue." As a result the Ninth Circuit overturned Poehlman's federal conviction.

The Poehlman case demonstrates that law enforcement must be very careful not to induce someone who has no previous propensity to commit a crime during their online activities. It is also important to note that the entrapment defense in the United States is only available to those who have not committed the crime before their interaction with law enforcement. Law enforcement using Internet techniques to investigate a crime that has already committed only have entrapment concerns about new crimes that may be committed after their interactions with the target. Even then their concerns are less as the target in these cases has already demonstrated a propensity for criminal behavior.

Basic undercover procedures

Undercover procedures require that the investigator follow the agency or company policy for undercover operations. Basic procedures by many law enforcement agencies may already exist and can be referred to for guidance when conducting online investigations. However, many companies and agencies have not developed separate policies regarding conducting online investigations, and even fewer have developed specific guidance for working undercover on the Internet. One of the primary reasons for the lack of guidance in conducting online undercover investigations is many organizations never contemplated conducting undercover actives prior to the Internet. This is particularly the case for corrections (pretrial services, probation, and parole) and corporate organizations, as their primary function is not law enforcement. They only now are contemplating undercover investigations as it seems so "easy" with the Internet. After all "online role playing" seems to be a regular occurrence, which can be done by anyone. Make no mistake. Online role playing is not the same as working undercover online. The stakes and consequences are much higher and accordingly working on these investigations should not be taken lightly. The following items are things that the investigator should consider when developing their procedures for conducting undercover Internet operations:

1. Type of investigation
   a. The level of undercover preparation would reflect the level of the investigation that the case requires. General intelligence gathering is different than conducting an investigation. Proactive investigations are also different than reactive investigations.
2. Prepare undercover profiles for a range of suspects, based upon the scope of your agency's mission. Here is a nonexhaustive list of possibilities:
   a. Pedophile
   b. Teen girl
   c. Teen boy
   d. Warez or carder
   e. Intellectual property thief
   f. Fence/theft
   g. Gang member
   h. Terrorist
3. Document your profiles.
   a. Traditional methods of profile documentation are to use a form designed to prepare/document the persona. The form is then used by the investigator to refer to while undercover. Other options include automated tools like those in Vere software WebCase. WebCase has dedicated modules for streamlining the process for the investigators to record and provide access to the investigator's undercover identity.
4. Learn online terminology from targeted offenses as well as commonly used vernacular used by the intended profile.
5. Set up undercover accounts for each persona (as required):
   a. Mailboxes
   b. Email accounts
   c. Gamer tags
   d. Cell phones.

Developing your undercover persona

Depending upon the online operation being conducted, the investigator has several things to consider when developing the appropriate Internet persona. Name, address, age, and date of birth would seem the simplest of the persona building process. However, determining a name for your undercover identity can be problematic. Is the name and age of your new identity similar to that of a living person? Is that living person geographically located in the investigator's region? The investigator needs to think about this as in an issue when developing the persona so as not to allow for the possible confusion with the false identity and a real person. Why would this be of concern to the investigator? Well depending on the case being investigated, a real person with the same name could be identified by another law enforcement agency as a potential perpetrator of a crime. Or a suspect might identify that person as the investigator and possibly do them harm. The liability for the investigator is too high to ignore. This is not to say you can't use the real identity of a person in an investigation. In fact during an identity "Take Over," that is exactly what the investigator does. In such situations, a signed consent needs obtained waiving liability and giving permission to the investigator to operate that profile during the investigation. Such waivers should reflect how the profile is going to be used and for how long and that the person consenting to its use will not attempt to regain or circumvent control of the profile. Additionally, once consent is obtained the investigator should immediately change the password to the account to prevent the person from interfering with the investigation.

PRINCIPLES 8 AND 9: TAKING OVER AN ONLINE IDENTITY

Recall from the last chapter, the Online Investigations Working Group (Working Group) principles for concerning online investigations. Principle 8 discusses assuming another's online identify and notes that this can occur… "if that person consents, if the communications are within the scope of the consent, and if such activity is authorized by agency guidelines and procedures." (pg. 42)

However, what about where the person doesn't consent, what then? Let's suppose a terrorist has been arrested or even killed, unbeknown to his confederates. Can law enforcement assume the terrorist's online identify to obtain information, particularly if it is a life or death scenario? Principle 9 covers this kind of situation, which it refers to as "appropriating online identity." In a pre-911 world, the Work Group noted:

"Appropriating online identity" occurs when a law enforcement agent electronically communicates with others by deliberately assuming the known online identity (such as the username) of a real person, without obtaining that person's consent. Appropriating identity is an intrusive law enforcement technique that should be used infrequently and only in serious criminal cases. To appropriate online identity, a law enforcement agent or a federal prosecutor involved in the investigation must obtain the concurrence of the US Attorney's Office's "Computer and Telecommunications Coordinator" (CTC) or the Computer Crime and Intellectual Property Section…. In rare instances, it will be necessary for law enforcement agents to appropriate online identity immediately in order to take advantage of a perishable opportunity to investigate serious criminal activity. In those circumstances, they may appropriate identity and notify the Computer Crime and Intellectual Property Section within 48 hours thereafter. (pg. 45)

Clearly both assuming and appropriating another's online identity is appropriate, depending upon the circumstances. Again, these principles are for federal law enforcement. As always consult your legal authority for specific guidance.

Other things to consider when building the persona are how deep of an identity do you need to create? For instance, general intelligence gathering personas only need to be further developed if they will be used to actively interact with targets. Especially with online undercover identities, designing personal family information can aid in your ability to quickly and effectively communicate and

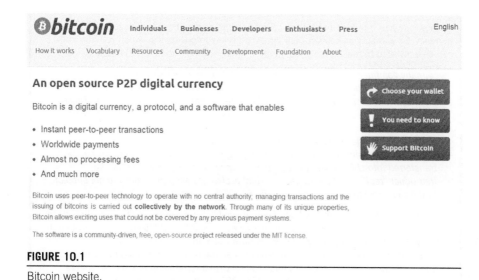

FIGURE 10.1

Bitcoin website.

make your identity believable. Information on the identities of direct family members, friends, school, and/or work can be developed ahead of time allowing the investigator to better think on his feet and respond in online conversations. The depth of the persona can include email addresses and contacts, phone numbers, building undercover banking or credit card accounts, and online fund transfer methods, such as Paypal or Bitcoin (Figure 10.1).

WHAT THE HELL ARE BITCOINS?

In 2009, Satoshi Nakamoto, an anonymous (as in a hacker pseudonym not part of the hacker group anonymous) hacker created a digital peer to peer currency that is not backed by any government. This digital currency, known as Bitcoin, is automatically "mined" on a set schedule using Bitcoin user's computers around the world. Basically, the user's computers are running a program that creates the digital currency. The exchange of this currency is all controlled by computer and it can't be traced. The amount to be mined is set at 21 million. What is the big deal? It after all is not "real." Well, the currency is being used to actually buy things in the real world, and there are actually sites that have set up an exchange rate for Bitcoins to dollars, to pounds, etc. (Sanders, 2013).

Imagine the possibilities for using Bitcoins for criminal activity. Drug dealers could convert real currency into Bitcoins and then back to real currency, or not. Think this is far-fetched? Well in 2013, Liberty Reserve, was charged by the United States with operating a $6 billion cyber money laundering. "It traded in virtual currency and provided the kind of anonymous and easily accessible banking infrastructure increasingly sought by criminal networks..." (Santora, Rashbaum, & Perlroth, 2013). Additionally, Bitcoins were discussed being used to purchase The Anarchist Cookbook by self-proclaimed anarchists who were later arrested for plotting to bomb an Ohio bridge (Chick, 2012).

Now put your mind around this one. Bitcoins can also be bought with gaming or virtual currency. So gamers can convert their virtual currency into Bitcoins, which you now know can be converted to real currency. As Regli, Mitkus, and D'Ovidio (2012) note:

...many gaming companies have created digital currencies that are meant to facilitate transactions within the virtual world. Some companies even contemplated that their virtual currencies would be transferrable into real world currencies. There are even currency exchange platforms that allow users to trade in and out of virtual currencies in the same way they could trade foreign currencies in the real world. Individuals provide virtual goods and services — everything from new dresses for an avatar to virtual prostitution — and money paid for these goods and services can be transferred into U.S. dollars through the currency exchange. However, unlike traditional "real" world banks, these virtual exchanges and operations are not subject to the same regulatory oversight. (pg. 5–6)

So digital and virtual currency have value. It would also make sense that virtual goods in gaming environments, such as a "sword" or special "shield," would likely also have value. If digital and virtual currency and virtual goods have value and they are stolen, do the victims call the "virtual police"? Nope, they are likely to call the real police to investigate who stole it. That is exactly what happened in Finland when virtual furniture and other items were stolen in the virtual world of Habbo Hotel (BBC, 2010). Brave new world ain't it!

Regardless of what persona is created, law enforcement investigators should run local and state checks to ensure your undercover identity does not match an actual person. The civilian investigator should do the same due diligence by checking with your corporate counsel about the use of undercover personas and researching the persona online to determine if there is any potential match in your locale. Whatever method is used to confirm information about the identity should be documented in the investigator's case file. The identity can always be used in other investigations if it is not revealed and can be built on to improve its effectiveness as the investigator's online persona.

The undercover role

Determining the need for an undercover identity is mainly dictated by the type of investigation being conducted. In general there are two types of roles, (1) proactive identities and (2) reactive identities. Common proactive identities could include:

- Minor boy/girl
- Adult with access to kids
- Adult trader of children
- Adult seeking kids
- Adult willing to trade child pornography
- Adult seeking prostitutes
- Adult seeking cardez
- Corporate Executive seeking Insider (Corporate Spy).

Reactive investigations frequently involve assuming another's identity, such as the victim or a sex offender's profile to facilitate the investigation of other pedophiles. An investigator's predesigned identity might also be used. For instance, if the victim was a minor female and the investigator's predesigned identity of another minor female might be used to further investigate or target the offender.

Online undercover accounts

When the investigator builds the online identity, he will look at obtaining various accounts and profiles from popular online sites. Adding several accounts can add in the depth of the identity and its believability. The investigator should be aware though that long periods of inactivity with the account could indicate to the investigation target that the account may be a phony. Another consideration is obtaining only the accounts required for that persona's level of technology understanding. Having multiple email accounts and social networking sites might not fit the persona's identity. However, having gamer tags and numerous accounts on Twitter and Facebook might fit the technology astute user and fit into the online community being investigated.

Other considerations when developing the undercover persona include the collection of false identity, undercover credit cards, untraceable cell phone, false business cards and letter head, and potentially a mailing address to use to accept packages and or traditional correspondence. Mailboxes require identification and can complicate the investigations. Law enforcement investigators can enlist the support of the Postal Service Investigators for this purpose. Internet Service accounts can be established with large companies using the same undercover identification. Simple use of Internet access at the local Starbucks or Barnes and Noble store can sometimes suit the investigation's needs. However, remember that as you trace the targets they can also trace you. Ensure that your use of an Internet service fits your persona. If your persona is a 10-year old boy, accessing the Internet from Starbuck's probably won't fit.

Finishing touches to your persona

Before you go live with your persona have it reviewed by several individuals in your agency or company to check for areas that are potential problems or inconsistencies. Recently, an undercover sting case targeting sex offender was lost due to an unscrutinized picture. In this case, a picture of a very young looking female police officer, posing as a minor, was sent to the target. Unfortunately, no one realized the young officer was wearing a wedding band, until the arrested target noted he believed it was all fantasy and the minor was an adult because he saw the band. Check and double check all facets of the developed persona to make sure there are no loose ends.

Once the persona is finalized it needs to be fully documented, such as in a notebook or binder, or in an automated tools such as WebCase, for easy reference (Figure 10.2). This is particularly important in case the person who commenced an undercover operation can no longer continue the activity. Additionally, this

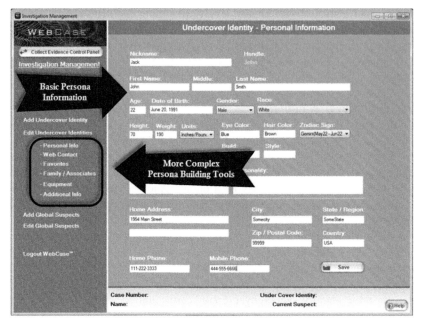

FIGURE 10.2

WebCase undercover identity module.

reference can be provided if others are required to take on certain facets of the operation. For instance, a male agent has developed a minor female persona and sometime during the operation a female is needed to speak to the target via a cell phone. This persona profile, as well as other records, such as chat logs, will help insure the female agent accurately portrays the persona during the call.

In cases involving an identity "Take Over," investigators should interview the cooperating person, gathering and documenting all facets, that may be needed to accurate impersonate them online. In cases, where "appropriating the online identity" is necessary, the investigator should likewise research and document as much as possible about the real person to facilitate the impersonation. Again, this information should be in a ready format for quick review if the need arises.

The investigator should also pay attention to the numbers and types of personas he maintains. Keeping track of the different personas is a required task when working on multiple undercover cases. If the investigator does not track and manage the personas, he could potentially use conflicting information in an investigation. Additionally, are these personas used in cases that another agency might be investigating? The term "deconfliction" has come about as a method law enforcement uses to identify whether or not another investigator is undercover in someone else's case. (The ICAC Task Forces regularly have investigators check for deconfliction.)

Countermeasures

Diligence in protecting your online persona can mean the difference between failing to solve the crime investigated and a successful apprehension of a criminal. Steps can include being cautious of your mail drop when picking up items. Criminals often apply the same techniques law enforcement and civil investigators do. Surveillance works both ways. Pay attention to the location when checking or picking up items from a drop box location. Investigations on the Internet are about real people and real places. Eventually when these cases come to a conclusion, the investigator has to get off the Internet and into the real world to place handcuffs on someone. When connecting to your ISP, make sure you are in the correct geographical location for your operation. If you state that you are in Austin, you do not want your IP Address resolving back to Los Angeles.

When using the cell phones to contact the suspect, be aware of caller ID and call return capabilities. There are services like Google phone numbers that can be applied to assist in hiding the investigator's identity, but they are employed by the targets too. The investigator should set up and use anonymous email accounts as much as possible. These can be throwaway accounts that can be used repeatedly or abandoned if they are compromised. Yahoo mail, Google mail, and Windows Microsoft Live are popular free email services. Using an email account from a business or a local or regional Internet service can play both ways. It can assist in identifying the persona and legitimizing it to the target or it may have the opposite chilling effect if not part of the persona.

USE OF IMAGES FOR PROFILES

Some novice online investigators think it is okay to use images of minors pulled directly from the Internet for their profile. Along the same lines, some of these same investigators, concerned over the copyright issues, will go the extra step and purchase an image. They think that by purchasing it they are free to do whatever they want with the image, including using it for their undercover online persona. These are very bad ideas. Here is why. There are websites out there, such as, TinEye.com, a reverse image search engine, that will allow individuals to compare your image to hundreds or thousands of similar images for a match. This website will allow the user to: find out where an image came from; research or track the appearance of the image online; locate web pages that make use of an image; and discover modified or edited versions of an image. In this way, your target could identify that the image is a fake or worse go after the real person whose image you used. Purchasing the image also does not give you the right to use the image for an undercover operation, particularly if the real person is inadvertently harmed by your activities. In an extreme case, a "defense" expert purchased stock images of minors for use in courtroom demonstrations to show how supposedly easy it was to "morph" innocent images into child pornography. Notwithstanding the potential criminality of such activity, the expert was successfully sued for misusing the purchased images, and the minors were awarded $300,000 in civil damages (Van Voris, 2012).

Instead of using an image of a person, take a picture of a landscape or some inanimate object and use it. In cases where you need a minor's image, consider getting consent from one of your colleagues to use a picture of them when they were younger or use age regression technology to make an authorized adult image look young again. However, make sure there is nothing in the background that may "date" the image.

Undercover cell phones and credit cards

In today's environment, getting the tools to support the identity such as cell phones and credit cards is much simpler for the investigator than in the past. Just as hiding on the Internet has become much easier, so has concealing your financial transactions and communications. Obtaining a traditional "cold phone," one that is not identifiable to the agency or company, is fairly simple today. Walk into any Walmart store or your favorite Radio Shack and simply buy a "Tracfone." The purchase can be a cash-only transaction along with the purchase of the minutes for the phone. Criminals have figured this out and are now regularly using this as a means of communication. If it is compromised, they can just remove the battery (and SIM card if it has one) and toss the phone in a nearby trash can. Undercover credit cards can be purchased through "Green Dot" kiosks at local stores or through the use of Visa or Mastercard gift cards.

IS VIOLATING THE TERMS OF SERVICE (TOS) AN "OTHERWISE ILLEGAL ACTIVITY"?

Online companies have attempted to prevent false identities on their sites since the beginning of the Internet. Law enforcement investigators have spent years making up false identities to use on the Internet. So the question is can this be an issue later in court? Facebook has stated publically that any account that they find that is not real will be closed, even if it is a law enforcement undercover account. Other social media networks, such as LinkedIn, also require users to use their real name. Additionally, social media networks also frequently prohibit users from allowing others to use their accounts, which obviously would seem to preclude identity takeovers. What can happen is upon discovery the fictitious account is deleted, along with all the work that went into developing it.

In one criminal case, *U.S. v. Drew*, charges were filed due to the creation of a false identity, which was used to harass a minor, who later committed suicide. The defendant, Lori Drew was indicted for conspiracy and hacking for creating and using a false MySpace identity, which was a violation of the TOS (Lemos, 2008). This was the first case drawing primarily on the fact that someone had fabricated an identity on a social networking site and was prosecuted by the federal government for doing so. Ultimately Drew was acquitted of the charges but not before bringing to the forefront that "cyberbullying" was real and required to be addressed legally. Missouri, where Drew lived, later added to their state law penalties for harassment by computer. The question remains where does the Internet crimes investigator's activities fall within this situation? Is the act of making an identity simply a violation of the TOS or is it a more deliberate law violation? In a real world analogy, it is perfectly acceptable for a police officer to "speed," thereby breaking the law, to catch a criminal. However, even in this scenario, a police officer can't ignore administrative guidelines and continue without regard to the public's safety. Clearly, corporate investigators have even more to consider. Again, consultation with the appropriate authority is the key to insuring you are on firm legal ground.

Social networking site undercover challenges

Selecting appropriate social media sites for undercover personas is critical in today's operations on the Internet. There are a few more challenges though with social media than simply getting an email address for the persona. The investigator should review the sites' TOS. Many sites actually prevent the use of their sites with false identities. In fact Facebook has specifically stated that they will make no exception for even law enforcement using undercover accounts on their service.

> *Facebook spokesman Simon Axten said that the site's rules forbid people from using fake names and that Facebook would not make an exception for police officers working undercover. Facebook is based on a real name culture, so fake names and false identities are actually a violation of the terms of use."* *Axten wrote in an email. "We disable the accounts of people operating under pseudonyms."[2] (Masis, 2009)*

Some social media however understands that law enforcement's presence online, even in an undercover capacity, can make the Internet environment safer. As such they have no issue with an undercover profile being created, as long as they are notified of its creation. However, depending upon the investigative focus, this prior notification may not be possible. Again, the investigation dictates and legal concerns will guide whether prior notification should be made.

Using social media accounts during online undercover investigations is almost a necessity these days. However, these are complicated tools to use effectively and make believable. The investigator has to consider how they will get and make "Friends" requests as a start. Building the social media piece of the persona without them makes them less believable. The investigator needs to request "Friends" who are not investigation subjects, are not law enforcement friends or connected directly or indirectly to law enforcement, or connected to the investigator's real identity. This certainly complicates the building of the identity because the persona has no real friends or family to connect to. The whole purpose of social media is to connect to people you know. Other things to consider regarding setting up your social media undercover accounts is will your online interactions with other "Friends" or "Friend's" page compromise your investigation? One way to make your social network persona more realistic is to consider networking with your colleagues personas profiles. In this manner you are "legitimatizing" each other's profile to make is appear to be real. However, doing so could expose the identities of one or more of them if anyone of the identities is later revealed as a law enforcement investigator. At some point this will occur if the identity is used in a prosecution or litigation.

Social media services are constantly updating and changing their security, functions, and online services. Setting up a practice account on the social networking site you are considering using can be an effect way to identify issues with the service and its effective use prior to deploying your undercover identity on that service. Spending time observing how the social networking service operates can also prepare you for its effective use in your investigation.

---

[2]Facebook also has a policy against allowing sex offenders to use their site. Seems kind of ironic that with this stated policy they are making it harder for law enforcement to catch repeat sex offenders who are illegally using their site to look for children to victimize.

Computer equipment for undercover operations

Preparing the computer system for undercover operations needs have the same importance as any other undercover operation in the real world. The computer you use, the Internet service you select, and the browser you use, all tell a tale of who you are. First, the equipment should only be used for undercover operations. Accessing the Internet for an agency or a company owned system may reveal your real identity. Personal information and/or agency or company information should never be stored on the undercover computer. This prevents the possibility of an adversary identifying your true identity if they offensively work back to your computer. The computer should not be connected to any network system within the agency or company. The investigator should plan for and prepare for the possibility that the undercover system could be accessed by a target while you are connected to the Internet.

IDENTIFYING THE SUSPECT ONLINE

1. In Instant Message or chat session have the target do a "Direct Connect" with you
   a. Use NETSTAT to grab his IP addresses
2. Have the target email you and analyze the headers
3. Have the target send you a file type that might contain Metadata (Microsoft Word document, an image file). Examine Metadata for possible incriminating information
4. Have the target provide you other means of contacting him that could potentially be traced
   a. Email addresses
   b. Instant Message accounts
   c. Telephone numbers
5. Direct the target to a website you control and capture their IP address when they visit.

CONCLUSIONS

In the "real world," undercover operations are a strong tool to identify targets in criminal investigations. They can also be effective tools in investigating Internet crimes. However, investigators need to be aware of their agency or company policy regarding conducting undercover online investigations. Besides investigative planning, undercover online investigations require: a clearly defined purpose, identification of the means for conducting the investigation, defining time resources, identifying documentation requirements, and planning for the unexpected. Building undercover personas is a somewhat complicated concept especially when dealing with social media investigations. There are also unique issues associated with an identity take over. Investigators also need to be familiar with the concepts required to conduct undercover operations on the Internet and the ethical considerations surrounding these operations.

Further reading

Bitcoin Exchange Rate/Value Calculator. (n.d.). *Bitcoinexchangerate.org*. Retrieved from <http://www.bitcoinexchangerate.org/>.

Chick, L. (2012, May 2). Bomb plot reveals hidden dangers of the occupy movement. *Breitbart.com*. Retrieved from <www.breitbart.com/Big-Government/2012/05/02/bomb-plot-reveals-hidden-dangers-of-the-occupy-movement>.

Code of Ethics & Bylaws. (n.d.). *High Technology Crime Investigation Association (HTCIA)*. Retrieved from <http://www.htcia.org/code-of-ethics-bylaws/>.

Consortium of Digital Forensic Specialists. (n.d.). *Consortium of digital forensic specialists*. Retrieved from <http://www.cdfs.org/objectives.php>.

Facebook Policies. (n.d.). *Facebook*. Retrieved from <https://www.facebook.com/policies/?ref=pf>.

Fleishman, G. (2000, December 14). Cartoon captures spirit of the Internet —New York Times. *The New York Times—Breaking News, World News & Multimedia*. Retrieved from <http://www.nytimes.com/2000/12/14/technology/cartoon-captures-spirit-of-the-internet.html>.

Foran, T. (n.d.). *Famous quotes at BrainyQuote*. Retrieved from <http://www.brainyquote.com/quotes/quotes/t/thomasfora191172.html>.

HTCC—Mission and Goals. (n.d.). *High Tech Crime Consortium (HTCC)*. Retrieved from <http://www.hightechcrimecops.org/mission.html>.

ICAC Home. (n.d.). *Internet Crimes Against Children Task Force*. Retrieved from <https://www.icactaskforce.org/Pages/Home.aspx>.

Integrated Units. (n.d.). *Royal Canadian Mounted Police*. Retrieved from <http://bc.rcmp-grc.gc.ca/ViewPage.action?siteNodeId=342&languageId=1&contentId=1570>.

Investigations involving the Internet and computer networks. (2007). US Dept. of Justice, Office of Justice Programs, National Institute of Justice.

Lemos, R. (2008, May 16). Legal experts wary of MySpace hacking charges. *SecurityFocus*. Retrieved from <http://www.securityfocus.com/news/11519>.

Masis, J. (2009, January 11). Police increasingly use social networking websites in detective work—The Boston Globe. *Boston.com—Boston, MA News, Breaking News, Sports, Video*. Retrieved from <http://www.boston.com/news/local/articles/2009/01/11/is_this_lawman_your_facebook_friend/?page=full>.

Mitchella, K., Finkelhorb, D., Jonesa, L., & Wolaka, J. (2010). Growth and change in undercover online child exploitation investigations, 2000−2006. *Policing and Society: An International Journal of Research and Policy, 20*(4), 416−431.

New Membership: Code of Ethics. (n.d.). *The International Association of Computer Investigative Specialists (IACIS)*. Retrieved from <https://www.iacis.com/new_membership/code_of_ethics/>.

Police Investigate Habbo Hotel Virtual Furniture Theft. (2010, June 1). *BBC—Homepage*. Retrieved from <http://www.bbc.co.uk/news/10207486/>.

Regli, B., Mitkus, M., & D'Ovidio, R. (2012). *Our digital playgrounds: Virtual worlds and online games: Criminal threats are emerging in online communities where adults and children play* Camden, NJ: Drakontas LLC.

Sanders, T. (2013, June 12). The Wild Wild West of Digital Currency. *Informationintersection.com*. Retrieved from <www.informationintersection.com/2013/06/the-wild-wild-west-of-digital-currency/>.

Santora, M., Rashbaum, W., & Perlroth, N. (2013, May 29). Liberty Reserve operators accused of money laundering—NYTimes.com. *The New York Times—Breaking News, World News & Multimedia*. Retrieved from <http://www.nytimes.com/2013/05/29/nyregion/liberty-reserve-operators-accused-of-money-laundering.html?pagewanted=all&_r=0>.

Tetzlaff-Bemiller, M. (2011). Undercover online: An extension of traditional policing in the United States. *International Journal of Cyber Criminology, 5*(2), 813–824.

The Department of Justice's Principles for Conducting Online Undercover Operations. (n.d.). *Public intelligence*. Retrieved from <http://publicintelligence.net/the-department-of-justices-principles-for-conducting-online-undercover-operations/>.

TinEye Reverse Image Search. (n.d.). Retrieved from <www.tineye.com/>.

USDOJ: Project Safe Childhood. (n.d.). *United States Department of Justice*. Retrieved from <http://www.justice.gov/psc/>.

Undercover With the New F.B.I.—NYTimes.com. (1981, November 29). *The New York Times—Breaking News, World News & Multimedia*. Retrieved from <http://www.nytimes.com/1981/11/29/opinion/undercover-with-the-new-fbi.html>.

Undercover Policing: Interim Report: Thirteenth Report of Session 2012–13: Report, Together with Formal Minutes, Oral and Written Evidence. (2013). London: Stationery Office

U.S. v. Poehlman, 217 F. 3d 692 (Court of Appeals, 9th Circuit 2000).

User Agreement (n.d.). *LinkedIn. World's Largest Professional Network*. Retrieved from <http://www.linkedin.com/legal/user-agreement>.

Voris, B.V. (2011, October 22). Facebook Claimant's lawyer must pay award in child porn lawsuit—Bloomberg. *Bloomberg—Business, Financial & Economic News, Stock Quotes*. Retrieved from <http://www.bloomberg.com/news/2011-10-21/facebook-claimant-s-lawyer-hit-with-morphed-child-porn-images-judgment.html>.

Wolak, J., & Mitchell, K. (2009). Work exposure to child pornography in ICAC task forces and affiliates. Durham: Crimes against Children Research Center. Retrieved from <http://www.unh.edu/ccrc/pdf/Law%20Enforcement%20Work%20Exposure%20to%20CP.pdf>.

Conducting Reactive and Proactive Internet Investigations

11

For the first time federal, state and local bureaus of investigation are coordinating their effort, to serve as eyes and ears and protect us against further attacks.

George Pataki, American Politician and former New York Governor

Reactive versus proactive investigations

According to a recent United Nations survey, over 90% of responding countries indicated that cybercrime most frequently comes to law enforcement's attention through reports by individual or corporate victims. Generally, when the police respond to a crime that has already occurred we call that reactive. The vast majority of investigations are reactive in nature. The same United Nations report reflects that the proportion of cybercrime acts detected through proactive investigations was low, although some countries are focusing on undercover or proactive operations. Proactive investigations occur before and during the commission of the offense. In Chapter 10, we discussed covert online investigations, which can start as either reactive or proactive investigations. However, they are not the only or even the primary component to conducting Internet investigations or providing an online enforcement presence. There are other reactive and proactive investigative activities, which also need to be woven into agency or company's online enforcement presence. This chapter will discuss these other components and their importance in addressing Internet crimes.

Reactive investigations

In noncyber offenses, a victim realizes a crime has occurred and notifies the police. A patrol officer is assigned to take the report, which may include being dispatched to the crime scene or the victim's location. Generally the officer conducts some initial data collection, possibly some follow-up and completes a report. He makes the first assessment of victim/witness information, specifically its validity and reliability. He may also collect available physical evidence at the scene for later review. He may also collect victim and witness statements about the crime and possibly review and collect general police intelligence about the suspect (conduct an FBI/NCIC check and a local wants and warrants check).

Frequently, in a reactive investigation, after the patrolman completes the report, it is submitted through the record's section to the detective unit. The report is reviewed by a supervisor and if warranted assigned to a detective to review and follow-up. The detective's fundamental task is to establish who did what to whom, when, where, how, and why. Brown (2001) notes reactive investigations typically fall into the following three categories:

1. A Walk Through (solved at scene—by the patrolman).
2. A "Who done it?" (don't know who the suspect is and requires follow-up).
3. Where are they? (the suspect is known but they need to be found).

Now let's take a look at the typical reactive Internet investigations conducted by law enforcement. Just like a traditional crime, a report should be taken by a patrol officer and a detective is assigned to follow-up. Unfortunately, this might not always occur as there is still a misconception by some local law enforcement that the Internet is simply not their jurisdiction. Bill Siebert, a computer forensics legend, liked to retell the story of a conversation he had with a police administrator at the annual International Association of Chief of Police (IACP) conference. Bill indicated that this administrator insisted the Internet was not his jurisdiction. Bill asked him if the victims or possibly the suspect were in his town and if so how could the crime not have occurred in his community? The chief perplexed still could not accept that something occurring on the Internet was in any way connected to his community.

The result of this kind of jurisdictional blind spot is the victim may be redirected to some other agency. If the victim does not get discouraged and takes the effort to go to the second agency, they may likely become disheartened if the larger agency does not follow up as the crime may not meet their investigative threshold. Eventually, victims begin to believe that reporting an Internet crime is useless as either the local police can't investigate as it is "not their jurisdiction" and larger regional or federal law enforcement will not investigate as it doesn't meet their guidelines. Victims may also start to conclude that the cybercrime investigations are beyond the capabilities of their local police department.

In situations where the local police do take a report, in many cases little is done to further the initial investigation because patrolman or report takers lack the basic knowledge and training regarding Internet crimes. This prevents the initial traditionally done follow-up, and in most cases no basic evidence collection occurs. After the report is taken, it might not always go to the pertinent crime unit for that offense type. If it is a theft, vice, and/or fraud-related Internet crime, those reports might not go to the corresponding unit investigating those offenses, such as the Burglar, Vice, or Fraud Unit. Oftentimes these cybercrime reports go to the agency's High Tech Crime Unit, get referred to federal task forces such as the

United States Secret Services Electronic Crime Task Forces or the FBI's Regional Computer Forensic Laboratory. Some unfortunately just plain get ignored.

"There are no procedures which can embody truth and fairness (or justice) without sacrificing one to the other, and both to cost" (Nobles & Schiff, 1997). This applies to Internet investigations as well. The problem law enforcement faces with reactive Internet investigations is the general lack of training in on-site digital collection methods and pertinent initial questions to ask victims or witnesses. Although a report and a statement may be taken, the first responder may not have the training to understand the appropriate questions to ask the victim. This delay in getting initial details can leave perishable online evidence uncollected and a frustrated victim. Ironically, in many cases only a little training and effort is needed to properly collect on-site physical or digital evidence and interview victims/witness (Figure 11.1).

The importance of proper initial interviewing and evidence collection in Internet crime investigations cannot be overstated. In 1975 the US Department of Justice commissioned the Rand Corporation to conduct a study on US criminal investigative practices. This study found the most important factor in solving a crime was the initial information collected by the patrolman responding to the crime. Of particular note was that if a suspect was not identified in the initial patrolman's investigation the likelihood of future identification diminished greatly. The Rand Corporation Study recommended that patrolman:

- investigate crimes,
- conduct witness and victims interviews,
- collect physical evidence and prepare investigative report,
- decide if the case should be continued for investigation or suspended.

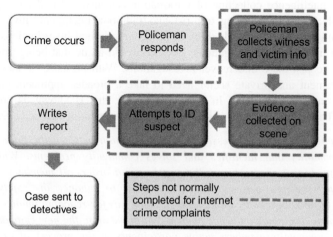

FIGURE 11.1

Reactive law enforcement: traditional versus Internet investigations.

These factors are no less important for Internet crimes, particularly in view of how evidence can be altered or destroyed. It is therefore imperative that all first responders have a firm grasp of initial questions that are important in investigating Internet crime. We have provided such questions in Chapter 5 of this book. Additionally, first responders should be familiar with specific cybercrime statutes in their jurisdiction. They should also be familiar with how "traditional" statutes can be brought to bear on the Internet crimes. For instance, a theft by deception statute may be used to prosecute an Internet fraud.

First responders should also be able to identify evidence source containers, such as computers, laptops, cell phones, mobile devices, and gaming systems. Once identification has been made, there are several decisions that have to be made. Is there violable data (evidence) present which must be collected before a device is turned off or can the device be "bagged and tagged" and examined by someone else? We have provided details on numerous tools that can be used for collecting live data in Chapter 6. However, each agency or company must provide clear policy directing trained first responders to collect such evidence or pointing them to those who can collect digital evidence in a timely manner.

Proactive investigations

Proactive Internet investigations involved actively seeking information and persons on the Internet who may be committing crimes. There are a variety of proactive investigation types. These include your typical undercover investigations looking for child pornographers or traditional vice violations. The investigator can look into various peer-to-peer networks for the sharing of contraband or the illegal trade in music or videos. Proactive investigations on the Internet can also include traditional "Sting" operations. Intelligence collection of information can also fall under the proactive category which can include gang, terrorist, and traditional intelligence investigations.

Frequently, when individuals think of proactive criminal investigations they are thinking of undercover investigations. But, we would argue that being proactive is not limited to just these undercover investigations. With presence of social media, law enforcement and private sector need to take a broader approach, getting the community at large involved. In law enforcement, this is known as community policing. The Bureau of Justice Assistance, US Department of Justice (1995) noted:

> *Community policing is, in essence, a collaboration between the police and the community that identifies and solves community problems. With the police no longer the sole guardians of law and order, all members of the community become active allies in the effort to enhance the safety and quality of neighborhoods. Community policing has far-reaching implications. The expanded outlook on crime control and prevention, the new emphasis on making community members active participants in the process of problem solving, and the patrol officers' pivotal role in community policing require profound changes within the police organization. The neighborhood patrol*

officer, backed by the police organization, helps community members mobilize support and resources to solve problems and enhance their quality of life. Community members voice their concerns, contribute advice, and take action to address these concerns. Creating a constructive partnership will require the energy, creativity, understanding, and patience of all involved.

(BJS, 1994, p. vii)

Community policing in cyberspace

In 1996, the Chicago Tribune reported that a Chicago Police Department Sergeant was a "trailblazer" for having created a police department webpage (Searcey, 1996). In 2013, there are countless city, state, and local government communicating online. In less than 20 years, the concepts of community policing has changed to require the inclusion of the Internet as part of an agency's interaction with its citizens. This change is no doubt due to the general population's migration from somewhat static websites to an interactive Internet populated by social media sites. Citizens can now interact online with law enforcement much easier than they could when a static website was considered the "avant-garde" of modern cyberpolicing.

In 2012, LexisNexis Risk Solutions, in partnership with PoliceOne, conducted an online survey of 1,221 law enforcement officers. The findings revealed four out of five officers were using social media platforms, such as Facebook, YouTube, and Twitter to help solve crimes. Fifty percent of the survey participants used social media on at least a weekly basis and two-thirds believed that social media was helping to solve crimes more quickly. Law enforcement's use of these sites were not just limited to investigative techniques discussed thus far but also included proactive activities, such as anticipating crimes that may be occurring and understanding criminal networks. Wyllie (2012) noted that one survey participant cited the detection of an online threat, leading to the discovery of a "Columbine"-type scenario, anecdotal evidence that a police presence on social media can prevent serious crime. Samantha Gwinn, Government Solutions Consultant for LexiNexis Risk Solutions, noted: "Investigation and analysis of social media content provides a huge opportunity in terms of crime prevention and offender apprehension" (Wyllie, 2012).

Community policy according to COPS Office of the US Department of Justice is "... a philosophy that promotes organizational strategies which support the systematic use of partnerships and problem-solving techniques, to proactively address the immediate conditions that give rise to public safety issues such as crime, social disorder, and fear of crime." Most of what we have discussed so far is creating those organizational strategies that can make use of online technology to enhance an agency's ability to communicate and collaborate with its citizens. Cyberspace, or the Internet in general, is an effective tool for any agency or company to employ as a communication protocol in multiple venues. We have spent most of this text discussing the use of the Internet for investigative purposes as that is our book's purpose. However, from a general communications position, the Internet provides an unparalleled method for accessing the public. Investigators can use the Internet for general access to the agency. A simple webpage can provide the public basic general information, such as contact details and hours of operation for an agency or company. Various social media tools, from Facebook to Twitter, can further enhance timely communication by providing information on upcoming events and wanted persons, and access directly to various departments. When engaging the problem-solving processes of community policing, the agency needs to consider how the Internet and the various communication tools fit into the process. Evaluating community problems must include how the Internet affects the issue. When developing the response and evaluating the success of the problem-solving process, the Internet and the various social media sites and other tools need to play a factor.

Social media policy considerations

In February 2013, the Bureau of Justice Assistance (BJA), Office of Justice Programs, US Department of Justice, in collaboration with the Global Advisory Committee of the US Attorney published, *Developing a Policy on the Use of Social Media in Intelligence and Investigative Activities: Guidance and Recommendations*. This document recognizes the proactive and reactive uses of social media by law enforcement in the United States. Accordingly, the guide concludes law enforcement's use of social media should reflect an authorized purpose, limitations of using social media information, and the appropriate manner social media sites may be accessed, such as during normal working hours or via agency systems. The guide references the following three distinct investigative uses of social media, each of which is more intrusive and accordingly should necessitate a higher level of justification and authorization.

- Apparent/Overt use is where an officer accesses public areas of the Internet, such as "Googling" someone and searching social media sites (Facebook, YouTube, etc.). This activity may be targeted at a particular individual of interest or generally searching of a social media site, such as Twitter, to develop a situational awareness for the jurisdiction.
- Discrete use occurs where law enforcement takes steps to conceal its online investigative activities with use of undercover techniques noted in Chapter 9 of this book. Specific steps are also taken to conceal the investigator's IP address from the subject or groups under investigation. Discrete use also includes searching and retaining information from public access sites.
- Covert use is considered the most intrusive investigative use of social media. It involves not only concealing the investigation but the creating of an undercover persona as outlined in Chapter 10 of this book. Additionally, unlike discrete use, this investigative type also involves interaction with the subject. Covert use may also involve lawful interceptions of communication through a court order or other legal process.

This guide also provides seven key elements for law enforcement considering developing a social media policy. Many of these elements have been restated in this book in the context of dealing with other areas of online investigation. However, they are worth restating in the context of using social media. They are as follows:

1. "Articulate that the use of social media resources will be consistent with applicable laws, regulations, and other agency policies.
2. Define if and when the use of social media sites or tools is authorized (as well as use of information on these sites pursuant to the agency's legal authorities and mission requirements).
3. Articulate and define the authorization levels needed to use information from social media sites.
4. Specify that information obtained from social media resources will undergo evaluation to determine confidence levels (source reliability and content validity).
5. Specify the documentation, storage, and retention requirements related to information obtained from social media resources.
6. Identify the reasons and purpose, if any, for off-duty personnel to use social media information in connection with their law enforcement responsibilities, as well as how and when personal equipment may be utilized for an authorized law enforcement purpose.
7. Identify dissemination procedures for criminal intelligence and investigative products that contain information obtained from social media sites, including appropriate limitations on the dissemination of personally identifiable information (PII)" (BJA, 2013, p. 9).

Social media monitoring

"Social media monitoring is the active monitoring of social media channels for information about a company or organization" (Financial Times Lexicon, 2013). Dyer (2013) further notes "... over the last decade, social media monitoring has become a primary form of business intelligence, used to identify, predict, and respond to consumer behavior." Additionally, some organizations, such as the Australian Securities Exchange, are requiring its member companies to actively monitor social media for disclosures of confidential information that may require an official announcement to inform investors (Robertson, 2013).

Law enforcement is also turning to social media monitoring as a proactive investigative tool. The United Kingdom's Metropolitan Police Department (Met) has created a unit to monitor social media for intelligence gathering, referred to as social media intelligence or Socmint (Wright, 2013). Umut Ertogral, Head of the Met Opensource Intelligence Unit, noted "[Social media] almost acts like CCTV on the ground for us. Just like the private sector use it for marketing and branding, we've developed something to listen in and see what the public are thinking" (Wright, 2013). Social media monitoring is also occurring in the United

States. In 2011, the New York Police Department formed Facebook and Twitter units in order to track down and monitor criminals and criminal behavior on social media sites (Parascandola, 2011). Both the FBI and the US Department of Homeland Security are also using social media for intelligence and investigative purposes (Rushe, 2012; Stone, 2012). Fusion Centers, DHS supported "... focal points within the state and local environment for the receipt, analysis, gathering, and sharing of threat-related information..." are also using social media monitoring tools (DHS, 2013).

At a basic level, monitoring can be conducted simply by having an account on social media and being connected with the community. More advanced techniques involve the use of social monitoring tools which capture data and monitor social media sites via webcrawlers and word search functions. Some law enforcement agencies are defining how social monitoring tools are to be used. For instance, the Georgia Bureau of Investigation social networking policy requires the following information be included in all requests to use these tools:

1. "A description of the social media monitoring tool;
2. Its purpose and intended use;
3. The social media websites the tool will access;
4. Whether the tool is accessing information in the public domain or information protected by privacy settings; and
5. Whether information will be retained by the GBI and if so, the applicable retention period for such information" (BJA, p. 33).

Social media monitoring is somewhat like computer forensics in that it is both an art and a science. The tools to be effective require search parameters and terms be properly defined. If the geographic area is too broad information will be collected that is not prurient to a jurisdiction. Likewise, if the search terms are too broad, the monitoring will produce data that contains false positives and too large a data stream to be useful in a timely manner. However, if the terms are too narrow important information might be missed.

Using a single social media profile or a social media management tool, which combines numerous profiles into one user interface, can also be problematic. Unlike tools that are just merely data gatherers, these methods allow the user to also interact with social media. This kind of community interaction requires the user have a clear understanding of the agency or company's mission. The user in charge of such outlets must also not disclose sensitive information or provide contradictory statements in the quest to develop sources or get information. Equally troubling is security concerns. If a profile or social media management tool is compromised, the resulting communication can be very damaging for the agency or company. Recently, Burger King's Twitter account was hacked, resulting in bogus statements that the company had been bought out by McDonald's (Manker, 2013). The results of a law enforcement social media account being hacked could be disastrous for the community it serves.

Developing a social media presence for law enforcement is beyond the scope of this book. Readers interested in exploring this area are directed to Social Media the Internet and Law Enforcement (SMILE) Conference, http://smileconference.com/, which brings law enforcement together for training on this topic. Additionally, ConnectedCOPS, http://connectedcops.net/ is a website designed "... to enhance law officers' ability to succeed with social media tools by providing insight, encouragement, education and the overall support required."

SOCIAL MEDIA MONITORING TOOLS

One of the simplest social media tools is Google Alerts (http://www.google.com/alerts). Google Alerts will email updates based on your search criteria of Google results (web, news, etc.). These alerts can be set to the following preferences: *send as they happen, once a day,* or *once a week.* The following are additional social media monitoring tools for consideration.

Free

Icerocket, http://www.icerocket.com/
Plancast, http://plancast.com/
Socialpointer, http://www.socialpointer.com/
Socialmention, http://www.socialmention.com/
Twitterfall, http://twitterfall.com/

Commercial

Netbase, http://www.netbase.com/
Topsy, http://topsy.com/
Trackur, http://www.trackur.com/

Law Enforcement Specific

BrightPlanet, http://www.brightplanet.com
3iMind, http://www.3i-mind.com/law_enforcement
Geocop, http://www.hmstech.com/geocop/
Geofeedia, http://corp.geofeedia.com/
TACTrend, http://www.hmstech.com

Policy considerations for undercover operations

Internet undercover investigations focus usually on a single type of crime such as Internet Crimes Against Children (ICAC), Online pharmaceuticals, prostitution, and so on. These crimes allow the investigator to assume the role of a provider, seller, or consumer of illicit goods or services, and employ a *sting* or *buy-bust* strategy to detect and apprehend criminals.

Proactive undercover investigations should be governed by cost versus benefit analysis. Is the cost of the crime to the community higher than the expense of undercover resources (time, personal, equipment, etc.) needed to detect and investigate it before it is known and reported to police? Obviously, one of the reasons why ICAC undercover investigations are at the forefront of proactive investigations is, we as a society have concluded that the prevention of harm to even one child justifies the expenses associated with these operations. The other part of this analysis is, will the expense of the undercover resources produce beneficial results, such as the apprehension and prosecution of criminals and overall improvement to a community?

This cost versus benefit analysis is second nature to those in the corporate world. Instead of community protection, they are concerned with protecting company assets. Obviously, a company may initiate an undercover investigation to detect theft, both internal and external. But at a proactive level, can a company justify expending resources to detect small loses before they occur? Again, the question becomes, does the benefit (preemptively catching the perpetrators) offset the expenditure of resources to run an undercover operation? Common with major software vendors as well as the music/video industry is the use of undercover Internet investigation to detect piracy. In this case, the asset being protected is frequently not only the company's intellectual property but it's very brand. After all, if the market becomes flooded with counterfeit, substandard goods, consumers may opt for another brand as opposed to the risk of getting a cheap imitation. These undercover investigations are not only protecting the company's assets but also its market share and even future existence.

Undercover Internet investigations require a different skill set, equipment, and training than traditional investigation. We have discussed these issues in previous chapters. In some cases, the corporate world takes a lead in an undercover investigation, particularly when it comes to piracy and counterfeiting of their product. Obviously, having a vested interest is one reason but the other is likely that they have specific knowledge that is required about their product to make the investigations successful. The simple fact is law enforcement and corporations frequently need to work together in the investigation of advanced crimes.

LAW ENFORCEMENT AND PRIVATE SECTORS WORKING TOGETHER

In 1984, industry security managers approached the Santa Clara County District Attorney's Office over their concern that the then fledgling high technology industry was suffering significant losses and public law enforcement had limited expertise and training to address the growing problem. As a result, the Clara County District Attorney Les Himmelsbach applied for and received a grant from the California Office of Criminal Justice Planning Project, which resulted in the start of the District Attorney's Technology Theft Association (DATTA). This group grew to include over 49 law enforcement jurisdictions (local, state, and federal agencies) in California. In 1986, representatives from Southern California law enforcement and security personnel from private industry came together with the assistance of an established DATTA to form the entity called the High Technology Crime Investigation Association (HTCIA). We are both proud past presidents of HTCIA, which has grown to be the largest worldwide nonprofit professional organization of its kind, built on the power of networking between law enforcement and private sector.

Managing undercover Internet investigations

Internet undercover strategies can be as controversial as real world operations. In addition to the entrapment issue raised in the last chapter, there can be unique issues, specific to the nature of cybercrimes. One such example is the "fantasy" defense, frequently raised by offenders charged with sexually enticing a minor over the Internet, where there is no minor but a police officer. This defense is usually not effective in the courtroom. However, managers need to be able to articulate to their superiors that these investigations are not focused on "fantasy" but on individuals who clearly are intent on doing criminal acts in the real world.

Another unique issue also associated with these kinds of undercover investigations is the strain it may bring to bear on a community's legal resources. For instance, a small police department commences conducting undercover online operations to catch sexual predators in their community. However, by using the Internet to arranged meetings between the offender and the "minor," they have expended their operations to not only their community but also literally to the entire world. In short order, they not only catch sexual predators who reside in their community, but those who live in adjunct jurisdictions, and even several states away. They quickly have increased the workload of the entire justice system in their area. Now the tax payers are paying for prosecutions of nonresidents who but for the fact of the police's undercover sting operation, may have never traveled to their community. Clearly, law enforcement managers need to be aware of these issues and coordinate such investigations with their local prosecutors to insure they are not biting off more than they can effectively chew.

Other things to think about in preparation for conducting undercover investigations include the agency policy regarding undercover investigations. These policies require management fully understand Internet investigations and the liability and rewards they may bring for the agency/company. Management needs to evaluate the organization's internal capabilities, including its ability to support these investigations. They need to identify what capabilities currently exist within the organization to further Internet investigations and what additional resources, equipment, personnel, as well as training may be needed to conduct them effectively. Cost evaluations of equipment and personnel require the agency to determine their ability to financially support these kinds of operations.

Internet investigation policy

An agency or company policy regarding Internet investigations should clearly lay out guidance for supervision of these operations and the staff's conduct during their execution. Looking to traditional undercover investigation practices, the Internet investigators can identify commonality between these two types of covert activities. Traditional undercover investigation will have a supervisor managing the operation. The supervisor monitors all activities on the undercover operation including overseeing the undercover investigator's surreptitious body wire communications. In other words, the supervisor is intimately involved in the operation's management and the undercover investigator's actions. All of this direct monitoring is intended to prevent the investigator from making a mistake and keeping the investigator safe.

Internet undercover investigations are a little different. Commonly during an undercover online operation, the supervisor isn't sitting over the investigator's shoulder watching hours of online chat. The supervisor generally reviews content after the investigators take actions. Their review of the Internet investigation is done after the fact and from reports of the investigator's conduct. The need for direct monitoring during an Internet investigation is not an officer safety issue from the supervisor's point of view.

From a practical implementation point of view, the traditional undercover investigation has more supervisory input and management. This is normally because of the need for officer protection, but still it is a better practice than the typical Internet investigation. The Internet investigation policy should address the supervisory role managers play during the investigation. Internet investigation managers should have a hands-on role. Undercover operations regardless of their location can still be a risk to the investigator. Remember at some point the target has to be arrested and handcuffs can't be put on remotely. Managers should be engaged throughout the operation to ensure the overall operation's goals and objectives are met. They should also be verifying that the agency policy is being complied with during the operation.

MODEL POLICY

Included in the appendices are three separate model policies that an agency or company can use to help draft internal policy for investigations. The three model policies include a Model Policy for LE Investigative Use of Social Networking, Model Policy for LE Use of Social Networking, and Model Policy for Off-Duty LE Use of Social Networking.

Operational planning

Operations planning for Internet investigations require the same kinds of information needed for investigations in the real world. Going online in an undercover capacity to investigate a crime requires pre-thought and planning. The investigator in consultation with their superiors need to identify the intent and scope of the undercover operation, identify the legal restrictions around the undercover operation, determine the limits of the investigator's authority while on the Internet, identify the available resources to support the undercover investigation, prepare a risk assessment of the operation, and identify data collection requirements. All of these help the investigator determine the direction the undercover operation will take and contribute to its likelihood of success.

1. Identify the intent and scope of the undercover operation.

    Each undercover investigation on the Internet is different. The investigator needs to collect information up front about the case. Including the kind of investigation, the potential locations for working undercover on the Internet, the depth of the persona required, estimates of the resources needed to support the investigation, the time estimated to complete the investigation, and the personnel commitment needed to support the investigation.

2. Identify the legal restrictions around the undercover operation.

   During an undercover Internet investigation, the legal requirements related to the investigation need to be identified. Does your jurisdiction support this kind of investigation? Does your agency have a policy for conducting undercover investigations on the Internet?

3. Determine the limit of the investigator's authority while on the Internet.

   The limit of the investigator's authority deals with identifying the investigator's legal ability to conduct certain investigative tasks online. Again agency policy will help to dictate the limits.

4. Identify the available resources to support the undercover investigation.

   The investigator needs to evaluate the personnel required for the operation, the equipment required (the undercover computer is only one cost), and the time investment (depending on the type of the investigations the time investment can be significant). Identifying this early can help managers understand the financial and resource commitment an Internet investigation requires.

5. Prepare a risk assessment of the operation.

   Preparing a risk assessment, specifically a cost versus benefit analysis, is probably the most overlooked part of the planning process. The risk assessment is a management process for the investigation to determine whether or not the investigations should be conducted and to what benefit the agency or company will get out of the investigation. The basis for the risk assessment includes identifying the potential for success. This can mean the likelihood of a prosecution of an offender or the recovery of stolen property and the accountability of the investigators during the investigation.

6. Identify data collection requirements.

   What are the requirements for documenting and collecting the required evidence to support a prosecution? A printed email may be entered in as a piece of evidence that is authenticated by the sender or receiver, but the metadata from the header in the email may tell a different version. How the investigator collects the data can provide the difference between a well-documented investigation and one that poorly represents the facts of the case.

OPERATION FAIRPLAY

Operation Fairplay was a closely held secret for the longest time among the investigators seeking to identify those trading child pornography through the peer-to-peer networks. Law enforcement had figured out that the peer-to-peer networks used a common method to identify and transfer files through its program. The method employed was the use of a hash, a mathematical algorithm that fingerprints the individual file. The hash was used in the network to identify files to be transferred between users. This hash, if known, could be used to identify these known files and track them through the network. The child investigators learned they could track the IP address of the users downloading specific files through that hash. Operation Fairplay as a method of identifying criminals using peer-to-peer on the Internet is no longer a secret but the exact investigative methods used are still a closely guarded.

Internet crime analysis

Internet crime analysis is in its infancy. Internet crime is not tracked nor is it reported well. As we addressed earlier in Chapter 1, poor documentation and no standard for reporting these offenses hamper efforts to grasp the extent of Internet crime. However, there are various reports and reporting agencies that can give us a clearer picture of the incidents of Internet crime. Reports from the National White Collar Crime Center's (NWCCC) Internet Crime Complaint Center (ICCC), the Computer Security Institute, and Norton's Cybercrime Study can give us a better understanding of the cybercrime problem. From the cybercrime perspective we can begin to measure the effectiveness of our investigative responses. Traditional crime response effectiveness is measured by looking at the number of crimes reported and identifying the number of crimes solved in comparison. This is a simple statistical measure. With Internet-related crimes we can identify similar effectiveness of the reported crimes. Effective understanding of an agency or company's response to cybercrime depends on its ability to record the known crime. With the known numbers of cybercrimes committed, a clear solution rate can then be identified.

CONCLUSION

This chapter introduced the concepts of reactive and proactive Internet investigations. We know generally that traditional reactive investigations are frequently better handled by patrol officers and report takers than Internet reactive investigations. We have to improve. Managers and supervisors have to understand that these offenses are not going to go away and their line staff must be prepared to handle them in the earliest stages of the investigation. Being prepared requires not only providing training and resources but also a commitment from upper management that Internet crimes do fall under their jurisdiction. Additionally, we hopefully expanded the concept of proactive investigations beyond just undercover online investigations. Social media clearly presents new and challenging opportunities for community policing. We also drove home that management needs to also take an active role in overseeing and supporting Internet undercover investigations. Finally, we again stressed that management needs to work on Internet crime analysis so they can adjust their reactive and proactive investigative efforts accordingly.

References

3i-MIND. (n.d.). 3i-MIND. Retrieved from <http://www.3i-mind.com>.
BrightPlanet | Deep Web Intelligence. (n.d.). *BrightPlanet | Deep Web Intelligence*. Retrieved from <http://www.brightplanet.com/>.
Brown, M. F. (2001). *Criminal investigation: Law and practice* (2nd ed). Boston, MA: Butterworth-Heinemann.

Chaiken, J. M., Greenwood, P. W., & Petersilia, J. (1976). June *The criminal investigation process: A summary report* Santa Monica, CA: The Rand Corporation.

Community Policing Dispatch. (n.d.). COPS Office: Grants and Resources for Community Policing. Retrieved from <http://www.cops.usdoj.gov/html/dispatch/january/>.

Developing a Policy on the Use of Social Media in Intelligence and Investigative Activities: Guidance and Recommendations. (2013). Washington, DC: Bureau of Justice Assistance, Office of Justice Programs, US Department of Justice (BJA) and Global Justice Information Sharing Initiative.

Dyer, P. (2013, May 13). 50 top tools for social media monitoring, analytics, and management. *Socialmediatoday.com.* Retrieved from <http://socialmediatoday.com/pamdyer/1458746/50-top-tools-social-media-monitoring-analytics-and-management-2013/>.

Geofeedia—Search & Monitor Social Media by Location. (n.d.). *Geofeedia—Search & Monitor Social Media by Location.* Retrieved from <http://corp.geofeedia.com/>.

Google Alerts—Monitor the Web for interesting new content. (n.d.). *Google.* Retrieved from <http://www.google.com/alerts>.

HMS Technologies, Inc. | GEOCOP. (n.d.). HMS Technologies, Inc. | *IT Systems Integration.* Retrieved from <http://www.hmstech.com/geocop>.

Horvath, F., Messig, R. T., with the assistance of Lee, Y. H. (November, 2001). *A National Survey of Police Policies and Practices Regarding the Criminal Investigation Process: Twenty-five years after Rand* [Electronic version] (United States Department of Justice, National Institute of Justice, NCJRS Publication No. 202902). Rockville, MD.

HTCIA | High Technology Crime Investigation Association. (n.d.). HTCIA | *High Technology Crime Investigation Association.* Retrieved from <http://htcia.org>.

Manker, R. (2013, February 19). Burger King apologizes for Twitter hack: Account was changed to look like McDonald's. *Chicago Tribune.* Retrieved from <http://articles.chicagotribune.com/2013-02-19/business/ct-burger-king-twitter-hack-0219-20130218_1_tweets-mcdonalds-hack>.

Meltwater IceRocket. (n.d.). *Meltwater IceRocket.* Retrieved from <http://www.icerocket.com/>.

Nobles, R., & Schiff, D. (1977). The never ending story: Disguising tragic choices in criminal justice. *Modern Law Review, 60,* 299.

Parascandola, R. (2011, August 11). NYPD forms new social media unit to mine Facebook and Twitter for mayhem. *NY Daily News.* Retrieved from <http://www.nydailynews.com/new-york/nypd-forms-new-social-media-unit-facebook-twitter-mayhem-article-1.945242#ixzz2XiL4RCsu>.

Pataki. (n.d.). *BrainyQuote.com.* Retrieved from <http://www.brainyquote.com/quotes/quotes/g/georgepata274179.html>.

Plancast—Find Things to Do & Upcoming Local Events | Event Planning & Promotions | Plancast. (n.d.). Retrieved from <http://plancast.com/>.

Robertson, A. (2013, June 7). Beware of tweeters and bloggers: New social media rules for listed companies-—*Business—ABC News (Australian Broadcasting Corporation)* ABC.net.au. Retrieved from <http://www.abc.net.au/news/2013-06-04/beware-of-tweeters-and-bloggers-new-social-media/4733374?section=business>.

Rushe, D. (2012, January 26). FBI to step up monitoring of social media sites amid privacy concerns. *Latest US news, world news, sport and comment from the Guardian* | guardiannews.com | The Guardian. Retrieved from <http://www.guardian.co.uk/world/2012/jan/26/fbi-social-media-monitoring-privacy>.

Searcey, D.(1996, February 2). Web surfers gain cop in cyberspace—Chicago Tribune. *Featured Articles From The Chicago Tribune.* Retrieved from <http://articles.chicago-tribune.com/1996-02-19/news/9602190148_1_home-page-police-sergeant-southwest-side>.

SMILE Conference. (n.d.). *SMILE Conference.* Retrieved from <http://smileconference.com/>.

Social Media Monitoring, Analytics, Engagement & Publishing For RTM—NetBase.com. (n.d.). *Social media monitoring, analytics, engagement & publishing for RTM—NetBase.com.* Retrieved from <http://www.netbase.com>.

Social Media Monitoring Definition from Financial Times Lexicon. (n.d.). *Financial Times Lexicon—The Definitive Dictionary of Economic, Financial and Business Terms.* Retrieved from <http://lexicon.ft.com/Term?term=social-media-monitoring>.

Social Media Monitoring Tools & Sentiment Analysis Software | Trackur. (n.d.). *Social media monitoring tools & sentiment analysis software | Trackur.* Retrieved from <http://www.trackur.com/>.

SocialPointer—Real-Time Social Media Marketing Tools Campaign & Tactics. (n.d.). *SocialPointer.* Retrieved from <http://www.socialpointer.com/>.

State and Major Urban Area Fusion Centers Homeland Security.(n.d.). US Department of Homeland Security. Retrieved from <www.dhs.gov/state-and-major-urban-area-fusion-centers>.

Stone, A. (2012, February 16). DHS monitoring of social media under scrutiny by lawmakers. Breaking news and opinion on *The Huffington Post.* Retrieved from <http://www.huffingtonpost.com/2012/02/16/dhs-monitoring-of-social-media_n_1282494.html>

Topsy—Instant social insight. (n.d.). *Topsy—Instant Social Insight.* Retrieved from <http://topsy.com/>.

Twitterfall. (n.d.). *Twitterfall.* Retrieved from <http://twitterfall.com/>.

Understanding Community Policing: A Framework for Action. (1994). Washington, DC: Bureau of Justice Assistance.

United Nations. (2013). Comprehensive Study on Cybercrime Draft: February 2013New York, NY: United Nations.

US Department of Homeland Security (2013). *Civil Rights/Civil Liberties Impact Assessment: DHS Support to the National Network of Fusion Centers Report to Congress March 1, 2013* Washington, DC: Office for Civil Rights and Civil Liberties, U.S. Department of Homeland Security.

Webster, R. (n.d.). *ConnectedCOPS.net—Law Enforcement's Partner on the Social Web.* Retrieved from <http://connectedcops.net>.

Wright, P. (2013, June 13). Meet prism's little brother: Socmint (Wired UK). *Wired.co.uk Future Science, Culture & Technology News and Reviews (Wired UK).* Retrieved from <http://www.wired.co.uk/news/archive/2013-06/26/socmint>.

Wyllie, D. (2012, July 31). Infographic: How police investigators are using social media. *Police Officers, Cops & Law Enforcement | PoliceOne.* Retrieved from <http://www.policeone.com/investigations/articles/5885971-Infographic-How-police-investigators-are-using-social-media>.

Internet Resources for Locating Evidence

12

Some say Google is God. Others say Google is Satan. But if they think Google is too powerful, remember that with search engines unlike other companies, all it takes is a single click to go to another search engine.
Sergey Brin, Google Co-Founder; Jarboe, 2003

Sources of online information

There are many sites that have been around for some time that can be great resources for the investigator. But, online sources are always changing and the investigator needs to be aware of new ones that can assist his investigations. If you find a good site or resource page don't be afraid to bookmark it and use it. The basics of searching for people, telephone numbers, or businesses online include to always use more than one site. Each site uses different methods and algorithms to identify the data based on your input. Using more than one site increases the likelihood of finding the information you are seeking. Always be sure to evaluate the online resource before relying on the site for investigative purposes. Some sites can advertise certain effectiveness, but when tested against a search engine's returns you may find it not worth the time or effort to use it. There are pay sites that can give the investigator access to more information than the Internet can, but even these need to be evaluated for their content. Be aware that some pay sites rely on databases that may contained outdated information.

As the investigator spends more time using Internet-based tools to identify information they will find that there are some common search truths. The more common the name, the more likely you will get search returns that may not be correct. The more unique the name, the less search results but the greater the probability the hits will be germane to the investigation. Most free sites have a pay site component which provides more information. Even pay sites frequently allow a basic search to determine whether or not the site has information about your search subject. The information they contain can be substantial or limited. You won't know until you pay. Costs vary from a onetime payment for one search to a monthly or an annual subscription fee. These sites generally purchase or have access to different public and private databases, the accuracy or timeliness of which may vary. However, many of the sites use the same data brokers as their source of information.

Search services

Many people mistakenly believe that one search is as good as another or that one particular search engine will list everything that is available on the Internet. These misconceptions are simply not true. Kotch (2007) notes there are three types of Internet search services, (1) search directories, (2) search engines, and (3) metasearch engines, each varying in its provided results.

Search directories are hierarchical databases with references to websites. These directories contain websites that are selected by human beings, which in turn list and classify according to a particular search service's rules. Kotch describes Yahoo! Directory as the "mother of all search directories."[1] Directories do not search webpages but the text contained in the site title and description. This information is composed by the directory editors, which is often based upon content provided by the site owners.

Search engines are "... 'engines' or 'robots' that crawl the Web looking for new webpages. These robots read the webpages and put the text (or parts of the text) into a large database or index that you may access" (Koch, 2007). No one search engine covers the entire Internet. In June of 2013, Google had 66.7% of the US user's market share, compared to Bing's 17.9% and Yahoo! an 11.4% (comScore, 2013). It is interesting to note that Microsoft's search engine Bing powers Yahoo! searches (Kaushal, 2011). Clearly, Google has the lion's share of the market place. But what does that mean in size of their respective databases?

It is impossible to know how big Google or Bing's databases are as that information is considered proprietary. However, try this quick rough comparison. Type in the word "the" into both Google and Bing's search engines. In July 2013, Google returned 25,270,000,000 results to Bing's 3,260,000,000. There are likely to be some differences due to how their engines work and collect data, but it would be a safe bet to conclude that Google has a larger database. However, larger does not mean Google contains all the information of Bing and then some. Bing likely has information that Google does not have. Other search engines, such as Ask Network and AOL, Inc., with 2.7% and 1.3%, respectively, of the US market share (comScore, 2013), may also contain information that neither Google or Bing possesses. The important thing to note is that search engines are your best option when you know exactly what you are seeking.

Koch's last category is metasearch engines. These services search both engines and directories at the same time providing relevant hits from all of them. They can provide a general idea of what is out there. The problem is not all search engines

---

[1]Yahoo! Directory (http://dir.yahoo.com/) is not the same as Yahoo! (http://www.yahoo.com). If one goes to the later and enters a search term, a search engine will be used to produce the results.

interpret user's queries in the same manner. The metasearch engine "... has to try to 'translate' your query into a language that each search engine will understand. More often than not, they will not try to do so" (Koch, 2007). For a more complex search, the user needs to go to a particular search engine.

Some metasearch engines do have some neat features. For instance, Clusty (http://clusty.com) will group the hits into "clusters." These clusters, known as clouds, sources, sites, and time, are farther broken down. For instance a Clusty search of the term cybercrime will provide a list of website types this term appears, which is further broken down, such as .gov, .edu, so on. Dogpile (http://www.dogpile.com/), known as Webfetch, in Europe (http://www.webfetch.com/) searches Google, Yahoo!, and other search engines simultaneously. Pandia (http://www.pandia.com) not only conducts simultaneous queries, it also has a pretty comprehensive listing of the various search directories, engines, and metasearch engines out there.

TIPS FROM THE NATIONAL SECURITY AGENCY

Zetter (2013) reported that the National Security Agency (NSA) released its 643-page manual "Untangling the Web: A Guide to Internet Research" pursuant to a Freedom of Information Act Request. This guide is a PDF document and is available at http://www.nsa.gov/public_info/_files/Untangling_the_Web.pdf. Written in 2007, it is a bit dated, but nevertheless it has a wealth of information and tips. Here are a few for conducting Internet research:

1. Studies have found little overlap among major search engines. As a general rule use more than one search engine.
2. Information on the web is gaining in quality and reliability. However, one must weigh the validity, accuracy, currency, and overall quality of the collected information before acting on it.
3. Be careful in using Boolean expressions, such as and or, unless you know exactly what you looking for and you understand that search engine's Boolean rules. Use of these expressions can interfere or defeat the statistical approach used by the search engine to provide results.
4. Learn the search syntax for the search engines you frequently use. They are not all the same.
5. Keep in mind that search engines give more weight to popular or pay-for-placement webpages. The more popular the website the more likely it will be at the top of the results list.
6. The default operator for all major US search engines is now AND.
7. HTML does not have a "date" tag. Date can mean creation, last modified date for a page, or the date the page was found by a search engine. Refrain from searching by date unless you are searching a weblog, news, or newsgroup search engine.

PANDIA'S RECOMMENDATIONS FOR INTERNET SEARCHES

Pandia, a megasearch engine service, provides a helpful tutorial, which also includes recommendations for conducting Internet searches (http://www.pandia.com/goalgetter/recommendations.html). Many of them are consistent with the NSA suggestions. Below we have condensed them down for the reader's consideration:

1. Consider what you are attempting to find. Try writing it down and picking out keywords and use them (and relevant synonyms) in your search query.
2. If you are looking for specific information, use a search engine first. If you are looking for general information on a broader topic start with a search directory.
3. Use several search services as none of them cover entire Internet.
4. Read the search services help pages.
5. Use nouns and objects as query words. Avoid using common verbs, adjectives, adverbs, pronouns, prepositions like "and, in, or, of," unless they are part of a phrase, because they are often ignored by search engines.
6. Be as specific as possible. If you are looking for information on German Shepherds, do not search for dogs. Unless part of a specific phrase, avoid common terms like Internet or people.
7. Try synonyms if you do not find what you are looking for. Use the OR-operator: (pot OR marijuana).
8. Check spelling! Then recheck it. Also be aware of alternate spellings or alternative words in various forms of English: (colour OR color), (money OR currency).
9. Use at least two keywords in a query. The more keywords, the smaller and more focused the hit list will be.
10. Use phrases enclosed by quotation marks in order to reduce the number of results.
11. Use the AND or + operator in order to reduce the number of hits.
12. Normally use quotation marks and capitals when searching for names: "John Quincy Adams". There may be several variations of the same name, though: "Johnny Quincy Adams" OR "John Q. Adams". Also consider reversing the order to capture alphabetical listing.
13. Consider truncating words in order to find both singular and plural versions of nouns.
14. Put the main subject first as search engines often list based upon matching the first keyword at the top of their findings list.
15. Do not make your queries too complicated. Avoid complex nesting with too many brackets.
16. Consider using field searching to get more relevant hits. For instance, search for words that might be in a webpage's title, title: "investigations".

Searching with Google

Searching with Google can be one of the most effective tools the investigator uses during his research. Google was created in 1995 by Larry Page and Sergey Brin at Stanford University, California. Believe it or not Google is actually a word and stands for 1 googol which equals 10 to the power of 100 or 1 followed by 100 zeros. How Does Google do it all? Google has a series of data centers with an undisclosed number of servers in multiple locations around the World (Google, History).

Google Basics

Using Google is as simple as putting in your search terms and pressing enter. The investigator can then scroll through the returns and click on the hyperlinks associated with the returns. The Google results page provides the user with multiple hits on a single page as well as multiple pages. Google searches can often return thousands of result pages. Each page contains links to web artifacts responsive to the search term. That artifact can be a webpage, a document, or an other searchable hyperlinked item found by Google during its web crawling. The blue texts are hyperlinks to the web artifact that was found by Google. Indented links are multiple links to pages within the first webpage found (Figure 12.1).

Google also has additional information in a drop-down box at the end of the link that connects to a "cached" page. The cached page is the last copy of the webpage that Google crawled. It could be within days if not weeks of the current page but is also subject to being overwritten and replaced with a newer webpage version. The top of the cached page includes the date and time of the Google web crawl. For the investigator this can be a valuable piece of information. Depending on when Google crawled the site, the last page may contain information different than the current page. Documenting and capturing Google's cached page of a webpage can therefore be important step to ensure this time snapshot is preserved. Bing's search also has a cache feature which may not be the same date that Google's cache page was created. Bing's cache copy can yet be another piece to an investigative timeline puzzle, warranting similar documentation and preservation (Figure 12.2).

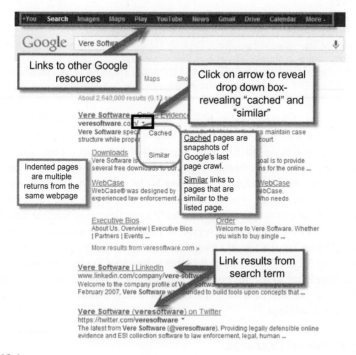

FIGURE 12.1

Google results page explanation.

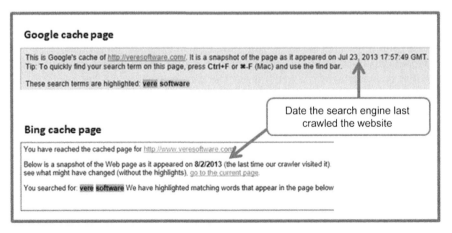

FIGURE 12.2

Google and Bing cached page notice the search was completed the same day.

WANT GET TO GOOGLE'S CACHED "TEXT-ONLY" VERSION OF A WEBPAGE?

First cut and paste the following into the top of your web browser:

    http://webcache.googleusercontent.com/search?strip = 1&q = cache

Now add the interested webpage onto the end: For example, to view the text of vere software.com, your web browser should now look like this:

    http://webcache.googleusercontent.com/search?strip = 1&q = cache:veresoftware.com

Now hit Enter. The cache version reflected will now only display text (Haynal, 2013).

Google has an Advanced Search page in addition to its general search page. After a query is completed, at the bottom of the page results, an Advance Search option is shown. Clicking on Advance Search will bring up a page which assists the user refining their query. Some of the Advanced Search options are the ability to limit the query by excluding certain words, by using an exact phrase, or the inclusion of a number range. The number range can be a year date range to include returns only between two specific dates. Additional functions include limiting the hit returns to a specific language, a region or just a specific website or domain.

Clicking "More" at the top of Google's search screen will produce a pull-down menu. Selecting "Even More" from this menu provides several additional options that can be beneficial to the investigator. For instance, this section has an area for Patent as well as Scholar searches, the latter of which includes access to not only articles but legal opinions.

Google's Advanced Operators

Using advanced operators with Google can provide the investigator with an ability to search for and locate more precise information about the specific query terms directly from the search box. We have provided a few of these operators in

Table 12.1 Useful Investigative Google Advanced Operators

	Advanced Operator Example
Definitions	define:term
News headlines	News:topic
Google cached pages	cache:url
Search within site	site:domain.com
Search for links	link:domain.com
Term(s) in URL	inurl:term
Term(s) in title	intitle:term
Term(s) in body text	intext:term
Term(s) anchor text	inanchor:term
Specific file type	ext:filetype
Related sites	related:url
URL-related info	info:url

Table 12.1. A good resource for understanding Google's Advanced Operators is their guide at http://www.googleguide.com/advanced_operators_reference.html, which provides lists of additional advanced operators and how they are used.

TouchGraph

Sometimes seeing relationships between individuals is not easy. It can be tough to see connections merely from gathering data and looking at a list, particularly when one is dealing with large numbers. A common law enforcement practice for years has been to place photos on a bulletin board and either organize the photos or draw lines to reflect how they are related. Perez (2008) refers to this as visualization, which "... is a technique to graphically represent sets of data." Visualization makes the relationships easier to detect and understand. One particular website, TouchGraph SEO Browser (http://www.touchgraph.com/TGGoogleBrowser.html) graphs and "... reveals the network of connectivity between websites, as reported by Google's database of related sites" (Figure 12.3).

Clicking a result icon will provide details about it, such as the URL where the information was found, a brief description, and additional related sites. The website also allows you to export the data out to a .csv file that can be opened in a spreadsheet to better utilize the information. The data exported includes the URL where the information was found and the title of the site's page where it was found.

Searching with Bing

Bing, previously known as Live Search, Windows Live Search, and MSN Search, was unveiled in 2009 and was designed "... with a new approach to user experience and intuitive tools to help customers make better decisions, focusing initially

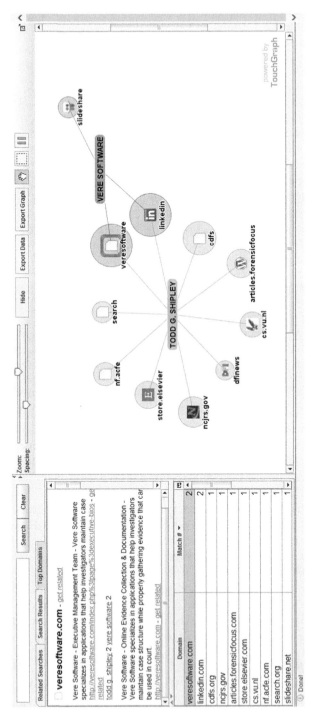

FIGURE 12.3

TouchGraph search results.

on four key vertical areas: making a purchase decision, planning a trip, researching a health condition or finding a local business" (Paczkowski, 2009). Bing's focus is simply providing results that lead users to decisions to purchase goods or services.

In 2012, Bing started presenting its search results in three columns, (1) search results, (2) a "snapshot" of related searches with associated ads, and (3) a social networking interface, which if approved will connect to a user's own Facebook profile (Peterson, 2012). According to Harry Shum, a Vice President of Microsoft, this revamping enables "information to flow from search to social networks" (Peterson, 2012). For investigators the first column results are usually the most important results.

Bing is remarkably similar to the layout of Google (Figure 12.4). As with Google simply input in your search terms and press enter. Returns are presented which can be scrolled through. Clicking on the hyperlinks, also shown in blue, will take the investigator to webpage associated with the search hit. The operators are somewhat different. For instance, in Google to query on two terms one uses the + sign. Bing however does a search on all words, without regard to the + sign. Bing provides a cache version of the webpage with a drop-down box at the end of the link that goes to a "cached" page. Bing has its own version of advanced operators, which are referred to as advanced keywords. See Table 12.2 for some of the useful ones. However, Bing does not have its own advanced search page like Google. Finally the resources to locate how to search on Bing are as not numerous as they are for Google.

FIGURE 12.4

Bing results page explanation.

Table 12.2 Useful Investigative Bing Advanced Keywords

	Advanced Keyword Example
IP: Finds sites hosted by a specific IP address. Type the ip: keyword, followed by the website's IP address	IP: 97.74.74.204
Prefer: Adds emphasis to a search term or another operator to help focus the search results.	cybercrime Prefer: FBI
ext: Returns only webpages with the specified filename extension.	cybercrime ext:docx
Filetype: Returns only webpages created in the specified file type. specify.	cybercrime filetype:pdf
inanchor: or inbody: or intitle: These keywords return webpages that contain the specified term in the metadata, such as in a website's the anchor, body, or title, respectively. Note: specify only one term per keyword. You can string multiple keyword entries as needed.	inanchor: cybercrime inbody:FBI inbody:Justice
Site: Returns webpages that belong to the specified site. Use a logical OR to group domains to focus on two or more domains. The site: keyword can be used to search for web domains, top level domains, and directories that are not more than two levels deep. It can also be used to search for webpages that contain a specific search word on a site.	To see webpages about cybercrime from the US Justice Department or FBI websites, type cybercrime (site: justice. gov OR site:fbi.gov) To find webpages reflecting Ohio on HTCIA's website type site: site: www. htcia.org ohio

BING'S CONNECTION TO SOCIAL NETWORKING SITES

The third column of Bing's search engine provides hits from social media. By granting Bing access to one's Facebook account, the search is expanded to include all of the user's friend's public posts and pictures. Facebook deletes Bing queries within 24 hours, and the search queries are not shared with a user's Facebook friends (Adhikari, 2010). Facebook results are reflected first in the third column, which are proceeded by those from the public access area of other social media, such as Twitter or Quora. If one does not provide access to their social networking profile, the results are limited to public posts on various social media. Results from Facebook can include hits from posts several years old. Additionally, for Facebook hits to be included, the search term must be in a post. For instance if you search for "Bonnie", the results will only include posts where Bonnie appears in the text. The results will not list all of your contacts who may have the Bonnie in their profile name. However, for other media, such as Twitter, hits will be reflected if the term is found in either the profile or post text.

Bing also will reflect images from your Facebook connections. For instance, if you search for baby, images associated with a post where the term baby appears will be reflected. This also goes for Albums. However, it gets a bit more confusing. If the Album is labelled baby and there is no text comment, the pictures in the Album will not be returned in the results. However, the Album could be called anything but if baby is noted in the associated comment, pictures will be returned in the results, even if they have nothing to do with a baby. This is because Bing is searching the posts and not the labels or images themselves. The result limitations make connecting an undercover Facebook account to search each target profile associated with that account of little value. Remember Bing is about getting the user information from their social connects to make decisions about buying things. It is not about giving the user all results possible from their social networking connections. Investigators will find using Bing enabled with their Facebook connections of little use for their activities, unless they are looking for tips on the best pizza, donuts, cigars, or beer.

Finding information on a person

Use multiple sites when Internet searching for an individual will get you a better well-rounded response and data set. There are many sites available on the Internet that can provide the investigator with information on a person. Each varies in the information provided and the requirements for doing a query. Using multiple sites can provide the investigator with a complete picture of the targeted individual. It is best to consider searching as a process, with each following search requiring more specific details for quality results.

These details fall into two general tiers of criteria. Tier one criteria is something that is very specific to that person, such as a photo, birth date, age, home address, telephone number, email address, screen or profile name, close relative, property ownership, or party to a civil or criminal case. These things are not always easy to know but if discovered can later lead to high-quality searches and information.

Tier two criteria is a bit more general and is frequently easier to know. They include such things as employment, occupation, general location (city/state/country), education, hobbies, and associates. These factors coupled with the individual's name may lead to more specific or tier one information, which again leads to quality searches and information.

Consider for a moment you have a name and where they graduated from high school. With this information you may be able to find an alumni site and find the year they graduated. With the year they graduated you now have their age narrowed down. Additionally, with their high school name you may be able to search for their profile on a social media site, which may lead to photos, where they are located, age/birth date, email address, and their relatives and associates.

Again, all of these can help the investigator identify information about a person. Using a search term of two names in quotes with a plus sign such as "Todd Shipley" + "Art Bowker" can provide the investigator with sites where the two names appear together. (For Bing the search term would be "Todd Shipley"

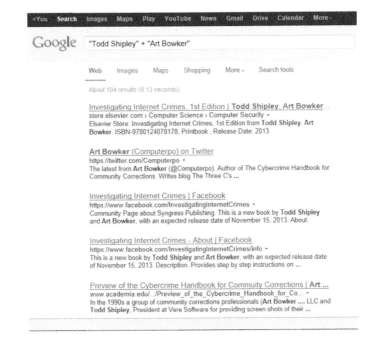

FIGURE 12.5

Google search with two names.

"Art Bowker", without the plus sign.) This same technique can be used with a name and employment, location, etc (Figure 12.5).

Generally, consider the search process as involving the following: (1) search engine inquiries (2) specific site searches, such as a social networking directory or an identified website, and (3) biological search site, which require one other factor beside names, such as address, age, or relatives to narrow the results. Online court records, inmate searches, and sex offender queries are increasingly available too. They can be considered a biological search as the location where a person lives or lived, along with the date of birth is needed to narrow the results to the target of interest.

At the start of the process is the use of a general search engine (Google, Bing, etc.) or a people search engine, such as Pipl (www.pipl.com). Simply by typing the target's name into the search box will provide individual page links that contain the name query. However, unless that person's name is unique you are likely to get results from all over the place, which need to be further refined. Add either a tier one or two level criteria you possess to narrow the results. If there is information present you should have located it. Harvest additional criteria for your searches and document your results. If not, attempt to search a social networking directory. Again, harvest additional criteria for your following searches. Only when you have a tier one level criteria, such as address, age, or relative attempt a biological search using one of the below sites, most of which require a fee to obtain more detailed information:

- 411.com, http://www.411.com
- BRBPub.com, http://www.brbpub.com/
- Dru Sjodin National Sex Offender Public Website, http://www.nsopw.gov/[2]
- Federal Bureau of Prisons Inmate Search, http://www.bop.gov/iloc2/LocateInmate.jsp[3]
- SearchBug, http://www.searchbug.com
- Search Systems, http://www.searchsystems.net
- ZABASEARCH, http://www.zabasearch.com
- ZoomInfo, http://www.zoominfo.com

Don't forget we have previously discussed the Vere Software Toolbar and its inclusion of multiple sites that can be used for identifying persons on the Internet. Finally, do not consider the search process as a one-direction linear activity. For instance, your site-specific search or biological search reveals some new criteria that you did not possess when you did the search engine queries. You are not precluded from taking that new criteria and doing another search engine query, which may lead to even more leads.

Finding business information

The Internet has provided the opportunity for every company on the planet to make a world-wide presence through the use of websites and social media. With this opportunity most businesses have made liberal use of the Internet to present their products/services and information about their company and its employees. Other sources on the Internet regularly collect information on companies and post it to their websites. Government agencies also routinely make available information about companies. Again, commence your inquires with search engines and progress to these other websites. Be aware that negative results on a government site may reflect that entity is very new, non-compliant with reporting requirements and/or outright fraudulent person or entity. Accordingly document negative results and what government database was searched.

---

[2]Not all countries have registered sex offenders. Additionally, those that do may not always make the data available outside of the law enforcement community.

[3]In the United States, many of the state correctional systems also have online access to names in their inmate and/or parolee databases. Other countries restrict this information but some provide it online. Do a Google search to locate if an online inmate database exists in the country of interest.

US government sources

Secretary of State's offices in the United States provide online access to corporation registration records. However, be aware that some states limit how much information is provided online or regular a fee payment. Also consider checking foreign entity records for companies doing business in one state but incorporated in another. The US Security and Exchanges Commission provides online access to a variety of required filings from US Companies. Using these resources, an investigator can identify huge amounts of information about a company or corporation.

In the United States, labor unions which represent private sector employees or are representing US Postal Service employees are required to file annual financial reports and to provide copies of their bylaws/constitution. Additionally, under some circumstances employers and labor relations consultants are required to file disclosure reports. Collective bargaining agreements covering 1,000 or more workers are also on file with the US Department of Labor. All of these records are online and can be searched. One interesting query will allow the user to search by payee for payments from labor organizations. Many states also require unions which represent solely public employees within their state to file annual financial reports.

The US Internal Revenue Service's website provides information on charities and nonprofit organizations that file the Form 990. These forms can provide information on the targeted organization. Additionally, many states provide online access to professional licensing information on variety of occupations. The following are some useful US government websites to research companies, nonprofit entries, and labor unions:

- Internal Revenues Service (Tax Exempt Organizations), http://www.irs.gov/ Charities-&-Non-Profits/Exempt-Organizations-Select-Check
- National Archives, http://www.archives.gov/
- Office of Labor Management Standards, US Department of Labor, http:// www.dol.gov/olms/regs/compliance/rrlo/lmrda.htm
- Securities and Exchange Commission, http://www.sec.gov/cgi-bin/srch-edgar?

Non-US government sources

The United States is obviously not alone in providing its citizenry online information about businesses operating in their jurisdictions. Many countries mandate companies register and file annual reports with a government agency. Increasingly these records are publicly available and online. Locating these sites can be as easy as doing a Google search (corporation + registration + country of interest). However, we have provided some of the larger sites below:

- Australian Security and Investment Commission, https://connectonline.asic. gov.au/RegistrySearch/faces/landing/bn/SearchBnRegisters.jspx?_adf.ctrl-state = t5t9t1hry_13
- Corporations Canada (provides search for federal corporations as well as links to provincial registries), http://www.ic.gc.ca/eic/site/cd-dgc.nsf/eng/cs01134.html
- European Business Register (EBR), http://www.ebr.org/section/1/index.html
- The Registrar of Companies (England, Wales, Northern Ireland, and Scotland), http://www.companieshouse.gov.uk/

Non-government sources

Individuals and companies need to make sound business decisions and that often requires "due diligence" inquiries on potential partners and investments. Fortunately, governments are not the only entities maintaining records on businesses and non-profit organizations. Some large data brokers, such as LEXIS-NEXIS®, mentioned in Chapter 6, have information on businesses and nonprofits in their databases. Another such data broker is IRBSearch (www.irbsearch.com). Access to these databases requires the payment of fees and/or a subscription. However, there are other online sites which provide a variety of business data for free or at a small cost. Below are some of the notable ones:

Other business search sites
- Canadian Council of Better Business Bureaus (both businesses and charities), http://www.bbb.org/canada/
- Council of Better Business Bureaus (US) (both businesses and charities), http://www.bbb.org/us/
- CreditRiskMonitor, http://crmz.com/directory/
- Fran Finnegan & Company, http://www.secinfo.com/
- Hoovers, A D&B Company, http://www.hoovers.com
- Manta Media, Inc., http://www.manta.com/
- Search Systems, http://www.searchsystems.net
- Zoom Information, Inc., http://www.zoominfo.com/

Charity/nonprofit resource sites
- Charity 101, http://charitycheck101.org/
- Charity Navigator, http://www.charitynavigator.org/
- GuideStar Nonprofit Directory, http://www.guidestar.org/
- NOZA 990-PF Database Listing, http://www.grantsmart.com/
- Noza Search (Donors), https://www.nozasearch.com/

Finding telephone numbers and email addresses

Finding information about telephone numbers on the Internet can be a little unsatisfying. Unfortunately most records on telephone ownership require the use of legal service on the provider that owns the number. Additionally, some websites may provide dated information on telephones, which can lead to erroneous owner identification. This does not mean the investigator cannot identify certain information about a telephone number. Websites like FoneFinder, http://fonefinder.net/ and PhoneNumber.com, http://PhoneNumber.com can provide the city and state that the number is originally from as well as the service provider controlling the number. This can provide the investigator with the company to send legal service to identify the telephone owner. From an investigative perspective, a search on Google or other search engines can provide the user with places on the Internet that the telephone number has been posted. This may lead to the identity of the person or company connected to the number.

Email addresses likewise can be identified by using search engines to reveal locations where the email has been used on the Internet. Humans are creatures of habit and will use and reuse nicknames, descriptive screen names, or slight variations of these in their email addresses. For instance the person using osubuckeyefan1@yahoo.com may also use osubuckeyefan1@gmail.com. Consider searching by everything prior to the @ symbol for additional leads. Websites like Email Finder, http://www.emailfinder.com/, can be useful at finding email address information on the Internet. My Email Address, http://my.email.address.is/, is a multiple email search engine that can help to identify an email address. Mail Tester, http://mailtester.com, allows the investigator to identify the MX (Mail transfer) records of the email address including the server that hosts the mail service. JigSaw, http://www.jigsaw.com/, is a business contact service that can also provide information on email addresses.

NAME 2 EMAIL

An interesting technique for identifying an email address is described by Rob Ousbey of Distilled.com. He has developed a spreadsheet, called name2email, which he makes freely available as a Google document. Using this spreadsheet a person can make multiple variations of a first and last name and a domain name. He can then use these email address variations with the Gmail plugin from Rapportive.com to identify a particular user's email. His posting at http://www.distilled.net/blog/miscellaneous/find-almost-anybodys-email-address/ includes a video of how to use the tool. Try using this with multiple domains such as Gmail.com, Yahoo.com, and Live.com to determine the user's possible email addresses.

Searching blogs

Comments on blogs have become a regular source of complaint. Personal anonymous comments made on one of the tens of thousands of blogs that exist can be problematic to find. Searching through that many blogs can sometimes be a monumental task. Google is as always a good start for any searching. Many blogs allow for anonymous posting which can be a near dead end for an investigator. Some blogs may record poster's IP addresses, but this is only available by legal service to the blog owner or blogging site. There are some sites, although few, that actually record the poster's IP address. This is not always visible in the browser. The investigator may have to look at the blog's source code to identify the IP address. Blogs sometimes include the IP address in the blog source code but do not make it visible on the page. Investigators should check the source code for possible inclusion of the poster's IP address (see Chapter 13 for further details on viewing source code).

As noted in Chapter 9, there are ways to conceal one's IP address, which defeats this identifying technique. Again, be aware that some blog posters will reuse screen names on different blogs. They will also post similar information or use a catch phrase routinely in their postings. The screen name or these other user habits can become search engine queries, which may reveal more posts on different sites, which might lead to some piece of information that leads to the blogger's identification. The following sites can be good information resources for the investigator to locate blog postings:

- Blogs.com, http://www.blogs.com/
- Blogdigger.com, http://www.blogdigger.com/index.html
- Blogsearchengine.com, http://www.blogsearchengine.com/
- Feedster.com, http://www.feedster.com/
- Google Blog Search, http://www.google.com/blogsearch
- Technorati.com, http://technorati.com/
- Yahoo.com, http://blog.search.yahoo.com

Professional communities

Professional social networking communities are another great source of information for the investigator. Persons using these sites generally are intending to make a good business or professional presentation. Much of the information presented is related to their education and previous employment. However, it is not unheard of to see partial dates of birth, telephone numbers, and email addresses. Additionally, the investigator can identify additional insight into the user's account by reviewing groups that they belong to. Some users also feel compelled to provide their itineraries. These sites generally have a public profile and a member's only accessible profile containing access to additional information. Information can be identified from the public profile as in the example of Figure 12.6. Additionally, information can also be viewed from a search engine's cache result of the public profile page. However, more information is usually reserved for other social media site members. The investigator can login and see

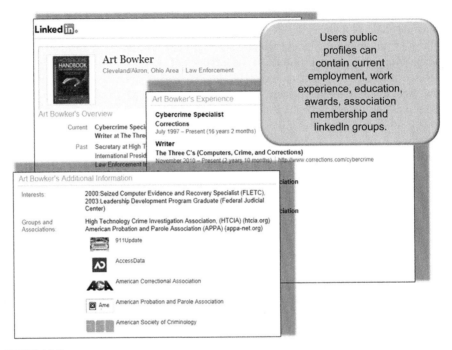

FIGURE 12.6

LinkedIn public profile.

additional information about the site member. The investigator needs to be aware that the site might alert the user that someone has looked at their site and the user who reviewed the site. Undercover accounts used for this purpose should be consistent with the target's background. The following are some common professional networking sites:

- Jigsaw.com, http://www.jigsaw.com/
- Linkedin.com, http://www.linkedin.com/
- Spoke.com, http://www.spoke.com/
- Ryze.com, http://www.ryze.com/
- Xing.com, http://www.xing.com/
- Zoominfo.com, http://www.zoominfo.com/

News searches

From an investigative purpose, news-related articles about target individuals and companies can be of significant benefit to an investigation. Searching Google as usual can provide a significant amount of information. Also consider Google and Bing's news search engines (https://news.google.com/ and http://www.bing.com/news) There are several search sites the investigator can make use of that are dedicated to news-related information. Additionally, with today's video popularity news is no longer just print news or blogs. Investigators need to consider searching sites like YouTube (a Google company). Below are some useful search sites for news:

- Newsvine.com, http://www.newsvine.com/
- Onlinenewspapers.com, http://www.onlinenewspapers.com/
- Reddit.com, http://www.reddit.com/
- Stumbleupon.com, http://www.stumbleupon.com/
- Techdirt.com, http://www.techdirt.com/

Video news

- ABC News, http://abcnews.go.com/
- Aljazeera, http://www.aljazeera.com/
- British Broadcasting Corporation, http://www.bbc.co.uk/news/video_and_audio/
- Cable News Network, http://www.cnn.com/video/
- CBS News, http://www.cbsnews.com/
- Fox News, http://video.foxnews.com/
- LinkTV, http://www.linktv.org/
- NBC News, http://www.nbc.com/news-sports/
- Newsy, http://www.newsy.com/
- Public Broadcasting Corporation, http://www.pbs.org/search/
- Reuters News, http://www.reuters.com/news/video
- The Real News, http://therealnews.com/t2/
- USA Today, http://www.usatoday.com/media/latest/videos/news/

INTERNET SEARCH TIP

Put your initial search terms in a Word or Note Pad document and save it. Copy those terms into your search queries. Save the used search queries and where they were used to the document. As you find new search terms paste them into this document and save it, along with the source you found for the new term. Continue the process of documenting new terms and search queries. In this way you have a record of what searches you did and where you found your results. You can also use the form in the appendix titled "Basic Investigation and Documentation of a Person Online" for this purpose.

CONCLUSIONS

This chapter provided the investigator with useful Internet resources. We discussed the differences between search directories and search and metasearch engines. We noted that search engines are frequently the first choice in looking for information on individuals, companies, and telephone/cell numbers, and email address. We further provided a general investigative process which commences with search engine inquiries, then specific site searches, ending with biological search sites. Each of the provided websites can provide information that the investigator can use to further their investigation. The investigator can utilize the resources here and on the Internet to effectively identify and locate information on the targets as well as the victims in an investigation.

Further reading

411.com—Official Site. (n.d.). *411.com—Official Site*. Retrieved from <http://www.411.com>.

42 Bing Search Engine Hacks. (n.d.). *ivanwalsh.com*. Retrieved from <www.ivanwalsh.com/google-tips/42-bing-search-engine-hacks/>.

ABCNews.com—Breaking News, Latest News & Top Video News. (n.d.). *ABC News*. Retrieved from <http://abcnews.go.com/>.

Adhikari, R. (2010, October 14). Facebook and Bing Do the Search Two-Step. *TechNewsWorld: All Tech—All The Time*. Retrieved from <http://www.technewsworld.com/rsstory/71036>.

Al Jazeera English—Live US, Europe, Middle East, Asia, Sports, Weather & Business News. (n.d.). *Al Jazeera News*. Retrieved from <http://www.aljazeera.com/>.

BBB Consumer and Business Reviews, Reports, Ratings, Complaints and Accredited Business Listings, U.S. (n.d.). *Council of Better Business Bureaus*. Retrieved from <www.bbb.org/us/>.

BBC News—One-minute World News. (n.d.). *BBC—Homepage*. Retrieved from <http://www.bbc.co.uk/news/video_and_audio/>.

Bing. (n.d.). *Bing*. Retrieved from <http://bing.com>.

Bing Advanced Search Keywords. (n.d.). *Online Help*. Retrieved from <http://onlinehelp.microsoft.com/en-us/bing/ff808421.aspx>.

Blachman, N., & Peek, J. (n.d.). Google Search Operators—Google Guide. *Interactive Online Google Tutorial and References—Google Guide*. Retrieved from <http://www.googleguide.com/advanced_operators_reference.html>.

Blogdigger: Blog Search Engine—Search Blogs. (n.d.). *Blogdigger*. Retrieved from <http://www.blogdigger.com/index.html>.

Blogs.com. (n.d.). *Blogs.com*. Retrieved from <http://www.blogs.com>.

Blog Search Engine. (n.d.). *Blog Search Engine*. Retrieved from <www.blogsearchengine.com/>.

BOP: Inmate Locator Main Page. (n.d.). *BOP: Federal Bureau of Prisons Web Site*. Retrieved from <http://www.bop.gov/iloc2/LocateInmate.jsp>.

Breaking News Headlines: Business, Entertainment & World News—CBS News. (n.d.). *CBS News*. Retrieved from <http://www.cbsnews.com/>.

Business Profiles and Company Information: ZoomInfo.com. (n.d.). *Business Profiles and Company Information: ZoomInfo.com*. Retrieved from <http://www.zoominfo.com>.

Cached Link—Search Help. (n.d.). *Google*. Retrieved from <https://support.google.com/websearch/answer/1687222?hl=en&p=cached>.

Charity Navigator—America's Largest Charity Evaluator. (n.d.). *Charity Navigator.* Retrieved from <http://www.charitynavigator.org/>.

Clusty.com—Clusty Search Engine. (n.d.). *Clusty.com—Clusty Search Engine.* Retrieved from <http://clusty.com>.

Companies House. (n.d.). *Companies House.* Retrieved from <http://www.companieshouse. gov.uk/>.

comScore Releases June 2013 US Search Engine Rankings—comScore, Inc. (2013). *Analytics for a Digital World—comScore, Inc.* Retrieved from <http://www.comscore. com/Insights/Press_Releases>.

Connecting You to the World: Link TV. (n.d.). *Link TV.* Retrieved from <http://www. linktv.org/>.

CNN Video—Breaking News Videos from CNN.com. (n.d.). *CNN.com—Breaking News, US, World, Weather, Entertainment & Video News.* Retrieved from <http://www.cnn. com/video/>.

Do a Charity Check Before You Donate. (n.d.). *CharityCheck101.or*g. Retrieved from <http://charitycheck101.org/>.

Dogpile Web Search. (n.d.). *Dogpile Web Search.* Retrieved from <www.dogpile.com>.

EBR—European Company Information Online. (n.d.). *EBR—European Company Information Online.* Retrieved from <http://www.ebr.org/section/1/index. html>.

Email Search—Email Address Search—Find Email Addresses. (n.d.). *My.Email.Address.Is.* Retrieved from <my.email.address.is/>.

Email Search & Reverse Email Lookup. (n.d.). *emailfinder.com.* Retrieved from <www. emailfinder.com/>.

EO Select Check. (n.d.). *Internal Revenue Service.* Retrieved from <http://www.irs.gov/ Charities-&-Non-Profits/Exempt-Organizations-Select-Check>.

Explore More. Web pages, Photos, and Videos: StumbleUpon.com. (n.d.). *StumbleUpon. com.* Retrieved from <http://www.stumbleupon.com/>.

FeedsterSearch—Home. (n.d.). *FeedsterSearch—Home.* Retrieved from <http://www.feed-ster.com>.

Find (Almost) Anybody's Email Address|Distilled. (n.d.). *Distilled: Online Marketing, PPC & SEO Agency in London, Seattle & NYC.* Retrieved from <http://www.distilled. net/blog/miscellaneous/find-almost-anybodys-email-address>.

Fone Finder Query Form. (n.d.). *Fonefinder.Net:Primeris, Inc.* Retrieved from <fonefinder. net/>.

Fox News Video. (n.d.). *Fox News.* Retrieved from <http://video.foxnews.com/>.

Free People Finder and Company Search: SearchBug. (n.d.). *Free People Finder and Company Search.* Retrieved from <http://www.searchbug.com/>.

Free People Search Engine: ZabaSearch. (n.d.). *Free People Search Engine; ZabaSearch.* Retrieved from <http://www.zabasearch.com>.

Free Public Records: Search the Original Resource Worldwide. (n.d.) *Free Public Records: Search the Original Resource Worldwide.* Retrieved from <http://www.searchsystems. net>.

Google. (n.d.). *Google.* Retrieved from <http://www.google.com>.

Google Advanced Search. (n.d.). *Google.* Retrieved from <http://www.google.com/ advanced_search>.

Google Blog Search. (n.d.). *Google.* Retrieved from <http://www.google.com/blogsearch>.

Google News. (n.d.). *Google.* Retrieved from <https://news.google.com/>.

GuideStar Nonprofit Reports and Forms 990 for Donors, Grantmakers and Businesses. (n.d.). *GuideStar*. Retrieved from <http://www.guidestar.org/>.

Hagedorn, E. (n.d.). *Newsy: Multisource Video News*. Retrieved from <http://www.newsy. com/>.

Haynal, R. (2013, March 1). *Cached Issues. Russ Haynal—Home Page*. Retrieved from <http://navigators.com/cached.html>.

Home—Canadian BBB. (n.d.). *Canadian Council of Better Business Bureaus*. Retrieved from <www.bbb.org/canada/>.

Hoover's Company Information. (n.d.). *Hoover's Company Information, Industry Information, Lists*. Retrieved from <http://www.hoovers.com>.

lineUSA. (n.d.). Videos, Photos—USATODAY.com. *USA TODAY: Latest World and US News—USATODAY.com*. Retrieved from <http://www.usatoday.com/media/latest/vide>.

IRBsearch. (n.d.). *IRBsearch: Information Exclusively for Investigative Professionals*. Retrieved from <http://www.irbsearch.com>.

Jarboe, G. (2003, October 15). A "Fireside Chat" with Google's Sergey Brin. *Search Engine Watch (#SEW)*. Retrieved from <http://searchenginewatch.com/article/2064259/A-Fireside-Chat-with-Googles-Sergey-Brin>.

Jigsaw Business Contact Directory of Business Contacts and Company Information. (n.d.). *data.com*. Retrieved from <www.jigsaw.com/>.

Kaushal, N. (2011, October 24). Now Bing Powers Yahoo Organic Search. *SearchNewz, Search Engine News*. Retrieved from <http://www.searchnewz.com/now-bing-powers-yahoo-organic-search-2011-10>.

Koch, P., & Koch, S. (2007). Search Engine Tutorial by Pandia—a Free Guide to Web Searching. *Pandia Search and Social*. Retrieved from <http://www.pandia.com/goalgetter/index.html>.

MailTester.com. (n.d.). *MailTester.com*. Retrieved from <http://mailtester.com>.

Manta. (n.d.). *Manta—Big finds from Small Businesses*. Retrieved from <http://www.manta.com>.

Microsoft's New Search at Bing.com Helps People Make Better Decisions. (n.d.). *Microsoft Corporation*. Retrieved from <http://www.microsoft.com/en-us/news/press/2009/may09/05-28NewSearchPR.aspx>.

National Archives and Records Administration. (n.d.). *National Archives and Records Administration*. Retrieved from <http://www.archives.gov/>.

NBC.com—News & Sports—NBC Official Site. (n.d.). *NBC.com*. Retrieved from <http://www.nbc.com/news-sports/>.

Newsvine. (n.d.). *Newsvine*. Retrieved from <http://www.newsvine.com/>.

NOZA 990-PF Database Listing. (n.d.). *Grantsmart.com*. Retrieved from <http://www.grantsmart.com/>.

NOZA—Charitable Donations Database and Prospect Research. (n.d.). *NOZA*. Retrieved from <https://www.nozasearch.com/>.

Our History in Depth—Company—Google. (n.d.). *Google*. Retrieved from <http://www.google.com/about/company/history>.

Paczkowski, J. (2009, May 28). Microsoft Bing: The full press release—John Paczkowski—D7—AllThingsD. *AllThingsD*. Retrieved from <http://allthingsd.com/20090528/micro>.

Pandia Search and Social. (n.d.). *Pandia Search and Social*. Retrieved from <http://www. pandia.com>.

Perez, S. (2008, March 31). The Best Tools for Visualization. *ReadWrite*. Retrieved from <http://readwrite.com/2008/03/13/the_best_tools_for_visualization>.

Peterson, T. (2012, May 10). Microsoft Revamps Bing with Social Sidebar|Adweek. *Adweek—Breaking News in Advertising, Media and Technology*. Retrieved from <http://www.adweek.com/news/technology/microsoft-revamps-bing-social-sidebar-140302>.

Pipl—People Search. (n.d.). *Pipl—People Search*. Retrieved from www.pipl.com.

Phone Number and Reverse Phone Search. (n.d.). *PhoneNumber.com*. Retrieved from <PhoneNumber.com>.

Public Records. (n.d.). *Public Records*. Retrieved from <http://www.brbpub.com/>.

Pyle, C. H., & WarIsACrime.org. (n.d.). *The Real News Network—Independent News, Blogs and Editorials*. Retrieved from <http://therealnews.com/t2/>.

Rapportive. (n.d.). *Rapportive*. Retrieved from <http://rapportive.com/>.

Recommendations on Net Searching. (n.d.). *Pandia Search and Social*. Retrieved from <http://www.pandia.com/goalgetter/recommendations.html>.

Reddit: the Front Page of the Internet. (n.d.). *Reddit*. Retrieved from <http://www.reddit.com/>.

Registrars—Corporations Canada. (n.d.). *Corporations Canada*. Retrieved from <www.ic.gc.ca/eic/site/cd-dgc.nsf/eng/cs01134.html>.

Ryze—the Original Social Network for Business. (n.d.). *Ryze*. Retrieved from <http://www.ryze.com/>.

Search. (n.d.). *PBS: Public Broadcasting Service*. Retrieved from <http://www.pbs.org/search/>.

SearchBug. Retrieved from <http://www.searchbug.com>.

Search Business Names Register. (n.d.). *Australian Security and Investment Commission*. Retrieved from <https://connectonline.asic.gov.au/RegistrySearch/faces/landing/bn/SearchBnRegisters.jspx?_adf.ctrl-state=t5t9t1hry_13>.

Search Historical SEC EDGAR Archives. (n.d.). *US Securities and Exchange Commission*. Retrieved from <http://www.sec.gov/cgi-bin/srch-edgar?>.

SEC Info. (n.d.) *SEC Info—the Best EDGAR Online Database of Securities and Exchange Commission Filings & IPOs*. Retrieved from <http://www.secinfo.com/>.

SEO Keyword Graph Visualization|SEO Browser—TouchGraph.com. (n.d.). *TouchGraph.com*. Retrieved from <http://www.touchgraph.com/TGGoogleBrowser.html>.

Spoke: Discover Relevant Business Information. (n.d.). *Spoke*. Retrieved from <http://www.spoke.com/>.

Techdirt. (n.d.). *Techdirt*. Retrieved from <http://www.techdirt.com/>.

Technorati. (n.d.). *Technorati, Inc*. Retrieved from <technorati.com/>.

Thousands of Online Newspapers on the Web: World Newspaper Directory: Listed on OnlineNewspapers.com. (n.d.) *Online Newspapers on the Web*. Retrieved from <http://www.onlinenewspapers.com/>.

Top Stories—Bing News. (n.d.). *Bing*. Retrieved from <http://www.bing.com/news>.

United States Department of Justice National Sex Offender Public Website. (n.d.). *United States Department of Justice National Sex Offender Public Website*. Retrieved from <http://www.nsopw.gov/>.

Untangling the Web: An Introduction to Internet Research. (2007). Washington, DC: National City Agency, Center for Digital Content.

U.S. Department of Labor—Office of Labor-Management Standards (OLMS)—Online Public Disclosure Room: Union Reports and Collective Bargaining Agreements. (n.d.). *United States Department of Labor*. Retrieved from <http://www.dol.gov/olms/regs/compliance/rrlo/lmrda.htm>.

Video—Top News Videos, Business & Entertainment Videos: Reuters.com. (n.d.). *Business & Financial News, Breaking US & International News: Reuters.com.* Retrieved from <http://www.reuters.com/news/video>.

WebFetch. (n.d.). *WebFetch*. Retrieved from <www.webfetch.com>.

World's Largest Professional Network: LinkedIn. (n.d.). *LinkedIn*. Retrieved from <http://www.linkedin.com/>.

Worldwide Directory of Public Companies. (n.d.). *CreditRiskMonitor—Search for a Public Company*. Retrieved from <http://crmz.com/directory/>.

XING—Das professionelle Netzwerk. (n.d.). *XING*. Retrieved from <http://www.xing.com/>.

Yahoo!. (n.d.). *Yahoo!*. Retrieved from <http://www.yahoo.com>.

Yahoo! Blog Search. (n.d.). *Yahoo! Blog Search*. Retrieved from <http://blog.search.yahoo.com>.

Yahoo! Directory. (n.d.). *Yahoo! Directory*. Retrieved from <http://dir.yahoo.com/>.

YouTube. (n.d.). *YouTube*. Retrieved from <https://www.youtube.com/>.

Zetter, K. (2013, May 8). Use These Secret NSA Google Search Tips to Become Your Own Spy Agency. *Threat Level: wired.com*. Retrieved from http://www.wired.com/threatlevel/2013/05/nsa-manual-on-hacking-internet/>.

Investigating Websites and Webpages

13

All they need to do is to set up some website somewhere selling some bogus product at 20% of the normal market prices and people are going to be tricked into providing their credit card numbers.
Kevin Mitnick, reformed hacker

Webpages and websites

Webpages are the Internet's heart as we know it. We described earlier in Chapter 3 how the Internet works and how Internet protocol (IP) addresses are the basis for most Internet connections. Webpages are the graphical representations of the data stored on a webserver as viewed through a browser on our local computer or computing device (tablet or cell phones). The main protocol used for communication between a web browser and a webserver is Hypertext Transfer Protocol. This protocol was designed to enable document, images, and other types of data to be transferred between a website and a user's browser. The data resides on the webserver in folders, just like other data resides on your local computer. You enter a domain name into your browser, which is translated to an IP address, and the browser sends a request to the webserver asking for the page at the requested address. The webserver that resides at the IP address responds, providing access to the requested data if authorized (Figure 13.1).

How webpages work

Webpages "live" on what we refer to as the World Wide Web (WWW). WWW is a collection of servers around the world that host pages of information that are connected to each other using hypertext. We regularly click on hypertext links, identified as blue colored text on a webpage. These pages are historically written in HTML, a common IP language. There are more languages being used on webpages now than just HTML. Modern browsers also use Java, ActiveX, and other scripting languages to show image files, video, and animation.

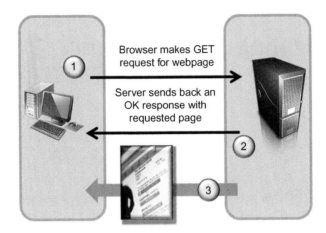

Server sends back an
OK response with
requested page

FIGURE 13.1

Simplified browser request for webpage.

Website structure

There are several basic structures that can be used to design a website. The first page is called the home page and other pages are organized in one of three possible structure types: tree, linear, and random. The tree structure is laid out in a hierarchical manner with the information presented on each page going from general to more defined or specific information. A linear structure is one where each page follows the home page one after the other. The random structure is one without any structure where the pages are connected to each other in a random fashion (Figures 13.2 and 13.3).

These structures help the website designer lay out the website and organize the design. From an investigative point of view, it can give the investigator an understanding of how the data is laid out on the website. The investigator has to remember that the data stored on the hosting website server is located in folders and files that link to the data laid out in the webpage.

How markup languages work

We have previously discussed how browsers connect to a webpage and the communication protocol is sent between the two when the connection is made. What we have not discussed is the data that the browser interprets as the page. HTML is the common language used to build a webpage and is the data interpreted by the browser which is ultimately displayed on the investigator's monitor. The markup languages contain two things, content and instructions on how to format the content, which are called tags. Markup languages are NOT programming languages themselves and they do not execute a program on the investigator's

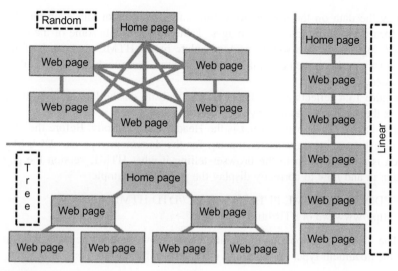

FIGURE 13.2

Basic website structures.

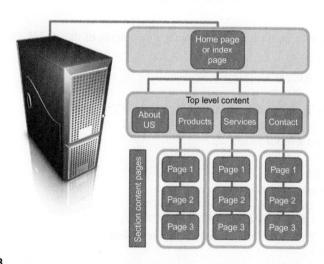

FIGURE 13.3

Generic website structure.

computer. There are programming and scripting languages that execute on the investigator's computer if allowed, but the HTML itself does not execute any code. The common types of markup languages include HTML, XHTML, DHTML, and XML. The tags provide the browser with instructions on how to display the data on the screen, from font and size to color and even the display and location within the page of images. Table 13.1 presents some of the common HTML tags found in a webpage. A complete list of HTML tags can be found at http://www.web-source.net/html_codes_chart.htm from which this table was compiled.

Figure 13.4 reflects a very basic HTML website on the left side. On the right side is the same code as displayed by a browser.

The basic HTML page format is the Header and the Body. Before the Header, the investigator may encounter the tag for the document type as <DOCTYPE> which is an instruction to the browser telling it what HTML version the page is written in and how to correctly display the page. For example:

```
<!DOCTYPE HTML PUBLIC "-//W3C//DTD HTML 4.01//EN"
"http://www.w3.org/TR/html4/strict.dtd">
```

The <head> tag contains information about how the document describes itself like the document type, the title, and other meta information. For example:

```
<head>
    <meta content = "text/html;
    charset-UTF-8" http-equv = "Content-Type"/>
    <title>This is My Targets Website</title>
</head>
```

The <body> tag in the page contains the contents of the HTML document.

```
<body>
    <h1>This is My Targets Website</h1>
    <p>
        It has content here regarding the case.</p>
        <p>It contains <em>emphasized text</em>
        and a blockquote:</p>
    </p>
    <blockquote>
        <p> Find evidence here!!!</p>
    </blockquote>
    <h2> Here is a subheading </h2>
    <p>This is the end of the text in the website</p>
    <hr/>
</body>
```

Website reconnaissance

Before you actually visit a website, there is a significant amount of information that can be obtained about the site prior to actually connecting a browser to a

Table 13.1 Basic HTML Tags

Type	HTML Language	Description of Tag
Tags	\<html>\</html>	Creates an HTML document
	\<head>\</head>	Sets off the title and other information that isn't displayed on the web page itself
	\<body>\</body>	Sets off the visible portion of the document
Attributes	\<body bgcolor = "yellow">	Sets the background color, using name or hex value
	\<body text = "black">	Sets the text color, using name or hex value
	\<body link = "blue">	Sets the color of links, using name or hex value
	\<body vlink = "#ff0000">	Sets the color of followed links, using name or hex value
	\<body alink = "#00ff00">	Sets the color of links on click
	\<body ondragstart = "return false" onselectstart = "return false">	Disallows text selection with the mouse and keyboard
Text tags	\<hl>\</hl>	Creates the largest headline
	\<h6>\</h6>	Creates the smallest headline
	\<b>\</b>	Creates bold text
	\<i>\</i>	Creates italic text
	\<strong>\</strong>	Emphasizes a word (with italic or bold)
	\<font size = "3">\</font>	Sets size of font, from 1 to 7
	\<font color = "green">\</font>	Sets font color, using name or hex value
Links	\<a href = "URL">\</a>	Creates a hyperlink
	\<a href = "mailto:EMAIL">\</a>	Creates a mailto link
	\<a href = "URL">\<img src = "URL"> \</a>	Creates an image/link
	\<a name = "NAME">\</a>	Creates a target location within a document
	\<a href = "#NAME">\</a>	Links to that target location from elsewhere in the document
Formatting	\<p>\</p>	Creates a new paragraph
	\<p align = "left">	Aligns a paragraph to the left (default), right, or center
	\ 	Inserts a line break
	\<ol>\</ol>	Creates a numbered list
	\<div align = "left">	A generic tag used to format large blocks of HTML, also used for stylesheets

(Continued)

Table 13.1 (Continued)

Type	HTML Language	Description of Tag
	<img src = "name">	Adds an image
	<img src = "name" align = "left">	Aligns an image: left, right, center; bottom, top, middle
	<img src = "name" border = "1">	Sets size of border around an image
Tables	<table></table>	Creates a table
	<tr></tr>	Sets off each row in a table

FIGURE 13.4

HTML source code compared with browser display.

web address. Investigators can scout and collect valuable information on the site's ownership, other sites associated with the target site, and possibly other victims of similar crimes. The section will introduce a process that can reveal more data about the website before it is actually accessed online by the investigator.

URL traits

We have already looked at what makes up a domain in Chapter 8. We know that the web address gives us the domain's name and the Top Level Domain (TLD) suffix, such as .com, .gov, or .xxx, provide information about the entity behind the site. Even a site ending with a country code, such as ".dk" (Denmark) or ".se" (Sweden), can provide clues about the site's location. The question the investigator needs to ask "Is the domain extension appropriate for the content of the material you are looking for?" If you are looking at a government site, the extension should be .gov or .mil, educational sites should be .edu, and a nonprofit organization should be .org. Check the area of the URL between "http://www." and first "/". This is the domain. Have you heard of the domain name before? If not, open your favorite search engine and do a search of the domain name. Besides the domain returns itself, what sites reference the targeted domain? Do these links reflect anything additional about the target's website? The investigator needs to be aware though that a TLD such as .tv or .co can be registered by anyone anywhere in the world. So location of the domain may not originate with the TLD's registered country.

SEARCH ENGINE RESEARCH

- Use a search engine (Google (www.google.com), Bing (www.bing.com), or Yahoo (www.yahoo.com)) to search the domain name or company name being investigated.
- Other references and information regarding the company or person(s) under investigation can normally be found through a simple web search.

Another technique the investigator can use to discover information prior to accessing the site is to use the "link:" operator in a search engine like Google. This can provide you with what other sites consider your target site relevant enough to link to it. Go to Google.com type in "link:", type or cut and paste the URL of the site immediately following "link:", click on "Google Search" or press the Enter Key. This will provide a list of sites linked to the targeted site. What do the results tell the investigator? How many links are there? Many links can mean that this site is of value to others. Only a few can mean it is either new, unknown or not relevant to other sites. The investigator should then check the domain extensions of the linking sites. What types of sites link to the target page? Review the information about the sites that link to the page. Is the linked site pertinent to the target site or to the target website's topic? Maybe the linked site complains about the target site and identifies negative information that can lead to additional victims.

Domain registration

Previously, we discussed tools to determine basic information and ownership of a website or an IP address by accessing its domain registration. Prior to going to a page, the investigator should do a lookup of the domain and identify site ownership information. Any of the previously mentioned references such DNS Stuff (http://www.dnsstuff.com/) or Network Tools (http://network-tools.com/) are good resources to conduct the lookup. The domain registration provides the investigator with useful information which can include the company the domain was registered through, the registrant, their address, and email and telephone contacts for the owner. As previously stated, this information is an input by the user during domain registration and can be falsified. However, this step can provide the investigator with information to further the webpage investigation. The investigator should begin by doing a search on the registration information details. If the company name is listed, search the name for an additional information on the company. Do the same with the registrant's name, the telephone numbers listed, and the email address. Record and document this information using the tools we have previously described.

Website ranking and search engine optimization (SEO) sites

Another way to find information about a website is based on the site's Internet traffic. A website with the most traffic is ranked 1. Determining website rank is dependent upon the service used. Ranking sites collect a variety of information about individual sites, which can also be a good investigative source. Data collected frequently has a marketing focus, such as demographic information. However, these sites also collect linked sites as well as mentions by other websites and blogs. Notable website ranking sites include Alexa Traffic Ranking (http://www.alexa.com); Quantcast (http://www.quantcast.com/); and Website Outlook (http://www.websiteoutlook.com).

Search engine spiders also parse data similarly when they crawl a website and identify certain information from the site including the title, metadata, and keywords. A spider is a program that visits websites and reads their pages and other information in order to create entries for a search engine index. This is the general process that Google and other search engines use to build their databases of websites crawled. Search Engine Spider Simulator (http://www.webconfs.com/search-engine-spider-simulator.php) and Spider Simulator Tool SEO Chat (http://www.seochat.com/seo-tools/spider-simulator/) are two free search engine spider simulators for investigators to remotely view a website. Simply input the target URL and the spider simulator displays such items as content, meta descriptions, keywords, and internal and external links. Ranking and SEO sites can provide the investigator with webpage information prior to actually connecting to the site.

Website history research

In Chapter 12, we discussed using the Google and Bing's cache feature. This provides a snapshot of a website created the last time a search engine crawled the website. Again, it can provide clues to the investigator about any changes that might have been made to the website since the last search engine crawl. As the created cache is subject to replacement, it must be documented and preserved at the time it is collected. These website caches are only a short-term snapshot, which is replaced as soon as the search engine crawls the site again.

However, there exists a more long-term website archival system on the Internet. Since 1996, the Internet Achieve (http://archive.org) has been collecting and cataloging websites, which to date exceeds 240 billion webpages or almost 2 petabytes of data. It is currently growing at a rate of 20 terabytes per month (archive.org). It is a US 501(c)(3) nonprofit organization, which is supported by donations but collaborates with institutions such as the Library of Congress and the Smithsonian. The Internet Archive's website, the "Wayback Machine",[1] has an easy-to-use interface to search for website information. The site provides the date and times of when the site has been crawled, as well as a capture of the site, so the investigator can see how the site has changed over time. These achieved webpages may provide the investigator with additional useful information. This could include ownership information in the archived "About Us" section that may have been deleted or later changed to prevent the current webpage from disclosing website ownership.

Just like any other webpage, the investigator can also look through the HTML source code of the achieved page to look for possible usable information. Investigators should be aware that the site does not crawl and record everything found on a website or webpage. It does not record every page if the Robot.txt file is set to tell search engines not to crawl the page. Additionally, certain Java code and other newer active content scripting are not collected. The Internet Actives FAQ page lists circumstances when the site does not collect information on a particular website or page. Regardless of some limitations, this is still a hugely valuable tool for the investigator to identify past website information (Figure 13.5).

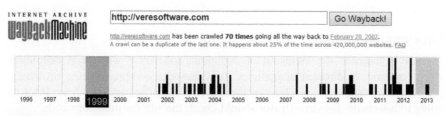

FIGURE 13.5

Wayback machine example search.

---

[1]The Wayback Machine is named in reference to the famous Mr. Peabody's WABAC (pronounced way-back) machine from the Rocky and Bullwinkle Cartoon Show (archive.org).

BACKUP OF THE INTERNET ARCHIVE

The data stored through the Wayback Machine project also has a mirrored site in Alexandria, Egypt. Bibliotheca Alexandrina maintains the only copy and external backup of the Internet Archive. The Internet Archive at the Bibliotheca Alexandrina includes the web collections from 1996 through 2007. It represents about 1.5 petabytes of data stored on 880 computers. The entire collection is available for free access to researchers, historians, scholars, and the general public.

The Bibliotheca Alexandrina Internet Archive is the first center of its kind established outside US borders. It is designed not only as a backup for the mother archive in San Francisco, but also as a hub for Africa and the Middle East.

AUTHENTICATION AND THE INTERNET ARCHIVE

The Internet Archive is a nonprofit organization and as such is not in the business of responding to requests for affidavits, or authenticating pages or other information from their Wayback Machine. Accordingly, they ask, prior to requesting authentication and an affidavit on the results, investigators to consider the following:

1. Seek judicial notice or simply ask your opposing party to stipulate to the document's authenticity.
2. Get the person who posted the information on the URLs to confirm it is authenticate.
3. Or get the person who actually accessed the historical URL versions to confirm that they collected and it is an accurate copy of what was accessed. (This is what this text has been stressing: proper collection, preservation, and documentation of the process, is a must in authenticating online evidence.)

However, if investigators are determined to obtain an affidavit and authenticating printouts, they provide procedures for doing so on their website (http://archive.org/legal/). Fees are $250 per request plus $20 for each extended URLS, except those which contain downloadable/printable files. Such URLs (e.g., .pdf, .doc, or .txt) cost instead $30 per extended URL. Copies are not automatically notarized. If the investigator wants the affidavit notarized, there is an additional $100 fee.

Checking for malicious code on a site

In today's Internet, the inclusion of malicious code on a website is becoming more common. Redirected or malicious websites can compromise the investigation or the investigator's machine, if they are not identified as hazardous. Prior to going to a website, the investigator should check the site for malicious code.

One sign that a web address might be problematic is if it is shorted. Websites like bitly (https://bitly.com/), Google URL Shortener (http://goo.gl/), and TinyURL!™ (http://tinyurl.com/) allow users to input a long URL and shorten it. These redirect services are designed to condense long URLs because of the limits imposed on some social media services such as Twitter. However, online criminals use this technique to obfuscate the address and hide the actual intent and location of the website. A typical shortened website URL using tinyulr.com can look like:

URL to Shorten:
http://veresoftware.com/index.php?page=eLearning
Shortened URL:
http://tinyurl.com/kc7sj5l

The original URL has a length of 48 characters, and using TinyURL!™ to shorten the URL resulted in a URL of 26 characters. The investigator can use several different websites to decipher shortened websites. Sites like Unshorten.com (http://www.unshorten.com/) and Unshorten.It! (http://unshorten.it/) expand an address to identify its real location. Once the URL is expanded, the investigator can use other Internet tools to identify if the site has malicious code or other possible threats, such as web bugs, which will be discussed shortly.

Sites like Zulu URL Risk Analyzer (http://zulu.zscaler.com/) (Figure 13.6), Web Inspector (http://www.webinspector.com/), and VirusTotal (https://www.virustotal.com/) provide a look into the URL. These sites check the URL for malicious activity by connecting to the URL with a virtual machine and downloading the page. The downloaded data is scanned for malicious activity. The sites also pass the URL through various "Black Lists" that record known and potentially malicious sites. These sites can provide other information about the site's activity, potential malicious content, and past known history of malicious activity. The investigator should be aware that scanning sites are not always a complete review of a website's code. Scanning sites review the page input only and also may not be able to review all types of active content or other code found at the URL.

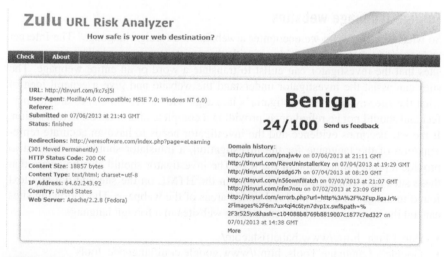

FIGURE 13.6

Example response of URL inspection by Zulu URL risk analyzer.

Webpage examination

So we finally point our browser at the website, what exactly can we find on a website? After collecting the website, we can review the website's various pages for useful investigative information. We can also review the HTML itself and the underlying code for comments by the web tool used to make the page and any comments or references in the page to other sites (redirects) or images linked or other pages. We can then review the pages themselves as how the browser produces the pages. The investigator can look for who wrote the page, look for links that reflect "About Us," "Philosophy," or "Background." Look for names of people, organizations, or groups that claim responsibility of the website or its design. If you have a long page with forward slashes separating the pages, truncate back the URL trying to find the main page and additional information on the site (e.g., http://www.weather.com/newscenter/stormwatch/index.html). Is there an email address for the person, company, or organization for further contact? The investigator can research this address through a search engine to see if it is used elsewhere on the Internet. Is the text grammatically correct and free of typos? From an investigative point of view, this might indicate the level of understanding of the language used. The website might be built by someone that does not speak that language natively. This could be a possible indication of a fraudulent site. The investigator should look for words like "Links," "Additional Sites," "Related Links.". These could be references to unknown investigative details such as additional victims and/or suspects. The investigator should check the links to determine if the links work and/or are relevant to the investigation.

Foreign language websites

So what happens when we encounter a website in a foreign language? The Internet and its many resources provide us with the assistance we need. There are many sites that the investigator can enlist to translate a word or an entire webpage. The sites can assist the investigator understand the website and give a general idea of what the site says in the investigator's language. However, these sites are not perfect and should not be relied on as providing a complete and/or accurate translation. If the site becomes evidence and the investigator needs to have an accurate representation of the language for the investigation, a translator should be enlisted to provide a proper translation of the text. The investigator should also be aware that these sites only translate the text found in the HTML on the site and not any text found in images or other nonhtml-coded areas of the webpage. The following sites can aid the investigator who is examining websites in a foreign language:

- Babel Fish, http://www.babelfish.com/
- Google's Language Tools, http://www.google.com/language_tools
- Online Translation Tools, http://www.emailaddresses.com/online_translation.htm
- Yahoo's Transliteration, http://transliteration.yahoo.com/

Reviewing source code

The code written by a programmer in HTML to form a webpage is readable by people. The investigator can take advantage of this as there can sometimes be information in the source code of the page that could be of use to the investigation. We have mentioned before that the browser interprets this language as the webpage we see. In Microsoft's Internet Explorer, you can view the source code by going to "View" and select "Source" or holding the "Control" button down and selecting the "U" key. Opened in notepad will be the HTML source code for that individual page. Web-Source (http://www.web-source.net/html_codes_chart. htm) provides a good guide for translating a webpage's source code. Figure 13.7 provides an example of a webpage's source code.

Webpage tracking bugs

Buried in webpages can be code that identifies the browser and information about the computer connecting to the webpage. From a marketing point of view, this is a popular way of identifying information about people and their surfing habits. A page's code can vary from legitimate marketing tools like Google Analytics to web bugs that track IP address of people going to a page. Looking through the

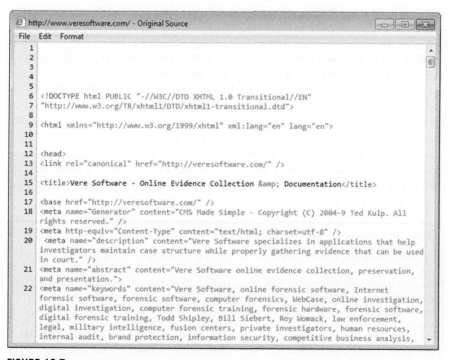

FIGURE 13.7

Example source code.

source code can identify the presence of such tracking devices. MySpace trackers still exist to allow the page owner to identify the IP addresses of persons looking at their page. Most other social media sites don't allow this because you don't have access directly to the HTML of the user page. Facebook and other social media sites lock this access down and prevent users from making changes to their pages. General websites though can add whatever data they want to the page and tracking software can easily be implemented that identified through the browser or other software such as Flash or Java the IP address and other information about the user connecting with a webpage.

Documenting a website's multimedia and images

Often overlooked places for evidence are images and videos on a website. Obviously, pictures or videos may show images that are important for what they show or reflect. Images or videos may identify suspects or evidence of illegal activity. They may provide clues to a suspect's location, a missing victim, or where some questionable activity took place. However, many times pictures and videos can provide additional information that is not shown in their images. This unseen information is called metadata. Digital forensic investigators understand that within the image and video files exists metadata that further describes the file. Internet investigators need to understand that there is the potential for valuable information within the image file. Image files and video files can have embedded information contained in the file that can give you potentially valuable leads in the case. Exif Data or Exchangeable image file format (Exif) is a specification for the image file format used by digital cameras. This Exif Data holds camera settings used to take the picture. Most digital cameras support Exif and save the data in the file's header information. Examples of metadata that can be found include a camera's model and serial number, creation time/date, and even global positioning coordinates. However, when an image is edited, the Exif data may be automatically removed by the software. This requires investigators to obtain images and videos and preserve them without making any changes that may obliterate Exif data.

WEB SEARCHING USING A PICTURE

Another investigative tactic to employ is the search of an image for similar pictures on other websites. This is easily done now through image search engines like Tineye.com or using Google's image search functions. Both tools allow the investigator to upload an image and then the search engine looks for matching and similar images to the upload. This can be a significant resource in identifying if the image has been posted on other sites. If it is an image of a person, the investigator might find other sites or social media locations that have the image. This can help to determine if the image belongs to the target's identity or is just an image that the target grabbed off of the Internet for use in their identity. Note: This concept and use of image search engines is not intended for the investigation of child pornography. Consult you local ICAC unit for assistance.

To examine an image from a website, right click on the image on the page and save the file to a folder on the investigator's local machine. Examining the Exif Data can easily be done in Microsoft operating systems. A subset of the Exif information may be viewed by right clicking on the image file and clicking "Properties." In the Properties dialog, click the "Summary" or "Details" tab. The investigator needs to be aware that damage can occur to Exif headers if changes are applied and that this method does not reveal all the potentially available Exif data. There are many tools available to review the entire Exif data such as Stuffware's Photostudio (http://www.stuffware.co.uk/photostudio/). This small, free program can review images and their Exif data. Also there are online resources that include Jeffrey's Exif Viewer (http://regex.info/exif.cgi) or online photo Exif metadata reader (http://www.findexif.com/) that can assist in identifying Exif data. The investigator should remember when using these services that they are uploading the images from their investigation to an unknown server.

Capturing website videos

Videos are now often not embedded on the page that you view the video from. Youtube.com presents many videos that it streams from another location to the viewer's browser. To download certain streaming web videos, you need to track the video to its source. Several tools exist to assist the investigator with grabbing video files from the web. Tools like YouRipper grabs videos from YouTube (http://www.remlapsoftware.com/youripper.htm) and URLSnopper grabs Streaming Video (http://www.donationcoder.com/Software/Mouser/urlsnooper/index.html) which can assist the investigator collect videos from their websites. Another good tool for this purpose is Replay Media Catcher located at http://www.applian.com. These tools are intended to aid the investigator in downloading files in their native format. There are sites on the web that will allow for downloading a copy of a video, but they may convert the file into a different format and delete any possible metadata.

If metadata is important in other investigations, can video metadata be a similar potential treasure trove? Todd in his classes has extolled the examination of metadata during Internet investigations because finding metadata in online documents or images can be incredibly damaging evidence. For example, Todd recently was asked to examine a website setup on a "free" domain to find out who the owner might be. Examination of the website failed to ascertain anything until Todd downloaded the files embedded in the site. A quick look at the files' metadata ascertained their author—who was well known to the plaintiff.

Two video metadata types

Video metadata does exist and it is clearly important. To deal with video metadata, we have to understand where it comes from. Good (2008) notes that there are two metadata sources, operational information and human-authored metadata. He describes them as:

(a) *"Operational, automatically gathered video metadata*, which is typically a set of information about the content you produce, such as the equipment you used, the software you employed, the date you created your video, and GPS coordinates of shooting location.

(b) *Human-authored video metadata,* which can be created to provide more search engine visibility, audience engagement, and better advertising opportunities for online video publishers."

Most of what we are currently dealing with in metadata examination is the "operational" metadata. However, human-authored metadata may become more important. Interestingly enough, video metadata is getting some heavy discussion from a marketing point of view. Online video providers are looking at the use of video metadata to describe the video better for two reasons: first, better coverage in the search engines, and second, end users have more descriptive information about the video. Additionally, video-sharing sites seek to make videos more "social" by enabling users to add metadata to the videos they host. For instance, Metacafe's Wikicafe section allows all its users to add "human-authored" comments to video metadata.

Although few standards currently exist for video metadata, this is changing as video delivery becomes more important. Acceptance of standards such as the Dublin Core Metadata Element Set is becoming common. With standards in the metadata, investigators will have an ability to look for common items of information in the file. Standard metadata also makes it easier to build tools to extract this data. The continuing conversation, and the acceptance of "human-authored" metadata, will undoubtedly provide investigators with additional information regarding videos they find on the Internet during investigations.

File formats and what they contain

Search Google for "video metadata forensics," and you won't find much of anything useful. It is mentioned in some places that video has metadata, but little describes the metadata in depth. However, search for Resource Interchange File Format (RIFF) and you will find a lot more. RIFF, the term similar in usage to Exif data, is the format that describes the usage of metadata in many video and audio files.

The amount of RIFF data available depends on the file format. RIFF data is a proprietary format originally developed by Microsoft and IBM for Windows 3.1. The format was released in the 1991 in the Windows Multimedia Programmer's Reference. RIFF was never adopted as a standard and few new video formats have adopted the file format since 1990s. Common file formats still in use that use RIFF include .wav and .avi. Microsoft has been using the Advanced Systems Format (ASF) since 2004 in its .wma files. From the Microsoft ASF specifications, we can find that the ASF file can contain potentially valuable information. However, as images have the Exif standard, there is no real standard for maintaining metadata in video files. There are other standards in the field including the newer MPEG-7 standard and the XMP Dynamic Media Schema developed by Adobe. What this all means is there is an underlying structure for the metadata present in video files. The question now becomes, how do we look at that data if it is there? There are a few free tools out there to assist you. Let's talk about three.

Gspot

Gspot has been the heavy lifter for most investigators looking at metadata in video files. It provides a single screen view of the available data in a video file (of the files it can translate). Most of the data is "operational" data found in the file, but it does provide you with the "human-authored" data if it is present. Gspot has an export function to allow the user to save the metadata information for inclusion in a report or to add to WebCase. Another good part of GSpot is that the investigator can export a report of its findings that can be included in the investigator's report. Gspot's failing is that it has had no recent updates since 2007 (Figure 13.8).

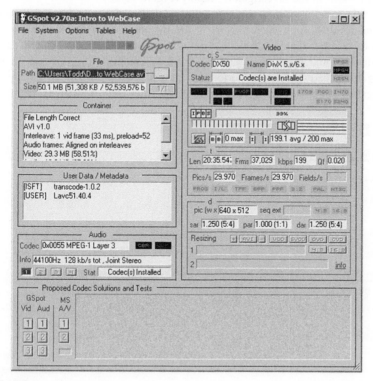

FIGURE 13.8

Gspot showing video metadata.

Mediainfo

MediaInfo is a newer tool. Its basic presentation is much simpler than Gspot's, but it offers several different views of the data that allow you to determine what metadata is present. The "tree" view lays out all of the metadata present in an easy-to-view screen. The export options for reporting also allow the user to quickly make reports in a text or html format for inclusion in their reports or to add to a tool like WebCase. MediaInfo also adds during installation a right click function to Windows Explorer to easily access the tool. Finally, the program can also export a report of its findings in a txt, html, or CSV format that can be included in the investigator's report (Figure 13.9).

Video inspector

This program is a very basic tool and provides the user with the basic metadata present in the video file. The export function allows for exporting a text document with the metadata it finds, but it is limited. The tool was designed to assist the user in identifying missing codecs required to play the video, so reading all the available metadata is not its main function. Video Inspector also has a report that can be included in the investigator's report (Figure 13.10).

There is some usefulness in reviewing video files for metadata. Something to remember is that some sites may strip the metadata when posted online. Also, other tools used to download videos from the Internet, like savevid.com, save the video in flash and not the original file format containing the original metadata. Investigators need to find the original video uploaded to get to the metadata. Investigators may encounter challenges when they review images from social

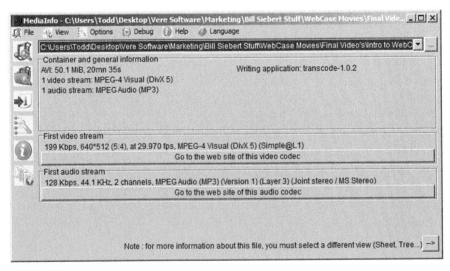

FIGURE 13.9

MediaInfo showing video metadata.

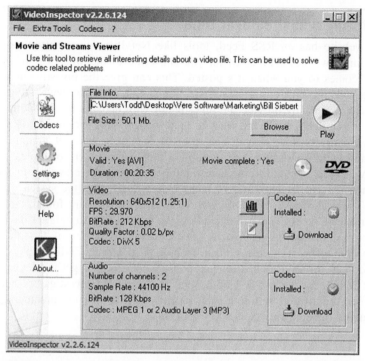

FIGURE 13.10

Video Inspector showing metadata.

media sites. One example is Metacafe's attempt to add metadata to videos it hosts. Its Wikicafe section allows all its users to add "human-authored" comments to video metadata. Other sites simply strip the Exif metadata from the image or video prior to posting on the site.

The legal process of identifying a website

Internet Service providers (ISPs) hosting webpages have no requirements to store data about its users or their action when online. However, they most often store a significant amount of usable data for the investigator. This data can include the site's owner, address and credit card information, dates and times logged on to the ISP. The proper legal service required for obtaining information from an ISP varies by jurisdiction. Contact your legal counsel for advice on serving an ISP. A great resource for information on the legal contacts for ISPs is maintained by SEARCH, a federally funded nonprofit organization, we have previously mentioned. You can find most ISP legal contacts at: www.search.org/programs/hightech/isp/.

Monitoring websites over time

If the website has an RSS Feed, tools like Netvibes (www.netvibes.com) or NewsBlur (www.newsblur.com) let you subscribe to the websites so that new content comes to you when it's posted. This can give the investigator an alert on up-to-date changes on the target site. Google Alerts (http://www.google.com/alerts) can also easily provide the investigator with updated information without having to regularly check the website or webpage. This service, available only with a Gmail account, provides updates of the latest relevant Google results (web, news, etc.) based on the investigator's choice of query or topics. Google Alerts will send an email to the investigator while they are crawling the Internet and when the investigator's query name or topic is found, the system sends an email. These alerts can be configured to be sent as they are found, on a daily basis or once a week. This can also allow the investigator to monitor developing news stories on the target. Some great investigative uses of Google Alerts include monitoring a company name or individual target. Civilian investigators can keep current on a competitor or industry concept and get the latest on the queries referenced on a site Google crawls. Corporate investigators may also find it helpful to detect individuals posting questionable or threatening comments about the company and/or key officers.

CONCLUSION

This chapter has provided the reader with the understanding of how a website is built and the programming languages used to design websites. The reader was provided an outline of how to look at a website and the information that can be provided by examining a website. There is a significant amount of data that can be found on a website and should not be overlooked by the investigator. With a little understanding the investigator can identify who owns the site, information about the contents, and potentially useful metadata from the source code as well as images and other items embedded on the site.

Further reading

Alexa—The Web Information Company. (n.d.). *Alexa—The Web Information Company*. Retrieved from <http://www.alexa.com>.

Applian Technologies: Video Downloaders, Media Converters, Audio Recorders and more. (n.d.). *Applian Technologies*. Retrieved from <http://www.applian.com>.

ASF (Advanced Systems Format). (n.d.). *Digital preservation (Library of Congress)*. Retrieved from <http://www.digitalpreservation.gov/formats/fdd/fdd000067.shtml>.

BabelFish—Free Online Translator. (n.d.). *BabelFish*. Retrieved from <www.babelfish.com/>.

Bing. (n.d.). *Bing*. Retrieved from <http://www.bing.com>.

Bitly. (n.d.). *Bitly*. Retrieved from <https://bitly.com/>.

DNS Tools: Manage Monitor Analyze, DNSstuff. (n.d.). *DNS Tools*. Retrieved from <http://www.dnsstuff.com/>.

Download Online Videos Save Direct Easily—Savevid.com. (n.d.). *Savevid.com*. Retrieved from <http://www.savevid.com/>.

Dublin Core Metadata Element Set, Version 1.1. (n.d.). *DCMI Home: Dublin Core®Metadata Initiative (DCMI)*. Retrieved from <http://dublincore.org/documents/dces/>.

English to Hindi. (n.d.). *English to Hindi*. Retrieved from <http://transliteration.yahoo.com/>.

Extracting and preparing *metadata to make video files searchable meeting the unique file format and delivery requirements of content aggregators and distributors*. (2008). Nevada City, CA: Telestream, Inc.

Find Exif Data—Online exif/metadata photo viewer. (n.d.). *Find Exif Data—Online Exif/metadata photo viewer*. Retrieved from <http://www.findexif.com/>.

Free Online Translation Tools. (n.d.). *Free email address directory: Guide to free email and other services*. Retrieved from <http://www.emailaddresses.com/online_translation.htm>.

Google. (n.d.). *Google*. Retrieved from <http://www.google.com>.

Google Alerts—Monitor the Web for Interesting New Content. (n.d.). *Google*. Retrieved from <http://www.google.com/alerts>.

Google Translate. (n.d.). *Google*. Retrieved from <http://www.google.com/language_tools>.

Google URL Shortener. (n.d.). *Google URL Shortener*. Retrieved from <goo.gl/>.

GSpot Codec Information Appliance. (n.d.). *GSpot Codec Information Appliance*. Retrieved from <http://gspot.headbands.com/>.

HTML Cheatsheet: Webmonkey, Wired.com. (n.d.). *Webmonkey—The web developer's resource, Wired.com*. Retrieved from <http://www.webmonkey.com/2010/02/html_cheatsheet/>.

HTML Codes Chart. (n.d.). *Web page design and development*. Retrieved from <http://www.web-source.net/html_codes_chart.htm>.

International School of Information Science (ISIS). (n.d.). *Home—Bibliotheca Alexandrina*. Retrieved from <http://www.bibalex.org/isis/frontend/archive/archive_web.aspx>.

Internet Archive: Digital Library of Free Books, Movies, Music & Wayback Machine. (n.d.). *Internet Archive: Digital Library of Free Books, Movies, Music & Wayback Machine*. Retrieved from <http://archive.org>.

Internet Archive: Legal: Requests. (n.d.). *Internet Archive: Digital Library of Free Books, Movies, Music & Wayback Machine*. Retrieved from <http://archive.org/legal/>.

Jeffrey's Exif Viewer. (n.d.). *Jeffrey's Exif Viewer*. Retrieved from <regex.info/exif.cgi>.

KC Softwares. (n.d.). *KC Softwares*. Retrieved from <http://www.kcsoftwares.com/?vtb>.

Kevin Mitnick Quotes—BrainyQuote. (n.d.). *Famous quotes at Brainyquote*. Retrieved from <http://www.brainyquote.com/quotes/authors/k/kevin_mitnick.html>.

MediaInfo. (n.d.). *MediaInfo*. Retrieved from <http://mediainfo.sourceforge.net/en>.

Metacafe—Wikicafe. (n.d.). *Metacafe—Online video entertainment—Free video clips for your enjoyment*. Retrieved from <http://www.metacafe.com/wikicafe/>.

Netvibes: Social Media Monitoring, Analytics and Alerts Dashboard. (n.d.). *Netvibes Social Media Monitoring, Analytics and Alerts Dashboard*. Retrieved from <http://www.netvibes.com>.

NewsBlur. (n.d.). *NewsBlur*. Retrieved from <www.newsblur.com>.

Photo Studio. (n.d.). *StuffWare*. Retrieved from <http://www.stuffware.co.uk/photostudio>.

Quantcast Measure. (n.d.). *Quantcast*. Retrieved from <https://www.quantcast.com/>.

Search Engine Spider Simulator. (n.d.). *SEO tools—Search engine optimization tools.* Retrieved from <http://www.webconfs.com/search-engine-spider-simulator.php>.

Spider Simulator—SEO Chat. (n.d.). *Spider Simulator—SEO Chat.* Retrieved from <www.seochat.com/seo-tools/spider-simulator/>.

The Official Blitz Website. (n.d.). *The Official Blitz Website.* Retrieved from <http://www.blitzbasic.com/codearcs/codearcs.php?code=2582>.

TinEye Reverse Image Search. (n.d.). *TinEye Reverse Image Search.* Retrieved from <http://tineye.com/>.

TinyURL.com—Shorten that Long URL into a Tiny URL. (n.d.). *TinyURL.com.* Retrieved from <http://tinyurl.com/>.

Traceroute, Ping, Domain Name Server (DNS) Lookup, WHOIS. (n.d.). *Traceroute.* Retrieved from <http://network-tools.com/>.

Unshorten—Get the Real Location of a Short URL. (n.d.). *Unshorten—Get the real location of a short URL.* Retrieved from <http://www.unshorten.com>.

Unshorten that URL!—Unshorten.It!. (n.d.). *Unshorten.It!.* Retrieved from <http://unshorten.it/>.

URL Snooper—Mouser—Software—DonationCoder.com. (n.d.). *URL Snooper—Mouser—Software—DonationCoder.com.* Retrieved from <www.donationcoder.com/Software/Mouser/urlsnooper/index.html>.

Video Metadata Key Strategic Importance For Online Video Publishers—Part 1. (n.d.). *Professional online publishing: New media trends, communication skills, online marketing—Robin Good's MasterNewMedia.* Retrieved from <http://www.masternewmedia.org/video-metadata-key-strategic-importance-for-online-video-publishers-part-1/>.

VirusTotal—Free Online Virus, Malware and URL Scanner. (n.d.). *VirusTotal—Free Online Virus, Malware and URL Scanner.* Retrieved from <https://www.virustotal.com/en/>.

WebP Container Specification—WebP Google Developers. (n.d.). *WebP Container Specification—Webp Google Developers.* Retrieved from <code.google.com/speed/webp/docs/riff_container.html>.

Website Security with Malware Scan and PCI Compliance: Web Inspector. (n.d.). *Web Inspector.* Retrieved from <http://www.webinspector.com/>.

Website Value Calculator and Web Information. (n.d.). Website Value Calculator and Web Information. Retrieved from <http://www.websiteoutlook.com/>.

Whitney, S. (2012, July 29). *How to understand Google safe browsing diagnostic page.* Retrieved from <25yearsofprogramming.com/blog/2009/20091124.htm>.

World Wide Web Consortium (W3C). (n.d.). *World Wide Web Consortium (W3C).* Retrieved from <http://www.w3.org/>.

Yahoo!. (n.d.). *Yahoo!.* Retrieved from <http://www.yahoo.com>.

YouRipper. (n.d.). *Remlapsoftware.com.* Retrieved from <http://www.remlapsoftware.com/youripper.htm>.

Zscaler Zulu URL Risk Analyzer—Zulu.(n.d.). *Zscaler Zulu URL Risk Analyzer—Zulu.* Retrieved from <http://zulu.zscaler.com/>.

Investigating Social Networking Sites

14

There's a danger in the Internet and social media. The notion that information is enough, that more and more information is enough, that you don't have to think, you just have to get more information - gets very dangerous.

Edward de Bono (physician, author, inventor, and consultant)

Social networking's impact on legal systems

Social network use among the public has reached the point where it can no longer be ignored as a passing fad, or considered a high-tech crimes investigation specialty. Detectives, patrol, intel, and gang officers, administrators, private and corporate investigators, prosecutors and corporate counsel need to know who's online, what kinds of crimes they're committing, what evidence they're leaving and, where it can be found. More importantly from a legal standpoint is obtaining online evidence in a manner so that it can be used to win convictions or in litigation. Why is it that we need to care about social networking sites? The answer is that is where the people are and it is where the criminals will go to victimize them. Let's look at some social networking statistics for some perspective on the issue. GlobalWebIndex reported that Facebook has 701 million active users, with Google Plus and Twitter at 359 and 297 million active users, respectively. (Watkins & Presse, 2013) Seventy-two percent of online US adults use social networking sites. (Brenner & Smith, 2013) Surely, the sheer number of users is large and obviously has an impact. But that is only part of the concern. Specifically, how much are these users on social media and how much data is being generated as result? Smith (2013) provides clues to these questions, with the following user stats for Facebook and Twitter:

- Average number of monthly posts per Facebook user page: 36
- Average number of friends per Facebook user: 141.5
- Average time spent per Facebook visit: 20 minutes
- Average time spent on Facebook per user per month: 8.3 hours
- Average followers per Twitter user: 208
- Average number of tweets per user: 307
- Average amount of time on Twitter per month: 170 minutes

These stats represent another investigative concern, specifically the number of profiles a target may have on various social networking sites. Having more than one profile on a social networking site can occur as well as having profiles on a number of different sites. A social networking investigation can involve a lot of data particularly if the target and those associated with the target (the victim, witnesses, and associated targets) have more than one social media profile.

If the target or victim is a corporation the investigator needs to be aware that most corporations will have more than one social networking site account. Owyang (2011) details a 2012 Altimeter Group survey, which received responses from 140 companies with over 1,000 employees. The survey found that the respondent companies averaged 178 official social networking accounts per company. This includes 39.2 Twitter accounts, 31.9 Blogs, 29.9 Facebook accounts, 28 LinkedIn accounts, and many others on various forums, message, image, and video sites. The point here is a social media investigation, without focus, without a plan, could easily become an Odyssey with no clear accomplishment.

Social networking investigations are not without other challenges. Many officers do not know how to navigate the myriad of social networking sites. To compound the investigative issues many government agencies have restricted access to those sites out of fear of what employees will say or do online. To address these issues, they need to understand effective investigative techniques as well as a suitable policy. Receiving detailed social network training becomes very critical in today's Internet-connected society.

A SOCIAL NETWORKING SITE DEFINITION

Boyd and Ellison (2008) defined "... social network sites as web-based services that allow individuals to (1) construct a public or semi-public profile within a bounded system, (2) articulate a list of other users with whom they share a connection, and (3) view and traverse their list of connections and those made by others within the system. The nature and nomenclature of these connections may vary from site to site."

Law enforcement, social media, and the news

In the last few years articles have claimed to expose a new offensive by the FBI to invade the privacy of people on the Internet. (McCullagh, 2010; Parrack, 2010) The Electronic Freedom Foundation (EFF) filed suit, along with the Berkeley Law School, against various Federal agencies trying to expose their investigative use of social networking. Using a Freedom of Information Act, the EFF obtained their smoking gun. They obtained a US Department of Justice PowerPoint presentation discussing the general issues surrounding social networking and how to go about using it effectively as an investigative tool. Nothing earth shattering, but apparently many in the press seemed to be surprised that the FBI was doing their job. The EFF was so impressed with the revelation that they have made their own webpage "FOIA: Social Networking Monitoring" just to track their progress at exposing law enforcements' use of social networking to the world.

Social networking has changed many things when it comes to our online lives. Immediate postings of user activities, locations, and the divulging of individual's feelings are common. Everyone realizes that all of this is posted for the world to see otherwise they would not be doing it. We are becoming a bunch of Internet exhibitionists. With that exposure comes those that would take advantage of our openness. Criminals tend to congregate where victims increasingly gather. Law enforcement is starting to recognize this and is also gathering in the social networking sphere. So with online crime comes policing of the Internet. So, the police, and the FBI, will go where the criminals go. Ergo, the FBI is working undercover on Facebook to catch criminals and terrorist. This is shocking to only those blind to how law enforcement functions.

Social networking's impact is not just as new undercover tool. On February 18, 2010, Joe Stack, flew his plane into a federal building as both a suicide and antigovernment gesture (Brick, 2010). The story quickly made national headlines. Social media made private citizens into scene reporters telling the world in real time about events as they unfolded. Traditional news media gathered this information and reportedly after confirming it, included it their own coverage of the incident (Gonzalez, 2010).

Austin Police Chief Art Acevedo, apparently unhappy that information was flowing in this matter retorted "There's a lot of speculation. I can tell you right now that those reports are inaccurate and it is irresponsible journalism to put out information that is not confirmed through law enforcement." YNN News Channel 8, agreed in their commentary but correctly observed "But law enforcement needs to keep up with the speed of citizen journalism using social media" (Gonzalez, 2010).

We don't know for sure what context the Chief's single quote was regarding, but it is a little arrogant to think that his department is the only source for correct information. Social media has changed many things and citizens are regularly using it to report news as well as track crimes. The fact that a person can live stream information from an incident like that changes how we receive our news and how journalists are viewing their position in the reporting of that news. Law enforcement is going to have to adapt to the changing speed of the information flow. Private citizen's use of social media necessitates that law enforcement respond more quickly. Law enforcement public information officers will also need to learn to track social media at the scene of an incident and respond to the information more timely. Investigators will need to start tracking this information to identify leads related to an incident. Social media has changed dramatically how law enforcement will need to respond to incidents and the news media in the future. The question is how quickly law enforcement can adapt to the changing social media landscape.

The Boston Marathon Bombing is an example of both advantages and disadvantages of law enforcement's using social media to solve crimes. The FBI posted photos of Suspect 1 and Suspect 2 from surveillance footage to social media, seeking the public's assistance in identifying the individuals in the photos. Unfortunately, the public erroneously identified one of the subjects as an innocent bystander, requiring a quick correction by law enforcement. Ultimately, law enforcement obtained a clearer picture and was able to identify the correct suspect through their YouTube page (Presutti, 2013).

Many investigators are probably thinking that these kinds of social media events only happen to big cities like Austin and Boston. This is simply not true and the below example should be a sobering warning that law enforcement does have to "keep up with the speed" of its citizen's use of social media.

Social media in small town USA
Steubenville, OH, birth place of Dean Martin and Jimmie the Greek, was founded in 1797, along the Ohio River in Jefferson County. During its peak in the 1940s−60s, it was popularly known as "Little Chicago," a nickname evoked, not only for its prolific industry and downtown bustle, but also for its reputation for crime, gambling, and corruption (Forbes, 2013).

However, in the twenty-first century, Steubenville ranked as Ohio's #101 largest city, with a population of 18,659 (USA.com, 2013). Its police force has 38 officers and 3 dispatchers (The Intelligencer and Wheeling News-Register, 2013). Jefferson County, where it is located has a population of 69,709 and covers 408 square miles. (State and County QuickFacts, 2013) Jefferson County's Sheriff's Office size is commensurate with the size of the population is serves. Forbes considers Steubenville's Metro population, encompassing nearby Wheeling, West Virginia at 123,200. By any standard Steubenville is a not large city, not even comparable to Austin or Boston. Nevertheless, this did not stop Steubenville from finding itself in the social media cross-hairs, the result of a brutal crime committed by some of Jefferson County's youngest citizens.

On August 11, 2012, teenagers from several nearby high schools meet for an end-of-summer party, which also kicked off the coming football season. High school football is a big event in this area. As too frequently occurs the party also involved alcohol. Teenage party goers used social media to announce the party. However, it did not end there. During the evening a teenage girl, unconscious from drinking was sexually assaulted by several members of Steubenville's Big Reds football team. Social media posts, videos and photographs started circulating, documenting that the unconscious girl had been sexually assaulted over several hours, while some watched the crime occur without intervening (Dissell, 2012).

The victim, because of her state, did not initially recall what happened to her that night. However, as the information supported by the social media posts came to light, she and her parents realized what had occurred. They took a flash drive full of social media postings indicating that the victim had been assaulted to the police. Police seized cell phones of the teenage suspects and found more digital traces that corroborated the victim's story. Two teenager offenders were arrested (Macur and Schweber, 2012).

However, it did not end there. The citizens began taking sides and expressing their views via social media. The story got the attention of Alexandria Goddard, a local web analyst with a national crime blog, who started writing about the case in her blog. This further fueled the discussion, particularly how could only two individuals be arrested for this crime (Macur and Schweber, 2012). From there it took on a life of its own, gaining worldwide attention, including a cell of the hacktivist collective Anonymous, who promptly inserted itself into the social media circus by posting its own information (Abrad-Santos, 2013).

The two juveniles were convicted of the sexual assault and sentenced. However, it did not end there. Two additional teenagers, ages 15 and 16, were charged with intimidation over social media posts they allegedly made concerning the victim. The local sheriff noted after those arrests "And I can assure you we've been monitoring Twitter for 24 hours and continue to. If there's anybody else there crosses a line and makes a death threat, they're going to have to face the consequences." Ohio Attorney General Mike Devine, whose office handled the locally sensitive case noted: "People who want to continue to victimize this victim, to threaten her, we're going to deal with them and we're going after them. We don't care if they're juveniles or whether they're adults. Enough is enough" (Pearson, Carter, & Brady, 2013).

One can only imagine the investigative resources that this case required. Would your department be prepared to handle this kind of case, where social media not only provides evidence but fuels intense feelings in not only your community but the world?

Social media around the world

Social media is not a United States-centric problem. Law enforcement investigators around the world are grappling with the social media associated issues. Recent studies in Europe have identified similar issues regarding the complexity of social media.

Denef, Bayerl, and Kaptein (2012) examined law enforcement's use of social media based on interviews and focus groups of European law enforcement experts in 10 countries. Their report found three cross-European variations: (1) implementation strategies, (2) media selection/integration, and (3) communication with the public. They found that police agencies adopt social media as needed, some from the bottom-up, officers utilizing social media without restrictions and others from the top-down.

Top-down agencies create general guidelines before deploying the social media resources. They also identified three common social media deployment methods, selective, centralized, and modular. The selective approach meant the agency picked the most popular services to follow and use. The centralized approach utilized their agency website as the primary central location for social media. The modular approach identified each social media tool with an individual strategy.

Additional recent European studies have identified that acceptable use of social media in law enforcement differed by country and the type of job an officer was assigned (Bayerl, 2012). To aid in the understanding and deployment of social media in use by policing agencies in Europe the European Commission has published the "Best Practice in Police Social Media Adaptation." This best practices guide identified and detailed the following categories as the principles to use by police when adopting social media:

1. Social media as a source of criminal information
2. Having a voice in social media
3. Social media to push information
4. Social media to leverage "crowd" the wisdom
5. Social media to interact with the public
6. Social media for community policing
7. Social media to show the human side of policing
8. Social media to support police IT infrastructure
9. Social media for efficient policing.

The Demos ThinkTank, a British cross-party organization, published a paper focusing on an analysis of Twitter posting between the Metropolitan Police and the public following the murder of British Army soldier, Drummer (Private) Lee Rigby (Bartlett & Miller, 2013). Of interest to the investigator is the detailed analysis of the Social Media Intelligence (SOCMINT) that the police received through a single social tool. The analysts extracted from the @metpoliceUK's twitter account 19,344 tweets over the period of May 17−23, 2013. The study came up with recommendations which should come as no surprise to law enforcement or corporate investigators familiar with the power of social media. Dealing with social media is no longer a thing for investigators to avoid but a requirement to engage in and understand. The recommendations were:

1. Each constabulary should have the human and technological infrastructure to deal with social media aftermaths in emergency scenarios.
2. A centralized SOCMINT "hub" should be created.
3. The Home Office should create a clear legal framework for collection and use of SOCMINT.

Social media evidence in the courts

Worldwide social networking use has increased, compelling more courts to consider and accept Internet-based evidence. However, authentication as with any evidence is still required. The problem becomes one of Internet evidence documentation in a manner that will be acceptable to the courts. Online or Internet evidence is digital evidence, with the same concerns as any evidence collected from a computer. The digital forensic field has for years followed court accepted methodologies for getting electronically stored information (ESI) admitted or accepted as evidence. The process includes the proper collection, preservation, and presentation. It is done so through logging examiners and/or investigator's actions, collecting the evidence, date and time stamping it, and hashing the saved digital files. Lastly in the process is the presentation of the collected Internet evidence in a manner usable by the attorneys and the courts. In Chapter 4, we discussed ***Lorraine v. Markel Am. Ins. Com***, 241 F.R.D. 534, 538 (D. Md., 2007) and other legal issues related to online evidence. Those issues and concerns are valid for all online ESI, regardless of whether it is found on a social networking site or a website. Courts will no doubt continue to wrestle with online ESI, particularly as social networking sites are increasing in prevalence and usage.

Starting a social networking site investigation

Social networking sites are different than most websites. This is mainly due to these sites' content driven environment. A website in general provides text, images and downloads of documents or other material stored on the site for later viewing. They provide a means to communicate information to the person viewing the site. Social media sites, however, provide a means for the members to communicate among themselves. This information sharing can include traditional website text, images, and downloads. However, social networking sites focus on sharing information in real time. This focus is accomplished through messaging, email among the users, and user security/privacy features limiting sharing to only approved content and/or to specified users. This real time, and the sharing between multiple user's components, means investigators have a much larger task in documenting social networking site data. The task requires that investigative planning becomes far more important than simply snapshotting a webpage and downloading the source code.

The other significant preplanning factor in social networking collection and documentation is the fact that today most individuals do not have one social networking account, but several, across different social networking platforms. Without a directed collection and investigation plan the investigator could easily miss relevant information or simply go on collecting data without a sense of need to support the ongoing investigation.

Planning

We can start the planning by identifying the basics (who, what, and where) to help us determine the information we are looking for and how to collect it.

Who:
1. What is the target's real name? This sometimes is not known and we may have to move to the next step.
2. What is the target's usernames?

3. Research the name through search engines and social media site search engines. Get a clear picture of the location that are to be included in the plan.

What:

4. What is the information that we need to collect in the case?
   a. Are we simply looking to identify the user behind the account?
   b. Are we attempting to locate information about the user's activities (online or offline), which can be images, comments, posts, comments, etc.?

Where:

5. Where are the sites that the target uses?

6. Were the sites located geographically, are they in the same country as the investigator? Check with your prosecutor of counsel as to the collection methods available for the investigator's use in the case.

Answers to these questions will dictate the manner in which the investigator accesses and collects online ESI. Collection of any online ESI from a social networking site requires preplanning of the process and identifying the proper and authorized access method. The following are the four primary methods to access social networking sites in order to collect online ESI:

1. Available public information: This is the easiest to prepare for and collect. The available public information is content that the user (or the social networking site) allows to be seen by anyone viewing the user's page on the site. Collection and documentation planning begins with identifying the user's site, documenting the information with the tools we have described previously in the book and preparing collection reports.

2. Available "Approved Friend or Associate Information": Collecting information on the social networking site as an approved or friend or associate can be accomplished in two manners:
   a. A cooperating witness, who is a friend/associate allows the investigator to use their profile to collect content that the target user has shared or allowed them to view. This can be short-term access, limited to content that exists at the time the cooperating witness granted consent or it can be continuing which is an undercover operation involving an identity takeover (see Chapter 10). An identity takeover requires significant investment in the investigation by the investigator and his agency/company. The problem with consent is it can be revoked prior to the online ESI collection is completed.
   b. The second option requires the target's acceptance of the investigator as a friend/associate. This obviously requires direct communication with the target to have them allow you access. Usually this is with an undercover account and requires all the basic background required to produce an undercover persona as we have described previously. This option is much more involved than even the identity takeover and is certainly more difficult and requires more preparation than collecting public information. Undercover operations again require a significant investment in the investigation by the investigator and his agency/company.

3. Available private information: This collection is possible with the target's cooperation. The investigator is given access by the target through there username and password and collects the available information through the means we have discussed previously and throughout this chapter. Again, the problem with consent is it can be revoked prior to when the online ESI collection is completed.

4. Available information through legal service: This option requires that there be sufficient legal authority to require the social networking site to provide all the available information under the target's account directly from the social networking site's legal compliance department. Online ESI that was collected through options 1–3, as well as other investigative procedures may provide the legal basis (probable cause, etc.) to justify access via compulsory legal process (see Chapter 4). The legal service method frequently has the added benefit of providing details, such as IP addresses or global positioning information at the time the target user accessed and/or posted to their account. Such information is usually not available under options 1–3.

Preplanning the social networking investigation is an important step in a successful Internet investigation. The investigator that follows these concepts will be better prepared and have a more successful social networking collection and investigation.

TEST YOUR APPROACH

Investigators need to remember the Internet is not static and things change very fast. What you did last month or last year on a social networking site might not work today. Also the tools you use today may not work on that social networking site. Part of the planning process needs to include the testing of any processes and/or tools intended to document the online ESI found on a social networking site.

1. Outline the process to be used for collection and documentation of the social networking site.
2. Test the approach on another user account unrelated to the investigation.
3. Validate that the approach functions according to the plan.
4. If an issue arises in the approach that does not function as designed, reevaluate the approach and retest the process. Repeat until the process acts as desired.

Social networking sites commonalities

Social networking sites have some investigative similarities that need to be discussed. As we know social media today, each member of a particular site must have a valid login to access the site's functions. Most allow some access by non-members but the online ESI provided may not be useful for the investigation. Generally the sites require a valid email account. The user has to provide a username (on some sites this data needs to be real, others don't care). Commonly a validation feature includes a telephone number (generally a cell phone) that can be used to verify the user is a live person, the information is real, and/or later account access is legitimate. Some accounts require an email account to be connected with the user's account. Also, many social networking sites can be interconnected. A Facebook user's account is connected to Twitter, Twitter connected to LinkedIn, etc.

Social networking sites all have a profile or user biography, all of which is self-identified information supplied by the account holder. They may contain the account holder's picture, a place to post messages to and from the account holder. Many sites also have places to post images or videos. Some sites, but not all, even leave the metadata in multimedia files, (think latitude and longitude if the camera collects this information). The profile may have a credit card associated with it to pay for membership or to gain additional features from the site. Additionally, most sites now offer access through mobile phones. All of this information, and the Internet Protocol addresses used to access the site, are available through legal service to the social networking site (Look to the ISP list maintained by SEARCH http://search.org/programs/hightech/isp/) for these contacts. The types of information maintained by the social networking sites varies from site to site. Additionally, the duration online ESI is maintained varies.

The top social networking sites

Every social networking site is different. The sites are all coded differently and each has their own method of user authentication. This make each unique and requires an individual approach to investigating the site. Searching for users can be done using the site's search function. Often through using one of the big three search engines, Google, Bing, and Yahoo can guide the investigator to the user they are interested in better than the site's own internal search function. There are other search tools that also can assist the investigator when looking for a target. Many of these search sites are specific to a particular social networking site and have a habit of coming and going. The investigator needs to be aware that these sites may also become ineffective due to changes that the social networking site makes to the site's infrastructure. It has to be remembered though that the target may not be using a real name or only a moniker on the site and having these details can improve the accuracy of the search when looking for the target.

The top three social networking sites have changed over the years. Facebook, with its 1 billion plus user accounts has stayed on top for some time. It wasn't that long ago in social networking history that MySpace was the big dog on the block and it still has a large following. Twitter with its minimalistic data posting ability has become a phenomenon that most would not have guessed. Each of these sites contains a large amount of data on its users and can easily be used in an investigation. A relative newcomer on the block is Google + . It has gained in popularity very quickly and has found its way to the top of the list. "As of July 2013, five of the ten biggest social networks in the world come from China: QQ,

Qzone, RenRen, Youku Tudou, and Sina Weibo." (Balolong, 2013) Clearly social networking has changed how many people in the world approach the Internet.

Any case the investigator has today can be supplemented with social networking site data. The social networking site information can be used as direct evidence. Or the information can be used as intelligence information as to whom the target's friends are and what they have been doing recently. It can also tend to provide the general attitude of the social media user, determine political affiliation, and determine if the user is anarchist. The sites can also tend to tell the investigator that the target is just a normal person posting information for their family and friends. The information can assist the investigator in profiling the targets thoughts, behaviors, and actions as they relate to the investigation. Overlooking social media in today's environment will limit the investigator's understanding of the facts of the case and cloud their investigative situational awareness.

The investigator needs to remember that access to a social media site needs the proper legal authority. If the user has public information it is fair game. They posted the information for everyone to see. However, if their social networking profile has information marked by the users as private, or available only to the "friends" or restricted users, the investigator cannot simply befriend them and gain access. Investigators need to consult their legal authority and consider the current case law governing access to the data before they proceed with the social media investigation.

USING COMMON SENSE

Investigators can be some of the most ingenious individuals on the planet when it comes to uncovering evidence. However, sometimes the methods used leave the general public wondering if there is nothing sacred. Social networking investigations, particularly undercover operations, allow individuals to push these limits. For years law enforcement have impersonated minors to catch predators. But what about a private investigator impersonating another to investigate a minor and her father over a civil manner?

In 2011, civil investigation had commenced after a minor's father filed a lawsuit against a relative over a dog attack, which had permanently injured his daughter. During the investigation and after the appropriate legal consultation, it was decided that an investigator would impersonate one of the daughter's real friends, who was also a Facebook friend, to get access to her restricted areas. The investigator, obtained this friend's username and password and without authorization accessed this person's account. It is unclear if this friend was an adult or minor. The investigator "...who otherwise would not have had access to (the minor's) private Facebook page, assumed the identity of another in order to get around (the minor's) privacy settings and view her private information reserved only for the viewing of her Facebook friends" (Koenninger, 2012).

Upon the discovery, the minor's father promptly sued the investigator, their firm and the attorneys and insurance company who approved this investigative activity. In 2013, the case was dismissed after the parties reached a settlement with the defendants paying the costs (Cuyahoga County Court of Common Pleas, Case CV-12-781824).

Clearly, investigators need to be cautious and use common sense about methods they intend to use as well as the legal advice they sometimes receive.

Examining social networking sites

As with any webpage, we can use a browser to locate content in the profile area, postings, images, etc. which is useful investigative information. Additionally, just like any webpage we can review the HTML code. However, viewing HTML coding on social networking sites does not reveal hidden comment or information generated by the user. This code is from the social networking site. Viewing and searching HTML code on some social networking sites can provide a different method to quickly locate investigative information. It can be faster to search and read text than waiting for a browser to load graphics and other extraneous information. Additionally, there are tools specific to certain social networking sites which allow data to be captured, analyzed, and/ or presented in a manner that makes it much easier for the investigator to process. The following is a review of the major social networking sites and methods for investigating them.

Facebook

Facebook's stated mission "...is to give people the power to share and make the world more open and connected" (Facebook, n.d.). As an online directory started in 2004, Facebook gives people a way to connect with individuals they know, went to school with, share common interests, and more. As we have previously noted it's currently the most popular social networking site in existence, with over one billion users.

Examining Facebook

It would seem that identifying a Facebook user is as simple as reading the name reflected on a post. However, that text name may not always be the name used for the account profile uniform resource locator (URL). For instance, if the user has a vanity name, the account will have the vanity name in the profile URL. Later searching by text name, particularly if it is common, can produce numerous profiles before the correction profile is found, if ever. The best way to identify the account associated with a post is to hoover over it with your mouse, which will reveal the Friend's profile page, which can be written down. Documenting the address can also be accomplished by right clicking the "Friend" name, selecting "Copy Link Address," and pasting the address into a text document.

Facebook is the one site which can reveal useful information by viewing the page's HTML code. Login into Facebook and proceed to the user's page of interest. Once on the profile, examine the source code via your particular browser's option as we described in Chapter 13 (With Internet Explorer go to "View" and select "Source." In Chrome go to the settings button and select "Tools" and then "View Source). Opened in notepad will be the HTML source code for that individual page. The investigator can then use their browser's search function to look for certain artifacts of possible investigative use. Here are some useful ones:

- Searching for ""**user**":" will find the Facebook user's ID number.
- Searching for "URL = /" and "title id = "pageTitle"" will find the Facebook user's name for the account.
- Searching for a friend's page can be found by searching the source code for the term"**?hc_location = timeline**." In the source code at each location the term is found the investigator will find a "friend" listed on the page.
- Searching ""id":" will help locate a stream of data looking like this:

```
"1000000xxxxxxxx":{"id":"1000000xxxxxxxx","name":"John
Smith","firstName":"John","vanity":"noletide","thumbSrc":"https:
\/\/profile-b-sjc.xx.fbcdn.net\/hprofile-prn1\/s32 X 32
\/623859_1000000xxxxxxxx_10xxxxxxxx_q.jpg","uri":"https:\/\/www.
facebook.com\/noletide","gender":2,"type":"friend","is_friend":
true,"social_snippets":null,"showVideoPromo":
false,"searchTokens":["Smith","John"]}
```

This data stream translates as follows:

"1000000xxxxxxxx":{"id":"1000000xxxxxxxx"	Facebook user ID 1000000xxxxxxxx
"name":"John Smith","firstName":"John"	User's name on Facebook account John Smith
"vanity":"NeatGuy"	Vanity name attached to account "NeatGuy"
","thumbSrc":"https:\/\/profile-b-sjc.xx.fbcdn.net \/hprofile-prn1\/s32 × 32 \/623859_1000000xxxxxxxx_10xxxxxxxx_q.jpg"	Link to user's picture on Facebook
"gender":2	User's gender 1 = Female 2 = Male
"type":"friend","is_friend":true," "social_snippets":null,"showVideoPromo":false "searchTokens":["Smith","John"]}	Facebook friend to main account User's name

Internet tools for understanding a Facebook target

There are numerous marketing tools for obtaining information on a Facebook account. There are a few caveats though. These sites, like many Internet resources require you to set up an account with them. Additionally, some tools will not function properly if the user has placed privacy restrictions on their account. With these caveats in mind, here are links to a few such tools:

- Facebook Fan Page Analytics http://simplymeasured.com/freebies/facebook-fan-page-analytics
- Likealyser, http://likealyzer.com/
- Statilizer http://statilizer.com/

Network overview, discovery and exploration in excel

NodeXL is an Excel spreadsheet template that provides the investigator the ability to analyze certain social networking sites, including Facebook. NodeXL was not developed with the investigator in mind but it is certainly a tool that is easily adopted for investigative use. It actively worked as an open source community project and its main page is hosted on Codeplex.com. NodeXL is a project from the Social Media Research Foundation and is a collaborative effort among several organizations including Microsoft Research. Its investigative significance lies in its ability to collect information from certain social networking sites.

The created Excel template is used to access and download the data. Excel is the engine that runs the graphing. NodeXL and similar tools have been developed to assist researchers of social networking put together relationships between users. Its graphing ability allows researchers to sift through large amounts of data from a social networking site and find associations that might have been missed. Investigators will find its easy use a significant advantage when dealing with social networking sites compatible with NodeXL.

Using NodeXL

Download the NodeXL template from http://nodexl.codeplex.com/. In the downloaded zip is an installer that adds the template to your Windows start menu. Once installed go to the Windows Start menu select, "All Programs," then " NodeXL" then click on "NodeXL Excel Template." When the template is open select "Save As" another document name (that way you have the original template and if you mess something up playing with it you don't have to reinstall). You will notice that on the Excel tabs there is an additional tab called "NodeXL." Click in this tab and click on "Import." For the few social networks it collects data from, it is quick and very powerful. Facebook, Flickr, Twitter, and YouTube are the only current social networks programmed directly into the template. Selecting one of the import options for importing data offers various selections for the investigator (Figure 14.1).

FACEBOOK HAS A JAIL?

Well it's not the traditional bars and jailers but Facebook has consequences for certain actions it deems as unacceptable. The "penalty" is the user's account has restrictions imposed for a period of time (3 days). Becker provides the following examples of what can land you in Facebook Jail:

- Sending repeated Friend Requests => harassment
- Adding too many Friends, too fast
- Your friend requests that go unanswered
- Your friend requests that are marked as unwelcome
- Using Facebook to send message deemed SPAM

There is also a closed group page on Facebook for all the 1,400 plus formerly jailed Facebook members. (https://www.facebook.com/groups/439720179385480/).

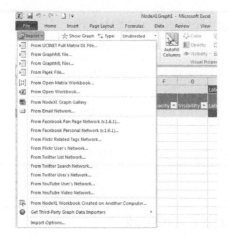

FIGURE 14.1

NodeXL import tools.

Google+

Google+ was launched in June of 2011. In less than 2 years it has become the second largest social networking site with 500 million users. Google has integrated Google+ into other member services.

Investigating user data

Google+ has its own search engine which is similar to using Google general search engine. The investigator can simply enter a term and review the returned information. Of interest to the investigator is the fact that Google+ search site even alerts you to new postings after your initial search. The search page provides the investigator with postings, links to people and pages, and what is trending. There are also links to Google+ posts, photos, communities, and page. Google+ has the following shortcuts that can be useful to the investigator:

J = scroll down
K = scroll up
/ = Select the search box at the top of the page
J = Move down in the stream
K = Move up in the stream
N = Move to the next comment on the current post
p = Move to the previous comment on the current port
Shift + Space = Scroll up the stream
? = Open the full list of keyboard shortcuts.

DOWNLOADING YOUR GOOGLE INFORMATION

If you have the user's login and password to Google, they have made collecting some of the account information simple. Google's new "Takeout" service (www.google.com/takeout) gives the account holder access to various Google account information other than the user's Gmail account. This includes Google+ , the user's contacts, location data, photo's voicemail, profile information, and YouTube data. The actual data when downloaded provides the investigator with a compressed file containing folders with the data. All the data can be of interest, but the location information can be extremely useful because most users are unaware it exists. The file is a java.json file and can be opened in Microsoft's WordPad to read the data, but it is not easy to review (Figure 14.2).

DOCUMENTING GOOGLE VOICEMAIL

As a means of communication Google has so many options. With your Google Voice account number your voicemails link right into your Gmail account where you can review the messages. From a collection and documentation point of view this is a little more challenging because it requires access to the account or submission of legal service to Google to obtain the messages. If you have the account owner's permission and login information you can collect the messages in the following manner:

1. Screenshot the login and access to the user's account.
2. Login into and access the users Google Voicemail account (if at the Gmail login select "More" and then "Voice."
3. At the Google Voice screen "Click" on the link on the left hand column of the Google Voice account linking to "Voicemails" (you can't access the voicemails from the inbox).
4. Under each voicemail listed there is the word "more" which links to a drop down arrow. Select "Download" to download the individual voicemail of interest.
5. Repeat #4 above for each Google voicemail that you need to collect.
6. Screenshot each voicemail to download.
7. Hash the file after download.
8. Document your actions.

Twitter

A Wikipedia page against a St. Louis school was recently found by a Twitter follower in Virginia, who discussed the incident with other followers. They collectively came up with a plan which resulted in the threat being relayed to a local police department. However, the police complaint taker was less than cooperative according to reports and noting the department "did not have access to the Web." Another neighboring agency was contacted and appropriate actions were taken to resolve the issue (Lasica, 2009). Obviously the initial police response to the Twitter complaint in a post-Columbine years was totally inappropriate, if not irresponsible.

Twitter "...is a service for friends, family, and co-workers to communicate and stay connected through the exchange of quick, frequent answers to one simple question: "What are you doing?" (NewsBlaze LLC, n.d.) For many new to the Twitterverse communicating in only 140 characters is a rather odd method of

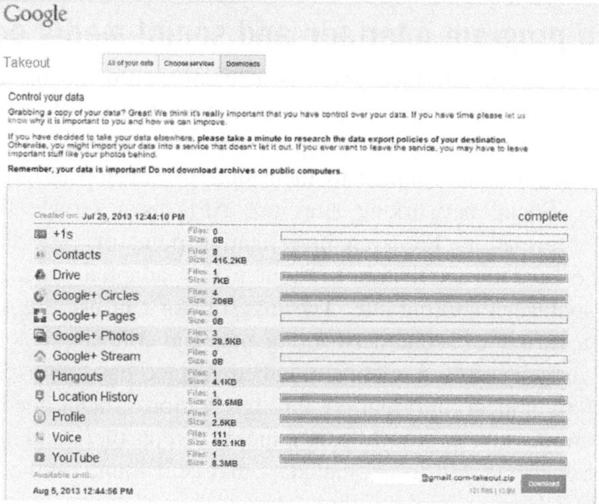

FIGURE 14.2

Google takeout.

updating your friends or world. The investigator new to Twitter only has to go to a website like We Follow (http://wefollow.com/), to grasp the number of people that are now communicating in a short abbreviated form. Just look at the millions of followers that hang on a celebrity's every Tweet. What exactly are the followers saying can be of huge interest to the investigator? Every Tweet and every follower of the tweets can provide the investigator with significant information. Not just what the tweet content is, but what data was it sent, what time and from what location. Who received the tweet and who forward the tweet (retweeted) to their followers? All of these can be of enormous use in the investigation when needed to verify times of events and establishing others awareness of the events in question.

Finding tweets

If you know the username go to www.twitter.com/{twittername}. The user's page has all their "tweets." The investigator can use the following other websites to search for and document tweets:

- Doesfollow (http://doesfollow.com): This site can find out if an individual twitter account is following another.
- Friend or Follow (http://friendorfollow.com): This site can search Twitter, Instagram, and Tumblr. It provides the investigator with an easy look at the accounts, followers, friends, and fans. The free plan is limited. The pay for plans allows the downloading of the same data.
- Trendsmap (http://trendsmap.com/): This site gives the investigator the ability to track tweets from a geographical location.

Application program interface and social media content

An application program interface (API) is a set of commands used by programmers to interact with a program or operating system. It gives the programmer the direction to take when asking the program for information. Most social media sites allow applications to connect to their sites to develop an API to facilitate communication. Social networking sites use APIs as a service that can assist user's access information. From an investigative point of view this provides a large hindrance to data acquisition without a tool adapted specifically for that API and that social networking site. The investigator can use this same information to access a variety of social networking sites and collect valuable information related to the investigation. A company called Apigee has a console that can be easily utilized to collect information through various social media APIs. The investigator can go to Apigee (https://apigee.com/console/) and access Twitter information through the API to get metadata that isn't found on the Twitter user's page. Figure 14.3 is an example of that data.

TWITTER IS OFFICIALLY "CREEPY"

Okay, this is a play on words, but it really is getting creepy. Yiannis Kakavas, a social media fanatic and software writer, published in 2011 a free tool to scare the pants off of most twitterphiles when they found out about it (Sullivan, 2011). But if you are updating your twitter page that much you probably won't really care. Kakavas's tool called "Creepy," is a social networking search tool or in his words a "*A geolocation information aggregator.*" More than just a search tool, it seeks out where users have posted from and triangulate the longitude and latitude of their posts, creating a pretty map of where users posted from each time. Can you say "stalker nirvana"? Now this requires that the individual used some device that collects lat/long when posting, like a smart phone or FourSquare (the user authorized that it be collected if using FourSquare). The tool is not collecting anything the users haven't already put online themselves. The tool has had several revisions since its initial release to keep up with Twitters changing its allowance to tools to collect this information. With the changes to Twitters API it is currently not working and at the time of this book's writing its website says it is currently under a major revision. The point here is that the data available behind the scenes in a Tweet can be a significant investigative find (Vere Software, 2011).

Other social networking sites of interest

There is a social networking type site for almost every kind of hobby or activity imaginable. Facebook and MySpace were not the first ones on the Internet. They happen to be some of the most used today, but many others exist. The investigator should not overlook these sites as they potentially could provide a valuable amount of detail in the investigation that might not be found elsewhere (Table 14.1).

A comprehensive list of the major active social networking sites is maintained on Wikipedia. This page has links to the major sites and has some background, the number of registered users.

FIGURE 14.3

Apigee twitter search.

Table 14.1 Other General Social Networking Sites of Interest

Site	URL and Details
MySpace	http://www.myspace.com
Hi5	http://hi5.com/
Bebo	http://www.bebo.com
Formspring	http://www.formspring.me
Pinterest	http://www.pinterest.com

LOCO CITATO ("IN THE PLACE CITED")

Investigators looking for tools to help them understand and evaluate social media data need to look at the tools offered by Thomas Whiteley at Lococitato (http://www.lococitato.com). He offers various tools to help the investigator understand and visualize the data found associated with a target's social networking username. There are tools available for Facebook, Twitter, and MySpace. Many of these tools are available only to law enforcement.

TO TRACK OR NOT TO TRACK

Social networking trackers first became available with MySpace. The notion of finding the IP address of visitors to a person's MySpace page is an attractive idea. This could be a stalker looking at a user's page or a predator's victim wanting to identify their perpetrator. Since MySpace first came on the scene, several tools, some useful and some not so, have been developed. Mixmap.com (http://www.mixmap.com/) has been in use for years as an investigative tool to identify who's visiting a MySpace page. The ability to utilize these kinds of trackers was because MySpace allowed the users to add HTML content to the user's page. These tools use HTML scripting to collect the incoming IP address of the visitor. This is unique to MySpace. Facebook does not allow this to occur and therefore prevents users from tracking each other. Tracking on other social networking sites is difficult because the user cannot change the page's HTML coding or add to it. The investigator with web programming tools can basically do the same thing. If a link is added to the social networking site to a webpage on a webserver the investigator controls the webserver can collect the IP addresses of the incoming connections.

Online social versus professional networking

People use social networking for a variety of reasons. Some may use them to get a date, expand their circle of friends, find people with similar hobbies or reconnect with old friends. The popularity has risen immensely over the past few years. However, professional eNetworking has a different purpose. Professional networking sites are used to connect people with contacts who can help them land a new or better job or lead to a business opportunity. These contacts include current and former colleagues, former bosses and coworkers, and even contacts not directly known to the user but from the same field. These professional sites offer similar functions to personal social networking sites such as "friends" referred to as contacts, email, public and private descriptions, pictures and groups with which to connect on various topics. Professional networking sites can have a significant amount of information about the person listed. Most of the information is listed on the "private" side of the user's account, but still there is a large amount of information that can be gleaned from the user's public account. Each of the professional sites requires an account on the networking site to access the "private" data listed on the user's account. Investigators need to be aware that some professional networking sites may inform the account holder who has been reviewing their profile. This is done to allow the user to connect with the viewer and start a dialogue between professionals. Another investigative aspect of these professional sites are user groups. These groups can inform the investigator about the types of interests a target has and can be useful in post arrest interviews and/or in locating additional victims.

Common business social networking sites

The most common business social networking sites include LinkedIn (http://www.linkedin.com), Plaxo (http://www.plaxo.com), and Spoke (http://www.spoke.com). Each of these sites offer similar services to their users. They intend to allow business networking between the users. Investigating each of these sites requires the investigator to obtain a user account. The investigator's personal account should not be used for this purpose. An undercover account should be used for this purpose that cannot identify the investigator as the one viewing a user's account.

Professional networking sites offer a large amount of user information to people using these sites and to add a significant amount of information about them to further develop their profile. Again, be aware that this is user-added content, which can be falsified. Professional networking sites generally have a public profile accessible by anyone and the private side containing additional information on the profile. Researching these sites is fairly simple. Most have a search function that allows you to identify the users by name. The benefit of these sites is that the users don't use a nickname. The sites require a full name. The investigator can find the current position held by the user, their work history and their education. All of this can be of great value to the investigator when researching a target.

IS THE SOCIAL MEDIA ACCOUNT REAL OR NOT?

When looking at a social media account during an investigation, how do we know that the account is real or fake? Facebook admits in their 2012 filing with the US Securities and Exchange Commission that their social networking site contains a large number of fake or duplicate accounts. CNN estimates there are 83 million false or duplicate accounts. So what can the investigator do to determine if the account is possibly a fake? Here are a few things to consider when reviewing a social media site to determine if it is real or fake:

1. Read the profile thoroughly: Does the age of the person match the job?
2. Review the profile picture: Run the profile picture through Google Imager search or TinEye to see if the picture is used elsewhere on the Internet.
3. Research the user's name and email (if it is reflected). Use your favorite search engine to research the user's name and identify if their name or user account is used elsewhere on the internet. Check to see if the email has also appeared elsewhere on the Internet.
4. Research the friends/contacts: If the account is not real are the friends made up? Is there a real relationship that the friends have and do they actually communicate with the target? If there are no friends this could be potentially a fake account. The friends could also be fake accounts. Review them also to determine their validity.

Finding individuals on social media sites

Looking for someone on a social networking site can sometimes be a challenge. Besides their name as a query term try searching using their email address to locate their profile. It sometimes is easier to locate a target's friend or associate and check their profile for possible connection to your target's profile. We previously have spoken about Spokeo and other sites that can assist in the search. There are other sites that can offer you additional options when searching for someone on a social networking site. These sites include:

General Social Networking Sites:
Social Mention, http://socialmention.com/

Addictomatic, http://addictomatic.com/
Who's Talkin, http://www.whostalkin.com/
Kurrently, http://www.kurrently.com
Social Seek, http://socialseek.com/
Ice Rocket, http://www.icerocket.com/
Social Buzz, http://www.social-searcher.com/social-buzz/
Topsy, http://topsy.com/
Twitter-Specific Search Sites:
Back Tweets, http://backtweets.com/
Nearby Tweets, http://nearbytweets.com/
Tweet Alarm, http://www.tweetalarm.com/
Twazzup, http://www.twazzup.com

MAKE SURE YOU CAPTURE EVERYTHING

When capturing a Facebook timeline, wall, or friend listing make sure you are getting everything. It is not enough to just go to a timeline, wall, etc. and capture it. Investigators must go through and expand all comments and display all posts. Otherwise, they will only capture what is being displayed by the browser and not what exists through the social media's feed to that user's account. This also applies to Twitter feeds. Expand the posts until you reach everything you need as evidenced by viewing it in your browser before you capture it.

Social media evidence collection

This text has stressed online ESI needs to be collected, preserved, and reported in a manner that allows it to be used as evidence. Online ESI found on a social media site is even more susceptible to user alteration or destruction than that found on a website. Frequently, users have continuous live access to their social media profile. Few website administrators are continuously logged on to their site. Additionally, social media, either with or without special applications, is accessible by all manner of mobile devices. The nature of social media dictates this kind of constant user access and ability to interact, anywhere at anytime.

In Chapter 4, we outlined proper online ESI collection procedures (collection, preservation, and its presentation). These procedures are not just for high-tech crimes and computer forensics specialists. Just as every patrol officer knows how to bag and log physical evidence found during a vehicle or personal search, it is also possible to teach patrol officers and detectives how to collect a YouTube video or series of Facebook status updates. Indeed, the courts have generally accepted evidence collected from the Internet as long as its authenticity can be established. We have previously discussed in other chapters the tools available to document and collect the evidence found on the Internet. The investigator should consider the documentation of the evidence he finds at the time they find it. This is particularly the case as online ESI found on social media can be, and more likely will be, changed.

IS THE PHOTOGRAPH ON THE USER'S PAGE ACTUALLY THE TARGET?

Have you wondered if the image on the user's page is related to another user's page or profile on the Internet? One of the ways the investigator can determine if the image on the target's business networking page is the target is by checking the image through one of the image databases. One such image databases is TinEye (http://TinEye.com). This site allows the investigator to up load an image and check their database of images for a similar picture. This can lead the investigator to identify the real name of the target or identify the fact the user account might be fraudulent because the image is found in other sites with other names. Google has a similar image search function that can be found at http://www.google.com/imghp. These tools have been successfully used to identify the original source of a photograph used on a fraudulent website.

Social networking through photographs

Photo sites can be an often overlooked networking tool. Users will post photos of their travels, work, and leisure-time activities in large numbers. These photographs can provide a glimpse into the target's life and provide the investigator with an understanding of the target's personal behavior. These sites list the photos and any user-added caption about the photographs. Additionally, most of the photograph networking sites, unlike regular social networking sites, keep the Exif data in the image (we discussed extracting Exif data in Chapter 13). This can be a gold mine of information for the investigator depending on the camera settings used to take the photograph. The investigator can download the images and use a tool to extract the Exif data for examination. However, not all sites pass the Exif data through to the user's pages. Facebook and others strip out the Exif data and reduce the image size for privacy and server space reasons. So the investigator may not have the Exif data available in that photo. Using the image search tools can assist the investigator in finding additional similar images that might in fact still retain the Exif data.

Flickr

Flickr (http://www.flickr.com/) is a photograph sharing social networking site. It has a feature that allows the geotagging of the images posted to the site. On the Flickr site a geotag is user-added information. This data can be public or private information. If it is public the investigator can easily identify the Exif data from the image. If it is private he may have to obtain the data by legal service or through some undercover connection to the user. Flickr has a search function that allows the investigator to search for names or usernames without logging into the service.

Photobucket

Photobucket (http://photobucket.com/) is another photograph sharing site similar to Flickr. It similarly allows for photo sharing as well as photo backup services, photo editing software, and printing services. Photobucket also has a search function that allows the investigator to search for names or usernames without logging into the service. Many other photo sharing sites exist and can be of use to the investigator. Some of those sites include:

- Deviant Art, http://www.deviantart.com/
- Shutterfly, http://www.shutterfly.com/
- Pbase, http://www.pbase.com/
- Photo.net, http://photo.net/
- Snapfish, http://www.snapfish.com/
- Smugmug, http://www.smugmug.com/

SOCIAL NETWORKING GENERAL SEARCH SITES

A couple of good general search sites to identify if a user or name has a social networking site is to use either yoName, (http://yoname.com) or Spokeo, (http://Spokeo.com). yoName searches 35 different social networking sites at once for a username. This can tell the investigator if the username is available or not on the multiple sites it searches. The investigator then can continue the search on those specific sites. Spokeo is often considered the ultimate social networking searching tool. It can provide investigators with the known social networking sites associated with the username or email address.

Social media investigations policy

We devoted much in this text to discussing policy and its need during Internet investigations. Social Networking investigations are no different. In Chapter 11, we discussed the need for policy on the use of social media during investigations. This emerging area has a great investigative capacity and requires that the investigators, their supervisors, and the agency/company management understand the requirements of using and documenting social networking data appropriately. The investigator should understand the agency/company policy regarding using social media during an investigation prior to commencing work on a case. A properly designed social media use policy for investigations should address how the agency/company communicates information on the investigation to the community it serves as well how the social media tools will be leveraged during the investigation. Obviously undercover social media has its own concerns as an investigative tool, which we noted in Chapters 10 and 11.

Training on investigating social networks

Policy is only a first step toward effective investigation of social networking sites. It must be backed up by training. There is a lot of focus in the commercial marketing world on how to use social networking as a marketing and sales tool. However training on the investigation and use of social networking as a community policing tool is something that is offered by very few organizations. Discussion within law enforcement really began relatively recently with the advent of conferences like the SMILE "Social Media In Law Enforcement" conference first held in April 7–9, 2010, in Washington DC. Even consultants are appearing in the market to assist officers and agencies deal with rebranding themselves in the social networking space like the people behind Cops 2.0 (cops2point0.com).

POLICY AND THE FIRST SMILE CONFERENCE

Your coauthor Todd G. Shipley made the first presentation to the law enforcement community suggesting the development of policy regarding the investigative use of social media at the first SMILE conference. It was after this conference that he designed and provided to the law enforcement community the first model policies for the investigative use of social media for law enforcement. Those model policies are included in the appendices.

Regardless of your motives for moving into the social networking space, it like anything on the Internet needs to be understood to be employed correctly. Agencies must look at the policy they develop from both the community policing and the investigative perspective from a training point of view. Officers, new to social networking, need to be trained about what this part of the Internet is, its inherent risks and benefits, how an agency can benefit from being on social networking, and how to prevent exposing the agency or the officer to any liability. This training also needs to be provided to supervisors and managers, particularly as they are less likely than newer officers, to have used social networking sites.

Officers need to understand how the different social networks operate and where potential investigative information can be found. Officers also need to be aware of the agency's policy on collection of investigative information versus intelligence collection and the different manner in which they each need to be treated. Training is available from a number of law enforcement specialists, which are reflected in Table 14.2.

CONCLUSION

This chapter has provided the reader with the understanding of how social networking has changed the investigative process. Social networking is a valuable tool for the investigator and needs to be considered in almost every investigation.

Table 14.2 Social Media Training Sources

Course	URL
Vere Software's Cybercrime Survival courses	www.cybercrimesurvival.com
SEARCH, the National Consortium for Justice and Statistics	www.search.org
Inland Direct	www.advancedinternet.org
Hetherington Group	http://hetheringtongroup.com/training.shtml
Internet Crimes Against Children	www.icactraining.org
Federal Law Enforcement Training Center • Internet Investigations Training Program (IITP)	http://www.fletc.gov/training/programs/investigative-operations-division/economic-financial/internet-investigations-training-program-iitp
National White Collar Crime Center • Cyber Investigation 201—(BOTS)	www.nw3c.org
European Police College • Social network analysis training • Social media implications in law enforcement	https://www.cepol.europa.eu

Social networking evidence should not be a source of stress for the investigator. Proper understanding, provided through good policy and training will help the investigator find offenders, collect evidence, and bring a well-packaged case to their prosecutors or legal counsel for whatever the litigation may be. Social networking sites, both personal and professional, can provide the investigator with intelligence that can further their understanding of targets and victims. Online ESI found on social networking sites is even more susceptible to user alteration or destruction than that found on a website because users frequently have continuous access which is possible by the availability of today's mobile devices. However, with proper policy, procedures, and training, online ESI can be collected and preserved in a manner that allows it to be used as evidence in any legal proceeding.

Further reading

Abrad-Santos, A. (2013, January 2). Inside the anonymous hacking file on the Steubenville "Rape Crew." *The Atlantic Wire.* Retrieved from <http://www.theatlanticwire.com/national/2013/01/inside-anonymous-hacking-file-steubenville-rape-crew/60502/>.

Addictomatic: Inhale the Web. (n.d.). Retrieved from <http://addictomatic.com/>.

Advanced Internet Investigations. (n.d.). Retrieved from <http://www.advancedinternet.org/>.

Apigee. (n.d.). *Apigee*. Retrieved from <https://apigee.com/>.

Balolong, F. (2013, July 29). Top 10 social networking sites in the world [INFOGRAPHIC]. *Social barrel: The latest social media news and marketing tips.* Retrieved from <http://socialbarrel.com/top-10-social-networking-sites-in-the-world-infographic/52658/>.

Bartlett, J., & Miller, C. (2013). *How twitter is changing modern policing: The case of the Woolwich aftermath* London: Demos.

Bayerl, P. (2012, September 29). Social media study in European police forces: First results on usage and acceptance. *Comparative Police Studies in the EU (COMPOSITE).* Retrieved from <www.composite-project.eu/tl_files/fM_k0005/download/SocialMedia-in-European-Police-Forces__PreliminaryReport.092012.pdf/>.

Bebo. (n.d.). *Bebo*. Retrieved from <http://www.bebo.com/>.

Becker, J. (n.d.). How to stay out of Facebook jail—Need to know tips for online marketers. *Julie Becker's Guide to Residual Income.* Retrieved from <http://igetpaidonline.biz/facebook-jail/>.

Boyd, D., & Ellison, N. (2008). Social network sites: Definition, history, and scholarship. *Journal of Computer-Mediated Communication, 13*(1), 210–230.

Brenner, J., & Smith, A. (2013 August 5). 72% of Online adults are social networking site users. Pew Research Center's Internet & American Life Project. Retrieved from <http://pewinternet.org/Reports/2013/social-networking-sites.aspx/>.

Brick, M. (2010 February 18). Man crashes plane into Texas I.R.S. office. *The New York Times.* Retrieved from <http://www.nytimes.com/2010/02/19/us/19crash.html?_r=1&/>.

Caeleigh Cope v. Steven D. Prince, et al., Cuyahoga County Court of Common Pleas, CV-12-781824.

Cops 2.0. (n.d.). Retrieved from <http://cops2point0.com/>.

CybercrimeSurvival.com—Learn the investigative tools you need to succeed. (n.d.). CybercrimeSurvival.com. Retrieved from <http://www.cybercrimesurvival.com/>.

Denef, S., Bayerl, P., & Kaptein, N. (2012). *Cross-European approaches to social media as a tool for police communication* Hampshire, UK: CEPOL European Police Science and Research Bulletin.

deviantART: Where ART meets application! (n.d.). *deviantART.* Retrieved from <http://www.deviantart.com/>.

Dissell, R. (2012, September 2). Rape charges against high school players divide football town of Steubenville, Ohio. *Cleveland OH Local News, Breaking News, Sports & Weather—Cleveland.com.* Retrieved from <http://www.cleveland.com/metro/index.ssf/2012/09/rape_charges_divide_football_t.html/>.

DoesFollow—Find out who follows whom on Twitter. (n.d.). *DoesFollow.* Retrieved from <http://doesfollow.com/>.

Edward de Bono. (n.d.). *BrainyQuote.com.* Retrieved from <http://www.brainyquote.com/quotes/quotes/e/edwarddebo124441.html/>.

Facebook. (n.d.). *Facebook*. Retrieved from <facebook.com/>.

Facebook Form 10-Q. (2012, July 31). *Securities and Exchange Commission.* Retrieved from <http://www.sec.gov/Archives/edgar/data/1326801/000119312512325997/d371464d10q.htm#tx371464_14/>.

Facebook Jail. (n.d.). *Facebook.* Retrieved from <https://www.facebook.com/groups/439720179385480/>.

Gonzalez, A. (2010, February 19). Social media forever changing the way we cover news. *YNN—Your News Now. NEWS—Austin/Round Rock/San Marcos.* Retrieved from

<http://austin.ynn.com/content/news/267483/social-media-forever-changing-the-way-we-cover-news/>.

Google Images. (n.d.). *Google*. Retrieved from <http://www.google.com/imghp/>.

Google Takeout. (n.d.). *Google*. Retrieved from <www.google.com/takeout>.

Hetherington Group—Training. (n.d.). *Hetherington Group—Welcome*. Retrieved from <http://hetheringtongroup.com/training.shtml/>.

hi5 (n.d.). *hi5*. Retrieved from <http://hi5.com/>.

Hofmann, M. (2010, March 16). Social networking monitoring. *Electronic Frontier Foundation*. Retrieved from <www.eff.org/deeplinks/2010/03/eff-posts-documents-detailing-law-enforcement/>.

Home CEPOL—European Police College. (n.d.). *CEPOL—European Police College*. Retrieved from <https://www.cepol.europa.eu/>.

ICAC Training and Technical Assistance. (n.d.). Internet Crimes Against Children Task Force. Retrieved from <http://www.icactraining.org/>.

ilektrojohn creepy @ GitHub. (n.d.). *ilektrojohn creepy @ GitHub*. Retrieved from <ilektrojohn.github.com/creepy/>.

Internet Investigations Training Program (IITP) at Federal Law Enforcement Training Center. (n.d.). FLETC: Federal Law Enforcement Training Center. Retrieved from <http://www.fletc.gov/training/programs/investigative-operations-division/economic-financial/internet-investigations-training-program-iitp/>.

Jefferson County QuickFacts from the US Census Bureau. (n.d.). *State and County QuickFacts*. Retrieved from <http://quickfacts.census.gov/qfd/states/39/39081.html/>.

Koenninger, K. (2012, May 4). Outraged dad says law firm and insurer snooped on injured girl's Facebook page. Courthouse News Service. Retrieved from <http://www.courthousenews.com/2012/05/04/46239.htm/>.

Kurrently Inc. (n.d.). *Kurrently Inc*. Retrieved from <www.kurrently.com/>.

Lasica, J. (2009, March 4). Social media and a school death threat. Socialmedia.biz. Social Media News and Business Strategies Blog. Retrieved from <http://socialmedia.biz/2009/03/04/social-media-and-a-school-death-threat/>.

Lorraine v. Markel AM. Ins. Com, 241 F.R.D. 534, 538 (D.Md. 2007).

Loco Citato. (n.d.). *Loco Citato*. Retrieved from <http://www.lococitato.com/>.

Macur, J., & Schweber, N. (2012, December 16). Rape case unfolds online and divides Steubenville. *The New York Times*—Breaking News, World News & Multimedia. Retrieved from <http://www.nytimes.com/2012/12/17/sports/high-school-football-rape-case-unfolds-online-and-divides-steubenville-ohio.html?pagewanted=all/>.

McCullagh, D. (2010, March 16). Feds consider going undercover on social networks.| Politics and Law—CNET News. Technology News. Retrieved from <http://news.cnet.com/8301-13578_3-20000550-38.html/>.

Meltwater IceRocket. (n.d.). *Meltwater IceRocket*. Retrieved from <http://www.icerocket.com/>.

Myspace. (n.d.). *Myspace*. Retrieved from <www.myspace.com/>.

MySpace Tracker—MixMap. (n.d.). *MixMap—MySpace Tracker*. Retrieved from <http://www.mixmap.com/>.

Nearby tweets: Search local tweets by location and keyword. (n.d.). *Nearby Tweets*. Retrieved from <http://nearbytweets.com/>.

NodeXL: Network Overview, Discovery and Exploration for Excel—Home. (n.d.). *NodeXL*. Retrieved from <http://nodexl.codeplex.com/>.

NW3C Home. (n.d.). *National White Collar Crime Center*. Retrieved from <http://www.nw3c.org/>.

Owyang, J. (2011, July 29,). Number of corporate social media accounts on rise: Risk of a social media help desk. *Social Media, Web Marketing. Web Strategy By Jeremiah Owyang*. Retrieved from <http://www.web-strategist.com/blog/2011/07/29/number-of-corporate-social-media-accounts-hard-to-manage-risk-of-social-media-help-desk/>.

Parrack, D. (2010, March 17). FBI tracks criminals via social networking sites. *Tech. Blorge.com*. Retrieved from <tech.blorge.com/Structure:%20/2010/03/17/fbi-tracks-criminals-via-social-networking-sites/>.

PBase.com. (n.d.). *PBase.com*. Retrieved from <http://www.pbase.com/>.

Pearson, M., Carter, C., & Brady, B. (2013, March 19). More social media trouble in Steubenville. *CNN.com—Breaking News, U.S., World, Weather, Entertainment & Video News*. Retrieved from <http://www.cnn.com/2013/03/19/justice/ohio-steubenville-case/>.

Photo Books, Holiday Cards, Photo Cards, Birth Announcements, Photo Printing: Shutterfly. (n.d.). *Shutterfly*. Retrieved from <http://www.shutterfly.com/>.

Photo Sharing. Stunning Photo Websites. SmugMug. (n.d.). *SmugMug*. Retrieved from <http://www.smugmug.com/>.

Photography community, including forums, reviews, and galleries from Photo.net. (n.d.) *Photo.net*. Retrieved from <http://photo.net/>.

Pinterest. (n.d.). *Pinterest*. Retrieved from <www.pinterest.com/>.

Plaxo—Your address book for life. (n.d.). *Plaxo*. Retrieved from <http://www.plaxo.com/>.

Presutti, C. (2013, April 26). Multi, social media play huge role in solving Boston bombing. *VOA—Voice of America English News—VOA News*. Retrieved from <http://www.voanews.com/content/multi-social-media-play-huge-role-in-solving-boston-bombing/1649774.html/>.

Real Time Search—Social Mention. (n.d.). *Real time search—Social mention*. Retrieved from <http://socialmention.com/>.

Real-time local Twitter trends—Trendsmap. (n.d.). *Trendsmap*. Retrieved from <http://trendsmap.com/>.

SEARCH High-Tech Crime—ISP List. (n.d.). *SEARCH: The online resource for justice and public safety decision makers*. Retrieved from <http://search.org/programs/hightech/isp/>.

SEARCH: The Online Resource for Justice and Public Safety Decision Makers. (n.d.). *SEARCH*. Retrieved from <http://www.search.org/>.

Smith, C. (2013, July 21). By the numbers: 20 amazing witter stats. *Digital Marketing Ramblings. The Latest Digital Marketing Tips, Trends and Technology*. Retrieved from <http://expandedramblings.com/index.php/march-2013-by-the-numbers-a-few-amazing-twitter-stats/>.

Smith, C. (2013, July 24). (August 2013 update) By the numbers: 39 amazing Facebook stats. *Digital Marketing Ramblings. The Latest Digital Marketing Tips, Trends and Technology*. Retrieved from <http://expandedramblings.com/index.php/by-the-numbers-17-amazing-facebook-stats/>.

Snapfish. Photo Prints, Photo Books, Photo Cards, Personalized Photo Gifts Occasion. (n.d.). *Snapfish*. Retrieved from <http://www.snapfish.com/>.

Social Buzz—Real Time Search for Facebook, Twitter and Google+. (n.d.). *Social Buzz*. Retrieved from <http://www.social-searcher.com/social-buzz/>.

Social Media Search Tool*WhosTalkin?* (n.d.). Retrieved from <http://www.whostalkin.com/>.

Social Networking Monitoring. (n.d.). *Electronic Frontier Foundation*. Retrieved from <https://www.eff.org/foia/social-network-monitoring/>.

Socialseek. (n.d.). *Socialseek*. Retrieved from <http://socialseek.com/>.

Spoke: Discover Relevant Business Information. (n.d.). *Spoke*. Retrieved from <http://www.spoke.com/>.

Spokeo People Search: White Pages, Find People (n.d.). *Spokeo*. Retrieved from <http://Spokeo.com/>.

Spring.Me.(n.d.). *Spring.Me*. Retrieved from <http://www.formspring.me/>.

Steubenville Under Siege—News, Sports, Jobs—The Intelligencer / Wheeling News-Register. (n.d.). *The Intelligencer / Wheeling News-Register*. Retrieved from <http://www.theintelligencer.net/page/content.detail/id/584526/Steubenville-Under-Siege.html?nav=511/>.

Steubenville, OH Population and Races. (n.d.). *USA.com: Location information of the United States*. Retrieved from <http://www.usa.com/steubenville-oh-population-and-races.htm/>.

Steubenville, OH—Forbes. (n.d.). *Information for the World's Business Leaders—Forbes.com*. Retrieved from <http://www.forbes.com/places/oh/steubenville/>.

Sullivan, B. (2011 April 15). Just how creepy is "Creepy"? A Test-drive. *NBC News.com. Breaking News & Top Stories*. Retrieved from <http://www.nbcnews.com/technology/just-how-creepy-creepy-test-drive-6C10406861/>.

TinEye Reverse Image Search. (n.d.). *TinEye Reverse Image Search*. Retrieved from <http://TinEye.com/>.

Topsy. (n.d.). *Topsy*. Retrieved from <http://topsy.com/>.

Twazzup—Twitter Real-time Monitoring and Analytics. (n.d.). *Twazzup*. Retrieved from <http://www.twazzup.com/>.

Tweetalarm.com. (n.d.). *Tweetalarm.com*. Retrieved from <http://www.tweetalarm.com/>.

Twitter. (n.d.). *Twitter*. Retrieved from <twitter.com/>.

Twitter Search: BackTweets. (n.d.). *BackTweets*. Retrieved from <http://backtweets.com/>.

Twitter WebCase WebLog. (2011, April 5). *Vere software—Online evidence collection & documentation*. Retrieved from <http://veresoftware.com/blog/?tag=twitter/>.

Watkins, T., & Presse, A. (2013, May 1). Google Plus is outpacing Twitter. *Business Insider. Business Insider*. Retrieved from <http://www.businessinsider.com/google-plus-is-outpacing-twitter-2013-5#ixzz2bh913KCy/>.

Wefollow: Discover prominent people. (n.d.). *Wefollow*. Retrieved from <http://wefollow.com/>.

Welcome to Flickr—Photo Sharing. (n.d.). *Flickr*. Retrieved from <http://www.flickr.com/>.

What is Twitter?. (n.d.). *NewsBlaze LLC*. Retrieved from <http://tweeternet.com/>.

Who Unfollowed Me? | Friend or Follow. (n.d.). *Who unfollowed me?* Retrieved from <http://friendorfollow.com/>.

World's Largest Professional Network. *LinkedIn*. Retrieved from <http://www.linkedin.com/>.

yoName—People Search. Search for People Across Social Networks, Blogs and More. (n.d.). *yoName*. Retrieved from <http://yoname.com/>.

Investigating Methods of Communication

15

USENET is like a herd of performing elephants with diarrhea — massive, difficult to redirect, awe-inspiring, entertaining, and a source of mind-boggling amounts of excrement when you least expect it.
(Gene Spafford, Computer Science at Purdue University, Computer Science Professor)

Communicating on the Internet

There are various Internet protocols available that can be used to communicate online with other users. Most of us are familiar with the Instant Messaging as a communication tool. Some of the other traditional tools, such as Internet relay chat (IRC) and Usenet, popular ages ago, are not as known or used as they once were. This does not mean these protocols are not used by millions of people. A little known fact to most on the Internet, USENET has been increasing in use since the mid-1990s. According to TechSono Engineering, Inc., a USENET software tool manufacturer, 8 terabytes of data daily were moving through the USENET system in 2011. The communication methods are not limited to just voice and chat but also include data transfers. The methods we are going to discuss are based on the protocol and design of the specific communication system. We are going to break these methods into three separate categories based on the type of communication protocol utilized. These are broad and not individually descriptive of each technology, but help us to categorize the technology into understandable forms. These categories are: client server, peer-to-peer (P2P), and bulletin boards. The application of these tools and protocols are not dependant on a specific operating system.

Client server: protocols and tools

The client server model is one where connections and data are controlled through a server or series of servers that a user connects with through a software client. The communications are guided by the server processing connections to connect

FIGURE 15.1

Client server connections between servers and users.

one or more users together (Figure 15.1). The common types of communication protocols and programs in this category include:

- Instant Messaging (IM);
- Internet Relay Chat (IRC);
- File Transfer Protocol (FTP);
- chatrooms.

Instant Messaging

Instant Messaging, a real-time technology, has existed as an Internet protocol for some time. It's a way of communicating which requires immediate feedback or response. It is an alternative to email and newsgroups. Instant Messaging programs work independent of your computer's browser and allow the users to communicate with each other without interrupting other applications. Instant messaging allows two people to communicate over the Internet just as if they were having a face-to-face conversation. The programs allow the creation of contact lists, sometimes referred to as a "buddy list." Contacts are generated by contacting another user on the network and asking to be connected to that user. The user contacted has to accept the user as a contact to make a connection. This adds them as a contact in the Instant Message application for later use. Most Instant Messaging software allows you to track when another "friend" logs on or logs off of the Internet. There also is usually an option to not provide these notifications to the user(s). Video Instant Messaging allows for real-time video communication between users.

Instant Messaging configuration

Instant Messaging is generally configured in a peer-to-network configuration (this is also called client/server model). Peer-to-network configurations require a central server. This central server acts as the connector between users. When a user adds a connection, the central server alerts the user when that connection comes onto the network. This allows the two users to make a connection. The connection is through the central server which forwards the communications between the users. Examples include: AOL Instant Messenger, Yahoo!, ICQ, and Skype.

Instant Messaging can allow for P2P connections but only when transferring files. The P2P connections made through Instant Messaging allow users to connect directly to one another user without relying on a central server. These connections could expose each user's Internet Protocol (IP) address of the users. Each of the Instant Messaging services have developed their protocols independently. This causes an inability of the messaging services to interoperate. Open-source protocols were eventually developed under the Extensible Messaging and Presence Protocol (XMPP). There are several software programs, such as Pidgin or Trillian, that have brought several of the Instant Messaging protocols together in one application that allow the users to communicate between services.

Instant Messaging works by the user logging into the messaging server, i.e., Yahoo, AOL, or through the user's software on the local machine. The messaging server acknowledges the user's buddy list and advises which of the contacts are currently logged into the server. The user selects an online contact to chat with and tells the system to connect to the contact. The users then chat with each other by typing their communications back and forth between themselves (Figure 15.2).

Instant messages historically have been sent in plain text with no inherent encryption unless enabled by the user. This can make sessions vulnerable to packet sniffing, especially if the connection is not encrypted. Instant Messaging allows the transfers of files between users. This file transfer method, however, does not allow files to be scanned by antivirus programs as they arrive which creates a real risk for an attack. Instant Messaging differs from IRC as the latter is communication on a one-to-one basis where IRC is one-to-many communication. There are many popular Instant Messaging software applications that have little to no interoperability. Examples: of this include, AOL Instant Messenger, Yahoo! Messenger, ICQ, and Skype.

- AOL Instant Messenger® (AIM), http://www.aim.com/
- ICQ®, http://www.icq.com/
- Yahoo! Messenger®, http://messenger.yahoo.com.

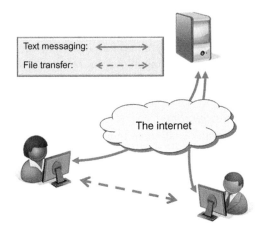

FIGURE 15.2

How Instant Messaging works.

There are other protocol independent instant messenger programs that allow communication between multiple Instant Messaging services. These can be useful to the investigator that is tracking targets and communicating with persons across multiple Instant Messaging platforms. Several of these cross platform tools are:

- Digsby, http://www.digsby.com/
- Miranda, http://www.miranda-im.org/
- Pidgin, http://www.pidgin.im/
- Trillian, https://www.trillian.im/.

WINDOWS LIVE MESSENGER

Windows Live Messenger retired in April 2013 and was replaced with the Microsoft purchase of Skype.

Web-based chat

Web-based chat program allows access to IM protocols through a web interface. Social media sites have integrated chat into their services and so have web-based email programs like Gmail. There are several web-based services the investigator can use to further their investigations. These make using Instant Messaging possible without having to install an application. They include:

- Communication Tube, http://www.communicationtube.net/
- EBuddy, http://www.ebuddy.com/
- IMO, https://imo.im/.

THE BASICS OF HOW INSTANT MESSAGING WORKS

1. User launches the Instant Messaging client.
2. Instant Messaging client finds the Instant Messaging server and logs in.
3. It sends communication info (IP address, etc.) to the Instant Messaging server.
4. Instant Messaging server finds user's contacts and sends him/her the communication info for the ones online.
5. Instant Messaging server also tells the contacts that the user is online; sends his/her communication info to them.
6. Now the user's and the contact's Instant Messaging clients are ready to communicate directly.
7. As new contacts come online, the Instant Messaging server informs them about the user being online. Multiple, simultaneous conversations are possible.
8. When the user logs off, his/her Instant Messaging client informs the Instant Messaging server.
9. The Instant Messaging server informs the user's contacts about the change to an "offline" status.

INSTANT MESSAGING SERVER

So why does an Instant Messaging require a server in the first place? And why doesn't the Instant Messaging client look for the user's contacts without the Instant Messaging server's help? Most Instant Messaging users do not have permanent IP addresses. They are assigned temporary IP addresses by their Internet service provider (ISP) each time they connect to the Internet (dynamically). The server-based Instant Messaging scheme removes the need of having permanent IP numbers to communicate to and from. It also gives users true mobility, allowing them Instant Messaging use from any Internet-connected computer that has a messaging application.

Internet Relay Chat

IRC relies on the existence of "channels," communication spaces dedicated to dialogue among a specific group of participants. This method involves a multiuser system of servers that are connected to each other to create networks. IRC is a well-documented protocol with several Requests for Comments guiding the systems. IRC was created in the late 1980s at the University of Finland (IRC, n.d.).

It is a real-time chat between two individuals or many individuals discussing a topic in a channel or room. Users can exchange files with each other and set up file servers to provide files to many users. The advantage to this communication method is that IRC usernames and "nicknames" are not verified by any central authority. An individual can truly be who they want to be on IRC. Why does the investigator care about IRC? Over 500,000 people a day connect to IRC channels (IRC, n.d.). With that many people using one protocol there is bound to be a victim somewhere and there surely will be a criminal to catch.

IRC participants communicate in user-created rooms. Any user can open a room and control the room. Individuals can send or trade photos or other files

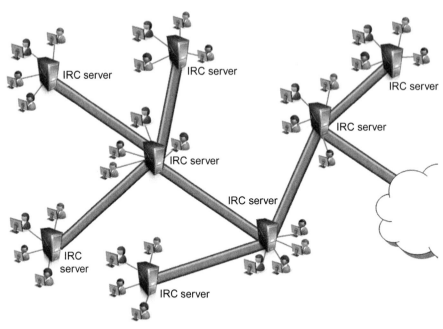

FIGURE 15.3

How IRC works.

with other users. IRC participants can also set up a server to automatically trade/ or distribute photos or files commonly referred to as an Fserve. In the chatrooms, multiple users can be in the same chat room at the same time. Each users is identified by a screen or "nick" name. Public chatrooms cover a broad range of topics, such as sports, cooking, and children. Each chatroom content is accessible by everyone in the chatroom while the conversation is taking place. Private chatrooms between users can be created and require an invitation by the channel owner to gain access (Figure 15.3).

Connecting to an IRC

The IRC network is a collection of servers linked together using the IRC protocol. Connecting to IRC requires using an IRC application. Users are then connected to an IRC server. The connecting IRC server is determined by the IRC network the user selects. The server knows who is on the network and what channel (room) users are in as they chat. The IRC server feeds the channels and the chatted text to the users connected to the server. The servers pass the user's chat in the various channels between the servers connected throughout IRC. User's can then chat with anyone in a channel anywhere in the IRC network. Internet latency and speed when using IRC depends on the location of the server in conjunction with the user. It is best to connect to a server geographically close to the user for a faster response. Some channels are *open* to anyone to access and chat with other channel members. Others are *private* and only accessible by invitation of the channel owner. Channels have topics set which are generally descriptive by the channel name. Investigators looking for a particular type of room can usually find them by a particular channel title.

Chat language

IRC early on in its existence began to build its own language. To make conversations faster users shortened up the words used by making acronyms out of terms and short sentences. "brb" or Be Right Back is an example of the shortening of the language used in the chatrooms. Over time a significant number of acronyms came into use and lists of the acronyms used were needed to identify what was being said. Table 15.1 contains a few of the more common acronyms developed to facilitate communicating over IRC. You'll recognize that many of them have come into mainstream use, especially in texting on cell phones.

Logging onto an IRC server

Fully accessing the IRC requires the investigator use a software application referred to as a client. IRC clients depend on the operating systems used. There are many applications to gain access to IRC. Both Windows and Apple Macintosh systems have software available for accessing IRC. Common on Windows systems is mIRC (http://www.mirc.com/) and on Macintosh is Ircle (http://www.ircle.com/). Both applications give the investigator access to the many features of the IRC protocol and the various servers containing the channels that might be of investigative interest. Two popular IRC server networks are DALnet (www.dal.net) and Undernet (www.undernet.org). The location the investigator actually goes to will ultimately depend on the facts of the case and the channel in use related to the investigation. mIRC has a logging feature that allows the investigator to select automatic logging of the channels and the chat.

Joining a channel (chatroom)

Effective access to IRC requires a desktop application. One of the most popular as mentioned is mIRC. This application allows access to all of the IRC servers. mIRC allows easy access to the IRC system through its user panel.

Channel operators, referred to as the "Bosses" or "ops," maintain absolute control of the channel. The "Ops" decide who gets to enter the channel, who gets kicked out, and who may talk. The Channel operators will have the "@" in front of their nickname. There are two ways to become a channel operator: (1) create a channel and (2) be made an operator by an existing channel operator. Users in the channel are designated by the "#" sign preceding their channel names. Channel names are not case sensitive.

Table 15.1 Chat Acronyms

brb = be right back	:-^) with flu
bbl = be back later	:-)^ choking
btw = by the way	:'-(crying
np = no problem	:-@ shouting
lol = laughing out loud	:-& can't talk
re = hi again, as in 're hi'	-:-) punk
rotfl = rolling on the floor laughing	|:-) fall sleep
bbiaf = be back in a flash	:-O waking up
ttfn = ta ta for now	0:-) angel
imho = in my humble opinion	:-D laughing
j/k = just kidding	:-X lips seal
wb = welcome back	:-Q smoker
Emoticons	:-/ skeptic
:) Smile	C = :-) chef
:-) Basic Smile	@ = nuclear bomb
;-) eye wink	*:O) clown
:-(sad	[:-) using walkman
:-I Indifference	(:I egghead
:-> Sarcastic	@:-) with turban
>:-> Diabolic	X-(just died
(-: left handed	:] friendly smile
%-) Drunk	:D laugh
8-) Uses glasses	:(again sad
B:-) Sunglasses on head	:O shouting
B-) dark sunglasses	[] hugs
8:-) little girl	:* kisses
:-() Mustache	:*,;* more kisses
:-()painted mouth	:*,:*,:*,:*, more and more kisses
{:-)with hair	

ROBOTS EXIST

IRC has robots called channel bots that are designed to help channel operators maintain control of their channel. They perform automated functions that allow operators to control the channel. Robots are also by criminals to control malware bots infecting computers worldwide.

HOW CAN YOU IDENTIFY A BOT?

Code writers intentionally make identifying bots harder. Bots can be programed to respond to another user and might appear real. Here are a few possible things to consider when trying to identify a "nick" as a bot:

1. Usually the bots are quiet, unless another user tries to talk to them, or something on the channel occurs that makes the bot react.
2. Seeing the same nick setting mode +o or kicking people (kicking them out of the room).
3. Never seeing the nick talking.
4. Look for "bot" or "srv" in the nickname or username (use the command/whois <nick> to get the users name).
5. Examine the username field for a "bot" command in parentheses.

EXAMPLE IRC COMMANDS

IRC commands are preceded by "/."

/whois <nickname>: Identifies the nicknames self-input information, channels they are ops on the server that they are logged into to access IRC and the hosts IP address.
/dcc send <nickname> [file1] [file2] [file3]...[fileN]: Sends the specified file (s>to nick.
/dcc chat <nickname>: Opens a dcc window and sends a dcc chat request to nickname.
/describe <#channel><action text>: Sends the specified action to the specified channel window.
/dns <nickname | IP address | IP name>: Uses your providers DNS to resolve an IP address.

Hiding in IRC

IRC can be accessed using a proxy server or through the Tor network. Using a proxy allows users to connect to chat servers sending the traffic through the proxy server. The proxy server forwards the chat messages from the user through the proxy server to the IRC server and channel. What is exposed is the IP address of the proxy server on the IRC server. This helps to hide the investigator's real IP address from others on the IRC channels investigated. Obviously the reverse is possible and the investigator should be aware that IP addresses found on IRC should not be immediately thought of as the target's actual IP address without significant investigation to determine that the IP is the target's actual IP address. You can find an updated list of proxy servers intended just for IRC at http://irc-proxies.blogspot.com/. The investigator can also use the list to determine if an IP address identified on IRC is potentially a proxy. You can connect to IRC through a proxy while using mIRC. You can set up a proxy in mIRC's Proxy settings section of the options dialog box (**ALT + O>Connect>Proxy**). The investigator needs to be aware that some IRC servers may ban the use of proxies and Tor if found.

IRC: THE INTERNET'S UNDERBELLY

Investigators going to IRC, particularly those working child exploitation cases, will unfortunately find, more than enough criminal activity to investigate. Seasoned investigators frequently described focusing on the most serious cases, those who appear to be actively victimizing children. There is just too much trading and simple possession in IRC channels to divert scare resources to its investigation.

Web browser access to IRC

Access to some IRC servers can be done through web interfaces. There are several websites that provide the investigator with access to some IRC servers. The investigator can use these as a quick means of accessing these IRC servers and channels of interest. Some of these websites include:

- freenode Web IRC, https://webchat.freenode.net/
- IRC.NETSPLIT.DE, http://irc.netsplit.de/about/
- irc2go, http://irc2go.com/
- Mibbit Chat Network, http://www.mibbit.com/
- The DALnet IRC Network, http://www.dal.net/
- Undernet IRC Network, http://www.undernet.org/webchat.php.

Tracking criminals in IRC

IP addresses can be identified for users while in IRC. The investigator can use the whois command to gain information about a possible target. Depending on the IRC server, the IP address can appear in the user's chat messages after their nickname. However, some IRC networks hide the user's IP address or hostname automatically on connection. For those that don't the IP address of users is exposed for everyone on the channel to see or query. This is of course if the user is not attempting to hide his address from others on the IRC channel.

When using mIRC as your IRC investigative tool, you can right click on the username and select "who is" or "info." This will provide the investigator with the IP address of the user, the server in use and channels where they are channel operators. An investigator who can act as a channel operator can monitor habits and methodologies of users which can be extremely useful in investigations. This of course means that the investigator spends enough time on the channel or channels in questions to become a well-respected member of the channel. The investigator has also to spent the time developing an undercover persona and preplanning the operational aspects of the investigation as we have discussed in previous chapters (Figure 15.4).

IRC resources

The following are some general resources that can assist the investigator understand IRC further:

- An IRC Tutorial, http://www.irchelp.org/irchelp/irctutorial.html

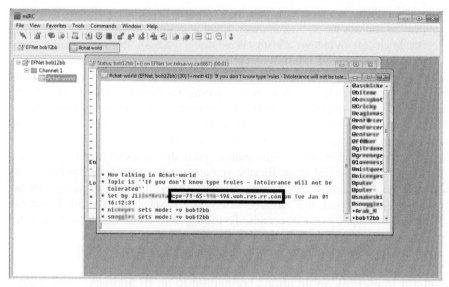

FIGURE 15.4

mIRC with IP address of users.

- IRC Beginner, http://www.ircbeginner.com
- #IRChelp, http://www.irchelp.org/
- mIRC, http://www.mirc.com/
- The IRC Prelude http://www.irchelp.org/irchelp/new2irc.html.

Identifying targets through communication protocols

Identifying targets on the Internet using the various communication protocols is somewhat of an investigative challenge. The investigator has to have an understanding of the communication protocol used and how the investigator's local machine communicates through that protocol to the target. However, there are opportunities for identification of a target which are discussed below.

Netstat

Netstat is a common TCP/IP networking utility command line available in most versions of Windows, Linux, Unix, and other operating systems. Netstat provides information and statistics about protocols in use and current TCP/IP network connections. It can be used to trap the target's IP address from incoming applications like Instant Messaging when sending a file between users. Something to remember when doing this technique is that it may not work due to networking complications. Additionally, the file transferred usually needs to be large enough to allow for Netstat to capture the IP address of the system transferring the file. Also with Client/Server applications, you may capture the Server's IP used with the application and not the client computer actually sending the file.

On Microsoft Windows (Vista, Windows 7 and 8), the investigator using Netstat can reveal active transmission control protocol (TCP) connections sent and received on the local machine. Close all tabs in your browser and all active connections except the chat application the investigator is using. Additionally delete all cookies from browser to prevent your browser from making previous connections. Doing these actions will limit the number of items making a connection so it will be easier to identify the connections of interest. Open a command prompt in Windows by clicking on the start button and in the "Search Programs and File" box type "CMD" and hit enter. Be sure you are accessing the local machine as an Administrator to have the tool work properly. Executing the following Netstat command line, "netstat -o 3" displays active TCP connections. The 3 tells Netstat to run the command every 3 seconds. To display active TCP connections and the process IDs using numerical form, type the following command netstat -no. Table 15.2 provides numerous Netstat command options (Figure 15.5).

Netstat to identify applications connected to an IP address

Netstat can be used to get IPs of anything and anyone, as long as there is a *direct connection* between you and the target (i.e., direct messages, file transfers, or ICQ chats in ICQ, DCC (Direct Client Connection) chat, and file transfers in IRC). This is of course also depends on the target not using any anonymous IP hiding technique. To get an IP address of an application using Netstat first identify the IP addresses of the local machine before connecting with the target. This will be a baseline of the IP addresses the local machine applications are already using and communicating with. Open a command prompt and run the Netstat command "netstat -bano". Copy and paste the data into a Notepad document and save the file. Open a new command prompt and run the command "netstat -bano 2." The "2" tells Netstat to run the command every 2 seconds. This is to allow for the capture of short-lived IP address connections.

Run the application being used in the investigation and communicate with the target using the application. Client/Server applications will be using the applications server to relay messages and any attempts to capture the IP address of a target require that a direct connection be made with the target. This direct connection can possibly allow for the recording of the target's IP address. Once the communication is over, stop Netsat. In the open command window, type Ctrl + C to stop the function. Again copy and paste the data into Notepad and save. Compare the Initial Notepad collection of the baseline of the local machine with the communication capture. The differences should be the IP addresses of the connections made with the application you are using. (Be sure to pay attention to the fact that other applications on the system will be making calls out too. Your antivirus and firewall programs regularly call out to update servers). With the unknown IP addresses, you can identify the ownership information and follow up as previously discussed.

Table 15.2 Netstat

-a	Displays all connections and listening ports
-b	Displays the executable involved in creating each connection or listening port
-e	Displays Ethernet statistics. This may be combined with the -s option
-f	Displays Fully Qualified Domain Names for foreign addresses (in Windows Vista/7 only)
-n	Displays addresses and port numbers in numerical form
-o	Displays the owning process ID associated with each connection
-p	Shows connections for the protocol specified. May be TCP or UDP. If used with the -s option to display per-protocol statistics, protocol may be TCP, UDP, or IP
-r	Displays the routing table
-s	Displays per-protocol statistics. By default, statistics are shown for TCP, UDP, and IP; the -p option may be used to specify a subset of the default
-t	Displays the current connection offload state (Windows Vista/7)
-v	When used in conjunction with -b, will display sequence of components involved in creating the connection or listening port for all executables (Windows XP SP2, SP3)
interval	Redisplays selected statistics, pausing interval seconds between each display. Press Ctrl + C to stop redisplaying statistics. If omitted, netstat will print the current configuration information once
Example	netstat [-a] [-b] [-e] [-f] [-n] [-o] [-p proto] [-r] [-s] [-t] [-v] [interval]
Data Copy	Adding the following to the example » C:\connections.txt dumps the data to a text file

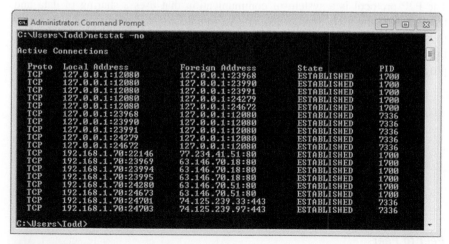

FIGURE 15.5

Netstat listing incoming and outgoing IP addresses.

Netstat the easy way

There are other tools available for collecting the TCP/IP connections of a local machine and the connections that it makes. Using these tools can make identifying a local machine's connections easier for the investigator. They each collect the TCP/IP traffic of the local machine and show connections in real time. Additionally, they identify the programs that made them and the current traffic on the local machine. Finally, they also display the returned data in an easier to view graphical user interface. Several of the available tools for this purpose are:

- CurrPorts, http://www.nirsoft.net/utils/cports.html
- X-Netstat – Professional, http://www.freshsoftware.com/
- TCPView, http://technet.microsoft.com/en-us/sysinternals/bb897437.aspx.

OTHER WAYS TO FIND A USER'S IP ADDRESS

A more sophisticated method of identifying an IP address of a person on the Internet is through a website. The investigator can set up their own web server and trap incoming IP address to a webpage stored locally on the webserver. Or they can use online servers like "What's their IP" (http://whatstheirip.com/). Services like this can assist the investigator in locating an IP address of a target, that is, of course if they are not using any anonymization techniques. Using websites like this are not without risk. Because they are services on the Internet the investigator has no control over the communication and identification of the target's IP address. The investigator needs to evaluate the security of the investigation against the exposure of himself or the investigation by using "free" sites on the Internet.

P2P: protocols and tools

The P2P protocol is a system of communication that uses a sharing of data and files amongst the users of the network. A software client is used to connect a user to the network and then the members of the network can share data between themselves (Figure 15.6). The common types of communication protocols and programs in this category include:

File Sharing Programs
- Bit Torrent Networks: BitTorrent, Inc., http://www.bittorrent.com/, and FrostWire, http://www.frostwire.com/
- eMule, http://www.emule-project.net/home
- Gnutella P2P Networks: Bearshare, http://www.bearshare.com/ and Limeware variations
- Shareaza, http://shareaza.sourceforge.net/: Supports the following P2P networks, Gnutella, Gnutella2, eDonkey, and BitTorrent).

Peer to Peer

P2P technology is one that uses multiple computers to share the data. Data is transferred between the participating users. Each of the users participates as a

FIGURE 15.6

P2P connections between servers and users.

sharing partner in the system. The networked system depends on the participation of the user's computers to process and forwards data among the network. This process is handled by the user's downloaded application which is installed to gain access to the network. P2P is used by many people on the Internet for legitimate purposes. File transferring is one of the most popular uses on the Internet for P2P technology. P2P technology became famous in 2001 when the then music file sharing company Napster was sued for violating the copyrights of records companies by allowing users to access the copyrighted music from Napster's servers (*A&M Records Inc. v. Napster, Inc.*, 239F.3d 1004 (9th Cir. 2001)). What this did for the P2P sharing community was to move the use of P2P technology from one that had centralized servers to a network technology that was decentralized. No longer could you stop illegal activity simply by taking out a master server with an index of data and users.

This presents an issue now for the investigator of P2P networks as no one person or server is responsible for the content being shared over the network. The data is spread over the network and not stored in one location. There are different P2P network variations in use today. The most popular is the Gnutella and Ares networks. Other P2P networks have appeared over the last decade and have been investigated, including Limewire, FastTrack, BitTorrent, eDonkey, and GigaTribe. Skype which is probably one of the most popular messaging programs on the Internet also uses P2P techniques for sharing of its user's communications. This technology changes all the time and applications come and go. Investigating P2P networks has become a mainstay of child pornography investigators. These investigations initially were a very tightly held investigative technique. Law enforcement early on identified that the P2P sharing concept was a protocol that could be successfully investigated. The use of the Peer Spectre software came to public knowledge after Flint Waters, then a Special Agent for the State of Wyoming, testified before Congress in 2007 about law enforcements investigations into the P2P networks. The use of P2P investigative software began in 2005 under the name Operation Fairplay. Waters (2007) stated in his testimony regarding law enforcement investigations into the trading of child pornography that the numbers of identified traders included:

> *There have been 1,519,791 unique IP addresses identified in the United States. If the breakdown were constant with the results in Wyoming that would indicate 504,947 individuals identified throughout the United States in the last 3 years. This is a rough estimate but again, it only pertains to one of many P2P systems and does not include other methods of trading child sexual abuse material.*

Investigating P2P networks

Investigating P2P is a complicated process that involves understanding the protocol and its operation. The function of the file sharing is based on the sharing of data files. The sharing is accomplished through the networks by identifying the hash values of the files traded. The programs then know if the file is on a particular user's computer (the file has the same hash value) and can then make that file available for sharing among the users connected to the network. The investigation of P2P is done through the collection and examination of these hashes and identifying which hash value matches known contraband. Some might think this collection of data is a violation of the 4th amendment. According to *United States v. Willard*, 2010 U.S. Dist. LEXIS 98216 (E.D. Va. September 20, 2010), the Peer Spectre program used to identify P2P downloaders of child pornography is not a wiretap nor does it violate the Fourth Amendment. The court noted: "Peer Spectre does not acquire communications contemporaneously with the transfer of data from one IP address to another. Instead, it reads publicly available advertisements from computers identified as offering images of child pornography for distribution and identifies their IP addresses."

P2P INVESTIGATIONS AROUND THE WORLD

The use of Peer Spectre and the other P2P investigation tools in US law enforcements inventory has spawned the development of other tools. EspiaMule (SpyMule) is a tool designed by Brazilian law enforcement for criminal investigations centering on Internet trading of child pornography through P2P networks. Other law enforcement agencies around the world have addressed the issues surrounding child pornography on the P2P networks. The NordicMule developed by The Norway National Criminal Investigative Service is based on the eMule software, which operates on the eDonkey network.

Accessing P2P sites Accessing a P2P network requires downloading the software for that network. The investigator should follow all the steps we suggest in Chapter 7 regarding setting up an investigative computer. Access these sites is not without possible exposure of the investigation to others on the network. Using the P2P software requires that the investigation connects to the network. Depending on the option of the software, the premise behind P2P is that the users share the resources of their attached computers to the benefit of the network. If the investigator installs the P2P software on his work machine, he could potentially be exposing the agency/company network to the P2P network and users. Be aware what options are being selected during the installation process and document them.

Each of the programs provides the user access to the network and provides access to the available files. This is usually done by a search function or a listing of files that the users can select which files are of interest and download the files. The software identifies the files of interest and downloads the files from other computers sharing space with the network. The shared files are contained on the user's local machine and available for others to access. Investigators can download the files and determine the file contents. Additionally, the investigative tools mentioned above work through the unique hash of the files stored throughout the network on the user's shared space. The networks know the individual files based on this file hash. This enables the file to be uniquely identified on the network. Law enforcement tools like Peer Spectre track the unique file hash for contraband files previously identified as child pornography. A similar process is also used by investigators tracking pirated software, music, and movies being traded on P2P networks.

Bulletin boards

Bulletin boards are similar to the client server model in that a server controls the communication, but in this instance the data is stored on a server and accessed by users. The data is posted for everyone to see and download through a web browser or a software client. Users do not make direct connections with each other but post information on the server that is accessible by other users (Figure 15.7). The common types of communication protocols and programs in this category include:

- Auction sites
- Newsgroups
- Usenet.

Bulletin boards prior to the advent of the public Internet in 1994 were one of the most popular means of communication. They still hold a fascination with Internet users and many bulletin board style websites have developed and matured the concept over the intervening years. Still in existence and use is the USENET more commonly referred to as Newsgroups Protocol RFC 3877 describes the Network News Transfer Protocol (NNTP).

Usenet along with various sites used to post information are still popular places among Internet users. Google has Google Groups, Craigslist is extremely popular and even the various auction sites such as eBay are as popular as ever. Across the world, sites like 4Chan give the Internet users a certain amount of freedom to post and say what they want and provide a rich field of information for the investigator. All of these various sites can have a huge impact on an investigation. Any place where people hang out there are going to be crimes and

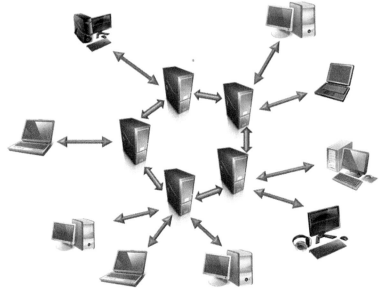

FIGURE 15.7

Bulletin board connections between servers and users.

evidence of the crimes. Posting sites have become places for prostitution and those that prey on prostitutes. In Boston, the infamous Craigslist killer looked to that site for his targets. Fraud has also been a common theme on bulletin board sites. Criminals have offered for sale items that don't exist and collected money from their victims without delivering the goods. Investigators can't overlook these sites as a source of information and investigation.

USENET newsgroups or bulletin boards

The traditional bulletin board protocol is USENET, which USENET uses the NNTP as its communication standard. These newsgroups are public discussion groups that generally require a client software to access the newsgroup feeds. There is a variety of newsgroup readers that the investigator can use to access newsgroups. The group discussion is in a hierarchical setup. The user subscribes to a group they are interested in and can then post and retrieve messages and attachments from the discussion board. The boards allow users to post a message and this permits every reader in that specific group to read the message and download any attachments. The topics range from computer certifications, new-born babies to very bazaar sexual related topics. Most ISPs have access to tens of thousands of different newsgroups. Each newsgroup can hold thousands of post-ings, which can contain just text, images, and other files. Anyone accessing a public newsgroup can view the postings and/or post their own responses. Private newsgroups can be created between users and require an invitation to gain access. These newsgroups can be moderated or unmoderated. Most are unmoderated with no control over what is said or posted.

Understanding USENET as an investigative tool

Prior to going onto newsgroups, investigators should thoroughly research their protocol. Choose a category and then select a topic. Be aware that "ALT," standing for alternative is where the nonstandard material is, i.e., "bad stuff", or in the investigator's case the most interesting. Users have no requirement or approval methods for forming a group. You will see variously named groups based on their content. Moderators name the group something attractive to get users into their rooms. This is much like an old-time carnival barker trying to attract patrons to a sideshow. These groups are unorganized, huge, and not suitable for minors (the Wild West of Usenet). For simple research on newsgroups, the investigator can go to Google Groups (http://groups.google.com/) to locate and review basic groups and information. However, Google Groups may not have all of the "Alt" content that may be required in your investigation. A serious investigation would require a USENET client to access all of the available sites possibly having the information the investigator is looking for as evidence. Generally, your ISP will have a news or NNTP server so you can access and investigate newsgroups.

COMMON USENET GROUPS

- comp (computers)
- humanities (arts and culture)
- misc (miscellaneous)
- news (news and current events)
- rec (recreational)
- sci (science)
- soc (social)
- talk (general discussion).

  The Common but Ugly groups

  The Alt world…
  - "Alternative"
  - Anything goes
    - Images
    - Movies
    - Text.

Investigate all newsgroups and chatrooms carefully before subscribing. Are you investigating a particular user or just trolling for crime? There are advantages and disadvantages with the exploring of Usenet. The investigator can quickly connect to a global network of individuals with similar interests. It can be a springboard for ideas and facts. Users can say nearly anything (very little you can't). Moderated groups could boot a user if the content was not appropriate. The disadvantages are that it is a global group. This can sometimes put the targets well out of the investigator's jurisdiction. It can also be very difficult to ascertain the quality of the information posted in a site. Anything goes and that includes telling the truth or not. USENET postings and users can easily be abusive in their posts. On unmoderated sites there is little in the way of repercussions for misconduct. The groups are complex and loosely organized. They also have had an ongoing frustration level with bots and spammers filling up groups with nothing.

Newsgroup had a lot to do with the origination of the terms "Netiquette" or "network etiquette." They are the unofficial rules defining the proper Internet behavior, e.g., sending spam and unwanted emails is bad netiquette. A "Flame" is an insult or derogatory message sent via email, USENET, or mailing lists to a person or group. Emoticons (smileys), "emotion icons," are used to represent human facial expressions and convey an emotion on the Internet. They are created from typing certain characters on your keyboard, e.g., ":-)" is a smile. Acronyms and abbreviation or Internet slang was first defined on USENET and is now in use as common parlance amongst many in the real world.

With the advent of instant messaging, AOL and Yahoo groups, blogs and other social networking, USENET isn't used by much of the Internet population. In fact many ISPs don't support USENET any longer. This is partly due to the fact that there are no controls and denying access USENET gave them a sense of control over the bad content. Accessing newsgroups now is usually done through one of the pay services, which is probably the best option for the investigator. These services provide better access to the newsgroups and most of them have browser interfaces. Below are a few such pay services:

- Astraweb, http://www.giganews.com
- GigaNews, http://astraweb.com/
- Newshosting, http://www.newshosting.com/.

Google Groups

Google Groups might look like it has the USENET all in one place, but it doesn't. It is a small subset of the data that passes through the USENET each day. It can be useful for some purposes and may contain the investigative data you are looking for but don't bet on it. Searching Google Groups does not require a login. Making your own group does, however, require the user to login using a Gmail account. Simply go to www.google.com, click on "More" drop down, access the Google products page and select "Groups." Google Groups have a search function that will provide a list of search term matches similar to their normal search engine (Figure 15.8).

Locating free Usenet servers

Free Usenet/News servers are still available. They are slow and may not be there tomorrow when you go back. Most of these servers are located outside of the United States and accessible from anywhere in the world. The following sites have been around for a significant amount of time and provide the investigator with a resource for finding USENET servers that can be accessed without a fee.

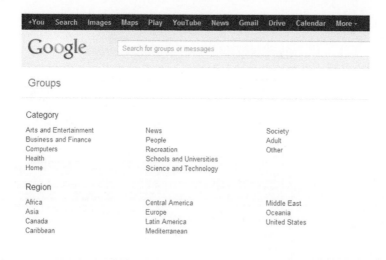

FIGURE 15.8

Google groups.

- List of Free NNTP News Servers, http://www.elfqrin.com/mine/nntpserv.html
- Newsbot, http://www.newzbot.com/
- Open Directory Free Server Listing, http://dmoz.org/Computers/Usenet/ Public_News_Servers/
- Premium-news (German site), http://www.premium-news.com/public.htm
- Public USENET Servers, http://usenet__servers.tripod.com/.

Investigative tools for USENET

Investigative accessing the USENET can be done using any of the freely available tools on the Internet. However, they all have a variety of user interfaces and your personal preference will drive what you use. Forte Agent News Reader (http://www.forteinc.com/) (Figure 15.9), Newsbin Pro (http://www.newsbin.com/), and Thunderbird Mail (http://www.mozilla.org/en-US/thunderbird/) are a few of the available news readers that can be employed by the investigator. USENET is an anonymous service and posts containing information such as the user's name and email can be false. Users can also access the newsgroup services through anonymization tools and Virtual Private Networks to hide their information and true IP addresses. In the USENET message is a header similar to an email header. The information has the email like received line and a line with the IP address of the poster at "NNTP-Posting Host." There is the user's email address which is self-reported (Figure 15.10).

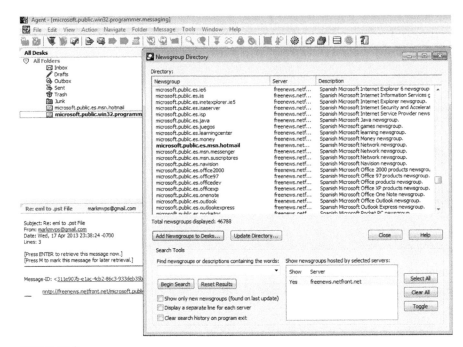

FIGURE 15.9

Forte agent news reader showing directory and subscribed groups.

```
X-Received: by 10.███.██.██ with SMTP id bu13mr490670wib.1.1375430073312;
    Fri, 02 Aug 2013 00:54:33 -0700 (PDT)
X-Received: by 10.██.██.1 with SMTP id ee1mr591911gb.5.1375430073142; Fri, 02
    Aug 2013 00:54:33 -0700 (PDT)
Path: news.netfront.net!news.unit0.net!feeder1.cambriumusenet.nl!feed.tweaknews.nl!209.85.212.216.MISMATCH!el7no1
Newsgroups: microsoft.public.win32.programmer.messaging
Date: Fri, 2 Aug 2013 00:54:32 -0700 (PDT)
Complaints-To: groups-abuse@google.com
Injection-Info: glegroupsg2000goo.googlegroups.com; posting-host=122.███.███.██;
    posting-account=5Mr4ggoAAAC_F6AtFVBNmVups2NinK_Aw
NNTP-Posting-Host: 122.███.███.██
User-Agent: G2/1.0
MIME-Version: 1.0
Message-ID: <874d5812-62af-445e-968d-2████████████d@googlegroups.com>
Subject: MAPI Calendar C++
From: ████ ████ <████████@gmail.com>
Injection-Date: Fri, 02 Aug 2013 07:54:33 +0000
Content-Type: text/plain; charset=ISO-8859-1
Xref: news.netfront.net microsoft.public.win32.programmer.messaging:2
X-Antivirus: avast! (VPS 130813-1, 08/13/2013), Inbound message
X-Antivirus-Status: Clean
```

FIGURE 15.10

USENET message header (IP addresses are obfuscated).

CONFIGURING THUNDERBIRD AS AN INVESTIGATIVE USENET READER

Mozilla's Thunderbird Mail client is a free tool that can be incorporated as a newsreader. To get started with Thunderbird as your investigative tool, follow these instructions:

1. Start Thunderbird and go to "File," then "New" and then "Other Accounts."
2. Select "Newsgroup Account" and click "next.
3. At this point it will ask for a name and email account. Be aware that this is what will be posted to the newsgroup. Insert your undercover persona name and email here.
4. Enter the address of the newsgroup server that you are investigating or using for access during the investigation.
5. Enter your under cover persona name for the account.
6. Once the account is configured, right click on the account name and select "Subscribe." Select the groups to join.
7. Modifying the account information can be done by right clicking the account name and select "Settings." Thunderbird will download the various pieces of large posts, but it may not put the pieces together such as an image broken up into multiple parts. Additional software may be required to put the image pieces together.

Online bulletin boards

Online bulletin boards have developed into popular online location for trading information, products, and personal contacts. Many of these sites started as small local or regional places to connect with other people. Some have grown into large corporations providing services to Internet users worldwide. These services can have very different methods of engaging their users. Auction sites like eBay (http://www.ebay.com/) have developed into regular places for users to purchase items and have facilitated some small business entry into worldwide market. Sites like Craigslist (http://www.craigslist.org/) have found a market to engage users at the community level. It facilitates the trading and connecting of users within their communities. Other sites like 4Chan (http://www.4chan.org/) have developed into communication mediums for the users in geographic regions that might not allow the freedom of speech that most western countries enjoy. Investigatively each of these sites has its own issues. The larger commercial sites have legal service sections that can be contacted to assist with identifying users who may have committed a crime on the service. They each will require legal service to obtain the user data (Figure 15.11).

As we mentioned in previous chapters, Exif data can still be an investigative tool used in bulletin board investigations. The investigator should attempt to identify if there is any Exif metadata available in postings that they are investigating. Sites like 4Chan that allow user's postings of images do not delete the Exif data of user's uploaded images.

Craigslist

Craigslist is a centralized network of online communities, which features free online classified advertisements of jobs, housing, personal ads, for sale/barter/

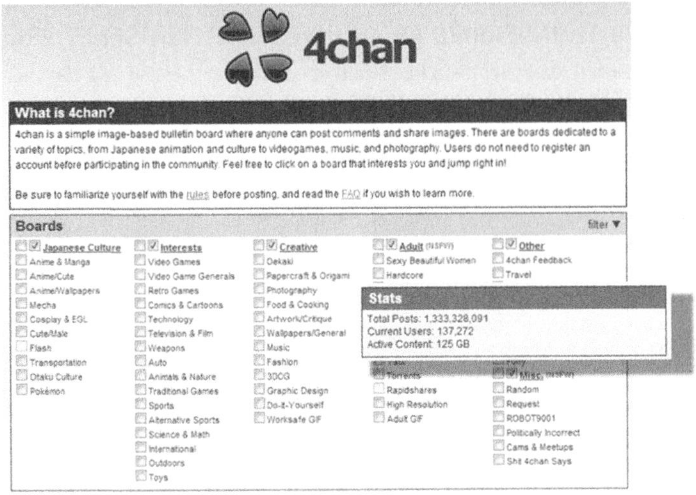

FIGURE 15.11

4Chan main page and stats.

wanted items, services, pet categories and forums on various topics. To search Craigslist, you don't need to make an account. Go to the Craigslist website, enter the geographic location (state and city) to search and enter the search term and select area to search (Figure 15.12). There are third party tools to assist with searching Craigslist like:

- CraigsList Notifier, http://craigslistnotifier.net/
- CraigsList Search, http://www.craigslistsearch.org/
- List-Alert, http://www.list-alert.com/
- TinkOmatic, http://www.tinkomatic.com/.

USING GOOGLE ALERTS FOR CRAIGSLIST INVESTIGATIONS

Investigators can also setup Google alerts for Craigslist. The investigator needs to have a Gmail account for this purpose but that can easily be done. Go to google.com/alerts and login. Simply set the alert for the term you are looking for and use the operator "Site:" with craigslist.com (<your search term> site:craiglist.com).

PORTABLE APPLICATIONS FOR INTERNET COMMUNICATIONS

Recall from earlier in this text our discussion of Portable Applications. Well, there are such applications to access P2P networks, Usenet, IRC, and instant message services. See Portable Applications (http://portableapps.com) for more information.

craigslist

US   Canada   Europe   Asia/Pacific/Middle East   Oceania   Latin America   Africa

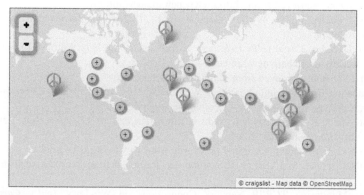

FIGURE 15.12

Craigslist.

CONCLUSION

This chapter has introduced to the investigator several different communication methods over the Internet. This introduction is intended to provide a basic understanding of messaging, chatting, and newsgroups. The amount of information available through these communication means require that investigators be familiar with them and understand their potential to contain useful information. What is important for the investigator to understand is that each of these Internet communication methods can be investigated. However, it takes some time and planning on the investigator's part to understand the technology and prepare for the investigation.

Further reading

A&M Records Inc. v. Napster, Inc., 239F.3d 1004 (9th Cir. 2001). Retrieved from <http://www.law.cornell.edu/copyright/cases/239_F3d_1004.htm/>.

Agent=Usenet+Email. (n.d.). *Agent=Usenet+Email*. Retrieved from <http://www.forteinc.com/>.

AIM Chat, Share, Connect. (n.d.). *AIM*. Retrieved from <www.aim.com/>.

Baloc's Public News Servers. (n.d.). *Baloc's Public News Servers*. Retrieved from <http://usenet__servers.tripod.com/>.

#Beginner—IRC Commands, the Basics. (n.d.). *#Beginner Website, Undernet—2003*. Retrieved from <http://www.ircbeginner.com/ircinfo/ircc-commands.html/>.

#Beginner Website, Undernet— 2003. (n.d.). *#Beginner Website, Undernet—2003*. Retrieved from <http://www.ircbeginner.com/>.

Beginner's Guide to Newsgroup Newsreaders. (n.d.). *Beginner's Guide to Newsgroup Newsreaders*. Retrieved from <http://www.newsreaders.info/>.

BitTorrent—Delivering the World's Content. (n.d.). *BitTorrent*. Retrieved from <www.bittorrent.com/>.

Caraballo, D. & Lo, J. (n.d.). *IRCHelp.org: Internet relay chat help*. Retrieved from http://www.irchelp.org/irchelp/new2irc.html/>.

4chan. (n.d.). *4chan*. Retrieved from <http://www.4chan.org/>.

Communication Tube—icq/gtalk/irc/msn Web-based Messenger!. (n.d.). *Communication Tube*. Retrieved from <http://www.communicationtube.net/>.

Craigslist Alerts at List-Alert.com. (n.d.). *Craigslist Alerts at List-Alert.com*. Retrieved from <http://www.list-alert.com/>.

Craigslist classifieds. (n.d.). *Craigslist*. Retrieved from <www.craigslist.org/>.

CraigslistNotifier.net. (n.d.). *CraigslistNotifier.net*. Retrieved from <http://craigslistnotifier.net/>.

CurrPorts: Monitoring TCP/IP Network Connections on Windows. (n.d.). *CurrPorts: NirSoft*. Retrieved from <http://www.nirsoft.net/utils/cports.html/>.

Digsby=IM+Email+Social Networks. (n.d.). *Digsby*. Retrieved from <http://www.digsby.com/>.

Electronics, Cars, Fashion, Collectibles, Coupons and More Online Shopping: eBay. (n.d.). *eBay*. Retrieved from <http://www.ebay.com/>.

eMule-Project.net—Official eMule Homepage. (n.d.). eMule-Project.net. Retrieved from <www.emule-project.net/home/>.

Extensible Messaging and Presence Protocol (XMPP): Core. (n.d.). *The XMPP Standards Foundation*. Retrieved from <http://xmpp.org/rfcs/rfc3920.html/>.

Fagundes, P. (n.d.). Fighting Internet child pornography: The Brazilian experience. *Police Chief Magazine*. Retrieved from <www.policechiefmagazine.org/magazine/index.cfm?fuseaction=display_arch&article_id=1892&issue_id=92009/>.

File-sharing programspeer-to-peer networks provide ready access to child pornography: *Report to the Chairman and Ranking Minority Member*, Committee on Government Reform, House of Representatives. (2003). Washington, DC: U.S. General Accounting Office.

Free music downloads—Download free music today with BearShare. (n.d.). *BearShare*. Retrieved from <http://www.bearshare.com/>.

Freenode IRC. (n.d.). *Freenode IRC*. Retrieved from <https://webchat.freenode.net/>.

Fresh Software. (n.d.). *Fresh Software*. Retrieved from <http://www.freshsoftware.com/>.

Frosted limes: The unintended consequences of shutting down LimeWire. (n.d.). *DFI News*. Retrieved from <http://www.dfinews.com/articles/2010/11/frosted-limes-unintended-consequences-shutting-down-limewire#.UgiCA5LVDpU/>.

FrostWire.com—Share Big Files—BitTorrent App, Media Player, Wi-Fi Sharing. Official Website. (n.d.). *FrostWire.com*. Retrieved from <http://www.frostwire.com/>.

Google Groups. (n.d.). *Google*. Retrieved from <groups.google.com/>.

History of IRC (Internet relay chat). (n.d.). *Daniel.haxx.se—Daniel Stenberg*. Retrieved from <http://daniel.haxx.se/irchistory.html/>.

How to find someone's IP address. (n.d.). *How to find someone's IP address.* Retrieved from <http://whatstheirip.com/>.

ICQ. (n.d.). *ICQ.* Retrieved from <http://www.icq.com/>.

Index of /history_docs/. (n.d.). *IRC.org—Home of IRC.* Retrieved from <http://www.irc.org/history_docs/>.

Instant Messaging and Group Chat App imo Messenger. (n.d.). *imo messenger.* Retrieved from <https://imo.im/>.

Internet Relay Chat—IRC—irc.netsplit.de. (n.d.). *IRC.NETSPLIT.DE.* Retrieved from <http://irc.netsplit.de/>.

Internet Relay Chat Help. (n.d.). *Internet Relay Chat Help.* Retrieved from <www.irchelp.org/>.

IRC Proxy Servers. (n.d.). *IRC Proxy Servers.* Retrieved from <http://irc-proxies.blogspot.com/>.

IRC.org. (n.d.). *IRC.org—Home of IRC.* Retrieved from <http://www.irc.org/history_docs/jarkko.html/>.

irc2go—Chat Rooms—Online Chat—irc2go.com. (n.d.). *irc2go.* Retrieved from <http://irc2go.com/>.

IRCHelp.org: An IRC Tutorial. (n.d.). *Internet relay chat help.* Retrieved from <http://www.irchelp.org/irchelp/irctutorial.html/>.

ircle.com. (n.d.). *ircle.com.* Retrieved from <http://www.ircle.com/>.

Laurie, V. (n.d.). *Netstat command and its application in Windows.* Retrieved from <http://commandwindows.com/netstat.htm/>.

Mibbit Chat Network. (n.d.). *Mibbit Chat Network.* Retrieved from <http://www.mibbit.com/>.

Microsoft Windows XP—Netstat (n.d.). *Microsoft Windows.* Retrieved from <www.microsoft.com/resources/documentation/windows/xp/all/proddocs/en-us/netstat.mspx?mfr = true>, <http://commandwindows.com/netstat.htm/>.

Miranda IM—Home of the Miranda IM client. Smaller, Faster, Easier. (n.d.). *Miranda IM.* Retrieved from <http://www.miranda-im.org/>.

mIRC: Internet Relay Chat Client. (n.d.). *mIRC.* Retrieved from <http://www.mirc.com/>.

mIRC: Personal FAQ. (n.d.). *mIRC: Internet relay chat client.* Retrieved from <http://www.mirc.com/khaled/faq.html/>.

Mozilla Thunderbird. (n.d.). *Mozilla.* Retrieved from <http://www.mozilla.org/en-US/thunderbird/>.

Multiple Craigslist Search; Monitor eBay, Kijiji, Oodle Classifieds. (n.d.). *Multiple Craigslist Search.* Retrieved from <http://www.tinkomatic.com/>.

Netstat. (n.d.). *Resources and tools for IT professionals: TechNet.* Retrieved from <http://technet.microsoft.com/en-us/library/ff961504.aspx/>.

News.astraweb.com—Usenet News Server. (n.d.). *News.astraweb.com.* Retrieved from <http://astraweb.com/>.

Newsbin Pro Software, Usenet Downloading Tool | NNTP Usenet Binary Newsgroup Robot. (n.d.). *Newsbin Pro Software.* Retrieved from <http://www.newsbin.com/>.

Newzbot! Public USENET Resources for the Masses. (n.d.). *Newzbot!* Retrieved from <www.newzbot.com/>.

Open Directory—Computers Usenet Public News Servers. (n.d.). *Open Directory—Computers Usenet Public News Servers.* Retrieved from dmoz.org/Computers/Usenet/Public_News_Servers/>.

Pidgin, the Universal Chat Client. (n.d.). *Pidgin*. Retrieved from <http://www.pidgin.im/>.

PortableApps.com—Portable software for USB, Portable and Cloud Drives. (n.d.). *PortableApps.com*. Retrieved from <http://portableapps.com/>.

Premium News—Premium Usenet Binaries Newsserver, Weltweit, Unzensiert, Anonym. (n.d.). *Premium News*. Retrieved from <www.premium-news.com/public.htm/>.

RadiusIM. (n.d.). *RadiusIM*. Retrieved from <http://www.radiusim.com/>.

RFC 1459—Internet Relay Chat Protocol. (n.d.). *RFC 1459—Internet Relay Chat Protocol*. Retrieved from <tools.ietf.org/html/rfc1459/>.

RFC 2779—Instant Messaging Presence Protocol Requirements. (n.d.). *RFC 2779—Instant Messaging Presence Protocol Requirements*. Retrieved from <tools.ietf.org/html/rfc2779/>.

RFC 2810—Internet Relay Chat Architecture. (n.d.). *RFC 2810—Internet Relay Chat Architecture*. Retrieved from <tools.ietf.org/html/rfc2810/>.

RFC 2811—Internet Relay Chat Channel Management. (n.d.). *RFC 2811—Internet Relay Chat Channel Management*. Retrieved from <http://tools.ietf.org/html/rfc2811/>.

RFC 2812—Internet Relay Chat Client Protocol (n.d.). *RFC 2812—Internet Relay Chat Client Protocol*. Retrieved from <http://tools.ietf.org/html/rfc2812/>.

RFC 2813—Internet Relay Chat Server Protocol. (n.d.). *RFC 2813—Internet Relay Chat Server Protocol*. Retrieved from <http://tools.ietf.org/html/rfc2813/>.

Russinovich, M. (n.d.). TCPView for Windows. *Resources and tools for IT professionals*. TechNet. Retrieved from <http://technet.microsoft.com/en-us/sysinternals/bb897437.aspx/>.

Search All of Craigslist: Tips and Tools, Advanced Searches. (n.d.). *craigslistSearch.org*. Retrieved from <www.craigslistsearch.org/>.

Shareaza—Bringing P2P Together. (n.d.). *Shareaza*. Retrieved from <http://shareaza.sourceforge.net/>.

Souza, J. and Silva, E.(2009) EspiaMule and Wyoming Toolkit: Tools repression of sexual exploitation of children and adolescents in peer-to-peer. *The International Conference on Forensic Computer Science*. Retrieved from <www.icofcs.org/2009/ICoFCS2009-PP14.pdf/>.

Spafford, G. (n.d.). *Gene Spafford's Personal Pages Quotable Spaf*. Retrieved from <spaf.cerias.purdue.edu/quotes.html/>.

State v. Mahan, 2011 WL 4600044 (Ohio Court of Appeals 2011) United State vs. Matthew Joseph Collins, Case Case 1:09-CR-00010-JEG-CFB, Southern District of Iowa, Court Order, November 24, 2009.

The DALnet IRC Network. (n.d.). Retrieved from <http://www.dal.net/>.

The Largest List of Text Message Shorthand (IM, SMS) and Internet Acronyms Found of the Web—Kept Current and Up-to-Date by NetLingo The Internet Dictionary: Online Dictionary of Computer and Internet Terms, Acronyms, Text Messaging, Smileys;-). (n.d.). *NetLingo The Internet Dictionary*. Retrieved from <http://www.netlingo.com/acronyms.php/>.

Trillian. (n.d.). *Trillian*. Retrieved from <https://www.trillian.im/>.

United State vs. Matthew Joseph Collins, Case Case 1:09-CR-00010-JEG-CFB, Southern District of Iowa, Court Order, November 24, 2009.

United States v. Willard, 2010 U.S. Dist. LEXIS 98216 (E.D. Va. September 20, 2010).

Usenet Free Newsgroups. (n.d.). *Newshosting*. Retrieved from <http://www.newshosting.com/>.

Usenet Newsgroups Service, News Servers, Usenet Access—Giganews. (n.d.). *Giganews*. Retrieved from <http://www.giganews.com/>.

Usenet Pumping 8 Terabytes per Day!. (n.d.). *TechSono Engineering, Inc*. Retrieved from <http://www.techsono.com/usenet/faq/usenet-traffic/>.

Waters, F. (2007) *Child sex crimes on the Internet. Prepared for House Judiciary Committee*. Retrieved from <judiciary.house.gov/hearings/pdf/Waters071017.pdf/>.

Web and Mobile Messenger for MSN, Yahoo, ICQ, AIM, Google Talk, Facebook. (n.d.). *ebuddy.com*. Retrieved from <http://www.ebuddy.com/>.

Welcome to the Undernet IRC Network. (n.d.). *Undernet IRC network*. Retrieved from <http://www.undernet.org/webchat.php/>.

www.ElfQrin.com—List of open NNTP servers. (n.d.). *ElfQrin.com Hacking Lab*. Retrieved from <http://www.elfqrin.com/mine/nntpserv.html/>.

Yahoo! Messenger—Chat, Instant message, SMS, Video Call, PC Calls. (n.d.). *Yahoo! Messenger*. Retrieved from <http://messenger.yahoo.com/>.

Detection and Prevention of Internet Crimes

16

...despite the serious problems being posed by the Internet to police everywhere, traditional, off-line evidence gathering and investigation will remain the primary tools of law enforcement.
Hiroaki Takizawa, Assistant Director, Economic and Financial Crime Sub-directorate, Interpol; Ghosh, 1997

Perception of law enforcement on the Internet

Cybercrime and its investigation is not new. The 1970s saw the first modern technology crimes when hacking the traditional telephone network with a cereal box whistle[1] was thought to be high tech. This was well before the creation of today's Internet or the World Wide Web. Their development ushered in an expansion in the scope and sophistication of criminal behavior. Clarke (1998) noted that "For law enforcement agencies to provide a credible threat against criminals, they need a number of capabilities; or at least they need to be perceived by potential criminals to have them." He further stated that "...a critical aspect of control over criminal activities is the credibility of law enforcement agencies' capabilities to detect and to investigate." The Internet has grown incredibly since that comment, bringing forth a corresponding explosion of high-tech crimes.

In Chapter 1, we provided a broad cybercrime definition as a criminal offense that has been created or made possible by the advent of technology, or a traditional crime which has been transformed by technology's use. We further defined Internet crimes as offenses committed or facilitated through Internet. In Chapter 2, we also explored how there is a convergence of online crime techniques and terrorist philosophies.

One thing that must be realized is that the Internet provides individuals bent on criminal activity or acts of terror, additional opportunities to fail without consequences. If the cyber terrorist/criminal fails in their attempt to commit the crime today, they do not automatically get arrested or die. They do however learn from what did not work, and they can use that knowledge against you and your

---

[1]John Draper, aka "Captain Crunch" discovered the give-away whistle in cereal boxes reproduces a 2600 Hz tone, allowing him to make free toll calls. (Kovalchik, 2008)

community again and again. We must remove these "free passes" for criminal experimentation. This chapter will focus on preventing Internet crimes from being successful and hopefully minimizing the criminal experimentation that targets our citizens, businesses, and governments.

Contributing factors to the problem

Increases in online crime are tied to three factors. First, there is a growing Internet dependence in our society. This dependence not only increases the victim pool but means more of a societal impact if a key service or organization is adversely effected by online criminal acts. Second, the Internet and technology have made committing crime much easier. Obviously, technology has made the actual commission much simpler. Online offenses, such as hacking, previously required a basic knowledge of programming and command line operations. Now there are downloadable programs that automatic Domain Name System (DNS) attacks. Additionally, the Internet has literally created a venue for worldwide fraud schemes, which even a novice can execute. Technology has clearly made offenses simpler to commit from an operational standpoint. However, its effect goes beyond just making execution easier.

The Internet's environment frequently reduces ethics or morals that might prevent such crimes from occurring in an "offline" environment. Consider the illicit trading and downloading of copyrighted software, music, and movies. Individuals are usually unwilling to go into a store to shoplift merchandise. However, many of these same individuals have no issue with downloading pirated materials. Even those who do understand it is wrong will still justify their actions by claiming as long as they don't download too much it is somehow okay. This is akin to saying it is okay to steal occasionally, just don't take too much.

Internet harassment is another example. Some offenders would not engage in such conduct if it required them to interact with their victim in the real world. The Internet provides an imaginary "shield of invincibly" reducing many individual's inhibitions to criminally act out. The same can be said about cybersex offenses. Countless sex offenders rationalize and minimize their illicit conduct by claiming it was merely "fantasy." The erroneous belief that Internet crime is not real provides a moral crutch, allowing some individuals to proceed with online criminal behavior.

The mere presence of law enforcement has long been held to be a deterrent to criminal behavior. One prong to US insanity defenses is the issue of "irresistible impulse," also known as the policemen at the elbow test (Frontline PBS, 2002). Basically, if an individual can't refrain from committing a criminal act based upon a mental illness, even in the presence of policemen, they may be found innocent by reason of insanity. Unfortunately, the Internet is perceived by many to lack that "policemen at the elbow." This perception translates into there being no restraint on illegal Internet conduct but for the user's morals and ethics.

The last contributing factor is a lack of general understanding of Internet security risks by the public, including some in law enforcement. No one would walk through a dangerous neighborhood, blind folded, while carrying a large bundle of $100 bills. However, countless individuals go online blindly, with unprotected computers containing credit and bank account information, as well as identifiers and passwords to access their entire financial wealth. Similarly, no one walks up to a stranger on the street, holding a sign that reflects the name of their financial institution and hands over cash for a deposit. Yet, countless phishing victims go to bogus websites and willing provide criminals access to their entire bank account.

The catalyst that aggravates these factors is an inadequate cohesive national strategy in the United States, let alone the world. We have discussed several groups, such as the Internet Crime Complaint Center (IC3) and past guidance from the White House on dealing with cybercrime. However, the IC3 data is based upon self-reported crimes by victims and does not come near to encapsulating the entirety of Internet offenses. In addition, it is US crime centric and does not cover the magnitude of the online crime internationally. In the United States, the White House Comprehensive National Cybersecurity Initiative has historically been the document referenced when the administrations talk about cybercrime response. This document reflects the following major goals designed to help secure the United States in cyberspace:

- "To establish a front line of defense against today's immediate threats by creating or enhancing shared situational awareness of network vulnerabilities, threats, and events within the Federal Government—and ultimately with state, local, and tribal governments and private sector partners—and the ability to act quickly to reduce our current vulnerabilities and prevent intrusions.
- To defend against the full spectrum of threats by enhancing U.S. counterintelligence capabilities and increasing the security of the supply chain for key information technologies.
- To strengthen the future cybersecurity environment by expanding cyber education; coordinating and redirecting research and development efforts across the Federal Government; and working to define and develop strategies to deter hostile or malicious activity in cyberspace." (Executive Office of the President of the United States, pp. 1–2).

However well-intentioned the document is regarding cybersecurity, it does not address the response to all Internet crimes. Specifically, the document effectively outlines the US national response to cybersecurity and infrastructure protection but fails to give guidance on how law enforcement at all levels should respond to nonhacker-type Internet crimes. Finally, the document is a US-based perspective on the worldwide problem of cybercrime. We do not want to minimize the impact of a DNS attack against a website and hacker intrusions into corporation and government systems. These are serious acts. But the vast majority of Internet crime affects individuals on a personal level, such as cyberfraud, identity theft, stalking/

harassment, and sexual exploitation offenses. Law enforcement and corporations need to prepare and educate their citizens and/or customers to those Internet crimes they are more likely to fall victim. The current strategy is like providing a plan to survive an earthquake while ignoring preparations for tornadoes, hurricanes, floods, fire, etc. Law enforcement and corporations need to educate their respective constitutes for all manner of online crime they may encounter. This education process will help prevent the successful completion of Internet crime. Additionally, the process will provide an avenue for investigators to interact and learn from their constituents. Overtime, these efforts will help establish that investigators are competent to handle these cases and demonstrate to the community that law enforcement has not abandoned the online world to criminals.

Law enforcement's response to internet crime

In the United States, the responses to Internet crime comes at many levels. Most of them are uncoordinated and make no unified effort to address online crime. The only exception is the US Internet Crimes Against Children (ICAC) Task Forces. We have mentioned them in previous chapters because they are the only real example in the United States of a coordinated response to any of the cybercrime issues. The reason is the common goals, policy, and coordination of the investigations. No other Internet crime has the same law enforcement response. The US federal agencies mainly focus on terrorism and the response to cybercrimes that affect businesses and the US infrastructure. Federal agencies also are recognizing the need to recruit engineers and computer scientists for their critical skills that can add to an effective response. Agencies, such as the FBI and Secret Service, are learning to deal with cybercrime by dedicating more agents to the problem and creating more task forces focused on cybercrime investigations.

State and local law enforcement agencies responses are very different. The response depends on the locale, its leadership's understanding of problem and funding. Beyond the ICAC's narrow focus (sex crimes against children), there is no consistent federal funding for the cybercrime problem. As a result, the nonchild cybercrime investigations are dependent on local funding sources. Recall in Chapter 11, the law enforcement perception frequently is that the "Internet is not our jurisdiction." With such an erroneous perception, it is little wonder that local agencies do not seek funding for a problem they consider someone else's concern.

Are there "broken windows" in cyberspace?

Recall in Chapter 1 our discussion of the "Broken Windows Theory." The question for us in the Internet's context is, does the theory apply? Just how different is policing the Internet from policing our own communities? Aside from the physical location being different, the Internet is a set of communities. Particularly with social media, the emphasis is with the community. They differentiate themselves by how one site builds its community's existence. For example, Internet Relay Chat has its own community identity different than those found on Google+. So, evaluating the "Broken Windows" theory in relationship to the Internet we have to accept that the online world has its own communities. Bill Siebert spoke on the need for law enforcement to invest in Internet investigations paraphrasing a description of this theory by noting: "Ignoring or just non-management of Internet crime sends a signal to certain elements that crime is safe because nobody cares, and soon it builds up to all sorts of crime." Given this approach, we can look at online crime in a very different way. Policing the Internet should be no different than policing the real world. Approaching Internet policing with this in mind, we can affect a positive change to make the online world safer. In this context, law enforcement needs to:

- Identify the communities to police.
- Contact the community members.
- Isolate the community's problems.
- Help set standards for the community.
- Seek out and prevent crime in the community.
- Stay visible in those communities.

If law enforcement reaches out to the online communities that serve their real-world community members they can effect change and reduce crime. The benefit to law enforcement will be a better understanding of the technology in use by its citizens. Additionally, law enforcement gains the opportunity to interact with the community and build relationships that allow the citizens to feel comfortable enough to report Internet crimes if they become victims.

Detection methods

How do we detect Internet crime? Well, the obvious answer is how we learn about most crime, via a victim compliant. We spoke in previous chapters about the need to take a report and the need to interview victims and get detailed information about the crime. There are other places that the investigator can get information about Internet crimes committed in their jurisdiction. Beyond receiving reports and proactive investigations, we note the following additional sources to detect Internet crime.

Internet Crime Complaint Center

Previously in Chapters 1 and 2, we discussed how the IC3 provides statistical data on cybercrime from receiving victim reports. However, they do not just collect, gather, and disclose data for annual reports. They provide victims a convenient and easy-to-use mechanism for reporting their victimization. These complaints are maintained in a central referral location, and they are eventually reviewed and forwarded to the appropriate law enforcement agency. However, for a law enforcement agency to receive such a report, it must first sign up with IC3. Signing up for these reports will alert law enforcement to how many of their citizens are becoming Internet crime victims. Additionally, it will help them detect patterns that may reflect a local nexus as opposed to one from across the globe. For instance, if five victims in a community all report a similar Internet crime occurred to them, a follow-up interview may reveal they all have some piece of information that points to a local suspect. Remember, just because a crime involves the Internet, doesn't mean that the suspect doesn't live near the victim. Finally, report collection which identifies local victims may be used as justification to secure additional resources or funding to address a problem that is affecting the agency's own community.

National Center for Missing and Exploited Children

National Center for Missing and Exploited Children's (NCMEC's) mission is to help prevent child abduction and sexual exploitation, find missing children, and assist victims of child abduction and sexual exploitation, their families, and the professionals who serve them. Additionally, it provides a cybertip line, allowing the public and electronic service providers the ability to report Internet-related child sexual exploitation (www.cybertipline.com). These cybertips are forwarded to participating law enforcements agencies, mainly ICAC participants. Finally, the NCMEC provides numerous resources which may be used to tailor Internet safety presentations.

US Federal Trade Commission

The Federal Trade Commission's (FTC's) mission is "... to prevent business practices that are anticompetitive or deceptive or unfair to consumers; to enhance informed consumer choice and public understanding of the competitive process; and to accomplish this without unduly burdening legitimate business activity." (FTC, 2013) The FTC has become very active with Internet cases where companies or individuals have engaged in deceptive or fraudulent practices online. Their first Internet case was *FTC v. Corzine*, CIV-S-94-1446 (E.D. Cal. filed September 12, 1994) and involved misrepresentations on America Online, that a "credit repair kit" would fix an individual's credit problems. Since that time, they have had numerous Internet cases including business opportunity scams, goods advertised but not furnished, pyramid schemes, hacked modem scams, bogus health products, and deceptive domain name registrars. Additionally, FTC is very active in identifying theft, providing the following:

- Resources to learn about identity theft, including detailed information to help individuals deter, detect, and defend against identity theft.
- An online location where consumers can file identity theft complaints.
- Maintenance of the FTC's Identity Theft Data Clearinghouse.

FTC investigations begin in a variety of ways, such as consumer or business letters, Congressional inquiries, or articles on consumer or economic subjects. If the FTC believes a law violation has occurred, they can obtain voluntary compliance by entering into a consent order with the company or individual.

Additionally, they can issue an administrative complaint which results in a formal hearing. If a violation is found, a cease and desist order or other appropriate relief may be issued. In some circumstances, the FTC will go directly to court and obtain an injunction, civil penalties, or consumer redress. In this way, the FTC can stop a fraud before too many consumers are injured.

FTC frequently works with law enforcement agencies who can also pursue criminal cases against the investigative targets. Checking with the FTC can alert law enforcement to other victims in their community who may have contacted them directly. The FTC is a powerful investigative ally. They have the ability to issue cease and desist orders and obtain injunctions, which can stop deceptive and fraudulent online conduct from continuing while the frequently longer criminal investigation progresses to its proper conclusion. Additionally, the FTC may be able to obtain consumer redress to citizens in your community, regardless of whether criminal charges are filed.

International Consumer Protection and Enforcement Network and E-Consumer

The FTC is not the only agency of its kind in the world. There are a multitude of similar consumer protection agencies in other countries, such as the Australian Competition and Consumer Commission, Competition Bureau Canada, and the United Kingdom Office of Fair Trading, to name a few. The International Consumer Protection and Enforcement Network (ICPEN) is made up of 50 such agencies.[2]

In April of 2001, 13 ICPEN agencies came together to respond to multinational Internet fraud and to enhance consumer protection and consumer confidence in e-commerce. The result was econsumer.gov, a joint effort to gather and share cross-border e-commerce complaints. Today, 28 countries[3] participate in this initiative. The econsumer.gov website allows consumers to report complaints about online and related transactions with foreign companies. These reports are entered into Consumer Sentinel, a database maintained by the FTC. The database is accessible to certified government law enforcement and regulatory agencies in all ICPEN member countries.

---

[2]Australia, Austria, Azerbaijan, Barbados, Belgium, Bulgaria, Canada, Chile, China, Colombia, Costa Rica, Cyprus, Czech Republic, Denmark, Dominican Republic, El Salvador, Egypt, Estonia, European Commission, Finland, France, Germany, Greece, Hungary, Ireland, Israel, Italy, Japan, Republic of Korea, Latvia, Lithuania, Luxembourg, Malta, Mexico, the Netherlands, New Zealand, Nigeria, Norway, Panama, Papua New Guinea, Philippines, Poland, Portugal, Seychelles, Slovakia, Spain, Sweden, Switzerland, Turkey, United Kingdom, United Nations, the United States, and Vietnam.

[3]Australia, Belgium, Canada, Costa Rica, Chile, Denmark, Dominican Republic, Egypt, Estonia, Finland, Hungary, Ireland, Italy, Japan, Latvia, Lithuania, Mexico, the Netherlands, New Zealand, Norway, Poland, South Korea, Spain, Sweden, Switzerland, Turkey, United Kingdom, and the United States.

Methods of prevention

So far we discussed investigating Internet crimes but we have not talked about the methods that can be used to prevent them. Like any crime there are many things we can do to approach the problem and prevent people from being victims. Clarke (1998) describes two kinds of Internet prevention methods, hard and soft, the latter being the more successful. This chapter will explore both methods in detail. For now, hard prevention is the use of technology to prevent Internet crime. Clarke (1998) advises that soft prevention comprises "... disincentives against criminal activity, and in particular:

- clear definition of criminal offenses;
- public awareness-raising and education;
- the perceived likelihood of discovery;
- the perceived likelihood of effective investigation; and
- the perceived likelihood of successful prosecution."

Hard prevention: using technology to stop internet crime

Hard prevention uses technical means, such as "... architecture, protocols and software that preclude, or render difficult, actions of a criminal nature from being performed." (Clarke, 1998) This is the building of better and safer computers, software, and hardware that will automatically prevent crime—a pretty neat idea but impractical for the vast majority of Internet crimes. Obviously, building more secure computers and systems can be done, but that will not have any impact on their direct use to commit a crime. Clarke (1998) observes that online, most criminal activities are only differentiated from noncriminal ones on the basis of the content or purpose of transmitted data. He concludes that designing Internet architecture or protocols in order to ensure that the Internet simply cannot be used for any criminal purposes is therefore problematic at best.

However, technological detection/blocking methods do have some successes. For years, corporations and governments have used block lists to prevent malicious websites from interacting with their systems. But methods are also being employed beyond just systems under an agency or corporations direct control. This is occurring particularly in the area of online child exploitation offenses. Technology is being deployed to detect child pornography on Internet Service Provider (ISP) networks or to block access at the national level of blacklisted websites or those which are found to contain images which match the hash values of known child pornography. Countries such as the United Kingdom, Norway, Sweden, Denmark, Canada, Switzerland, Italy, the Netherlands, Finland, New Zealand, and France have gotten ISPs to block child pornography from coming into their countries from known contraband sites. Additionally, large ISP companies such as Google (search results), AOL (email attachments), and Facebook (uploaded images) have developed their own systems to detect child pornography images (McIntyre, 2013).

In 2008, New York passed the Electronic Securing and Targeting of Online Predators Act (e-STOP) law, which requires convicted sex offenders to register all of their e-mail addresses, screen names, and other Internet identifiers with the state. In turn, this information is shared with various ISP, who purge these potential predators from their networks. It was first used to remove sex offenders from social media networks, and in 2012, it was expanded to online gaming platforms. Thousands of registered sex offenders in New York have had their accounts on these networks closed as the result of e-STOP.

It would be naive to think sex offenders would not use technology (use of proxy servers, changing one bit to overcome hash value detection, etc.) as well as other methods, such as lying on forms to bypass these detection/blocking methods. However, these initiatives do make some areas of the Internet safer and provide a barrier of sorts, making it harder for sex offenders to operate freely.

Blocking questionable websites is not limited to just child pornography. In the United Kingdom, various ISPs under court order are maintaining an antipiracy block list and initiating a proxy blockade against torrent sites found to trade in pirated music (Ernesto, 2013). Some may argue that this smacks of being too much like "Big Brother", particularly if the blocking is done under direct government control. From a pragmatic point of view, such methods only work until the site relocates or the end users employ one of the techniques noted in this book to access the website from another location. These "blacklists" of websites and IP addresses that are potentially used by criminals are increasingly the method of choice for ISPs to block potential criminal activity. However, useful and noncriminal sites added to these lists find it difficult to get themselves removed if they are put on the list through no fault of the owner. As such, constant vigilance is needed to keep the block lists up-to-date and accurate.

INTERNET WATCH FOUNDATION

The Internet Watch Foundation (IWF) is an "... dependent self-regulatory body, funded by the EU and the online industry, including internet service providers (ISPs), mobile operators, content providers, hosting providers, filtering companies, search providers, trade associations and the financial sector" which works with law enforcement partners in the United Kingdom and abroad to assist in child pornography distribution investigations (Internet Watch Foundation, 2013). Along with assisting investigations, IWF leads an industry initiative to protect users from inadvertent exposure to illegal content by blocking access through a dynamic list of child sexual abuse webpages. They report the following successes:

- By sharing intelligence with police, the IWF aided the identification and rescue of 12 children in the past 2 years.
- Less than 1% of child sexual abuse content is hosted in the United Kingdom since 2003, down from 18% in 1996.
- Child sexual abuse content is removed in the United Kingdom typically within 60 minutes.
- Time taken to remove child sexual abuse content hosted outside the United Kingdom was halved to 10 days in 2011.
- Over 400,000 webpages were assessed in 16 years.
- 100,000 URLs were removed for containing criminal content.

Soft prevention: education

Regardless of the investigative approach taken, both law enforcement and civil investigators need to understand that education helps prevent their communities from being victims. Preventive education hardens targets and helps provide disincentives against criminal activity. Clearly defining criminal offenses within the community allows the citizens to understand when they have been victimized. Education prevention helps raise public awareness to Internet crime issues and the perceived likelihood of its discovery. Education also leads to more effective investigations, which leads to a greater likelihood of a successful prosecution. Recall from Chapter 2 that a knowledgeable victim can be an asset to closing a case successfully. The investigator, either law enforcement or within their company, can conduct education prevention. Education outreach can also occur in various groups of online users.

We traditionally think about educating children of the dangers of certain Internet activities, but there are other groups needing attention. Parents need to understand how the technology and the Internet can pose a risk to their children. Businesses need to be informed of the risk technology can pose to the business and how to prevent the possibility of victimization. The elderly are an often overlooked group who need education on Internet hazards especially as they seek out and use more social media. Even local computer repair shops are a source requiring education. They may understand the technology, but they frequently don't understand their requirements for reporting certain behavior such as possession of contraband. Other places to educate and liaison include libraries, universities, and other areas which provide computers with open Internet use. Providing them tips for making sure their computers are not used for illegal purposes, such as locating computers in open public areas, can make criminals less likely to use their systems. Additionally, placing these computers in areas away from children reduces the chances that they will be exposed to inappropriate, if not illegal material.

Existing programs

There is a plethora of Internet sites dealing with online safety and/or security. Most are focused on educating children or providing information and guidance to parent/guardians and teachers. In addition, many of these sites provide instructional material and/or presentations for law enforcement to keep children safe online. Other sites are very specific, focusing exclusively on crimes such as cyberstalking or identity theft. Some sites focus on providing preventive information in a text format. Many have multimedia files for viewing and/or material for downloading, such as handouts or presentations. Still others are interactive, providing users the ability to take tests, play informative games, or post messages. Some sites are a webpage or two, off a main website, devoted to other endeavors, such as law enforcement or providing commercial goods or services. Many are stand-online websites devoted entirely to Internet safety/prevention. Sites tend to provide material for an entire country/region, although those focusing on a particular community or city are starting to appear. Online safety/prevention sites can generally be categorized by how they are supported, such as if they are government or business supported or a stand-alone entities such as a nonprofit corporation or private initiatives. Accordingly the following are five general online safety programs/sites:

1. Major law enforcement or other government agencies: Some examples include Cybersmart (http://www.cybersmart.gov.au/); FBI Safe Online Surfing (https://sos.fbi.gov/); IC3 Internet Crime Prevention Tips (http://www.ic3.gov/preventiontips.aspx); NCMEC Netsmartz (http://www.netsmartz.org/); Royal Canadian Mounted Police Internet Safety Resources (http://www.rcmp-grc.gc.ca/is-si/index-eng.htm); The Security and Exchange Commission's The Internet and Online Trading Safety Site (http://www.sec.gov/investor/online.shtml); and ThinkUknowNow (http://www.thinkuknow.co.uk/).
2. Nonprofit entities: ConnectSafely (http://www.connectsafely.org/); i-SAFE, Inc.(http://isafe.org); KidsSMART (http://www.kidsmart.org.uk/); SafeKids (http://www.safekids.com/); Web Wise Kids (http://www.webwisekids.org/); and Wise Kids (http://www.wisekids.org.uk/).
3. Corporations: Microsoft's Safety & Security Center (http://www.microsoft.com/security/family-safety/childsafety-steps.aspx); Google's Good To Know A Guide to Staying Safe and Secure Online (http://www.google.com/goodtoknow/); and Sprint's 4NetSafety (http://www.sprint.com/4netsafety/).
4. Private initiatives: Examples include Digital Stalking—Supporting Victims of Stalking, Harassment and Bullying (http://www.digital-stalking.com/); KL Greer Consulting, LLC (http://www.klgreer.com/); and Yoursphere Media, Inc.(http://internet-safety.yoursphere.com/).
5. Blended (two or more supporters): GetNetWise (http://www.getnetwise.org); Internet Keep Safe Coalition (iKeepSafe) (http://www.ikeepsafe.org/); OnGuardOnline.gov (http://www.onguardonline.gov/); United Kingdom Council for Child Internet Safety (UKCCIS) (https://www.education.gov.uk/childrenandyoungpeople/safeguardingchildren/b00222029/child-internet-safety); UK Safer Internet Centre (http://www.saferinternet.org.uk/); and Insafe (http://www.saferinternet.org/).

INTERNET SAFETY EDUCATION SITES

The variety of online safety sites out there is amazing. This is just a sampling of major ones for your reference. It does not include all the law enforcement sites which may provide Internet safety material or sites that may include Internet safety tips, alongside of other crime prevention information. Additionally, there are numerous software companies, particularly those selling antivirus or monitoring programs, which list online safety tips. The list also does not include those sites located at the local level. For instance in the United States, there is an ICAC Task Force in each state, which has its own website. Frequently, these ICAC websites have their own prevention initiatives and downloads. An example is the Ohio ICAC, which has a free iPhone app called Shaq Shield. The application, named after basketball great, Shaquille O'Neal, who promoted it, is designed to provide Internet safety tips and other information for the user. The point is: Please do your own research, particularly for resources that might be located locally.

Family/Children

Carnegie Cyber Academy (http://www.carnegiecyberacademy.com/)
ConnectSafely (http://www.connectsafely.org/)
Cybersmart http://www.cybersmart.gov.au/
Family Safe Computers, http://www.familysafecomputers.org/
FBI Safe Online Surfing (https://sos.fbi.gov/)
Enough is Enough (http://www.internetsafety101.org/)
Google's Good To Know A Guide to Staying Safe and Secure Online (http://www.google.com/goodtoknow/)
ICAC Training and Technical Assistance (http://www.icactraining.org/)
i-SAFE, Inc.(http://isafe.org)
Insafe (http://www.saferinternet.org/)
Internet Keep Safe Coalition (iKeepSafe) (http://www.ikeepsafe.org/)
KidsSMART (http://www.kidsmart.org.uk/)
Microsoft's Safety & Security Center (http://www.microsoft.com/security/family-safety/childsafety-steps.aspx)
National Center for Missing and Exploited Children (http://www.missingkids.com/)
NCMEC Netsmartz (http://www.netsmartz.org/).
SafeKids (http://www.safekids.com/)
Sprint's 4NetSafety (http://www.sprint.com/4netsafety/)
UK Safer Internet Centre (http://www.saferinternet.org.uk/)
UKCCIS (https://www.education.gov.uk/childrenandyoungpeople/safeguardingchildren/b00222029/child-internet-safety)
ThinkUKnowNow (http://www.thinkuknow.co.uk/)
Web Wise Kids (http://www.webwisekids.org/);
Wise Kids (http://www.wisekids.org.uk/).

Fraud

IC3, Internet Crime Prevention Tips (http://www.ic3.gov/preventiontips.aspx)
FBI—Internet Fraud (http://www.fbi.gov/scams-safety/fraud/internet_fraud)
The Security and Exchange Commission's The Internet and Online Trading Safety Site (http://www.sec.gov/investor/online.shtml)
USA.gov Internet Fraud Information (http://www.usa.gov/Citizen/Topics/Internet-Fraud.shtml)
USDOJ, Identity Theft and Identity Fraud, (http://www.justice.gov/criminal/fraud/websites/idtheft.html).

Cyberstalking

Digital Stalking, Victims of Stalking, Harassment and Bullying (http://www.digital-stalking.com/).

Multipurpose

GetNetWise (http://www.getnetwise.org)
OnGuardOnline.gov (http://www.onguardonline.gov/)
National Cybersecurity Alliance (http://staysafeonline.org/)
Royal Canadian Mounted Police Internet Safety Resources (http://www.rcmp-grc.gc.ca/is-si/index-eng.htm).

Developing your own prevention initiative

With all the wealth of resources available, the question now becomes why would anyone think about developing their own program? Having your own initiative, even if it is merely to provide regular presentations, reflects to your community that your agency is involved and engaged on the cybercrime front. This translates into more willingness to report Internet crime and to alert your agency to troubling cybertrends in your community. By all means, use the available resources with the understanding that may have some dated material. Consider them as the foundation that you will build on, not the final product. Also don't forget to check for "offline" resources, such as books. We now will focus on two types of initiatives you might consider.

Presentations

Preparing an Internet safety presentation is not a hard task, particularly with the number of available online sites noted. Some of these sites contain "canned" presentations or material that can be used, provided one tailors them to their audience and insures they are up-to-date. Presentations can be given in person or via webinars. They also can be recorded and made available for later viewing. Obviously, presentations focusing on keeping children safe online is a must, but also consider other venues and special topics, such as online fraud/identity theft; juvenile sexting, and gaming safety. Presentations should be available at any time of the year. However, special attention should be given to scheduling presentations to coincide with designated safety/presentation events. For instance, in the European Union, there is Safer Internet Day, held in February of each year. In the United States, there is National Internet Safety Month, held in June and the National Cyber Security Awareness Month, held in October. Also be aware of nonspecific cyberevents, such as the United States National Stalking Awareness Month held in January to provide presentations on cyberstalking as well as ICPEN's Fraud Prevention Month. Additionally, be prepared to provide presentations in the event there is a spike in online victimization among your constituents. Generally, the presentations should follow the below guidelines to maximize their effectiveness:

- Limit to 45–60 minutes in length and provide ample opportunity for questions.
- PowerPoint slides should contain no more than three "bullet-points," avoiding lengthy sentences as much as possible.
- For in person presentations, make sure material can be shown regardless of Internet access or audiovisual equipment.
- All presentations should include contact details for requesting additional information or to report a cyberincident.
- Make sure the presenter knows the material.
- Use plain language and avoid jargon.
- Include real-life examples.

- Limit the number and volume of handouts. If possible, provide links to presentation material as a way to establish and continue contact with the attendees.

Basic children online safety education Children online safety programs should include educating children that they should not give out identifying information such as name, home address, school name, or telephone number while online. Additionally, ensure they understand not to give photographs to anyone online without first checking or informing parents/guardians. Children should also not respond to messages, which are suggestive, obscene, belligerent or threatening, and not arrange a face-to-face meeting without telling parents or guardians. The training should also ensure that children understand that people online might not be who they seem. Also, stress that inappropriate online behavior is not limited to strangers. "Trusted" individuals, such as teachers, coaches, relatives, and so on have incorporated online communications as a way to groom victims. Additionally, it should be covered that digital images have an extremely long shelf life and are easily distributed. Finally, children online safety programs should include a component stressing cyberethics, to help develop good "netcitizens." The sidebar "Delivery Tips for Talking to Child Audiences" provides guidelines for tailoring presentations to children.

Basic parent online safety education Basic parental online education should include a brief discussion on the need to keep software updated and to use antivirus and anti-spyware programs, and firewalls. Additionally, parents should be informed about the pros and cons of content filtering and/or monitoring software to protect children from pornography, gambling, hate speech, etc. Education should also cover where to locate computers in the home, establishing time controls for their use. Providing information on how to check their children's online activities is also important. However, no amount of filtering, monitoring, or searching will prevent a child from obtaining unsupervised Internet access. As a result, the most important point to convene to parents is that they need to have and maintain open communication with their children.

Facebook and Twitter as well as other social networking sites can obviously also be used by criminals. Both children and adults therefore need to understand how social networking can be secured and that privacy settings need to be periodically reviewed and updated as social media providers frequently change settings and services.

DELIVERY TIPS FOR TALKING TO CHILD AUDIENCES

In approximately 2003, the High Technology Crime Investigation Association (HTCIA) partnered with Hewlett-Packard Company, LiveWWWires, the NCMEC, NetSmartz, and the United States Secret Service, to address HTCIA's membership's growing desire to conduct Internet Safety training in their geographic locations. As a direct result of this partnership, in 2004, the HTCIA Internet Safety For Children Campaign was created. Its strength recognized that prevention education was not a one-size-fits-all concept. Different ages have different interests, patterns of behavior, and understanding of themselves and the world around them. The result was the development of "Delivery Tips," which are reflected below:

General Tips (Apply to All Age Groups)

1. Schedule age groups together if possible (e.g., grade school, middle school, high school).
2. Tailor your presentation content to the group.
3. Don't make assumptions about computer use and the socioeconomic status of the group. Ask your group questions. Inner-city children sometimes have some of the same resources as those from middle class suburbs. Even families on welfare have computers at home and children can access computers from a variety of other places too (e.g., libraries, schools, friend's houses, Boys & Girls clubs, etc.).
4. Know your subject matter. A knowledgeable speaker is more interesting and will keep the audience's attention.
5. Show enthusiasm. This is especially important at the beginning of the presentation. Being interested in your own subject matter is contagious, especially with younger children.
6. Move around. This helps break down space barriers between you and your audience and can help children feel more comfortable. Remember, there is nothing more boring than a talking head.
7. Limit sessions to less than 1 hour.
8. Limit group size if possible. Up to 60 is optimal.
9. Save or reiterate the points you'd like your audience to leave with until the END of your presentation.

Younger Children—Ages 5–12 (Grades K–6)

- Interactive sessions are best. Children in general need stimulation to engage in a topic. Lecturing is only useful for a very limited time, especially with younger children. Involving children in the discussion can help enhance the impact of their learning. This can encourage them to talk about their own experiences. A speaker's personal approach will encourage audience participation.
- Speak slowly and clearly.
- Emphasize keywords.
- Maintain eye contact. This helps you gauge their reactions.
- Be straightforward.
- Praise correct answers. This encourages other children to share their experiences.
- Use age appropriate language and speak in a language your audience will understand.

Teen Groups—Ages 12–17 (Middle and High School)

- Use real-life stories and examples to make your point. If you have none of your own, use real stories you've gathered from the newspaper, magazines, and other sources. Try to use examples of stories about teens from the area, city, or at least the state where your audience is from. Although teen girls are heavily victimized online, boys are also targeted. Be sure to also include examples for both.
- Be direct. This is especially true for older audiences.
- Ask for their personal experiences.
- Don't be put off by a group who is not participative. Older kids are very worried about being embarrassed in front of their peers. Continue your presentation as usual. If no one participates, you supply the answers and examples you need to make your points. If one or more in the group took some safety tips away with them after your presentation, you were successful.

COMPUTER LEARNING FOUNDATION CODE OF RESPONSIBLE COMPUTING

Respect for Privacy: I will respect others' right to privacy. I will only access, look in, or use other individuals', organizations', or companies' information on computer or through telecommunications if I have the permission of the individual, organization, or company who owns the information.

Respect for Property: I will respect others' property. I will only make changes to or delete computer programs, files, or information that belong to others, if I have been given permission to do so by the person, organization, or company who owns the program, file, or information.

Respect for Ownership: I will respect others' rights to ownership and to earn a living from their work. I will only use computer software, files, or information that I own or that I have been given permission to borrow. I will only use software programs that have been paid for or are in the public domain. I will only make a backup copy of computer programs I have purchased or written and will only use it if my original program is damaged. I will only make copies of computer files and information that I own or have written. I will only sell computer programs which I have written or have been authorized to sell by the author. I will pay the developer or publisher for any shareware programs I decide to use.

Respect for Others and the Law: I will only use computers, software, and related technologies for purposes that are beneficial to others, that are not harmful (physically, financially, or otherwise) to others or others' property, and that are within the law.

Employer security awareness programs Any large organization, such as a corporation or government agency, should have an acceptable computer use policy in place, which all employees must acknowledge and adhere to on a continuing basis. However, these agreements are only part of the answer. Increasing employees are engaging in bringing your own device (BYOD) to the workplace. A Logicalis Group (2012) study found 57% of full-time employees engaged in some form of BYOD. These devices pose additional risks and challenges for employers. Unfortunately, the same study found that 17.7% of respondents noted that their employer's IT department was unaware of this practice and 28.4% actively ignored it. Clearly, computer use policies must now incorporate BYOD components. An employee's online safety, particularly when they are engaging in BYOD practices, now becomes more important to the employer. The theft of data from the employee may not be limited to just their identity but the employer's assets as well. Therefore, it becomes imperative that employers couple acceptable use policies with online safety and security awareness programs. The National Security Institute (2010) provides the following three essential ingredients to creating an effective security awareness program:

1. The program must convincingly demonstrate that security breaches don't just adversely affect the organization, but also harm individual employees.
2. It must focus and consistently reinforce strong security practices in different and creative ways.
3. It must appeal to issues important to employees.

The National Security Institute further notes that effective awareness programs can transform employees from a company's "greatest risk to greatest asset" by (1) continuous exposure to appropriate awareness training; (2) consistent positive reinforcement through well-articulated security messages, which are easily understood, digested, and applied to employees' everyday lives at work and at home; and (3) management ensuring that employees receive needed training and are motivated to use it. "Only when security becomes as second nature as buckling up your seatbelt, will it really be effective." (National Security Institute, p. 8).

Employer security awareness will naturally center on good work place practices. However, we would argue that those same practices are also important for employees to adopt at home to keep safe from identity theft, cyberfraud, and other online crimes. As such, employers need to stress to their employees that they should adopt the same preventive measures at home. Additionally, employers should likewise consider scheduling major awareness training events at the work site to coincide with online safety preventions occurring in their communities. Consider the impact of employees attending such training at the same time their children are receiving online safety tips at their school. This may very well enhance the retention of presented information by both the employees and their children because they have a shared learning experience they can talk about.

NATIONAL SECURITY INSTITUTE'S 10 TIPS FOR PROMOTING SECURITY AWARENESS

1. Train employees to recognize security-robbing behaviors in themselves and others.
2. Get management to buy into the program. Make sure the company's top executives understand and support security awareness initiatives.
3. Involve employees in setting security goals, and make sure everyone understands what the lack of good security can mean to them and the company.
4. Don't intimidate and use security as a big stick. Educate and inform.
5. Insure employees and management know there is a clear chain of security responsibility that everyone has a role and owns a piece of the problem and solution.
6. Make security fun. Have pizza Fridays or use games to raise awareness levels. Provide "trinkets," such as pens, stickers, and antistatic screen cloths with a security message attached.
7. Encourage security roundtable discussions, where employees and management discuss risks to the company based on news reports.
8. Bring in an outside speaker to motivate employees about security issues.
9. Offer computer-based security training and reward employees with certificates in recognition of their accomplishments.
10. Conflict resolution can deflate security problems: defuse issues before they become threatening security events.

Online presence

An online presence can be as simple as just listing cybersafety tips on a webpage. More complicated endeavors, such as creating a website or social media presence, require planning and resources. Who is the effort trying to reach and what will be the focus (a general Internet safety tips or a specific online crime)? What are the resources to create, maintain, and keep current the effort? Is the endeavor going to be merely a listing of tips or will it contain material that can be downloaded (handouts, presentations, etc.) or viewed online (multimedia)? Will the online presence be interactive and if so who will engage the target population? The sidebar, "Tips for Online Presence" provides some basic guidance on the pros and cons of the various elements to creating an online safety presence. One final consideration: Is it to be an in-house project or a collaborative effort with other interested parties?

TIPS FOR ONLINE PRESENCE

Webpages: Easily modified but can become static.

PDF/DOC: Good for handouts but can get outdated quickly requiring regular checking/modification.

Links: Good for providing additional information. However, they can go "dead" or the target site may not be kept up-to-date information or change the material without notice.

Powerpoints: Allow law enforcement and educators to have readymade presentations. However, they may become outdated.

Multimedia: Provide a more active presentation, expanding the quality of the website. However, if too long, the user may lose interest. They may become dated as well. Consider making them "portable" allowing them to be downloaded into presentations.

Social media/blogs: Allows online and timely exchange of information. Also permits interaction with public. However, requires someone to moderate.

Cybercommunity coalitions The National Cybersecurity Alliance, Infragard, and the Multi-State Information Sharing & Analysis Center have created a guide for building cybercommunity coalitions to help secure the Internet. The guide includes steps such as developing a vision/mission statement, getting buy-in from stakeholders and who to initially invite to participate in the coalition. The guide also provides a coalition website plan example, invite templates and agendas for first meeting, a defined framework with deliverables, and speaker ideas. Two noteworthy examples of cybercommunity coalitions are Washtenaw County Cyber Citizenship Coalition (http://washtenawcybercoalition.org/) and Securing Our eCity (http://securingourecity.org/).

The latter, located in Michigan, is being used as a model for such coalitions by the National Cyber Security Alliance. Securing Our eCity, located in San Diego, California, was recognized in 2010 along with My Maine Privacy, as the "Best Local/Community Plan" by Departments of Homeland Security and Commerce and the White House Cybersecurity Coordinator (Figures 16.1 and 16.2).

Investigator cybercrime education

Training on how to investigate Internet crimes is a must. You are starting that journey by reading this book and implementing its recommendations. However,

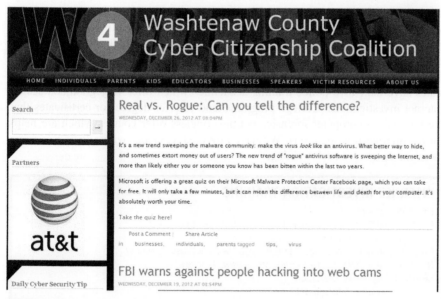

FIGURE 16.1

Washtenaw county cybercitizenship coalition main webpage.

FIGURE 16.2

Securing our city main webpage.

hands-on training is always a good addition to any text. There are groups that the law enforcement as well as corporate investigators can attend that can provide the basic skills needed to prepare for Internet investigations as well as to educate their constituents. Some law enforcement supported training will allow police from other countries to attend their programs. Additionally, in the United States, many states have their own police training academies which offer very good courses on Internet investigations. College programs tend to offer degrees or certificates that are focused on computer forensics but nevertheless offer courses which are helpful for Internet investigations. We have provided a sidebar with a listing of some locations to receive such training.

INTERNET INVESTIGATION TRAINING

Law Enforcement
FBI Regional Computer Forensic Labs, http://www.rcfl.gov
ICAC Task Forces, http://www.icactaskforce.org
National Computer Forensics Institute, http://www.ncfi.usss.gov/ncfi/
National White Collar Crime Center, http://www.nw3c.org
SEARCH, http://www.search.org
International Law Enforcement
Canadian Police College (CPC), http://www.cpc.gc.ca/en/home
European Police College (CEPOL), https://www.cepol.europa.eu/
Hong Kong Police College, http://www.police.gov.hk/
INTERPOL, http://www.interpol.int/Crime-areas/Cybercrime/Training
Metropolitan Police Crime Academy, http://content.met.police.uk/
Colleges and University Programs
Alliant International University, http://catalog.alliant.edu/preview_course_nopop.php?catoid=19&coid=28315
California State University, Long Beach, http://www.ccpe.csulb.edu/continuinged/course_listing/programdescription.aspx?Group_Number=236&Group_Version=2
Central Piedmont Community College, http://www.cpcc.edu/aaaf/digital-evidence/classes-offered
Champlain College, http://www.champlain.edu/cyber-security/online-computer-forensics-digital-investigation-degree
College of Policing, http://www.college.police.uk/en/578.htm
Cranfield University, http://www.cranfield.ac.uk/cds/postgraduatestudy/forensiccomputing/page15415.html
Defiance College, http://www.defiance.edu/pages/BASS_CF_courses.html
University of Central Florida, http://www.cs.ucf.edu/csdept/info/gccf/index.html
University of New Haven, http://catalog.newhaven.edu/preview_program.php?catoid=4&poid=510
Commercial Training
Cynthia Hetherington, Smarter Academy courses, http://hetheringtongroup.com/training.shtml
Toddington International, eLearning courses http://toddington.com/etraining/
Vere Software, Cyber Crime Survival courses, http://www.cybercrimesurvival.com
Nonprofit Organization
High Technology Crime Investigation, http://htcia.org

What can you do to detect and prevent online crime?

Within your company or agency, setting up a dedicated cybercrime investigation team should be a priority. The prevention of the various cybercrimes needs a dedicated and regular response. This is true for law enforcement as well as companies large enough to support a team. All investigators should be trained in how to investigate online crimes. Because the skill set for investigating Internet crimes is different than the digital forensic examiner, the two units should not be housed together. They certainly work in concert but the two functions are different. Unfortunately, for many years within law enforcement, the two functions have been done by the same individuals. No longer can the department's "computer guy" do everything technical. Internet investigations and digital forensics are different in their approach. The investigator familiar with digital forensics may certainly understand the Internet investigative process. However, maintaining currency in the field of Internet investigations requires going online and honing skills that frequently change due to the nature of the Internet. This is no different than as the digital forensic investigator who has to update and maintain their skills when it comes to understanding operating system changes and program updates. These Internet investigation units should likewise liaison and network on a regular basis with other similar units in their geographic area. Again HTCIA (htcia. org) provides a great venue to not only network but receive quality training at the same time.

What can you do to detect and prevent online crime? Well, the first thing is to encourage the reporting of Internet crimes. Whether it is in a law enforcement agency or a company, getting the victims to report the crimes is significant. If the crime is not reported, it can't be investigated. If you do not have an organized response in your agency or business, prepare a plan to address the issue and present it to your supervisor. Compare the cost of Internet crime to the cost of not investigating online crime by your agency or company. Include the expense of providing a response, such as personnel, equipment, and training costs. Provide the end result of committing to dealing with Internet crimes which can include the protection of your community and business assets as well as the potential for prevention of further crimes against your citizens or employees. The final point here is that if you are not addressing the investigation of Internet related crimes, you can't respond to the problems associated with it.

CONCLUSIONS

Detecting and preventing Internet crime should be an integral part of the investigator's standard processes. Early detection minimizes the number of victims that may be affected as well as leads to more successful prosecutions. Prevention initiatives provide a method to exchange information with an agency's constituents. This enhances trust and leads to more communication and cooperation. Additionally, it helps keep an agency up-to-date on the online risks facing those they serve. This chapter has provided both suggestions and resources for developing presentations and an online presence to educate and prevent Internet crime. One thing that we must continue to remind our communities is if it isn't reported law enforcement does not know it occurred!!! This lack of knowledge means resources will not be devoted to the problem and a viscous cycle begins. No one reports Internet crime because it is believed no one can do anything about it. The result is the criminals gain ground in the online world. Finally, we stressed that Internet investigators need to receive regular training to keep up-to-date on their skills as well as educate their constituents about emerging online threats.

Further reading

A Crime of Insanity—Insanity on Trial. (2002, October 2). *Frontline PBS*. Retrieved from <www.pbs.org/wgbh/pages/frontline/shows/>.

Attorney General Cuomo, Senate Majority Leader Joseph Bruno And Assembly Speaker Sheldon Silver Announce Bill To Protect New Yorkers From Sex Predators On The Internet | Eric T. Schneiderman. (n.d.). *Eric T. Schneiderman | New York State Attorney General*. Retrieved from <http://www.ag.ny.gov/press-release/attorney-general-cuomo-senate-majority-leader-joseph-bruno-and-assembly-speaker-1>.

Clarke,R. (1998, February 16). Technological aspects of internet crime prevention. *Australian Institute for Criminology's Conference on 'Internet Crime'*. Presented at Australian Institute for Criminology, Melbourne University, Melbourne, Australia. Retrieved from <http://www.rogerclarke.com/II/ICrimPrev.html>.

CJU 4030—Internet Crimes—Acalog ACMS™. (n.d.). *Alliant International University*. Retrieved from <http://catalog.alliant.edu/preview_course_nopop.php?catoid=19&coid=28315>.

Code of Responsible Computing, Computer Learning Foundation (2000). The advent of the computer delinquent. *FBI Law Enforcement Bulletin*, 69(12), 7–11. Retrieved from <http://www.fbi.gov/stats-services/publications/law-enforcement-bulletin/2000-pdfs/dec00leb.pdf>.

College of Policing: Covert Internet Investigations. (n.d.). *College of Policing*. Retrieved from <http://www.college.police.uk/en/578.htm>.

Commission Enforcement Actions Involving the Internet and Online Services. (2003). Washington, DC: *Federal Trade Commission*.

CybercrimeSurvival.com—Learn the Investigative Tools You Need to Succeed. (n.d.). *Vere software*. Retrieved from <http://www.cybercrimesurvival.com>.

Digital Evidence Class. (n.d.). *Central Piedmont Community College*. Retrieved from <http://www.cpcc.edu/aaaf/digital-evidence/classes-offered>.

Digital Forensic Science Courses. (n.d.). *Defiance College*. Retrieved from <http://www.defiance.edu/pages/BASS_CF_courses.html>.

Digital Stalking—Supporting Victims of Stalking, Harassment and Bullying. (n.d.). *Digital-stalking*. Retrieved from <http://www.digital-stalking.com/>.

econsumer.gov—Your site for cross-border complaints. (n.d.). *econsumer.gov*. Retrieved from <http://ECONSUMER.GOV>.

Enough is Enough. (n.d.). *InternetSafety101.org*. Retrieved from <http://www.internetsafety101.org/>.

Ernesto. (2013, June 11). UK ISPs secretly start blocking torrent site proxies. *torrentfreak.com*. Retrieved from <torrentfreak.com/uk-isps-secretly-start-blocking-torrent-site-proxies-130611/>.

Explorer (RT) (n.d.). Web security: tips to protect kids online. *Microsoft Protect. Microsoft Corporation*. Retrieved from <http://www.microsoft.com/security/family-safety/child-safety-steps.aspx>.

Family Safe Computers—Home. (n.d.). *Family safe computers*. Retrieved from <http://www.familysafecomputers.org/>.

FBI—Internet Fraud. (n.d.). *FBI*. Retrieved from <http://www.fbi.gov/scams-safety/fraud/internet_fraud>.

Federal Trade Commission—About Us. (n.d.). *Federal Trade Commission*. Retrieved from <http://www.ftc.gov/ftc/about.shtm>.

GetNetWise | You're one click away. (n.d.). *GetNetWise*. Retrieved from <http://www.getnetwise.org>.

Ghosh, R. (1997, October 31). Exclusive: Interpol's top internet crimefighter speaker out. *The American Reporter*.

Google's Good to Know a Guide to Staying Safe and Secure Online. (n.d.). *Google*. Retrieved from <http://www.google.com/goodtoknow>.

Hetherington Group—Training. (n.d.). *Hetherington Group*. Retrieved from <http://hetheringtongroup.com/training.shtml>.

High-Tech Crime Investigation: Loss Prevention and Cybercrime Certificate Program.(n.d.) *The College of Continuing and Professional Education, California State University, Long Beach*. Retrieved from <http://www.ccpe.csulb.edu/continuinged/course_listing/programdescription.aspx?Group_Number=236&Group_Version=2>.

High Technology Crime Investigation Association (HTCIA). (n.d.). *High Technology Crime Investigation Association*. Retrieved from <http://htcia.org>.

Home CEPOL—European Police College. (n.d.). *CEPOL—European Police College*. Retrieved from <https://www.cepol.europa.eu/>.

Home | CPC Canadian Police College. (n.d.). *Canadian Police College/Collège canadien de police*. Retrieved from <http://www.cpc.gc.ca/en/home>.

Home ConnectSafely. (n.d.). *ConnectSafely*. Retrieved from< www.connectsafely.org/>.

Home: Cybersmart. (n.d.). *Cybersmart*. Retrieved from <http://www.cybersmart.gov.au/>.

Home-KL Greer Consulting. (n.d.). *KL Greer Consulting*. Retrieved from <http://www.klgreer.com/>.

Home—Metropolitan Police Service. (n.d.). *Metropolitan Police Service*. Retrieved from <http://content.met.police.uk/>.

ICAC Training and Technical Assistance. (n.d.). *ICAC Training and Technical Assistance*. Retrieved from <http://www.icactraining.org/>.

iKeepSafe Home.(n.d.). *iKeepSafe*. Retrieved from <http://www.ikeepsafe.org/>.

Improving Security from the Inside Out. (2010). Medway, MA: National Security Institute. Retrieved from <http://www.nsi.org/pdf/improvingSecurity_InsideOut.pdf>.

Insafe. (n.d.). *www.saferinternet.org*. Retrieved from <http://www.saferinternet.org/>.

International Consumer Protection and Enforcement Network (ICPEN) Home. (n.d.). *International Consumer Protection and Enforcement Network (ICPEN)*. Retrieved from <https://icpen.org/>.

Internet Crime Complaint Center (IC3) | Prevention Tips. (n.d.). *Internet Crime Complaint Center (IC3)*. Retrieved from <http://www.ic3.gov/preventiontips.aspx>.

Internet Fraud Information. (n.d.). *USA.gov: The U.S. Government's Official Web Portal.* Retrieved from <http://www.usa.gov/Citizen/Topics/Internet-Fraud.shtml>.

Internet Investigation. (n.d.). *Cranfield University.* Retrieved from <http://www.cranfield.ac.uk/cds/postgraduatestudy/forensiccomputing/page15415.html>.

Internet Safety Resources—Royal Canadian Mounted Police. (n.d.). *Royal Canadian Mounted Police—gendarmerie royale du Canada—Bienvenue.* Retrieved from <http://www.rcmp-grc.gc.ca/is-si/index-eng.htm>.

Kidsmart Welcome. (n.d.). *Kidsmart.* Retrieved from <www.kidsmart.org.uk/>.

Kovalchik, K. (2008, August 30). True Crime: John Draper, the original whistle blower. *Mental Floss. Random, Interesting, Amazing Facts—Fun Quizzes and Trivia | Mental Floss.* Retrieved from <http://mentalfloss.com/article/19484/true-crime-john-draper-original-whistle-blower>.

Logicalis Commissions White Paper Study into BYOD. (2012, November 28). *Global IT Partner. Global IT Services, Solutions from Logicalis Group.* Retrieved from <http://www.logicalis.com/news-and-events/news/logicalis-white-paper-byod.aspx#.UfUb89LVC8C>.

McIntyre, T. (2013). *Child abuse images and cleanfeeds: Assessing internet blocking systems* (pp. 277−308). *Research handbook on governance of the internet* Cheltenham: Edward Elgar.

National Center for Missing and Exploited Children. (n.d.). *National Center for Missing and Exploited Children.* Retrieved from <http://www.missingkids.com/>.

National Cyber Security Alliance | StaySafeOnline.org. (n.d.). *National Cyber Security Alliance | StaySafeOnline.org.* Retrieved from <http://staysafeonline.org/>.

NCFI—Home. (n.d.). *National Computer Forensics Institute.* Retrieved from <www.ncfi.usss.gov/ncfi/>.

NetSmartz: Parents & Guardians. (n.d.). *NCMEC NetSmartz.* Retrieved from <http://www.netsmartz.org/>.

Novielli. M. Delivery tips for talking to child audiences (2004). *HTCIA Internet Safety For Children Campaign*, High Technology Crime Investigation Association (HTCIA).

NW3C Home. (n.d.). *National White Collar Crime Center.* Retrieved from <http://www.nw3c.org/>.

Ohio ICAC.org. (n.d.). *Ohio Internet Crimes Against Children Task Force.* Retrieved from <http://www.ohioicac.org/>.

OnGuard Online Home.(n.d.). *OnGuard Online.* Retrieved from <http://www.onguardonline.gov/>.

Online Computer Forensics—Bachelor's Degree. (n.d.). *Champlain College.* Retrieved from <http://www.champlain.edu/cyber-security/online-computer-forensics-digital-investigation-degree>.

Online Open Source Intelligence eLearning - Toddington International. (n.d.). *Toddington International Inc.* Retrieved from <http://toddington.com/etraining/>.

Program: Forensic Computer Investigation Certificate. (n.d.). *University of New Haven.* Retrieved from <http://catalog.newhaven.edu/preview_program.php?catoid=4&poid=510>.

Programs in Digital Forensics. (n.d.). *University of Central Florida.* Retrieved from <http://www.cs.ucf.edu/csdept/info/gccf/index.htm>.

Protect Your Computer from Cyber threats and Learn How to be Safe Online. (n.d.). *Securing Our eCity®*. Retrieved from <http://www.securingourecity.org/>.

RCFL: Regional Computer Forensics Laboratory. (n.d.). *RCFL: Regional Computer Forensics Laboratory*. Retrieved from <http://www.rcfl.gov/>.

Report Child Sexual Abuse Content to the Internet Watch Foundation (IWF). (2013). *Internet Watch Foundation (IWF)*. Retrieved from <http://www.iwf.org.uk/>.

SafeKids.com: Digital Citizenship, Online Safety & Civility. *SafeKids.com*. Retrieved from <http://www.safekids.com/>.

Safe Online Surfing. (n.d.). *FBI SOS*. Retrieved from <https://sos.fbi.gov/>.

A.G. Schneiderman's "Operation Game Over" Continues With Thousands Of Additional Sex Offenders Purged From Online Gaming Platforms | Eric T. Schneiderman. (n.d.). *Eric T. Schneiderman | New York State Attorney General*. Retrieved from <http://www.ag.ny.gov/press-release/ag-schneiderman%E2%80%99s-%E2%80%9Coperation-game-over%E2%80%9D-continues-thousands-additional-sex-offenders>.

SEARCH: The Online Resource for Justice and Public Safety Decision Makers. (n.d.). *SEARCH*. Retrieved from <http://www.search.org>.

Sprint™ 4NetSafety™. (n.d.). *Sprint*. Retrieved from <http://www.sprint.com/4netsafety/>.

The Carnegie Cyber Academy—An Online Safety site and Games for Kids. (n.d.). *The Carnegie Cyber Academy*. Retrieved from <http://www.carnegiecyberacademy.com/>.

The Comprehensive National Cybersecurity Initiative (2010). Washington, D.C: Executive Office of the President of the United States.

The Internet and On-Line Trading. (n.d.). *U.S. Securities and Exchange Commission*. Retrieved from <http://www.sec.gov/investor/online.shtml/>.

The Leaders in E-Safety Education. (n.d.). *i-SAFE*. Retrieved from <http://isafe.org/>.

thinkuknow. (n.d.). *Thinkuknow—home*. Retrieved from <www.thinkuknow.co.uk/>.

Training/Cybercrime/Crime areas/Internet/Home—INTERPOL. (n.d.). *Internet/Home—INTERPOL*. Retrieved from <http://www.interpol.int/Crime-areas/Cybercrime/Training/>.

UK—Safer Internet Centre. (n.d.). *UK—Safer Internet Centre*. Retrieved from <http://www.saferinternet.org.uk/>.

United Kingdom Council for Child Internet Safety (UKCCIS). (n.d.).*UK Department of Education*. Retrieved from <https://www.education.gov.uk/childrenandyoungpeople/safeguardingchildren/b00222029/child-internet-safety>.

USDOJ: CRM: About the Criminal Division. (n.d.). *United States Department of Justice*. Retrieved from <http://www.justice.gov/criminal/fraud/websites/i/>.

Washtenaw County Cyber Citizenship Coalition - Online Security. (n.d.). *Washtenaw County Cyber Citizenship Coalition*. Retrieved from <http://washtenawcybercoalition.org/>.

Web Wise Kids. (n.d.). *Web Wise Kids*. <http://www.webwisekids.org/>.

WISE KIDS: Promoting Innovative, Positive and Safe Internet Use. (n.d.). *WISE KIDS*. Retrieved from <http://www.wisekids.org.uk/>.

Yoursphere for Parents—Helping Families Live Healthy Digital Lives. (n.d.). *Yoursphere*. Retrieved from <http://internet-safety.yoursphere.com/>.

Putting It All Together

17

We passed important laws to give the authorities responsible for investigation wide powers to defend us.
George Pataki, Former Governor

Concepts in action

Investigating Internet crimes requires a basic skill set to identify where the evidence is and to track it to a possible perpetrator. We have laid out techniques and tactics to accomplish a successful investigation. We will now apply these new skills to various investigative scenarios. The intention is to demonstrate how the investigator can collect online evidence and identify the witnesses and potential suspects for various common Internet crimes.

Basic Internet investigative steps

The following steps and actions, adopted from the International Association Chief's of Police resource for investigating and identifying theft, are intended to be a guide for understanding the Internet crime investigative process. Every online investigation is different and needs to be evaluated based on the known facts. The steps given below can be added to or subtracted from depending on what the investigator determines during the investigation. Table 17.1 provides possible investigative actions corresponding with each step.

1. Review the initial reports of the incident or crime.
2. Contact the reporting party/victim and determine if reported information is correct and additional information is not documented in initial reports.
3. Validate that a crime involving the Internet actually occurred.
4. Prepare an investigative plan.
5. Identify initial investigative information.
6. Document Internet evidence.
7. Subpoena ISP or other online services to ID IP address usage by suspects.

Table 17.1 Basic Internet Investigative Steps

	Step	Investigator's Actions
1	Review the initial reports of the Internet incident or crime	a. Review details in the initial report. b. Rechecking known facts. c. Review fact to identify if they meet the elements of the crime classification.
2	Contact the reporting party/victim and determine if reported information is correct and additional information is not documented in initial reports	a. Investigator contacts victim and validates reported information and ascertains if new information is available. b. Identify if additional information/evidence not originally identified or collected is available.
3	Validate that a crime involving the Internet actually occurred	Review the reported facts and identify that an Internet crime actually occurred.
4	Prepare an investigative plan	a. Create a predication laying out the basic allegation, the source, and date the allegation was made. b. Delineate all elements to establish a law violation occurred. c. Identify investigative steps need to legally prove law violation.
5	Identify initial investigative information	a. Identify the basic facts from the reports, the "who, what, where, when, why, and how" based on the available information. b. With an Internet case this will depend on the Internet service used to commit the offense.
6	Document Internet evidence	The investigator needs to document the available evidence on the Internet as determined by the initial report if not initially collected.
7	Subpoena ISP or other online services to ID IP address usage by suspects	Identify information to subpoena, such as IP and email addresses, website, or blog information.
8	Assess additional cases of similar comparison	Review additional cases locally, through adjacent agencies or nationally through the ICCC for similar suspects or crime type.
9	Review collected data and determine sufficiency of evidence	After collecting the evidence, determine if there is sufficient information and evidence to proceed with a prosecution.
10	Submit evidence to counsel/prosecutor for potential prosecution	Prepare case and submit to prosecutor.

8. Assess additional cases for similar comparison.
9. Review collected data and determine sufficiency of evidence.
10. Submit evidence to counsel/prosecutor for potential prosecution.

Case studies

The following scenarios have been designed to provide the investigator with the concept of how to follow up on and investigate an Internet crime. These scenarios are based on actual cases, but the facts have been changed. Of course, every case is different and each case requires an evaluation of the known facts. The case examples are designed to provide a concept of the potential investigative possibilities and not what should be done in every case. The investigator should review the case examples as a guide to planning their own investigations and to identify possible actions. Each scenario listed is a different possible Internet crime that has occurred in the real world. For the purposes of the text, the examples are simplified and actual cases can tend to be more complex. Additionally, the evaluation as to whether an arrest is made, submission for prosecution or termination of an employee under the examples is beyond this text's substance. The intent here is to only provide the investigator with investigative concepts and how an Internet investigation and online ESI collection can occur in real life. The investigator should always have a clear understanding of the law related to the crimes he/she is investigating and consider including legal counsel's advice throughout the investigative process. Also, each of these Internet cases ends with the investigator contacting the target of the investigation in the real world. The investigation may start with facts known to have occurred through the Internet, but the scenarios all come down to the investigator being able to tie the investigation to a real person in a real place using a real computing device to commit the offense. Ultimately, any Internet investigation comes down to the investigator's ability to conclude the investigation by connecting a law violation to the person or individuals using the Internet as a smoke screen to hide their unlawful activities. The scenarios are broken down into the following three parts:

1. The case facts known at the time of the initial report. This is an outline of the information reported by the victim and provided to the initial report taker.
2. The investigator's follow-up. This section includes the actions that can be taken by the investigator during this investigation, based on the known facts and identified information.
3. Internet evidence to document and collect. This section provides the investigator with the possible online ESI that can be collected from the Internet or holders of the Internet data.

eBay fraud scenario

Case facts known at time of report	The victim buys a signed Mickey Mantle baseball on eBay for a small fortune. The buyer agrees to send the money through PayPal. The baseball never appeared.
Investigator's follow-up	a. Interview victim and obtain proof of payment.
	b. Prepare an investigative plan.
	c. Identify eBay article.
	d. Document the eBay article.
	e. Subpoena eBay for seller's information.
	f. Subpoena ISP owning seller's IP address.
	g. Research identified potential perpetrator.
	h. Interview perpetrator.
Internet evidence to document and collect	a. Document posting from eBay Craigslist website with screenshot or method to properly document information.
	b. Obtain records that payment was made through PayPal and to whom.
	c. Subpoena eBay asking for poster's information and IP address.
	d. Identify IP ownership.
	e. Subpoena ISP owning IP address.
	f. Subpoena PayPal for information on the receivers account and associated IP addresses.
	g. Identify IP ownership.

Craigslist stolen property scenario

Case facts known at time of report	A corporation selling widgets stored 100 boxes of them in a warehouse near their offices. The warehouse was broken into and the 100 boxes were stolen. The theft was reported to the local police department. No leads were available to follow up on so no further investigation was completed. The company has an Internet security team responsible for physical security and internal theft. One of the investigators was researching online for possible sales of widgets that were not by authorized resellers. A check of Craigslist found several entries for various used widgets and one for a case of widgets.
Investigator's follow-up	a. Identify any serial numbers or other unique identifying information about the stolen widgets.
	b. Prepare an investigative plan.

(Continued)

(Continued)	
	c. Prepare an undercover persona relevant to the case.
	d. Obtain undercover email account and telephone.
	e. Contact the seller through Craigslist and inquire about the widgets.
	f. Research the seller in an attempt to identify them and possible connections to the break-in.
	g. Attempt to get additional information on the widgets, pictures, or other useful information without alerting the target to verify the widget as the ones stolen from the company.
	h. Agree to purchase the widgets. Set up a meeting in a location that can be observed and controlled.
	i. Contact the detective assigned to the investigation. Arrange for assistance with the purchase meeting.
Internet evidence to document and collect	a. Document posting from Craigslist website with screenshot or method to properly document information.
	b. Subpoena Craigslist asking for poster's information and IP address.
	c. Subpoena ISP owning IP address.

Internet threat to company officer scenario

Case facts known at time of report	The investigator is informed that certain threatening statements have been posted about a company's senior-level executive on one or more websites. There is a concern for the executive's safety. At the time of the report, it was unknown who made the threat.
Investigator's follow-up	a. Prepare an investigative plan.
	b. Identify the locations on the Internet that the threats were made.
	c. Properly document those locations.
	d. Conduct Internet background search on the executive in an attempt to identify additional locations of possible threats.
	e. Interview executive to ascertain if there is anyone wishing him/her harm.
	f. Research background on poster. Use search engines to search poster's name and identify if IP address is associated with posting.
	g. Subpoena blog owner for poster's IP address.

(Continued)

(Continued)	
	h. Subpoena ISP owning the IP address received from blog posting.
	i. Research identified subject.
	j. Locate identified subject and plan initial contact and interview.
	k. Interview subject(s) identified as poster(s).
Internet evidence to document and collect	a. Blog posts or other threatening postings.
	b. IP information by posters.
	c. Domain information for IP address.
	d. Internet background research on the poster.

Cyberharrassment scenario

Case facts known at time of report	The investigator is advised that a female high-school student is being harassed on the Internet. The harassment is based on a posting the female victim made on a social networking site. She mentioned that she liked a particular male classmate. The harassment began by others in her class on the same social networking site demeaning her for liking the boy. Additional postings began to occur on other locations and became increasingly threatening and defaming. The victim's parents have started making posting on some of the same sites defending their daughter, which only exacerbated the situation.
Investigator's follow-up	a. Prepare an investigative plan.
	b. Interview the victim regarding her knowledge of who is posting these messages.
	c. Identify the social networking site(s) in question.
	d. Identify the additional sites where postings were made.
	e. Identify the victim's usernames.
	f. Identify the usernames on the sites of the harassing posters.
	g. Document each of the social networking users and postings.
	h. Research the identified user's names on the Internet.
	i. Identify poster's relationship with victim.
	j. Interview the posters.

(Continued)

(Continued)	
Internet evidence to document and collect	a. Postings on the social networking site. b. Subpoena social networking site for information on all relevant posters in the investigation including the victim. c. Document postings on other sites found in the research that are relevant to the investigation.

Internet murder scenario

Case facts known at time of report	A young woman is found dead in her apartment. The investigation has no leads as to the suspect. The victim's friends said that she had no threats or former boyfriends that would be likely suspects. The forensic review of the victim's computer identified that she was a regular visitor to various Internet chat sites, including those focused on sadomasochistic behavior. None of the victim's friends were aware of this behavior or predilection of the victim. There were several websites that were regularly visited by the victim. The computer forensic investigation identified a unique Gmail address and username for several of the sites used by the victim.
Investigator's follow-up	a. Prepare an investigative plan. b. The investigator subpoenaed the unique Gmail account found during the computer forensic analysis. c. The investigator reviewed the sites found through the computer forensic exam and identified several usernames that the victim regularly interacted with. d. Several conversation threads were found in the Gmail data returned through the subpoena between a user identified on one of the sites as a regular poster that the victim interacted with on the site. e. The investigator subpoenaed the websites legal contact for information on the usernames of interest, including the victims. f. The investigator subpoenaed Gmail for user accounts related to the investigation that matched the user account from the websites of interest. g. The investigator reviewed the Gmail data returned for IP addresses of the user's accounts and ran the IP addresses to determine the ISP hosting the IP addresses. h. The investigator served the ISP with subpoenas to identify the account holders using the IP addresses.

(Continued)

(Continued)	
Internet evidence to document and collect	a. Online accounts
	b. Gmail account
	c. ISP info
	d. Domain registrations

Email threat scenario

Case facts known at time of report	A divorced mother of two received an email from an unknown account threatening her life and making vile comments about her person and her ability to care for her children. The email was from a Yahoo account and the reporting officer collected the email as well as the headers associated with the email.
Investigator's follow-up	a. Interview victim.
	b. Prepare an investigative plan.
	c. Review the email header information and identify available information including IP addresses, ISP owning IP addresses.
	d. Document the IP and ISP information.
	e. Subpoena ISP for user of IP address at time email was sent.
	f. Research identified potential perpetrator.
	g. Interview perpetrator.
Internet evidence to document and collect	a. Email
	b. IP information
	c. ISP information on user

CONCLUSION

This chapter was intended to provide the reader with some basic approaches to conducting an Internet investigation. The scenarios are only guides and should only be used to grasp the concepts of an Internet investigation. Each example has provided a number of steps based on the facts known at the time and the type of evidence that could be collected. The investigator can use these case studies to better understand what it is that they need to plan for when investigating Internet crimes.

Further reading

Investigative Steps Identity Crime Toolkit for Investigators. (n.d.). *International Association Chief's of Police*. Retrieved from <www.theiacp.org/investigateid/investigation/nuts-and-bolts-of-investigation/investigative-steps/>.

Epilogue

18

This text has covered a significant amount of information, much of which was likely new to the investigator's first learning about Internet crimes. We intended to present an overview of what the Internet was, how it is abused by criminals, and how to investigate, document, and successfully solve online crimes. This text was never designed to cover every possible location or type of crime committed on the Internet. We tried throughout this book to provide the new investigator with a foundational perspective of Internet investigative techniques to enable them to further their ability to fight these new crimes. So the question is where does this leave us? The short answer is there is a lot more to do. The Internet is a vast and ever growing place. Many areas were not addressed in this text. Today's investigators interested in furthering their understanding of crime in the world need to prepare themselves with a background in Internet crime investigation. This text is a beginning to understanding that process. If you have gotten this far in the text, you will know that crime and criminals are prevalent on the Internet. It is a problem that needs to be addressed. Ignoring online crime with the misconception that the Internet is not your jurisdiction is obviously not a solution to this problem. Investigating online crime is no longer a problem that can be avoided by law enforcement or corporate investigators. We both agree investigators need to "make the Internet their regular beat." Doing so will change how everyone looks at Internet crime. More investigators online means more criminals are brought to justice. Additional investigators focusing on Internet crime means more victims who will be assured that their law enforcement can protect them, even when online. Experienced investigators taking the time to understand the issues with Internet crime will influence their agency or companies approach to the problem. Administrators will be influenced from the ground up by their employees that grasp the issues that surround Internet investigations. Those investigators brave enough to step forward into the unknown of Internet crime will be standard bearers in the future of how modern criminal investigations should be conducted.

As an investigator reading this, you have taken the first step to changing how we approach Internet investigations. So what can you expect next? There are many things to consider when approaching investigating online crimes. Things change rapidly on the Internet and new places show up for individuals to be victimized. Money laundering, human trafficking, theft in virtual worlds, and drug dealing in hidden places in the Tor network are all occurring on the Internet. Online gaming environments are increasing becoming locations where criminal activity is occurring. Additionally, the Biticoin's emergence was only briefly discussed in this text. Digital and virtual currencies pose unique challenges for law enforcement. Investigators need to spend the time learning about these places and technologies and what it will take to protect our communities. Remember, if you make the Internet your regular beat, your community will be safer, your citizens will be able to surf the Internet without fear, and you will be an effective investigator in today's connected world.

Appendices

Appendix A: HEX to ASCII Conversion Chart

HEX	Symbol	Description	HEX	Symbol	Description
0	NUL	Null char	33	3	Three
1	SOH	Start of Heading	34	4	Four
2	STX	Start of Text	35	5	Five
3	ETX	End of Text	36	6	Six
4	EOT	End of Transmission	37	7	Seven
5	ENQ	Enquiry	38	8	Eight
6	ACK	Acknowledgment	39	9	Nine
7	BEL	Bell	3A	:	Colon
8	BS	Back Space	3B	;	Semicolon
9	HT	Horizontal Tab	3C	<	Less than (or open angled bracket)
0A	LF	Line Feed	3D	=	Equals
0B	VT	Vertical Tab	3E	>	Greater than (or close angled bracket)
0C	FF	Form Feed	3F	?	Question mark
0D	CR	Carriage Return	40	@	At symbol
0E	SO	Shift Out / X-On	41	A	Uppercase A
0F	SI	Shift In / X-Off	42	B	Uppercase B
10	DLE	Data Line Escape	43	C	Uppercase C
11	DC1	Device Control 1 (oft. XON)	44	D	Uppercase D
12	DC2	Device Control 2	45	E	Uppercase E
13	DC3	Device Control 3 (oft. XOFF)	46	F	Uppercase F
14	DC4	Device Control 4	47	G	Uppercase G
15	NAK	Negative Acknowledgement	48	H	Uppercase H

HEX	Symbol	Description	HEX	Symbol	Description
16	SYN	Synchronous Idle	49	I	Uppercase I
17	ETB	End of Transmit Block	4A	J	Uppercase J
18	CAN	Cancel	4B	K	Uppercase K
19	EM	End of Medium	4C	L	Uppercase L
1A	SUB	Substitute	4D	M	Uppercase M
1B	ESC	Escape	4E	N	Uppercase N
1C	FS	File Separator	4F	O	Uppercase O
1D	GS	Group Separator	50	P	Uppercase P
1E	RS	Record Separator	51	Q	Uppercase Q
1F	US	Unit Separator	52	R	Uppercase R
20		Space	53	S	Uppercase S
21	!	Exclamation mark	54	T	Uppercase T
22	"	Double quotes (or speech marks)	55	U	Uppercase U
23	#	Number	56	V	Uppercase V
24	$	Dollar	57	W	Uppercase W
25	%	Procenttecken	58	X	Uppercase X
26	&	Ampersand	59	Y	Uppercase Y
27	'	Single quote	5A	Z	Uppercase Z
28	(	Open parenthesis (or open bracket)	5B	[	Opening bracket
29	)	Close parenthesis (or close bracket)	5C	\	Backslash
2A	*	Asterisk	5D	]	Closing bracket
2B	+	Plus	5E	^	Caret - circumflex
2C	,	Comma	5F	_	Underscore

HEX	Symbol	Description	HEX	Symbol	Description
2D	-	Hyphen	60	`	Grave accent
2E	.	Period, dot or full stop	61	a	Lowercase a
2F	/	Slash or divide	62	b	Lowercase b
30	0	Zero	63	c	Lowercase c
31	1	One	64	d	Lowercase d
32	2	Two	65	e	Lowercase e
66	f	Lowercase f	99	™	Trade mark sign
67	g	Lowercase g	9A	š	Latin small letter S with caron
68	h	Lowercase h	9B	›	Single right-pointing angle quotation mark
69	i	Lowercase i	9C	œ	Latin small ligature oe
6A	j	Lowercase j	9D		
6B	k	Lowercase k	9E	ž	Latin small letter z with caron
6C	l	Lowercase l	9F	Ÿ	Latin capital letter Y with diaeresis
6D	m	Lowercase m	A0		Non-breaking space
6E	n	Lowercase n	A1	¡	Inverted exclamation mark
6F	o	Lowercase o	A2	¢	Cent sign
70	p	Lowercase p	A3	£	Pound sign
71	q	Lowercase q	A4	¤	Currency sign
72	r	Lowercase r	A5	¥	Yen sign
73	s	Lowercase s	A6	¦	Pipe, Broken vertical bar
74	t	Lowercase t	A7	§	Section sign
75	u	Lowercase u	A8	¨	Spacing diaeresis - umlaut

HEX	Symbol	Description	HEX	Symbol	Description
76	v	Lowercase v	A9	©	Copyright sign
77	w	Lowercase w	AA	a	Feminine ordinal indicator
78	x	Lowercase x	AB	«	Left double angle quotes
79	y	Lowercase y	AC	¬	Not sign
7A	z	Lowercase z	AD		Soft hyphen
7B	{	Opening brace	AE	®	Registered trade mark sign
7C	|	Vertical bar	AF	‾	Spacing macron - overline
7D	}	Closing brace	B0	°	Degree sign
7E	~	Equivalency sign - tilde	B1	±	Plus-or-minus sign
7F		Delete	B2	²	Superscript two - squared
80	€	Euro sign	B3	³	Superscript three - cubed
81			B4	´	Acute accent - spacing acute
82	‚	Single low-9 quotation mark	B5	μ	Micro sign
83	ƒ	Latin small letter f with hook	B6	¶	Pilcrow sign - paragraph sign
84	„	Double low-9 quotation mark	B7	·	Middle dot - Georgian comma
85	…	Horizontal ellipsis	B8	¸	Spacing cedilla
86	†	Dagger	B9	¹	Superscript one
87	‡	Double dagger	BA	º	Masculine ordinal indicator
88	ˆ	Modifier letter circumflex accent	BB	»	Right double angle quotes
89	‰	Per mille sign	BC	¼	Fraction one quarter
8A	Š	Latin capital letter S with caron	BD	½	Fraction one half

HEX	Symbol	Description	HEX	Symbol	Description
8B	‹	Single left-pointing angle quotation	BE	¾	Fraction three quarters
8C	Œ	Latin capital ligature OE	BF	¿	Inverted question mark
8D			C0	À	Latin capital letter A with grave
8E	Ž	Latin captial letter Z with caron	C1	Á	Latin capital letter A with acute
8F			C2	Â	Latin capital letter A with circumflex
90			C3	Ã	Latin capital letter A with tilde
91	'	Left single quotation mark	C4	Ä	Latin capital letter A with diaeresis
92	'	Right single quotation mark	C5	Å	Latin capital letter A with ring above
93	"	Left double quotation mark	C6	Æ	Latin capital letter AE
94	"	Right double quotation mark	C7	Ç	Latin capital letter C with cedilla
95	•	Bullet	C8	È	Latin capital letter E with grave
96	–	En dash	C9	É	Latin capital letter E with acute
97	—	Em dash	CA	Ê	Latin capital letter E with circumflex
98	˜	Small tilde	CB	Ë	Latin capital letter E with diaeresis

HEX	Symbol	Description	HEX	Symbol	Description
CC	Ì	Latin capital letter I with grave	D7	×	Multiplication sign
CD	Í	Latin capital letter I with acute	D8	Ø	Latin capital letter O with slash
CE	Î	Latin capital letter I with circumflex	D9	Ù	Latin capital letter U with grave
CF	Ï	Latin capital letter I with diaeresis	DA	Ú	Latin capital letter U with acute
D0	Đ	Latin capital letter ETH	DB	Û	Latin capital letter U with circumflex
D1	Ñ	Latin capital letter N with tilde	DC	Ü	Latin capital letter U with diaeresis
D2	Ò	Latin capital letter O with grave	DD	Ý	Latin capital letter Y with acute
D3	Ó	Latin capital letter O with acute	DE	Þ	Latin capital letter THORN
D4	Ô	Latin capital letter O with circumflex	DF	ß	Latin small letter sharp s - ess-zed
D5	Õ	Latin capital letter O with tilde	E0	à	Latin small letter a with grave
D6	Ö	Latin capital letter O with diaeresis	E1	á	Latin small letter a with acute
D7	×	Multiplication sign	E2	â	Latin small letter a with circumflex

HEX	Symbol	Description	HEX	Symbol	Description
E3	ã	Latin small letter a with tilde	F1	ñ	Latin small letter n with tilde
E4	ä	Latin small letter a with diaeresis	F2	ò	Latin small letter o with grave
E5	å	Latin small letter a with ring above	F3	ó	Latin small letter o with acute
E6	æ	Latin small letter ae	F4	ô	Latin small letter o with circumflex
E7	ç	Latin small letter c with cedilla	F5	õ	Latin small letter o with tilde
E8	è	Latin small letter e with grave	F6	ö	Latin small letter o with diaeresis
E9	é	Latin small letter e with acute	F7	÷	Division sign
EA	ê	Latin small letter e with circumflex	F8	ø	Latin small letter o with slash
EB	ë	Latin small letter e with diaeresis	F9	ù	Latin small letter u with grave
EC	ì	Latin small letter i with grave	FA	ú	Latin small letter u with acute
ED	í	Latin small letter i with acute	FB	û	Latin small letter u with circumflex
EE	î	Latin small letter i with circumflex	FC	ü	Latin small letter u with diaeresis
EF	ï	Latin small letter i with diaeresis	FD	ý	Latin small letter y with acute
F0	ð	Latin small letter eth	FE	þ	Latin small letter thorn
F7	÷	Division sign	FF	ÿ	Latin small letter y with diaeresis

Appendix B: Stored Communications Act Quick Reference Guide: USDOJ Search and Seizure

	Voluntary Disclosure Allowed?		How to Compel Disclosure	
	Public Provider	**Non-Public**	**Public Provider**	**Non-Public**
Basic subscriber, session, and billing information •	No, unless §2702(c) exception applies	Yes	Subpoena; 2703(d) order; or search warrant	Subpoena; 2703(d) order; or search warrant
	§ 2702(a)(3)	*§ 2702(a)(3)*	*§ 2703(c)(2)*	*§ 2703(c)(2)*
Other transactional and account records	No, unless §2702(c) exception applies	Yes	2703(d) order or search warrant	2703(d) order or search warrant
	§ 2702(a)(3)	*§ 2702(a)(3)*	*§ 2703(c)(1)*	*§ 2703(c)(1)*
Retrieved communications and the content of other stored files#	No, unless § 2702(b) exception applies	Yes	Subpoena with notice; 2703(d) order with notice; or search warrant*	Subpoena; SCA does not apply*
	§ 2702(a)(2)	*§ 2702(a)(2)*	*§ 2703(b)*	*§ 2711(2)*
Unretrieved communications, including email and voice mail (in electronic storage more than 180 days) †	No, unless § 2702(b) exception applies	Yes	Subpoena with notice; 2703(d) order with notice; or search warrant	Subpoena with notice; 2703(d) order with notice; or search warrant
	§ 2702(a)(1)	*§ 2702(a)(1)*	*§ 2703(a), (b)*	*§ 2703(a), (b)*
Unretrieved communications, including email and voice mail (in electronic storage 180 days or less) †	No, unless § 2702(b) exception applies	Yes	Search warrant	Search warrant
	§ 2702(a)(1)	*§ 2702(a)(1)*	*§ 2703(a)*	*§ 2703(a)*

- See 18 U.S.C. § 2703(c)(2) for listing of information covered. This information includes local and long distance telephone connection records and records of session times and durations as well as IP addresses assigned to the user during the Internet connections.
† Includes the content of voice communications.
* For investigations occurring in the Ninth Circuit, *Theofel v. Farey-Jones*, 359 F.3d 1066 (9th Cir. 2004), requires use of a search warrant unless the communications have been in storage for more than 180 days. Some providers follow *Theofel* even outside the Ninth Circuit; contact CCIPS at (202) 514-1026 if you have an appropriate case to litigate this issue.

Source: Searching and Seizing Computers and Obtaining Electronic Evidence in Criminal Investigations, U.S. Department of Justice, Computer Crime and Intellectual Property Section Criminal Division. Page 138. Retrieved from http://www.justice.gov/criminal/cybercrime/docs/ssmanual2009.pdf

Appendix C: Online Crime Victim Interview

Online Crime Victim Interview Question Aid[1]

Evidence on the Internet can be volatile and may not be stored on a server for very long. An investigator needs to take prompt action to preserve evidence located on the Internet.

> The list below is simply a guide and not an exhaustive investigative list of potential questions. Some questions may not be appropriate for your particular investigation. Ask only the relevant questions based on the type of crime and allegations by the victim. This is intended as a reference to aid in your online investigation.

Date: _____   Case Number:_____

Investigator: _____ Victim:_____

VICTIM QUESTIONS	ANSWER
Internet Access	

1. Who is your Internet Service Provider (ISP)?
2. What kind of Internet service do you have?
      a. Dial up
      b. DSL
      c. Cable
      d. Wireless
3. Where did this occur? (your home, work, school, etc.)?
4. What are your e-mail addresses?
5. Who owns the computer you used? (you, your employer, school, parents, etc.)
6. Did you access the Internet through a network? (employer, school, etc.)
7. Did you access the Internet through a wireless network and is so where?	

Chat related crimes	
1. What was the chat service where this occurred? 2. What was the date and time this occurred 3. What is the chatroom(s) name where this occurred? 4. What is your screen name or nickname in this chatroom? What is the suspect's screen name or nickname? Do you know their real name? 5. Did the chatroom have an operator or moderator and if so, what is their screen name or nickname? Do you know their real name? 6. Did your recognize anyone else in the chatroom and if so, what is their screen name or nickname? What about their real name? 7. Did you save or printout out a copy of the	

---
[1] APCO Guide

conversation?
    a) If you saved it, can you provide a copy to us? (If possible, try to observe them saving it.)
    b) If they printed it out, try to get the original hard copy.	

Newsgroup related crimes	

1. What is the newsgroup's complete name?
 2. Do you access newsgroups via software or through a website?
 3. Did you save the posting to a computer?
    a) Can you provide an electronic copy? (If possible observe them saving it).
    b) If not, did you print a copy of the posting and can we have the original hard copy?
 4. Is this newsgroup available directly from your ISP?
 5. Which newsgroup service do you use?
 6. Which computer server did you use to access this newsgroup? What is the name of the posting?	

E-mail related crimes	
1. Do you have the e-mail(s) address of the person who sent the email, including the header information? 2. Did you save the e-mail(s)? Where? 3. Can you provide an electronic copy to us? (This copy needs to include the header information) 4. Do you have a printed copy of the e-mail? 5. Is your e-mail software or web based?	
Website related crimes	
1. What is the website(s) address (URL)? 2. Did you save a copy of the web page in question? 3. What was the date and time you visited the website? 4. What was it that you saw on the website?	
Chat room (IRC) related crime	
1. What is your profile name and which e-mail account is associated with it? 2. Where was the post made? your shared area or another user's area? 3. What profile name made the post? 4. Who else may have seen the post and what is their profile name (real name)? 5. Was the message sent to your profile and if so do you still have it (It may be very important to get access to this message, which will point to the originating profile.)?	

Note: Always ask for any passwords that you consider may be relevant.

Appendix D: Internet Investigations Report Format

Internet Investigations Report Format

Case Number:_____   Date:_____

Investigator:_____   ID #:_____

Case Type: _____

Victim:_____   Target:_____

Evidence:_____

Evidence Collection Method:

The investigator used the following tools to document the collection of the evidence collected in the Internet during this investigation:

- SnagIt
- WebCase
- Internet Explorer

Targeted Internet Protocols and Identifying Information:

1) Websites:
   a. www.......com
2) IRC:
   a. Username bob1234 on
   b. IRC Server xxxxx
   c. IRC channel "cardz"

Identified Target(s):

1) Bob Smith

Details:

This investigation is about internet content found at the following URL http://www........com hosted by a hosting service provider XXXXXX which appears to be hosted in the United States.

The domain is registered to:

The content on the URL appears to be....

Conclusion: (Brief description of the violations and evidence supporting they occurred.)

Appendix E: Digital Officer Safety Computer

Online Digital Officer Safety Computer Setup Checklist

	Investigator Task	Completed
1	Install Software Firewall and updates	
2	Install Antivirus programs and updates	
3	Install Spyware Detection Software and updates	
4	Installation of Browsers and browser Updates	
5	Block cookies	
6	Configuring the system's operating system and making sure it is up to date	
7	Preparing system backups	
8	Continuing Security Maintenance • Use of encryption • Operating system updates • Browser updates • Software updates, tools, system, anti-virus, anti-spyware programs, etc. • Keeping the system clean • Testing the security of the system. • Regular or programmed backups	

Appendix F: Router Setup Checklist

Router Setup Checklist

Required Items:
- A) **Wireless Router with power cord**
- B) **Two Ethernet cables**
- C) **Computer or laptop**

Note: The following is a general guide and the steps will vary depending on the make and model of the router. Always review the manufacturer's guidelines for installation details.

	Investigator Task	Completed
1	**Plug in the router and turn on the router** **Connect your Internet modem to the router.** Plug in Ethernet cable into the router Ethernet port named "WAN" or "uplink" or "Internet."	
2	**Turn the modem off** and turn it back on (This is to ensure the router is recognized).	
3	**Connect a computer to the router.** Plug and Ethernet cable into the network connection of the computer and the other end into an open port on the router.	
4	**Open the router's administration tool.** Open Web browser on the computer connected to the router. Check the bottom of the router or installation manual for IP address - Often the default address is http://192.168.1.1 or http://192.168.0.1.	
5	**Log in to the router.** Enter default username and password (These are provided in the router's documentation).	
6	**Change Default Administrator Passwords (and Usernames)**	
7	**Enter required Internet connection information**	
8	**Turn on Encryption**	
9	**Change wireless network name** (called SSID).	
10	**Enable MAC Address Filtering**	
11	**Disable SSID Broadcast**	
12	**Turn Off Auto-Connect to Open Wi-Fi Networks**	
13	**Assign Static IP Addresses to Devices**	
14	**Enable Firewall on Router (if installed)** 1. Verify the network connection is working	
15	**Verify your computer can connect to the Internet**	
16	**Configure additional network security features as required**	

Appendix G: Tracing Email Worksheet

Basic Email Tracing Worksheet

	Student Task
1	Identify the "Message-ID"
2	Identify the "From" Email Address
3	Identify the "To" Email Address
4	Identify the "Received from" Servers
5	Identify the "Received from" IP Addresses
6	Identify the ISP Owning IP Address
7	Identify the Legal Contact for the ISP

Appendix H: Undercover Persona Worksheet

Undercover Persona Worksheet

1	**First Name**	**Last Name**
2	**Age/Date of Birth**	**Gender**
3	**City**	**State** **ZIP**
4	**Email**	
5	**Email Password**	
6	**Instant Message Login** **Password**	
7	**Chat Name** **Password**	
8	**Newsgroup Login** **Password**	

Model Policy
for Law Enforcement
Investigative use
of Social Networking

Disclaimer: This is a model policy was designed to provide a guide to writing a policy related to social networking use. This model policy should be reviewed and revised based on your local legal requirements. Implementation of any of this model policy should be done so <u>only</u> after legal review by your agency attorney. Additionally, your policy prior to implementation will need to conform to any national or local laws, labor agreements and existing policy within the agency.

I. POLICY

That all *<Agency Name>* police department personnel use computers, computer applications, computer programs, Internet resources and network/Internet communications in a responsible, professional, ethical, and lawful manner. That conduct of its employees off off-duty has a reflection on the department. This policy is intended to guide employees conduct when it relates to their employment or representations of employment though the numerous social networking venues. The *<Agency Name>* police department has established guidelines for conducting surveillance, undercover, decoy, and raid operations. Investigations using Social Networking are specialized investigative operations requiring an understanding of the new technology and its impact on the community. These investigations can be very effective in determining criminal activities of individuals or groups both online and in our community. At times, social networking investigations may provide the only technique available to identify principals and co-conspirators involved in criminal activity. Social Networking investigations may be conducted against any type of crime including: organized crime, narcotics, burglars, vice suspects, stalking, child predators and other individuals or groups who commit criminal acts.

II. POLICY REVIEW

This policy will be reviewed by the *<Appropriate administrative level Supervisor>* or any person so designated by the *<Chief of Police, Sheriff or lead Law Enforcement Administrator>* on an annual basis to ensure that it is legally sound and reasonably enforceable.

III. POLICY TRAINING

All full-time officers, administrative staff, support personnel, student interns, volunteer staff and/or any other persons so authorized to use the police department computers will become familiar with and adhere to the provisions of this policy and receive training and notification pertaining to this policy by in-service training, internal mail, email, and/or occasional network log-on reminders.

IV. DEFINITION OF "SOCIAL NETWORKING"

Is defined as social network sites that use Internet services to allow individuals to construct a public or semi-public profile within that system, define a list of other users with whom they share some connection, and view and access their list of connections and those made by others within that system. The type of network and its design vary from site to site. Examples of the types of Internet based social networking sites include: blogs, networking sites, photo sharing, video sharing, microblogging, podcasts, as well as comments posted on the sites. *The absence of, or lack of explicit reference to a specific site does not limit the extent of the application of this policy.*

V. SOCIAL NETWORKING INVESTIGATIVE OPERATIONS:

Social Networking investigations have no different requirements when it comes to documenting the investigations. The techniques applied on the Internet still require the information be properly collected, properly preserved and properly presented in a report.

The objective of social networking investigations is to:

1. Determine the nature of the online criminal activity.
2. Identify all of the persons involved in the online criminal activity.
3. Legally obtain evidence for a search warrant or for prosecution.
4. Obtain evidence of the crime from social networking sites.
5. Verify investigators online actions.
6. Prevent the commission of further crime and apprehend subjects committing crimes through social networking sites.
7. Develop leads based on information from other sources.

VI. PROFESSIONAL CONDUCT ONLINE

Officers realize their obligation to the community and should strive to act in a professional manner while investigating crimes on the Internet in order to inspire the public trust and confidence. Maintaining professionalism, even while online, should be a primary goal our officers and will ensure the continued trust and respect of the community. All officers are public servants and shall keep all contacts with the public both professional and courteous.

VII. PREPARING FOR A SOCIAL NETWORKING INVESTIGATIVE OPERATION:

Prior to determining if a social networking investigative operation is necessary or useful, the designated supervisor or investigator in charge will conduct an analysis of all available information, which may include victim information, review of F.I. cards from the area, criminal intelligence data, confidential informant information, and information from police officers or police reports from the neighborhood or target area where officers will work.

The supervisor or investigator in charge of the specialized investigative operation will:

1. Closely supervise the operation.
   a. including any large scale undercover operation.
2. A Supervisor with the rank of Sergeant or above has the authority to conduct a small scale operation which encompasses his or her squad with the approval of the Divisional Commander.
3. Supply or have access to the computer equipment required for the investigation. The

equipment may include:
  a. Online Investigations computer
  b. Investigative Internet access (not tied to the agency)
  c. Online evidence collection software
  d. Any other equipment the supervisor determines to be necessary.

4. Determine operational procedures and guidelines for arrest, if applicable, including:
  a. Where the operation will start from.
  b. What is expected of each officer.
  c. When and where the arrest will take place.
  d. Any other information which is necessary to successfully complete the operation.
5. Obtain and authorize undercover identities.
6. Obtain false credentials when necessary.
7. Determine what funds need to be made available and provide funds as required to the undercover personnel. Requests for investigative funds will be handled as described by agency directive.
8. Determine what legal problems may be encountered and what action is necessary to resolve them.
9. The supervisor may require the investigator in charge of a large scale social networking investigations to complete a plan of the operation, which is not part of the case file, containing what is currently known about the suspect(s) and target areas. This may be accomplished through an analysis of the available information and should include, but is not limited to, the:
  a. Suspect(s) activities, habits, vices, occupation, hobbies, and crimes.
  b. Suspect(s) work and residential address, including the neighborhood environment using maps, aerialphotos, and/or driving in the area, if possible.
  c. Known vehicle(s).
  d. Family, associates and friends.
  e. Review of F.I. cards of persons who have had contact with the police.
  f. The plan of operation and all applicable information will be provided to all members participating in a large scale social networking investigation. Information of a sensitive nature may be withheld or distributed in a limited manner at the discretion of the supervisor or investigator in charge, as long as it does not compromise the safety of any involved member.
10. Assure the investigator is properly prepared for the assignment.
  a. The officer best suited for each particular operation will be selected.
  b. The officer will adapt review and understand the persona he has adopted online.

VIII. INVESTIGATIVE REPORTS

The assigned supervisor must review and approve all investigative reports and material, which are prepared and submitted by the investigative officer. Once approved, all investigative reports and material will become a part of a numbered investigative file. Officers must include all relevant information in their investigative reports concerning:

     a. Criminal activity
     b. Suspect identification and disposition
     c. Contraband information and identification
     d. All monies expended for evidence.
     e. Description and disposition of all property seized for forfeiture.

IX. UNDERCOVER SOCIAL NETWORKING INVESTIGATIONS

1) General Authority And Purpose

<Agency Name> police department may engage in undercover activities and undercover operations pursuant to these Guidelines that are appropriate to carry out its law enforcement responsibilities, including the conduct of preliminary inquiries, general crimes investigations, and criminal intelligence investigations. In preliminary inquiries, these methods may be used to further the objective of inquiry into possible criminal activities by individuals or groups who use social networking to determine whether a full investigation is warranted. In general crimes investigations, these methods may be used to further the investigative objectives of preventing, solving, and prosecuting crimes. In criminal intelligence investigations – i.e., racketeering enterprise investigations and terrorism enterprise investigations – these methods may be used to further the investigative objective of ascertaining such matters as the membership, finances, geographical dimensions, past and future activities, and goals of the enterprise under investigation, with a view to the longer range objectives of detection, prevention, and prosecution of the criminal activities of the enterprise. These guidelines do not apply to investigations utilizing confidential informants, cooperating witnesses or cooperating subjects, unless the investigation also utilizes an undercover employee.

Undercover operations will only be used by the law enforcement agencies where they judge such use to be proportionate to the seriousness of the offence(s) being investigated and the history and character of the individual(s) concerned. Online undercover operations should not be used as a speculative means of search for the existence of a criminal offense, where no other grounds exist to suspect that criminal offenses have been or are being committed.

2) DEFINITIONS

A. **"Undercover Activities"** means any investigative activity involving the use of an assumed name or cover identity by an employee of the agency or another Federal, state, or local law enforcement organization working with the agency.

B. **"Undercover Operation"** means an investigation involving a series of related undercover activities over a period of time by an undercover employee, whether on the Internet or not. For purposes of these Guidelines, a "series of related undercover activities" generally consists of more than three separate substantive contacts by an undercover employee with the individual(s) under investigation. However, undercover activity involving sensitive or fiscal circumstances constitutes an undercover operation regardless of the number of contacts involved. A contact is "substantive" if it is a communication with another person, whether by oral, written, wire, or electronic means, which includes information of investigative interest. Mere incidental contact, e.g., a conversation that establishes an agreed time and location for another meeting, is not a substantive contact within the meaning of these Guidelines.

NOTE: In the context of online communications, such as e-mail and Internet Relay Chat (IRC), multiple transmissions or e-mail messages can constitute one contact; much like a series of verbal exchanges can comprise a single conversation. Factors to be considered in determining whether multiple online transmissions constitute a single contact or multiple contacts include the time between transmissions, the number of transmissions, the number of interruptions, topical transitions, and the media by which the communications are exchanged (i.e., e-mail versus IRC).

C. **"Undercover Employee"** means any employee of the agency, or employee of a Federal, state, or local law enforcement agency working under the direction and control of the agency in a particular investigation, whose relationship with the agency is concealed from third parties in the course of an investigative operation by the maintenance of a cover or alias identity.

3) Types of Online Undercover Operations

Online Undercover Operations are the use of a pretext to gain the confidence of persons involved in criminal activities on the Internet. It implies anyone engaged in this type of activity must have the ability to establish a relationship with the suspect online in order to determine the nature of his or her activities. An Online undercover operation may encompass several types of assignments which may include, but are not limited to:

A. Single Operation Assignment: an online undercover operation on a gambling site, a prostitution website or posting on a bulletin board, illegal pharmaceutical drug sales, or a person who deals in stolen property.

B. Multiple Operation Assignment: an investigation of crimes encompassing several websites and or physical locations such as gambling operations or bookmaking, para-mutual betting operations, prostitution activity, or a sales of stolen property from a theft ring.

C. Long-Range Penetration Assignment: an operation directed toward the upper-echelon leaders of an illegal activity.

D. Intelligence Gathering Assignment: a type of online undercover operation which is not directed toward any specific type of illegal activity. The operation may be used as a listening post for general information in a general geographic location where illegal activities are believed to be occurring. Any collection of intelligence on specific persons or groups that fall within the guidelines as identified in 28 C.F.R. PART 23 need to comply with the Federal rules.

4) Online Undercover Operational Plans

Operational plans for the conduct of undercover operations on social networking are intended to guide officers through the execution of an enforcement action. They provide for the assignment of personnel, identification of suspects, equipment and locations (both physical and online) and play a significant role in the safety of officers involved.

A. An operational plan will be prepared for each significant social networking investigation or enforcement operation.
B. The operational plan will be generated on an established format and shall note the case and any deconfliction procedures taken. The operational plan will state a clear objective and detail the specific roles and assignments of each participating officer. A follow on plan should be completed when the operation moves to a physical arrest situation or a search warrant execution.
C. The operational plan will be reviewed by a supervisor or his designee prior to the execution of the enforcement action and maintained in the case file.

5) Deconfliction

Online undercover investigations have the very real potential for multiple agencies to be conducting similar investigations on the same criminal suspects, website, social networking sites or organizations at any given time. There are serious safety considerations in such situations that may bring law enforcement Investigators into high-risk situations without realizing the presence of other law enforcement Investigators. Similarly, such parallel investigations, conducted independently, are less efficient and effective than cooperative law enforcement efforts conducted in a coordinated manner.

A. All officers should attempt to utilize deconfliction, where practicable. Where formal deconfliction agreements with other agencies do not exist the officer, or his supervisor, should notify the appropriate law enforcement agencies within the area of operation, if identified through the investigation, to ensure appropriate deconfliction has been conducted.

B. On any investigative activity conducted by an officer outside his assigned area of responsibility, the supervisor shall notify the affected law enforcement agencies, either local or federal, of the desired investigative efforts within their area. This notification should occur prior to beginning the investigative activity or as soon as it becomes apparent that the online investigation has an identified suspect not in the local jurisdiction. It shall be the responsibility of the supervisor to ensure proper deconfliction is conducted.

C. Any investigative activity that takes an officer physically out of his assigned area of responsibility will require prior notification of the appropriate law enforcement agencies within the area of operation.

6) Conducting Online Undercover Operations

Covert undercover operations on the Internet and Social Networking are an effective investigative technique in establishing admissible, credible evidence in support of a criminal prosecution against suspects. The ultimate goal of any online undercover operation is a criminal conviction. To that end, every aspect of undercover operations should be well planned, deliberate and performed in compliance with all applicable policies. The actions of undercover officers on the Internet should always be appropriate, under the circumstances, and easily justified to prosecutors, judges and juries. Officers conducting covert Internet and social networking investigations to obtain evidence for criminal prosecution will conduct such investigations under the following guidelines:

A. Officers will obtain the approval of a supervisor prior to the initiation of an undercover involving social networking sites investigation.

B. Officers will corroborate undercover investigations with the assistance of other officers conducting surveillance of the case officer, informants and suspect(s).

C. When possible, officers will utilize investigative computer systems and software intended to record data from the Internet and audio and/or video recording in an evidentiary manner when contacting suspects. All video or audio recordings made from the social networking site being used in the investigation shall be considered as evidence and handled as such, regardless of the quality of the recording. All video and audio recordings will be maintained as evidence until the case receives a final disposition.

    D. Officers will not transfer or make available for download any files that they knowingly contain any malicious code or other type of file that would disrupt, delay, or destroy another person's computer system,

    E. Officers will follow all local guidelines and Federal law when conducing undercover operation on social networking sites.

    F. Terms of Service Social networking sites require that users, when they sign up, agree to abide by a terms of service (TOS) document. Agency employees are responsible for reading and understanding the TOS of the sites they use during an undercover investigation. TOS agreements may ban users who give false names or other false information during the registration process which may affect the investigation if the use of an undercover identity is discovered by the social networking site.

6. Participation in Otherwise Illegal Activity by Undercover Employees

Except when authorized pursuant to the agency's general Under Cover operation Guidelines, no undercover employee on the Internet shall engage in any activity that would constitute a violation of Federal, state, or local law if engaged in by a private person acting without authorization. For purposes of these Guidelines, such activity is referred to as otherwise illegal activity.

7. Review of Conduct

From time to time, during the course of the undercover operation, the Chief of Investigations shall review the conduct of the undercover employee(s) and others participating in the undercover operation, including any proposed or reasonably foreseeable conduct for the remainder of the investigation. Any findings of impermissible conduct shall be discussed with the individual and promptly reported to the designated Supervisor for a determination to be made as to whether the individual should continue his or her participation in the investigation. Any unacceptable conduct discovered in violation of this or other departmental policy shall be forwarded for review by the agency Internal Affairs Division.

8. Protecting Innocent Parties Against Entrapment

Entrapment must be scrupulously avoided. Entrapment occurs when the Government implants in the mind of a person who is not otherwise disposed to commit the offense the disposition to commit the offense and then induces the commission of that offense in order to prosecute.

9. Identifying and Managing Employee Stress

Investigative personnel encounter a range of assignment-specific challenges and strains based on their participation in undercover operations and contact with material that over time can be emotionally detrimental. The cumulative effects of these strains, together with repeated exposure to disturbing images and situations, may result in stress reactions that require the attention of agency managers. Supervisors managing employees working in an undercover capacity on the Internet will monthly evaluate the employee's ability to continue in that capacity. Referrals to agency approved Employee Assistance Program (EAP) at a minimum may be appropriate. Reassignment of employees to a less stressful position may be warranted based on the supervisor's evaluation of the employees needs.

Model Policy
for Law Enforcement
Off-Duty Employee use
of Social Networking

Disclaimer: This is a model policy was designed to provide a guide to writing a policy related to social networking use. This model policy should be reviewed and revised based on your local legal requirements. Implementation of any of this model policy should be done so <u>only</u> after legal review by your agency attorney. Additionally, your policy prior to implementation will need to conform to any national or local laws, labor agreements and existing policy within the agency.

I. POLICY

That all *<Agency Name>* police department personnel use computers, computer applications, computer programs, Internet resources and network/Internet communications in a responsible, professional, ethical, and lawful manner. That conduct of its employees off off-duty has a reflection on the department. This policy is intended to guide employees conduct when it relates to their employment or representations of employment though the numerous social networking venues.

II. POLICY REVIEW

This policy will be reviewed by the *<Appropriate administrative level Supervisor>* or any person so designated by the *<Chief of Police, Sheriff or lead Law Enforcement Administrator>* on an annual basis to ensure that it is legally sound and reasonably enforceable.

III. POLICY TRAINING

All full-time officers, administrative staff, support personnel, student interns and volunteer staff will become familiar with and adhere to the provisions of this policy and receive training and notification pertaining to this policy by in-service training, internal mail, email, and/or occasional network log-on reminders.

IV. DEFINITION OF "SOCIAL NETWORKING"

Is defined as social network sites that use Internet services to allow individuals to construct a public or semi-public profile within that system, define a list of other users with whom they share some connection, and view and access their list of connections and those made by others within that system. The type of network and its design vary from site to site. Examples of the types of Internet based social networking sites include: blogs, networking sites, photo sharing, video sharing, microblogging, podcasts, as well as comments posted on the sites. *The absence of, or lack of explicit reference to a specific site does not limit the extent of the application of this policy.*

IV. POLICY GUIDELINES

a) Self-Identification

Employees may identify themselves as representatives of the agency. However, if they do their actions are reflective of the agency and will conform to the agencies general internet use policy. Self-identification can include the acknowledgment in the user profile for work experience, job title, etc. by identifying oneself as an employee of agency. Posting on their or another's social networking sites the identification of their employment. If the employee identifies their employment with the agency they take on the responsibility for representing the agency in a professional manner from that period forward while still employed by the agency. If the employee does self-identify themselves as a member of the agency, the employee will at a minimum post on their social networking sites a disclaimers that make it clear that the opinions expressed are solely those of the employee and do not represent the views of the agency. An example of a disclosure to use in these circumstances is:

> "The posts on this site, including but not limited to images, links, and comments by left by readers, are my own and don't necessarily represent my employers positions, strategies or opinions."

b) Confidential and Law Enforcement Sensitive Information

You must take proper care not to purposefully or inadvertently disclose any information that is confidential or law enforcement sensitive. Consult the agency's other policies for guidance about what constitutes "confidential" or "law enforcement sensitive" information. Employees will also honor the privacy rights of our current employees by seeking their permission before writing about or displaying internal agency happenings that might be considered to be a breach of their privacy and confidentiality. Any employee who violates this policies regarding confidentiality can be subject to disciplinary action.

c) Terms of Service

Social networking sites require that users, when they sign up, agree to abide by a terms of service (TOS) document. Agency employees are responsible for reading, knowing, and complying with the TOS of the sites they use. For example, most TOS agreements prohibit users from giving false names or other false information.

d) Copyright

Employees at all times comply with the law in regard to copyright/plagiarism. Posting of someone else's work without permission is not allowed (other than short quotes that comply with the "fair use" exceptions). Other relevant laws that need to be complied with include those related to libel and defamation of character. Employees may not the agency's logos or other identifying items related to their employment without first obtaining written permission from the agency.

e) Productivity

Agency employees need to comply with the general agency Internet use policy and recognize that all time and effort spent on their personal site should be done on their personal time and should not interfere with their job duties.

f) Disciplinary Action

Employees should use common sense in all communications, particularly on a website or social networking site accessible to anyone. What you say or post on your site or what is said or posted on your site by others could potentially be grounds for discipline. If you would not be comfortable with your supervisor, co-workers, or the management team reading your words, do not write them. Recognize that you are legally liable for anything you write or present online. Employees can be disciplined by the company for commentary, content, or images that are defamatory, pornographic, proprietary, harassing, libelous, or that can create a hostile work environment. You can also be sued by agency employees or any individual that views your commentary, content, or images as defamatory, pornographic, proprietary, harassing, libelous or creating a hostile work environment.

g) Investigative Activities

No employees should conduct any activity related ongoing investigations through their personally owned social networking accounts. Employees should refer to their agency policy on conducting online investigations and the investigative use of social networking.

Appendix K: Investigating A Person Online

Basic Investigation and Documentation of a Person Online

I. Locating and Identifying a Person Through the Internet

Search Bug	http://www.searchbug.com/
Zabba Search	http://www.zabasearch.com/
The Ultimates	http://www.theultimates.com/
SkipEase	http://www.skipease.com/

Document your findings

Record the information obtained through the various searches

II. Researching the Social Networking Presence of a Person

Searching MySpace	http://www.icerocket.com/index?tab=myspace&q=
Searching YouTube	http://www.searchthetube.com/
Searching Blogs	http://technorati.com/
Searching IRC	http://searchirc.com/
News Groups/Usenet	http://www.binsearch.info/ and http://www.newzleech.com/
News group Archives	http://www.google.com

Document your findings

Record the information obtained through the various searches

III. Searching Business Connections

LinkedIn	http://www.Linkedin.com
Spoke	http://www.Spoke.com
ZoomInfo	http://www.Zoominfo.com
Ryze	http://www.Ryze.com
Xing	http://www.Xing.com
Jigsaw	http://www.Jigsaw.com

Document your findings

Record the information obtained through the various searches

IV. Find Email Addresses

Email Finder   http://www.emailfinder.com/

Document your findings

Record the information obtained through the various searches

Documenting a Person Online Checklist

	Action	Discovered Details and Notes		Action Completed	Properly Documented
1	Locating and Identifying a Person Through the Internet	Search Bug Zabba Search The Ultimates SkipEase	http://www.searchbug.com/ http://www.zabasearch.com/ http://www.theultimates.com/ http://www.skipease.com/		
2	Researching the Social Networking Presence of a Person	Searching MySpace http://www.icerocket.com/index?tab=myspace&q= Searching YouTube Searching Blogs Searching IRC News Groups/Usenet News Group Archives	 http://www.searchthetube.com/ http://technorati.com/ http://searchirc.com/ http://www.binsearch.info/ and http://www.newzleech.com/ http://www.google.com		
3	Search Business Connections -	LinkedIn Spoke ZoomInfo Ryze Xing Jigsaw	http://www.Linkedin.com http://www.Spoke.com http://www.Zoominfo.com http://www.Ryze.com http://www.Xing.com http://www.Jigsaw.com		
4	Find Email Addresses	Email Finder	http://www.emailfinder.com/		
6	Other Searches				

Appendix L: Investigating A Website Worksheet

Basic Investigation and Documentation of a Website

I.   **Website Registration Information**

Domain Registration and website specific information

Initially, to determine basic information and ownership of a website or IP (Internet Protocol) address we start with the Domain registration information commonly referred to as the Whois information. This can be done through numerous sources. However, the source of that information is the domain registrars. This is a system set up to control the registration of domains worldwide.
You can search domain names from the following common resources:

> **DNS Stuff** http://www.dnsstuff.com/

> **Network Tools** http://network-tools.com/

Information about the Whois can be found by typing the domain name of the website being investigated and clicking on search.

Document your findings

Record the Domain registration information obtained through the Whois lookup.

II.   **General Website Background Information**

Search Engine Research

Using Google (www.google.com) or Yahoo (www.yahoo.com), search for the domain name or company name being investigated. Other references and information regarding the company or person(s) under investigation can normally be found through a simple search of the web.

WebSite Ranking and Traffic

> **Alexa Traffic Ranking** www.alexa.com

Alexa provides Internet traffic ranking of websites based on the website's traffic. The website with the most traffic is ranked 1. The traffic is ranked through the millions of users of the Alexa tool bar, which is used to collect information about the websites that each Alexa tool bar user visits.

Light Speed Systems
http://www.lightspeedsystems.com/resources/CheckOurDatabases.aspx

Light Speed Systems is another useful website for giving the investigator information about the traffic to the website.

Quantcast http://www.quantcast.com/

Quantcast is an additional website useful for giving the investigator information about the traffic to the website.

Document your findings

Record the information obtained through the various web research.

III. Website History Research

Internet Archive http://www.archive.org/web/web.php.

The *Wayback Machine* archives copies of websites that go back several years.

Document your findings

Record the information obtained through accessing the Internet Archive.

IV. Foreign Language Websites

Babel Fish babelfish.yahoo.com/

Google's Language Tools http://www.google.com/language_tools

Both these sites aid the investigator who is examining websites in a foreign language.

List of translation websites http://www.emailaddresses.com/online_translation.htm

Document your findings

Record the information obtained through the language translation websites.

V. The Legal Process of Identifying a Website

What an ISP can provide?

Internet Service providers have no requirements to store data about its users or their action when online. However, most store a significant amount of usable data for the investigator. This data can include the users name, address and credit card information, dates and times logged onto the ISP and possibly the web surfing of the user.

The proper legal service required for obtaining information from an Internet Service Provider varies by jurisdiction. Contact your legal counsel for advice on serving an ISP. A great resource for information on the legal contacts for Internet Service Providers is maintained by SEARCH, a federally funded non-profit organization. You can find most ISP legal contacts on their website at www.search.org/programs/hightech/isp/.

Website Investigative Checklist

	Action	Discovered Details and Notes	Action Completed	Properly Documented
	What is the URL (Uniform Resource Locator)?			
1	Domain Registration (Whois)	Registration Date: Registrants Name: Address: City:　　　　State:　　ZIP:		
2	Search Engine Research			
3	Website Ranking and Traffic - Alexa Rating - Light Speed Systems	_____		
4	Website History (Wayback Machine)			
5	Foreign Language Translation			
6	ISP Legal Process Requests			

Appendix M: Chat and Text Messaging Abbr List

Chat and Text Messaging Abbreviations List

Abbreviation	Meaning
<3	heart
404	I haven't a clue
A3	Anyplace, anywhere, anytime
ADN	Any day now
AFAIK	As far as I know
AFK	Away from keyboard
ARE	Acronym-rich environment
ASAP	As soon as possible
A/S/L?	Age/sex/location?
B4N	Bye for now
BAK	Back at the keyboard
BAS	Big a** smile
BBIAB	Be back in a bit
BBL	Be back later
BBN	Bye bye now
BBS	Be back soon
BEG	Big evil grin
BF	Boy friend
BFD	Big f***ing deal
BFN	Bye for now
BG	Big grin
BIBO	Beer in, beer out
BIOYIOP	Blow it out your I/O port
BL	Belly laughing
BMGWL	Busting my gut with laughter
BOTEC	Back-of-the-envelope

	calculation
BRB	Be right back
BTA	But then again...
BTDT	Been there, done that
BTW	By the way
BWL	Bursting with laughter
BWTHDIK	But what the heck do I know...?
CICO	Coffee in, coffee out
C&G	Chuckle and grin
CNP	Continued in next post
CRB	Come right back
CRBT	Crying real big tears
CU	See you
CUL	See you later
CUL8ER	See you later
CYA	See ya
CYA	Cover your ass
CYO	See you online
DBA	Doing business as
DFLA	Disenhanced four-letter acronym (that is, a TLA)
DL	Dead link
DLTBBB	Don't let the bed bugs bite
DIKU	Do I know you?
DITYID	Did I tell you I'm distressed?
DOM	Dirty old man
DOS	Dozing off soon
DQMOT	Don't quote me on this

DTRT	Do the right thing	GA	Go ahead
DWB	Don't write back	GAL	Get a life
E2E	exchange to exchange	GIGO	Garbage in, garbage out
E2E	e-business to e-business	GD&R	Grinning, ducking, and running
E2E	employee to employee	GF	Girlfriend
E2E	end to end	GFN	Gone for now
EG	Evil grin	GGP	Gotta go pee
EMFBI	Excuse me for butting in	GIWIST	Gee, I wish I'd said that
EMSG	E-mail message	GL	Good luck
EOM	End of message	GMAB	Give me a break
EOT	End of thread (meaning: end of discussion)	GMTA	Great minds think alike
ESAD	Eat s**t and die	GOL	Giggling out loud
ETLA	Extended three-letter acronym (that is, an FLA)	GTRM	Going to read mail
		GTSY	Glad to see you
EWG	evil wicked grin	H&K	Hug and kiss
F2F	Face to face	HAGN	Have a good night
FAQ	Frequently-ask question(s)	HAND	Have a nice day
		HHIS	Hanging head in shame
FC	Fingers crossed	HIG	How's it going
FISH	First in, still here	HT	Hi there
FLA	Four-letter acronym	HTH	Hope this helps
FMTYEWTK	Far more than you ever wanted to know	HUB	Head up butt
		IAC	In any case
FOMCL	Falling off my chair laughing	IAE	In any event
		IANAL	I am not a lawyer (but)
FTBOMH	From the bottom of my heart	IAW	I agree with or In accordance with
FUBAR	F***ed up beyond all repair or recognition	IC	I see
		IGP	I gotta pee
FUD	Fear, Uncertainty, and Doubt	IHA	I hate acronyms
		IHU	I hear you
FWIW	For what it's worth	IIRC	If I recall/remember/recollect correctly
FYI	For your information		
G	Grin		

ILU or ILY	I love you	L8R	Later
IM	Immediate message	L8R G8R	Later gator
IMCO	In my considered opinion	LD	Later, dude
IMHO	In my humble opinion	LDR	Long-distance relationship
IMing	Chatting with someone online usually while doing other things such as playing trivia or other interactive game	LHO	Laughing head off
		LLTA	Lots and lots of thunderous applause
IMNSHO	In my not so humble opinion	LMAFO	Laughing my f**king a** off
IMO	In my opinion	LMAO	Laughing my a** off
IMS	I am sorry	LMSO	Laughing my socks off
IOW	In other words	LOL	Laughing out loud
IPN	I'm posting naked	LRF	Little Rubber Feet (the little pads on the bottom of displays and other equipment)
IRL	In real life (that is, when not chatting)		
ITA	I totally agree	LSHMBH	Laughing so hard my belly hurts
ITIGBS	I think I'm going to be sick	LTM	Laugh to myself
IWALU	I will always love you	LTNS	Long time no see
IYSWIM	If you see what I mean	LTR	Long-term relationship
J4G	Just for grins	LULAB	Love you like a brother
JBOD	Just a bunch of disks (like redundant array of independent disks, etc.)	LULAS	Love you like a sister
		LUWAMH	Love you with all my heart
JIC	Just in case	LY	Love ya
JK or j/k	Just kidding	LY4E	Love ya forever
JMO	Just my opinion	MorF	Male or female
JTLYK	Just to let you know	MOSS	Member of the same sex
k	ok	MOTOS	Member of the opposite sex
KISS	Keep it simple stupid		
KIT	Keep in touch	MTF	More to follow
KOTC	Kiss on the cheek	MUSM	Miss you so much
KOTL	Kiss on the lips	NADT	Not a darn thing
KWIM?	Know what I mean?	NFG	No f*****g good

NFW	No feasible way or no f*****g way
NIFOC	Naked in front of computer
NP or N/P	No problem
NRN	No response necessary
OIC	Oh, I see
OLL	Online love
OMG	Oh my God
OTF	Off the floor
OTOH	On the other hand
OTTOMH	Off the top of my head
PANS	Pretty awesome new stuff (as opposed to "POTS")
PAW	Parents are watching
PCMCIA	People can't master computer industry acronyms
PDA	Public display of affection
PEBCAK	Problem exists between chair and keyboard
PIBKAC	Problem is between keyboard and chair
PITA	Pain in the ass
PM	Private message
PMFJIB	Pardon me for jumping in but...
POAHF	Put on a happy face
::POOF::	Goodbye (leaving the room)
POTS	Plain old telephone service
PU	That stinks!
QT	Cutie
RL	Real life (that is, when

	not chatting)
ROR	Raffing out roud (Engrish for "laughing out loud")
ROTFL	Rolling on the floor laughing
ROTFLMAO	Rolling on the floor laughing my a** off
ROTFLMAOWPIMP	Rolling on the floor laughing my a** off while peeing in my pants
ROTFLMBO	Rolling on the floor laughing my butt off
RPG	Role-playing games
RSN	Real soon now
RT	Real time
RTFM	Read the f***ing manual
RYO	Roll your own (write your own program; derived from cigarettes rolled yourself with tobacco and paper)
S^	S'up - what's up
S4L	Spam for life (what you may get when you become someone's customer or client)
SHCOON	Shoot hot coffee out of nose
SEG	S***-eating grin
SETE	Smiling ear to ear
SF	Surfer-friendly (low-graphics Web site)
SHID	Slaps head in disgust
SNAFU	Situation normal, all f***ed up
SO	Significant other
SOL	Smiling out loud or sh*t out of luck

SOMY	Sick of me yet?
SOT	Short on time
SOTMG	Short on time must go
STFU	Shut the f**k up
STFW	Search the f*****g Web
STW	Search the Web
SU	Shut up
SUAKM	Shut up and kiss me
SUP	What's up
SWAG	Stupid wild-a** guess
SWAK	Sealed with a kiss
SWL	Screaming with laughter
SYS	See you soon
TA	Thanks again
TAFN	That's all for now
TANSTAAFL	There ain't no such thing as a free lunch
TCOY	Take care of yourself
TFH	Thread from hell (a discussion that just won't die and is often irrelevant to the purpose of the forum or group)
TGIF	Thank God it's Friday
THX	Thanks
TIA	Thanks in advance (used if you post a question and are expecting a helpful reply)
TILII	Tell it like it is
TLA	Three-letter acronym
TLK2UL8R	Talk to you later
TB4U	Too bad for you
TMI	Too much information
TNT	Till next time
TOPCA	Til our paths cross again

	(early Celtic chat term)
TOY	Thinking of you
TPTB	The powers that be
TTFN	Ta-Ta for now
TTT	Thought that, too (when someone types in what you were about to type)
TTYL	Talk to you later
TU	Thank you
TY	Thank you
TYVM	Thank you very much
UAPITA	You're a pain in the ass
UAF	Until further notice
UW	You're welcome
VBG	Very big grin
VBSEG	Very big s***-eating grin
WAG	Wild a** guess
WAYD	What are you doing
WB	Welcome back
WBS	Write back soon
WDALYIC	Who died and left you in charge?
WEG	Wicked evil grin
WFM	Works for me
WIBNI	Wouldn't it be nice if
WT?	What/who the ?
WTF	What the F***!
WTFO	What the F***! Over!
WTG	Way to go!
WTGP?	Want to go private?
WU?	What's up?
WYSITWIRL	What you see is TOTALLY WORTHLESS IN REAL LIFE!

WUF?	Where are you from?
WYSIWYG	What you see is what you get
YBS	You'll be sorry
YGBSM	You gotta be s***tin' me!
YMMV	Your mileage may vary.
YW	You're welcome
:-)	smiley face (humour)
:-))	laugh
Smileys	
(-:	left handed smiley
;-)	wink (light sarcasm)
:-|	indifference
:->	devilish grin (heavy sarcasm)
8-)	big-eyed smiley
:-D	shock or surprise
:-/	perplexed
:-(	Sad
:-C	real unhappy
:-P	wry smile
;-}	leer
;-(	crying
:-*	kiss
:-X	big wet kiss
:-e	disappointment
:-@	scream
:-O	Yell
>;->	A very lewd remark was just made
:-&	Tongue tied

:-{}	wears lipstick
O:-)	Angel smiley
:-Q	Smoking smiley
:-[	Vampire smiley

This list of abbreviations are compiled from lists maintained at:

http://searchcrm.techtarget.com/sDefinition/0,,sid11_gci211776,00.html#

http://gei.aerobaticsweb.org/smileys.html

http://www.urbandictionary.com/

Appendix N: mIRC-commands

Quick Reference to mIRC's commands:

/ Recalls	The previous command entered in the current window.
/! Recalls	The last command typed in any window.
/action <action text>	Sends the specified action to the active channel or query window.
/add [-apuce] <filename.ini>	Loads aliases, popups, users, commands, and events.
/alias <alias name> <command(s)>	Adds the given alias to the Tools/Aliases list.
/ame <action text>	Sends the specified action to all channels which you are currently on.
/amsg <text>	Sends the specified message to all channels which you are currently on.
/auser [-a] <level> <nick|address>	Adds a user with the specified access level to the remote users list.
/auto [-r] [on|off|nickname[type]|address]	Adds (-r removes) auto-opping of a nick or address or sets it on or off totally. The type determines the used address syntax.
/away <away message>	Sets you away leave a message explaining that you are not currently paying attention to IRC.
/away	Sets you being back.
/ban [#channel] <nickname> [type]	Bans the specified nick from the current or given channel.
/beep [<number> <delay>]	Locally beeps 'number' times with 'delay' in between the beeps.
/channel	Pops up the channel central window (only works in a channel)
/clear [nickname|channel]	Clears the entire scroll back buffer of the (given) window.

/clearall	Clears all text in all open windows.
/close -icfgms [nick1] [nickN]	Closes inactive, chat, fserve, get, message or send windows.
/closemsg <nickname>	Closes the query window you have open to the specified nick.
/creq [ask | auto | ignore]	Sets your DCC 'On Chat request' settings in DCC/Options.
/ctcp <nickname> <ping|finger|version|time|userinfo|clientinfo>	Does the given ctcp request on nickname.
/ctcpreply <nickname> <ctcp> [message]	Sends a ctcp reply message to nickname.
/ctcps [on|off]	Sets the Tools/Remote/Commands section on or off or checks its status.
/dcc send <nickname> <file1> [file2] [file3] ... [fileN]	Sends the specified file(s) to nick.
/dcc chat <nickname>	Opens a dcc window and sends a dcc chat request to nickname.
/dde [-r] <service> <topic> <item> [data]	Allows DDE control between mIRC and other applications.
/ddeserver [[on [service name] | off]	To turn on the DDE server mode, eventually with a given service name.
/describe <#channel> <action text>	Sends the specified action to the specified channel window.
/disable <#groupname>	De-activates a group of commands or events in the remote section.
/disconnect	Forces a hard and immediate disconnect from your IRC server. Use it with care.
/dlevel <level>	Changes the default user level in the remote section.
/dns <nickname | IP address | IP name>	Uses your providers DNS to resolve an IP address.
/echo [N] <-s|a|[=]nickname|#channel> <text>	Displays the given text only to YOU on the given place (status, active window, query or channel) in color N.

/enable <#groupname>	Activates a group of commands or events.
/events [on|off]	Shows the Tools/Remote/Events section status or sets it to listening or not.
/exit	Forces mIRC to shutdown and close.
/finger <nickname | address>	Does a finger on a user's address... also if his nick is given.
/flood [<numberoflines> <seconds> <pausetime>]	Sets a crude flood control method.
/flush [levels]	Clears all nicknames from the Remote/users list that are currently not on your channels.
/flushini <filename>	Forces the specified INI file to be saved to disk.
/font	Activates the font selection dialog.
/fsend [on|off]	Shows fsends status and allows you to turn dcc fast send on or off.
/fserve <nickname> <maxgets> <homedirectory> [welcome text file]	Opens a fileserver.
/groups [-e|d]	Shows all (enabled or disabled) groups defined in the remote sections.
/guser [-a] <level> <nick> [type]	Adds the user to the user list with the specified level and address type.
/help <keyword>	Brings up the Basic IRC Commands section in the mIRC help file.
/ial [on|off]	Turns the Internal Address List on and off.
/identd [on|off] [userid]	Activates the IdentD server with the given userid.
/ignore [-rpcntiu#][on|off|nickname|address] [type]	Ignores a nick or address or sets ignore on or off totally. -r to remove.
/invite <nickname> <#channel>	Invites another user to a channel.

/join <#channel>	Makes you join the specified channel.
/kick <#channel><nickname>	Kicks nickname off a given channel.
/links	Shows the entire list of IRC servers in the network you are currently connected to.
/list [#string] [-min #] [-max #]	Lists all currently available channels, evt. filtering for parameters.
/load <-a|p<c|n>|r<u|v|s>> <filename.ini>	Loads Aliases, Popups, Remote items or Variables into mIRC.
/loadbuf [lines] <window> <filename>	Loads lines from a text file into the specified window. (like echo)
/log [on|off] [windowname]	Shows the logging status or sets it on or off for the window.
/me <action text>	Sends the specified action to the active channel or query window.
/mode <#channel|nickname> [[+|-]modechars [parameters]]	Sets channel or user modes.
/msg <#channel|nickname> <message>	Send a private message to this user without opening a query window.
/names <#channel>	Shows the nicks of all people on the given channel.
/nick <new nickname>	Changes your nickname to whatever you like.
/notice <nick> <message>	Send the specified notice message to the nick.
/notify [-sh][-ar][on|off|nickname]	Toggles notifying you of a nick on IRC or sets it on or off totally.
/onotice [#channel] <message>	Send the specified notice message to all channel ops.
/omsg [#channel] <message>	Send the specified message to all ops on a channel.
/part <#channel> <message>	Makes you leave the specified channel.
/partall <message>	Makes you leave all channels you are on

/perform [on|off]	Toggles the File/Options/Perform (on startup) section.
/play [-cp q# m# rl# t#] [channel/nick] <filename> [delay|linenumber]	Allows you to play text files to a channel.
/pop <delay> [#channel] <nickname>	Performs a randomly delayed +o on a not already opped nick.
/protect [-ar][on|off|nickname|address]	Toggles protection of a nick or address or sets it on or off totally.
/query <nickname> <message>	Open a query window to this user and send them the private message.
/quit [reason]	Disconnect you from IRC with the optional message
/quote [-q] <raw command>	Sends any raw command you supply directly to the server.
/raw [-q] <raw command>	Sends any raw command you supply directly to the server.
/remote [on|off]	Sets the entire Tools/Remote section on or off or checks its status.
/remove <c:\path\filename>	Will delete the requested file.
/rlevel <access level>	Removes all users from the remote users list with the specified access level.
/run <c:\path\program.exe> [parameters]	Runs the specified program, evt. with parameters.
/ruser [-r] <nick[!]|address> [type]	Removes the user from the remote users list.
/save [-apuce] <filename.ini>	Saves remote sections into a specified INI file.
/savebuf [lines] <window> <filename>	Saves lines from the buffer of a window to a file.
/say <text>	Says whatever you want to the active window.
/server [server # | server address [port] [password]]	(Re)connects to the server or a newly specified one.
/sound [nickname|#channel] <filename.wav> <action text>	Sends an action and a fitting sound request.
/speak <text>	Uses the external text to speech program Monologue to speak up the text.
/splay <c:\path\filename.ext>	Plays .wav and .mid files to you. (like /wavplay)
/sreq [ask | auto | ignore]	Sets your DCC 'On Send request' settings in DCC/Options.

/strip [+-burc]	Turns removal of color codes (see Options dialog) on/off.
/time	Tells you the time on the server you use.
/timer[N] <repetitions> <interval in seconds> <command> [| <more commands>]	Activates a timer.
/timestamp [-a|e|s] [on|off] [window]	For Turning on/off timestamping in windows or globally. (-s = for status window, -a = for active window, -e = for every window)
/titlebar <text>	Sets mIRC's title bar to the specified text.
/topic <#channel> <newtopic>	Changes the topic for the specified channel.
/ulist [<|>]<level>	Lists all users in the remote list with the specified access levels.
/unload <-a|-rs> <filename>	This unloads the specified alias or remote script file.
/url [-d|on|off|hide]	Opens or closes the URL window that allows you to surf the www parallel to IRC.
/uwho [nick]	Pops up the user central with information about the specified user.
/version	Tells you the version of the IRC server you use.
/wavplay <c:\path\filename.ext>	Locally plays the specified wave or midi file.
/who <#channel>	Shows the nicks of all people on the given channel.
/who <*address.string*>	Shows all people on IRC with a matching address.
/whois <nickname>	Shows information about someone in the status window.
/whowas <nickname>	Shows information about someone who -just- left IRC.
/window	This allows you to create and manipulate custom windows.
/write [-cidls] <filename> [text]	To write the specified text to a .txt file.
/writeini <inifile> <section> <item> <value>	To write to an .ini file.

Index

Printed and bound by CPI Group (UK) Ltd, Croydon, CR0 4YY

08/05/2025

01864873-0003